THE SASSOONS

David Sassoon (1792–1864)

THE
SASSOONS

Stanley Jackson

אמת ואמונה

CANDIDE · ET · CONSTANTER

1968

E. P. DUTTON & CO., INC. : NEW YORK

Library of Congress Catalog Card Number: 68-11386

For my Mother

CONTENTS

LIST OF ILLUSTRATIONS

In Old Baghdad we'll call a halt
At the Sâshun's ancestral vault;
We'll catch the Persian rose-flowers' scent,
And understand what Omar meant.

'Letter to S.S. from Mametz Wood'
From *Fairies and Fusiliers* by Robert Graves,
July 1916.

FOREWORD

As a family, the Sassoons are unique in many respects. Other houses, to mention only the Rothschilds, Vanderbilts and Astors, amassed vaster fortunes and played a more glittering rôle in international society. But none has more dramatically spanned two worlds, Oriental and Western, or generated so many virtuoso talents outside the commercial sphere.

The dynasty has long been a fruitful source of speculation and legend. Its ancient origins, followed by dealings in opium during the pioneering days, have together contributed to the colourful myths. Another factor is the depth of bitterness which separated various branches for over a century. This has created a confusion of testimony, reinforced by the two rival family firms' traditional secrecy in their business dealings.

Apart from Siegfried Sassoon's reminiscences of an early life which was more influenced by his Thornycroft strain, the only published history is Cecil Roth's interesting study which appeared nearly thirty years ago. Although a valuable source, particularly on the Edwardian period, it is now out of print and inevitably overtaken by events. Since it was published, the firms have experienced their greatest triumphs and reversals, both in India and China.

Professor Roth acknowledged frankly that there was nothing official about his volume, 'in the production of which the Sassoon family has had no part whatsoever'. I have been more fortunate in this respect, mainly because the old tribal vendettas have since lost much of their sting. The changes in financial structure have also tended to make excessive reticence superfluous.

I should, however, stress that the private papers, business documents and other data made available to me have not imposed any form of individual or collective 'censorship'. I have enjoyed full liberty in the selection and presentation of all material and take personal responsibility for any expressions of opinion.

My acquaintance with the subject-matter of this book dates back to undergraduate days in the late 'twenties when a close friend, Ralph Ezra, talked often of his kinswoman, Mrs Flora Sassoon. She presided over a remarkable salon in Bruton Street and had previously directed, almost single-handed, the firm's key branch in Bombay. Through her I first grew interested in other members of the clan, including Siegfried, who had already made a distinguished literary reputation; his aunt, Rachel Beer, who at one time owned and simultaneously edited both the *Sunday Times* and *The Observer*; Sir Philip, an enigmatic controversial figure in social and political circles; and others who became prominent as scholars, sportsmen and soldiers.

Much about them was on public record, but a great many gaps remained, both on the financial side and in the complicated network of inter-tribal relationships. It was left to Mrs Flora Sassoon's son, a celebrated scholar and bibliophile, to assemble diaries, records and miscellaneous jottings dating back to his grandfather's exodus from Bushire in the early part of the last century. His death in 1942 prevented him from editing and cataloguing his Letchworth Papers.

I owe his son, Rabbi S. D. Sassoon, my gratitude for giving me unrestricted access to his archives and permitting their use for publication. He was also kind enough to translate letters from the original Hebrew and Arabic and supplied much new information about the Jews of Baghdad.

Many other members of the family have provided photographic and documentary material or otherwise assisted with reminiscences. I am specially indebted to the late Siegfried Sassoon and his brother, Michael; Jacques Sassoon; Frederick Sassoon; Major Arthur Sassoon; Sir Victor's widow, Lady Sassoon, and his cousin, Lucien Ovadia; Lord John Cholmondeley; Major Desmond FitzGerald; and Mrs Mozelle Spielman. It was also a personal pleasure to renew my association with Ralph Ezra, now of Singapore, who fanned the spark which he had first ignited so many years ago.

Numerous friends, business associates and other Sassoon connections have also given me valuable assistance. I can only thank a small number individually; among them, Air Marshal Sir John Tremayne; Mme Zola Ponzio; Louis Polak of Amsterdam; Dr Frederick Hilton; Asher Barukh; Robert Heathfield; Miss G. F. Leeds; Miss V. M. E. Conolly; and Stanley J. Rowland. For intimate recollections of the two firms during their time in Shanghai, Bombay, and Hong Kong, I had generous help from Frank Lobel, Robert Stock and W. B. Bryden.

I must also acknowledge the assistance of many who provided research facilities or background data. They include Harold Evans, Editor of the *Sunday Times*; Tristan Jones, General Manager of *The Observer*; George D. Painter; William Frankel, Editor of the *Jewish Chronicle*, and his library staff; the Librarians of Walton-on-Thames and Tunbridge Wells; Harry Trehearne of Associated Newspapers; J. G. Curtis of Jardine, Matheson; J. H. Blake of the British Light Aviation Centre; the Head

Masters of Eton and Harrow; the Steward of Christ Church, Oxford and the Chief Clerk, Trinity College, Cambridge; the Hon. Secretary, Royal Bombay Yacht Club; and the Naval Historical Branch, Ministry of Defence.

My special thanks are due to George Sassoon and Robert Graves for kindly consenting to the use of copyright material.

To preserve readers from genealogical jaw-breaking, each chapter is preceded by a potted *dramatis personae*. A fuller family tree, but nevertheless pruned for easier reference, will be found on pages xiv and xv.

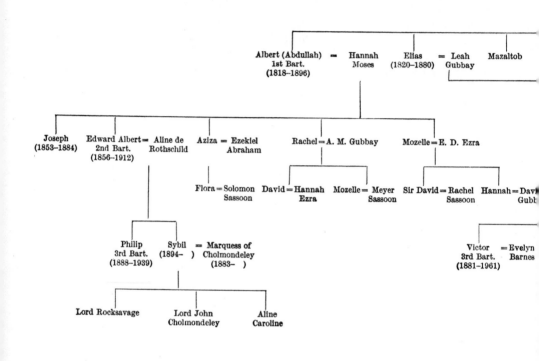

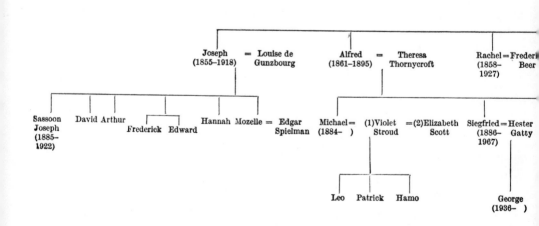

THE HOUSE OF SASSOON

A condensed genealogical table of family members mentioned in
the text. Descendants in the female line are generally omitted.

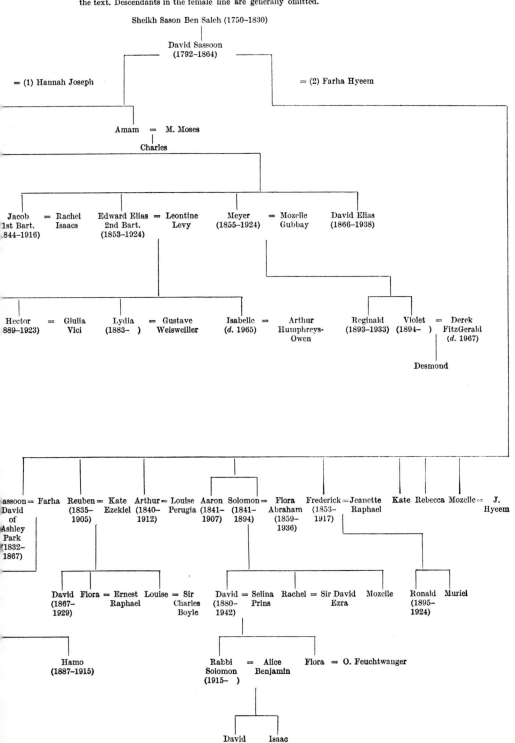

Prologue

At their peak of social and financial prominence, it was customary to describe the Sassoons as 'the Rothschilds of the East'. The label was loosely attached but convenient, since the two clans were leaders of the *haute Juiverie* and had marriage ties. In fact their origins were very different, and they contrasted as sharply by family tradition and temperament as in their business operations.

The Rothschilds arrived at the Court of St James's from the ghetto of Frankfurt-am-Main, where a small trader in old coins and medals became factor to the Landgrave of Hesse-Hanau and laid the foundations of a spectacular banking empire. They remained a close-knit clan of Europeans. The Sassoons were courtiers and merchant princes from their earliest days. Their corporate personality came to flower in the East without always transplanting too smoothly, despite Park Lane mansions, grouse moors in Scotland and a persistent entry at Eton and Christ Church, Oxford. Consequently, their destiny would prove more convulsive and off-centre than that of the less aristocratic, but relatively predictable, House of Rothschild.

The family flourished for centuries in Baghdad where their chieftain wore gold tissue to ride to the palace of the Pasha, those in the streets and outside the bazaars standing with bowed heads until he and his retinue had passed. Their days of ease and pomp ended with the decline in power of the ancient city of the caliphs. By the end of the eighteenth century, the clan was facing a threat of complete extinction.

Mesopotamia, 'the land between two rivers', had been the second homeland of the Jews from the time of their exile by Nebuchadnezzar. Only a small minority elected to return to the land of their fathers when the Persian armies overran the country. Many had grown rich in commerce and preferred to mourn in reasonable security by the waters of Babylon. With the coming of Islam in the seventh century A.D., they entered a long era of peace under the caliphs who valued a law-abiding, trading community closely linked with their co-religionists throughout the sprawling Ottoman Empire. Among other advantages, it made tax control simpler and eased the transmission of money over vast areas.

Baghdad also became a fountain of culture and scholarship for the most distinguished mathematicians, doctors, poets and theologians of that time.

A rich soil, irrigated by a complex network of canals, made it the granary of Arabia. Along the great caravan routes, often over steep mountain passes and across endless deserts, raw wool, cotton goods, copper, spices and sugar from China and the Indies were hauled by mule and camel. Ancient rafts, reinforced by goatskins, negotiated the tricky channels of the Tigris to disgorge pearls and silverware from the Persian Gulf into the vaulted bazaars.

The original city stood on the right bank of the river. Its avenues and modish coffee-houses were only surpassed in elegance by those of Constantinople itself. The peacock-blue, tiled mosques and spindly minarets have been lovingly captured by countless artists and sculptors who enjoyed the caliph's patronage. His ornate palace was set in three square miles of wooded parkland, with tinkling fountains and lakes alive with rare fish. Here he received the elders of Israel who came to offer homage and the substantial taxes needed to balance his military budget. They were resigned to anomalies like being debarred from army service while forced to pay an annual toll as the price of this 'exemption'.

Small colonies had settled from antiquity in India and China, but Baghdad remained the nerve centre of the exiled race. Over forty thousand were living in the city by the twelfth century, and the Sassoons were among an *élite* who claimed their pedigree from King David himself. From this period onwards, there are constant references to Jewish scholars and royal physicians in the Middle East, apart from the majority in commerce. The caliphs and viziers turned increasingly to these prosperous infidels when they needed funds for some private use which the Sublime Porte at Constantinople might not always have approved. It finally became practical to appoint the lay leader of the Jewish community as Sarraf Bashi or Chief Banker, who would also be responsible for collecting taxes from his co-religionists. Known as 'Nasi' (Prince of the Captivity), he was usually the wealthiest and most respected Jew in Baghdad. It was a satisfactory arrangement all round. The ruler had a shrewd adviser whom he would flatter with ceremonial honours and greet as 'brother', while the Jews had a friend at Court to air their communal grievances or protest when some venal official grew too rapacious.

Early historical sources are sketchy. It appears that the Sassoons were among the first of their race to settle in Babylonia, to be joined there after the Inquisition by a number of kinsmen from Spain. They are often mentioned in medieval literature, and the name 'Shoshan', meaning lily in Hebrew but afterwards corrupted to 'Sason' (joy), is found in the Talmud. Among their ancestors were the Ibn Shoshans, princes of the community in Toledo, where they were Court favourites and respected for their wealth and learning. As early as the seventeenth century, a scholar and mystic of Venice, Abraham Sason, proudly claims descent from Shephatiah, the fifth son of King David.

Sason ben Saleh, born in Baghdad in 1750, is the first member of the family of whom there is any significant documentary evidence. He traced his direct line back through five generations. Like several of his forbears, he held the office of Chief Banker and enjoyed the honorary title of Sheikh, but the Nasi no longer wore cloth of gold. The Pasha's palace was little more than a shell, while the beautiful city had crumbled into a mud-brown, fetid huddle of brick dwellings with the glinting tiles of a minaret mockingly reflected in derelict waterworks. Overrun and sacked by Mongols, Persians and finally Turks, its beauty raped by plague and flood, Baghdad was now only a sullen desert pashalik. Enemies of the Porte and other malcontents were sent there into semi-exile or given governorships with limited influence. And like disappointed officials everywhere, many grew capricious and cruel in decision.

The Sheikh Sason (his descendants would use the modern variation) became Nasi in 1778. He officiated for thirty-eight years, collecting the heavy military tax and other tolls levied on his people. He presided over a kind of benevolent Star Chamber in his house. (Preserved among the family papers are memoranda in Turkish and Arabic, recording orders for payment issued by two Governors between 1781 and 1811.) A council of ten managed communal affairs, but the Nasi had the final word in disputes over debts, benefactions and the niceties of synagogue precedence.

The community settled in the north-west section of the city, but this was not a ghetto in which the hated yellow star was worn as in Western Europe. Traders moved freely over the vast province of Mesopotamia, many itinerant goldsmiths and other craftsmen penetrating to Damascus, Aleppo and Basra on the Gulf. The family archivist, D. S. Sassoon, has found evidence of a merchant who travelled regularly from Baghdad to Kut during the early nineteenth century to sell his corals among the Arabs.

For centuries Israel and Ishmael dwelt amicably together. Arabic was the vernacular, and the Jews of Baghdad wore native dress, but Hebrew remained the community's fabric of all learning and ritual observance. At Passover they ate unleavened bread and bitter herbs to remind them of afflictions suffered under Pharaoh, and like all others throughout the Diaspora, awaited the coming of their Messiah with quiet certainty.

Sheikh Sason supervised the secular welfare of his people but also provided funds for religious education. With the rabbis he inspected ritual baths and ensured that the slaughter-houses and dairies conformed strictly to the dietary laws. Door-posts had to be checked every three years to see that the *mezuzahs* – the tiny scrolls of the Holy Law encased in metal strips – were in good repair. Orphan girls were given dowries; rabbis, travellers and pilgrims from the Holy Land, even from distant China, were welcomed in the Nasi's house where they took their ease in a walled courtyard shady with orange trees and shrubs.

The city was always a furnace in summer, baking in a hot simoom wind which might send the temperature up to 120° in the shade. By day they sought relief from the pitiless sun in underground *serdabs*, cooled by thick arched walls and windows latticed with camel's thorn. Here the cold water was stored, and the gold acquired through years of commerce. Ingenious trapdoors facilitated the rapid transfer of valuables or a hasty exit when the military made a surprise raid. In high summer the family slept peacefully on the terrace under mosquito nets, but if necessary they could race across a street-length bridge of roofs. In the twisting alleys below, laden wagons were hauled by buffalo with mud-caked hides, while camels kicked dust over walls once pink with oleander. Bells tinkled and the Kurd drivers cursed as their wretched overladen mules plodded into some hole in the road or rasped flesh against a jutting wall.

As Baghdad decayed, the position of minorities became so precarious that none could rely on official goodwill. The patriarchal head of the Jews had to go under cover early in the winter of 1772. A document still extant confirms that 'the Sheikh Sason cannot show himself or go about freely because of fear of the Governor of the city, cursed be his name'. This explained his absence from a meeting of the Beth Din, the tribunal to which he wished to present papers in connection with his wife's estate, almost certainly her dowry. He used to store documents and samples of merchandise on the ground floor of his house. Like all provident men of business, the Sassoons kept only the most valuable portables in their home, and these under constant guard, but their city bazaars and booths were always stocked from floor to ceiling. Bales of bright silks were shipped hundreds of miles on rafts by the mercers of Bushire; India and far-off Kabul sent cotton goods, horses, gold and silver ornaments, while coffers of spices and trinkets of every kind arrived by sea, or more usually by camel caravan, from Java and Singapore. Much was sold locally, but for generations the family had steadily built up an export business in hides, dates, metals and, above all, wool. As soon as the sheep-shearing began, their agents would be active among the Bedouin tribes of the interior who sold their wool in exchange for cotton garments, shoes and cameos.

Almost before celebrating their Barmitzvah or religious majority, by reading a portion of the Law in the synagogue, the younger Sassoons were equally fluent in Hebrew, Turkish, Arabic and of course Persian, the language of business. Early each day they were sent to the crowded *souks* to report on the arrival of goods, noting market trends and learning to calculate in different currencies, weights and measures. Before leaving for the city at first light, all males who had reached the Barmitzvah age of thirteen would already have chanted the morning litany. Cocooned in prayer shawls and swaying in a pious ecstasy, they carried the phylacteries ordained by orthodox doctrine. On the forehead under a skullcap each wore a black wooden cube containing quotations from the Torah. Another rested on the left biceps and pointed to the heart. The Sabbath was holy, and none dared to work or even kindle a light after dusk. Nothing might be carried in the pockets, not even a piece of string. In the synagogue Sason the Nasi occupied the first seat of a divan reserved for his family and the community elders. With heads covered by lace mantillas, the women worshipped apart in a curtained-off gallery.

The Sheikh had married Amam Gabbai, daughter of a fellow-merchant and synagogue treasurer. She bore seven sons, a comfort to the patriarch, since only male children might recite prayers for the dead or join any quorum for religious service. The eldest died in a plague, like the Sheikh's own father some years before. The others were undistinctive except the second son, David, who founded the modern dynasty. He was born in 1792, when the fate of his family and indeed that of the whole community was already at flash point throughout the province.

No longer a young man, the Sheikh found himself swimming upstream, harassed by the pashas but even more by some of his own community. Several took panic and either abandoned their faith or decided to leave Baghdad. A number made for the Persian Gulf and set sail for New South Wales to found a small Arabic-speaking colony in Sydney. A few of the elderly and devout mustered their strength and finally made the pilgrimage to the Holy Land. Many more, however, emigrated to India, hungry for the tolerance and trading benefits which, it was reported, might be enjoyed under British protection. Among early settlers in Calcutta was the Ezra family with whom the Sassoons would later be linked by marriage. Others quickly took root in Bombay, where the recent breach in the East India Company's monopoly had opened a dazzling vista for independent traders.

The Sheikh and his sons had first become aware of India's attractions through their friendship with Colonel Taylor, who represented the Presidency of Bombay. They were often entertained with other local dignitaries at his mansion overlooking the Tigris. The walls and ceilings of his lofty dining-room glittered with scores of small diamond-shaped mirrors reflecting the solid silver goblets and plate on which a retinue of forty sepoys served banquets of taste and magnificence. He exuded an aura of prestige without the arrogance which the viziers now openly showed towards all minorities, but particularly the moneyed Jews and Armenians.

David Sassoon had been placed in the family's counting-house almost as soon as he could read. He showed an early aptitude for business. At fifteen he was betrothed to Hannah Joseph, the daughter of a leading merchant. She was two years younger than himself, and he would have to wait eleven years until 1818 for a son and heir. He seemed assured of following his father as Nasi, although the associate office of Court Banker was becoming far less attractive. Some of the Sheikh's predecessors had cynically used tax-gathering to enrich themselves, while others acted as informers for the Pasha who could then blackmail rich members of the community or confiscate their property.

In his own troubled years of office when no fewer than eight governors rose and fell through intrigues and palace revolutions, the Sheikh Sason helped to sustain the poorer members of the community. His handsome benefactions enabled them to pay their taxes and also blocked the threat of apostasy. He restored a synagogue which was dedicated with a poem of tribute to the goodwill of Suleiman Pasha, then Vali of Baghdad, and the generosity of their own leader, 'the great Prince and the Head and Chief of the Diaspora. He is a crown of magnificence, his name is Sason, and he is Nasi . . .'

The Sheikh retired from public life in 1817. He was then almost seventy and exhausted by the intrigues against him. Any hopes of being succeeded by his son were quickly frustrated when Suleiman fled the city after being warned of a *coup d'état*. His successor was Daud Pasha, a former slave from Georgia, whose bid for power was supported by two Jewish brothers, Ezra and Ezekiel ben Rahel. Both were prominent in banking and commerce, though not as rich as the Sheikh Sason whom they envied and had steadily undermined. Ezra succeeded him as Nasi and Chief Banker, while his brother became the Sultan's Treasurer and Keeper of the Seal in Constantinople.

Ezekiel helped to hound Suleiman to his death and quickly opened an early type of Tammany Hall at the Sublime Porte. According to D. S. Sassoon, 'sometimes as many as fifty or sixty pashas crowded the antechamber of this high-standing Jew'. He blatantly sold official posts and sinecures all over the Ottoman Empire to the highest bidders. Daud Pasha, not yet officially confirmed in office, was among many who sought his favour. The new Nasi was equally anxious to consolidate his position in Baghdad and sent his son to Constantinople with a message for Ezekiel. A word was whispered in the Sultan's ear, and the Pasha was then given the full imperial mandate. It was the signal for a reign of terror and vicious extortion unknown even in the worst days. The Jews were the easiest and most obvious victims, but few Armenians were spared, and a number of the wealthier Arabs also felt his lash.

Daud's newly won status made him more and more impatient of control from Constantinople, where Ezekiel was soon afterwards executed. The news terrified Ezra who had enjoyed few of the sweets of office once the Pasha was securely in control. The wretched Nasi was now little more than a tax-collector for an insatiable master. Scorned alike by his fellow-Jews and the hostile Armenian traders who had long resented his influence, Ezra at last tired of the jackal's rôle. He was removed from office and imprisoned. Daud Pasha had found direct extortion more effective than the services of a Court Banker. At the same time, he became suspicious of any Jewish Nasi who might rally his people and threaten his own position. Few candidates offered themselves for the vacant office.

David Sassoon was among those who declined to stand. He acted instead as the community's unofficial leader and spokesman, relying on his father's name and prestige. The family's fortune was still considerable, but much of it dispersed in caravanserais throughout Asia, as the Pasha was perfectly aware. Daud might tighten the screws by taxation but obviously needed subtler methods. He therefore planned to arrest selected Jews whose ransom would probably be paid by their richer brethren.

David Sassoon, now in his thirties and more forceful than his aged sire, decided on positive resistance. His sons, Abdullah and Elias, were approaching manhood, and there could be little future for them or his two daughters unless he acted swiftly. His first wife had died, her vitality sapped by too rapid childbearing, and he had recently taken as his bride, Farha Hyeem, the daughter of a merchant and bibliophile who soon afterwards fled to Calcutta. Aware that the ex-slave Pasha was already in disfavour at the Porte, David ignored his father's counsels of prudence and angrily informed the Sultan of the grim situation in Baghdad. It was a perfect invitation for Daud to silence his enemy and simultaneously seize his family treasure. Within a few months of his second marriage in 1828, David Sassoon was arrested and gaoled with a fellow-conspirator, his wife's brother. As a public warning of what they could themselves expect, the renegade Ezra was then taken from his cell and strangled.

Daud Pasha had most accurately anticipated every move in the game, fully aware that the Sheikh Sason would not stand by and wait for the mutilated body of his beloved son to be delivered to him for burial. At the palace he pleaded for mercy, while the tyrant showed reluctance in order to inflate the ransom. A huge sum was finally agreed as the price of David Sassoon's life, but he would have to leave by the next boat for Basra, then governed by a minor satrap subordinate to the Pasha.

It was a tenuous reprieve. The Jews of Basra had always relied on their wealthier and better-placed brethren in Baghdad. They would be helpless to resist if Daud decided to take the exile back into custody. The Sheikh, seasoned in palace ways, guessed that the ransom would be only the first of a series of 'fines' which must end in the murder of his son and certain ruin for the whole family.

Afraid of treachery now that the money had been paid over, David could not risk waiting for the regular boat service. That very night, within hours of his release, his father chartered a vessel for a large sum and guaranteed the captain a similar amount on landing safely. Provisions were hastily put together, since this orthodox Jew would have fasted the five days or more rather than eat the infidel's victuals. The weeping servants packed his clothes, not forgetting his prayer shawl, his phylacteries and the copy of the Pentateuch which had sustained him during the dark days in prison. Under his billowing and padded *atamsouk* he wore a money belt. According to family legend, he also had a few pearls sewn into the lining of his cloak. He embraced the four children of his first marriage and his young wife, again assuring his father that he would not risk staying in Basra.

Only his eyes showed between the turban and a high-muffled cloak as he slipped through the gates of the city where generations of his kin had once been honoured as Princes of the Captivity. The captain of the waiting vessel alone knew his true identity. It was feared that the Arab crew might have been tempted to rob him and fling his body overboard had they guessed that this very tall and silent passenger, the only one aboard, was the son of the province's leading Jewish merchant. At dawn next day he stood alone on deck and facing in the direction of Jerusalem. When he put on his striped prayer shawl and a black skullcap, they doubtless imagined him to be some rabbi on his way to the Holy Land or perhaps one of the many Jews then in flight from the Pasha.

The minarets drifted from the skyline, and he wept as the green winding waters took him swiftly from his family, perhaps for ever. He offered up prayers for them and his brother-in-law, who was ransomed at the same time but had preferred to remain behind. After almost a week, he came at last to the Gulf port of Basra which swarmed with junks, laden with silks, tea and spices from China and the Indies. He paid off the captain and went nervously ashore, half expecting to be arrested. He then made himself known to the local Jews and joined in their evening prayers. He was tempted to stay, but had to keep faith with his father. Before noon he set sail from the same port as Sinbad of old.

Some days later, he learned of his good fortune. Daud Pasha had sent messengers by the next boat to bring him back to Baghdad, planning to squeeze another heavy ransom from the Sheikh. By the time they arrived at the customs house and began to search every Jewish dwelling in Basra, the fugitive was already in Bushire, Persia, free at last from the writ of the Vali and eager to make a new home for his family.

By 1829, Bushire was only slowly re-emerging as a commercial centre. The Portuguese had first established a fort and trading station, but later it became a dingy fishing port with a shallow-water landing stage from which ships had to anchor three miles offshore. David Sassoon picked his way through a honeycomb of narrow alleys, more sinister than anything in his native city, where the tiled mosques and fretwork of minarets gave some illusion of grandeur. The streets were squashed between high walls on which perched squat dwellings, their red roofs peeling like a leper's scabs in the sun.

He had no time for self-pity. His antennae, sensitive from apprentice years in bazaars, soon began to twitch with the promise of new enterprises. Although the roads to Shiraz and the sea were little better than cart tracks and the whole town seemed shuttered under its rampart-like cliffs, he felt a hum in the atmosphere. Caravans came snaking over dizzy passes to drop into the deep valleys with leather goods, carpets and metal-ware.

Messages of goodwill soon reached him from other communities in Shiraz, Aleppo and even distant Tiflis, yet the first exhilaration of freedom was already passing. His time in prison now seemed almost more acceptable than the loneliness of exile. He kept reproaching himself for having put his family in jeopardy and possibly making scapegoats of many others. He found comfort in prayer and was a little reassured by the news that slowly filtered through from Baghdad. Under pressure from the Porte, Daud Pasha was now too concerned with his own safety to mount the full-scale terror feared by the Jews. The aged Sheikh was also becoming active in the complicated financial network that radiated from Baghdad. Arab shipmasters and fierce-looking hillmen from the Mongolian trade routes began to arrive in Bushire with goods and the currency for transactions which the Sheikh Sason or others close to him had initiated. Several traders, who had long made use of the family's counting-house and its credit facilities, co-operated, but others were more cautious. Reports of spies in Bushire confirmed that Daud had not entirely given up hope of kidnapping his enemy.

Although his family name earned respect in the synagogue, David was still a newcomer. Some of the local merchants thought it almost quixotic for a mighty Sassoon from Baghdad to be trading on such limited capital. He was said to have spent his first nights in a wharf shed exterminating rats with his pistol. Fact or legend, it was consistent with a man who felt no shame in starting as a pedlar in the port of Bushire. He was at last seeing his birthright without the semi-feudal glaze of privilege. He was not too proud to accept the free tenancy of a small dwelling from Samuel Zacharia, a prosperous merchant who had come originally from Shiraz and knew most of the Persian traders. Zacharia generously lent him a little stock and guaranteed his credit.

He could soon hold his own in the bazaars. His mind was nimble for market prices and the seasonal fluctuations in a wide, but familiar, range of goods. Another asset was his fluency in several tongues, even some of the mountain dialects of Central Asia, but he lacked the leisure or inclination to learn English. The East India Company had for more than half a century maintained a factory and flourishing trading post in the port which was ideally placed for receiving a bush telegraph service. Judging from David Sassoon's friendly reception in Bushire, Colonel Taylor had probably acquainted the local Agent with something of the new arrival's character and background.

He started active trading from a very small quayside warehouse, owned by Zacharia. It was rat-free but far removed from the spacious ancestral *serdab* in Baghdad which at times bulged with merchandise like an Aladdin's Cave. The dhow captains slowly came to know him as a man of honour whose word could be trusted even in the smallest enterprise. He bought wharf space and rented it to traders who arrived by sea or overland to sell their goods and stock up. He added steadily to his capital but preferred to act as a middleman, particularly for Bombay merchants, rather than compete independently with local dealers who had more substantial reserves. It was the birth of a lifelong antipathy to all gambling transactions, however tempting. Cautiously he began to export a few horses, dates, sheepskins and small consignments of pearls to India, content with the lighter cargoes of silks and metal-ware that came back. With neither boats nor camels to distribute goods, he wisely decided to limit his imports.

His piety and learning earned the respect of his co-religionists, but a remarkable presence also impressed others, including the British Agent. Tall, spare, hard of muscle, with an El Greco face the colour of light cinnamon and fringed by a beard already flecked with grey, he looked very different from the wheedling Jew of tradition. There was a curious remoteness about him, and he was saddened when the candles were lit in some elder's home where he was a Sabbath guest. As the woman of the house bowed her head over the damask cloth on which lay the loaves of bread, plaited in symbol of a bridal wreath, he longed for the wife whose warmth he had so briefly enjoyed. But no part of his lonely exile was more bitter than the knowledge that his first-born, Abdullah, would shortly celebrate his Barmitzvah without him. He had resigned himself to forfeiting the pleasure of hearing him read from the Torah when he learned, to his great joy, that the Sheikh was making plans to join him in Bushire.

Few details are available of this exodus, after so many centuries in Baghdad. The Sassoon patriarch was far too prominent a figure to have kept his plan secret without paying over substantial bribes for safe conduct. Only a fraction of the family wealth was salvaged. Funds were certainly left behind which helped many in the Baghdad colony to survive the plague that soon claimed four thousand victims a day. The Tigris rose and flooded the city, destroying many houses already looted by the Pasha's soldiers.

David Sassoon led prayers in Bushire for those who had suffered so cruelly. He offered thanks for the near-miracle of being reunited with his family, but the octogenarian was worn out by his hard journey and had not long to live. Early in 1830, he died peacefully in David's arms just before the Barmitzvah of his grandson. The thirteen-year-old Abdullah was conducted by his father to a dusty courtyard where an awning shielded the congregation from the fierce sun. In flawless Hebrew perfected by long and anguished rehearsal, Abdullah dutifully read the Torah from a yellowing scroll which jingled with tiny silver bells as it was borne from the Holy Ark. He was now a Son of the Commandment, confirmed in his duty to wear phylacteries for morning prayer and to carry out all the other observances of his faith. He modestly accepted the congratulations of the mercers, the money-changers and pedlars among whom he expected to spend the rest of his days. It was the earliest public ceremony in the career of Sir Albert Abdullah Sassoon, First Baronet of Kensington Gore.

David Sassoon had already set his sights on India which offered his children a more liberal education than was possible in this backwater. A visit to some of his business associates in Bombay made him itch to transfer his activities to that fast-growing city, now the natural entrepôt for trade with all the Gulf Ports and East Africa. He could clearly see prospects in a two-way export and import firm operating between India and Persia.

Bombay had first come into British possession as part of the dowry of Catherine of Braganza on her marriage to Charles II, who sold it to the East India Company for £10 a year. It remained a mean and unhealthy settlement on a group of seven islands which the Company welded into one vast inland lake of stagnant water. The city had sprouted from miles of stinking mud flats sprawling round the Fort, but corpses were still buried in the sands of Back Bay to invite the attention of pariah dogs. The expectation of life for Europeans was always said to be spanned by two monsoons, but immigrants like David Sassoon were immunized by the heat and dirt of Baghdad. They would cheerfully accept worse hazards for the religious freedom and protection offered by the British flag.

After a squalid little port like Bushire, the island seemed a vast bazaar where Parsees, Moslems, Jews and Hindus all traded in apparent peace and harmony, while other centres, notably Madras and Calcutta, were riddled with caste and commercial snobberies. In the crowded streets he jostled Afghan horse-dealers with well-oiled hair; traders from Bokhara, dressed in tall sheepskin caps and gaberdines; and the high-cheeked Mussulman usurers whose green silk turbans bobbed among the tall shiny *khokas* of the rival Parsees. He soon identified and avoided the Armenians, hereditary enemies, who wore Persian dress like himself but were more conspicuous with their henna-dyed hair and whiskers.

The Jewish colony was settled mainly in a small network of dense alleys. Here the Nissims and Gabbais from Baghdad greeted him warmly, yet he was saddened by the hovel which had been converted into a make-shift synagogue. The majority of the immigrants had failed to prosper, although grateful enough to escape from Daud Pasha. Without capital and finding it difficult to master Hindustani or the strange ways of a new country, most were content to trade half-heartedly among themselves. They seemed to him spineless and far less self-reliant than the Parsee shop-keepers who thrived in Bazar Street.

The congested port was busy with a variety of craft, small and large, none without some bustling Parsee scurrying across the decks with his pointed shoes twinkling under the red silk pantaloons. They were most prominent on the busy wharfside where all the leading British merchants had their warehouses. The point was not lost on David Sassoon who had already inspected a small house in Tamarind Lane. It might be divided into an office and godown, with living quarters above, rather on the lines of his old home in Baghdad, but without the cool courtyard which his family would miss in this noisy, foul-smelling city.

He returned excitedly to Bushire. With local merchants he explored outlets for the silks, cotton yarn and metals which he proposed sending back to them. He also approached traders who might supply him with merchandise from Persia. The goodwill of the British Agent was discreetly sought and promised, while several friendly Arab captains were canvassed to seek him out when they anchored at Bombay. When his wife confided the joyful news that she was with child, her first, it seemed a good augury for starting a new life across the sea. Yet he still hesitated to take the step on reserves that might not prove strong enough. The final decision was apparently made when Samuel Zacharia and his son, returning with the Sassoons from synagogue one Saturday night, were importuned by a fortune-teller. He insisted on reading David's hand and advised him to leave at once for India where he and his children would be blessed with immense riches. Within a short time, the Zacharias enabled him to sail with enough goods to stock his first godown in Bombay.

No formal record of this transaction survives, but it has been echoed in talk and letters for well over a century. The versions vary slightly. According to the Sassoons, an interest-free loan of 10,000 rupees (then about £1,000) was advanced to their ancestor without even a note of hand, and fully repaid by him within three years. The Zacharia clan is emphatic that an unconditional gift was made. It resulted in mutually profitable trading between the two firms, but the Zacharias failed to flourish on the same scale. Some of their descendants would later work as clerks in the firm which prospered almost from the day David Sassoon first nailed his *mezuzahs* to the portals at 9 Tamarind Lane.

Part One (1832–1867)

Chapter One

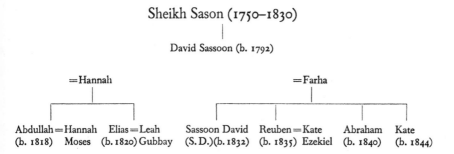

Sheikh Sason (1750–1830)

David Sassoon (b. 1792)

=Hannah · =Farha

Abdullah=Hannah	Elias=Leah	Sassoon David	Reuben=Kate	Abraham	Kate
(b. 1818) Moses	(b. 1820) Gubbay	(S. D.)(b. 1832)	(b. 1835) Ezekiel	(b. 1840)	(b. 1844)

David Sassoon opened the doors of his modest counting-house in the early months of 1832, the eve of a private commercial boom in Bombay, where many were eager to share the treasure enjoyed so long and exclusively by proud John Company. Its charter had recently been renewed for a further twenty years, but strictly on condition that others should also be permitted to trade freely in India and all foreign markets, notably China. Henceforth it would become little more than a political agent of the Crown, powerless to stop firms like Jardine, Matheson & Co., Forbes and the rest from widening that first wedge in its monopoly. Now the sun-worshipping Parsees would bask more openly in the warmth of a free enterprise soon to be briskly translated into textile mills and even more profitable real estate. It was almost inevitable that the first Sassoon born in India, later squire of stately Ashley Park in the county of Surrey, should be circumcised in a synagogue with a Parsee as landlord.

David Sassoon appreciated the friendly atmosphere of Bombay but was not impatient to compete with older and more solidly based merchants. He continued to trade on a relatively minor scale with the Gulf Ports through agents he could trust. Persia wanted the cotton goods which British exporters were quite as ready to barter for his hides, silks, spices and pearls. He also reopened the trade lines to his birthplace from which Daud Pasha had at last been driven by the Sultan. With some relaxation of pressure – the brother-in-law who had once shared his cell was briefly installed as Nasi – he could deal again with the bazaar-owners of Baghdad. More important, he was restoring his family name to the caravanserais along all the mighty overland silk routes. He was soon cautiously handling almost any commodity which might show some profit margin, however small.

Often it took five months to reach Bombay from England, but the new steamship services would surely send up the values of all foreshore property. With his first profits David Sassoon therefore began to buy up wharfages in Bombay. He was following in the tracks of the Parsees, but with one essential difference. They acted mainly as local middlemen and used their assets to buy land or lend money to the peasants. He preferred to nuzzle the warmth of foreign trade and was quickly among the captains of the bulging dhows which poured ceaselessly into the Bay of Bengal. By offering them dock space, he automatically had the first pick of goods before they reached the city booths. Many a trader would be stranded in port and short of money while waiting for the monsoons to pass. When they were ready to sail home, half their fresh cargoes would often be Sassoon merchandise. Some who had sold their own wares in Bombay were also tempted to invest in wools, gay chintzes, dye-stuffs and turquoises for the return journey. For this they needed additional capital or the services of a trusted go-between. Sassoon was at hand in both capacities.

Afghan traders would arrive after perilous journeys through Jalalabad and the snow-deep jaws of the Khyber Pass, their caravans gorged with indigo, dried fruits and shawls from Kashmir. Several also brought horses bred in Turkestan and fattened in their own sleek valleys. They found this Sassoon more congenial than the Hindus or some of the alien Parsees whose methods they suspected. They could speak freely to him in Persian and with a deep sense of kinship. Many of them, though Moslem, claimed descent from the Lost Tribes and shared certain ancient customs with the Jews.

When transactions did not turn out well, some preferred to store their unsold goods or sell on a commission basis rather than sacrifice them to the sly sharks on the waterfront. They were eager to load their caravans with merchandise for the long trek back to Afghanistan and even to Russia beyond. With little expectation of returning for many months from their orchards and bazaars, most were desperate for the credit which few Parsees cared to extend or only at ruinous rates of interest. David Sassoon was available and sympathetic. He accepted risks which seemed foolhardy to conservative British firms and even less attractive to the local money-lenders who liked to have their victims, mainly illiterate smallholders, within easy grasp. To the house in Tamarind Lane came merchants from far beyond the jurisdiction of British mercantile law. Their bills of exchange would often be guaranteed only by a goodwill and mutual confidence fostered throughout the years in Baghdad. Few cared to risk the bad joss of failing a Sassoon, but they expected the fullest integrity in return.

David Sassoon had soon discovered the advantages of having his capital and interest repaid in goods which he could then resell for an additional profit. His policy was more than justified, but it demanded harsh routine. In this new country he had first to master a primitive system of weights and measures which often varied from district to district. With a world market in prospect far beyond his previous experience, he familiarized himself with a wider range of prices and commodities and even started to explore the intricacies of the Stock Exchange. He acquired a working command of Hindi which he spoke with the measured diction of one naturally fastidious with words. He was almost as sparing in the use of Hebrew and Arabic, his two natural languages. A number of his letters have been preserved; they are incisive, very much to the point, and written in a clear script unusually free from the typical flourishes and affectations of the period.

He urged both his sons to interest themselves in the new markets which would open up with faster ships and a spreading network of railways. They became fluent in both English and Hebrew, the two languages in which the firm's cheques were stamped from the very first days in Bombay. Apart from observing the ritual of their faith and studying the Talmud, they learned British history and shared their father's deep loyalty to the régime.

One dusty forenoon in 1837 David Sassoon and his sons joined an excited throng on the Esplanade to hear the proclamation announcing the accession of Queen Victoria. They bowed with more than formal respect to the Governor, Sir Robert Grant, who composed Christian hymns but was no narrow zealot. The House of Commons rejected his Bill to remove civil disabilities on British Jews, but it had made him a heroic figure to the community long before he arrived in Bombay.

As they joined in chanting 'God Save the Queen', played by a military band in scarlet serge, the Sassoons looked conspicuous in their Baghdad-style costume, but certain refinements already reflected a ripening prosperity. The father wore a richly embroidered turban and flowing robes, dark in colour but obviously of fine material, with a broad sash at the waist. His sons, with mustachioes and fringe beards newly curled and perfumed, were dressed in shirts of good white muslin under their brocaded waistcoats. For this special occasion a striped pillbox, gay with tassel, replaced the customary black skullcap. Their billowing white trousers were bound at the ankle to display slippers of supple leather, curling elegantly to needle-point. The head of the house had made it a rule that his family must never wear western dress which might wean them from ancestral piety.

Several of his fellow-traders were misled by his natural reserve and an exceptional secretiveness in business matters. They made the mistake of underrating him. He was not invited to join the new Chamber of Commerce which had been set up for protection against the East India Company. The latter sniffed at these pushful intruders with their radical views on tariffs and continued to make things awkward for them. The Chamber survived, but at first served only the small fry. After only a few years, the minutes would record with regret that the Sassoons and other merchants of substance still 'stood aloof' from the Chamber.

The House of Sassoon was rising, brick upon brick, cemented by the family's own flesh and blood. The two sons had proved their capacity while still in their teens. They devoted themselves to detail, but the subtle executive gloss would come from their father. He taught them to restrain a natural Jewish emotionalism. They had always to appear calm and unhurried which would inspire confidence in times of crisis. In any transaction, great or small, each learned to play his cards close to the chest.

This triumvirate preferred to accept crushing personal burdens rather than delegate to strangers. Their meagre staff of warehouse clerks was recruited exclusively from ex-Baghdad Jews who would seldom be taken into private counsel. Many an ambitious employee, even when related to the family by marriage, would discover painfully that 'David Sassoon & Sons' meant precisely that. In policy and business routine, the young men reacted to their father and each other with almost a conditioned reflex. Physically, however, they had little in common except the hereditary mouth which turned down at the corners and often gave strangers an unfortunate impression of disdain.

Abdullah was nineteen when Queen Victoria came to the throne. Shorter than his brother and already tending to be portly – his calf seemed predestined to an aldermanic knee-breech – his genial manner made him popular with the salty Gulf captains. The Afghan traders also enjoyed his good-natured quips and used to present him with gifts of musk melons, quinces and boxes of grapes preserved in cotton. His junior by two years, Elias was not so voluble or demonstrative and took more after his father. He had a slightly withdrawn air, emphasized by myopic eyes gleaming behind his spectacles.

Both grew almost obsessively wary of impulse or experiment. Elias seemed to be ruled only by logic and a relentless devotion to percentages, while Abdullah smiled a good deal and never hurried. He was so sleek and affable to customers that nobody suspected him of an inner restlessness which had to be suppressed while his father was alive. For the present,

David Sassoon & Sons would be content to pile up their profits but without hoarding them. Shekels were automatically converted into more merchandise. The business broadened so unobtrusively that few in Bombay paid much attention when they took larger premises in Forbes Street.

As in Tamarind Lane, a room was set aside for daily prayers. There was now little difficulty in assembling a *minyan* or quorum of ten males from the staff. Under the whirring punkahs a legion of black alpaca mice scratched commodity prices and the names of new customers in hesitant Babu English and even weirder attempts at Mandarin. Cotton and opium; these two keys were at last unlocking the treasure which would soon make the firm a power from the Thames to the Tigris, and clear across Asia to the delta of the yellow Pei-ho itself.

India had grown raw cotton for centuries, using hand-looms for her local needs. The development of spinning in Lancashire created a keener demand, but transport to the coast was mainly by bullock carts over bad roads. Cleaning and ginning remained primitive. The cotton was often stored in pits plastered with cow-dung, although the East India Company had bought gins from the United States to improve cleansing.

On the dusty Green, cotton bales awaited shipment to Manchester and the Far East. The surrounding streets were always jammed from dawn onwards, and the marketing system chaotic. Lancashire brokers often complained of finding stones in the fibre, but bales still went out half-pressed and ruined the name of Indian cotton.

As soon as his sons were able to handle the now routine trade with Persia, Sassoon began to interest himself in the Cotton Exchange. He drove in a fringed *tonga* to the Apollo Bunder where brokers would sit and bargain for hours under the tamarinds. As he watched the bales being weighed and stamped, he sensed a new air of prosperity. The failure of an American crop had created a panic demand for Indian cotton. Lancashire spinners, already irritated by the high prices demanded by Alabama, were starting to order from Bombay. The market soon settled down again, but it had stimulated growers and many of the shrewder merchants to follow suit.

The Bank of Bombay had opened in 1840 mainly to cater for the port's expanding business in raw cotton and homespun. Lancashire more than doubled its supply of manufactured goods and trebled its outflow of yarn in the next decade. David Sassoon grasped this significance with both hands. Textiles and piece-goods could easily be funnelled into his usual markets in Mesopotamia and Persia, while China was now a potential outlet. Above all, the Lancashire merchants and other British traders might invest some of their profits in the carpets, spices and indeed the whole oriental cornucopia which his seamen and agents now emptied so regularly into his godowns.

His general policy was sound enough, although its full benefits would not be seen until the outbreak of the American Civil War. He decided to nibble at cotton himself, but only bit really hard after a Parsee had opened the first mill in Bombay. He was even more diffident of joining the scramble for Chinese markets when the East India Company's monopoly was finally breached. In the early 'thirties he had still lacked the capital to compete with concerns like Jardine, Matheson & Co., who were already established in Canton as independent merchants and acted as agents for firms in India. They sent out opium and shipped back tea in fifty-pound cedar-lined boxes. From 1819 onwards, they were already selling piece-goods in India by 'public outcry' or auction, but David Sassoon bought only modestly. His capital reserves would be far stronger a few years hence when China sprawled, prostrate and available, like some stranded whale.

Arab traders first introduced opium to the Chinese as a specific for gastric disorders and an antidote to leprosy. Portuguese seamen of the seventeenth century had then given the mandarins and a few rich officials a fashionable taste for *yang yien* (foreign smoke). With rapid national addiction, the drug developed into one of the East India Company's most profitable commodities. It became a very convenient medium of exchange when the Company began buying more tea and silk from the Cantonese who insisted on being paid in silver. Since exports of cotton could not balance the trade, opium was the only answer. The Imperial Government seemed less concerned with the growth of the habit than the huge silver drain to pay for it. They retaliated half-heartedly with an ineffectual ban on imports.

The Honourable Company's raw opium was first refined and then sold by public auction in Calcutta which had cornered the Indian output but still faced a threat from Turkish growers. Bombay moved swiftly into the lucrative traffic. The Company gave up transporting the drug, but continued to grant shipping licences to British and Parsee merchants as well as a few new exporting firms like the Sassoons. Small in bulk and imperishable, with a safe market and a satisfactorily rising demand, it yielded a net return of at least £100 a chest even after customs officials were bribed and the middleman had cut his slice.

By 1830, over eighteen thousand chests a year were being dumped more or less openly on China whose taels were pouring out in a silver torrent. By the time David Sassoon landed from Bushire, nearly one-third of the

Presidency of Bombay's trade came from the export of opium. The Manchu Government would sink a junk now and then and cry out against the 'foreign devils', but the newly-formed Bombay Chamber of Commerce admonished Lord Palmerston to deal more vigorously with 'the trickery and deceit of Chinese diplomacy'.

The East India Company's food ship *Lord Amherst* had docked at Shanghai in 1832 with members of a trade mission eager to buy tea and silk in exchange for their own piece-goods and opium. They were given a cold reception by officials acting on imperial orders. The opium clippers continued to establish smuggling bases at Lintin Island, off Canton, and other strategic centres like Hong Kong. The authorities had finally raided warehouses on Lintin and boarded several armed junks waiting offshore to take the drug in. They seized and burned twenty thousand chests worth upwards of £2 million. (Some outraged shippers valued their losses as high as £5 million.) It was the long-expected, and not unwelcome, signal for British warships to come to the aid of all honest merchants in the sacred name of free trade. They demolished the weak Chinese forces in an operation which would pay the plumpest of dividends for a full century.

At the end of the so-called 'war' in August 1842, a defeated Emperor signed the Treaty of Nanking. Five ports, Canton (previously the only one in which the British were allowed), Amoy, Foochow, Ningpo and Shanghai, were set aside for the conquerors. They would pay no taxes, while a modest tariff of up to five per cent on imports presented no obstacle to making one's fortune. Extra-territorial rights exempted them from the law of the country yet still gave jurisdiction over the Chinese in their Settlements or Concessions. The opium trade remained illegal, but a kindlier and half-blind eye was now turned on smugglers who promptly set up their main base on the island of Hong Kong, ceded to Britain. China had flowered overnight like a monstrous poppy.

Canton was hostile, and Shanghai appealed more to the 'barbarians'. The first fifty British traders, seven accompanied by wives, arrived on its mud flats, once an anchorage for junks. A handful of Americans followed, together with the Sassoons and some Parsees from Bombay, headed by Jejeebhoy and Cowasjee. In their wake came a horde of ruffians, free-booters and smugglers who saw no reason to pay even the five per cent tariff.

The first Sassoon had arrived in China in 1844. He was David's second son, Elias, who decided that Shanghai and Hong Kong offered by far the best prospects for opium and textiles. He had previously put up his sign in Canton and followed the example of Jardine, Matheson & Co. by financing shipments and giving small-scale merchant banking facilities to others, while sending his own goods up the coast. After leaving a deputy to manage the branch in Canton, he moved on to Hong Kong where some old ships' hulks near the river mouth had been speedily converted into warehouses for the brisk trade in opium. A crude but highly effective method was used to maintain a balance between supply and demand. The clippers would lie off the southern tip of the island until signalled to sail in by men posted on one of the peaks, known to this day as 'Jardine's Lookout'. To keep up the prices, vessels stayed out if the port was already over-stocked with opium.

Elias made Shanghai his personal base in 1850. Hong Kong seemed to him too dependent on slow mails and supercargoes of small clippers to handle a heavier volume of China trade. Already he saw lively potentialities beyond opium which was profitable but risky, and always strongly competitive. He therefore began to import metals, muslins and cotton while smoothly expanding the spice trade with the Indies, a lucrative sideline of the family business since their earliest years in Bombay. Moreover, the cold northern provinces offered a vast untapped market for the woollen yarns which his father was buying up in bulk.

He wisely decided to buy or build warehouses rather than pay rent. He also made sure of orderly delivery schedules, no easy task in those days of cynical opportunism. Others went for a quick turnover in opium, but this soft-voiced man with the wary brown eyes moved almost invisibly in the background and constantly expanded his stock-in-trade. Silk had long been grown in the hinterland of the walled native city. The profit from a chest of raw silk might be small, but it could easily be shipped down the coast together with nankeen, tea, hides and skins. Acting on this principle, he won the goodwill of the opium skippers who desperately needed cargo for their return trips to India.

There were many larger and older-established China traders than David Sassoon & Sons, but none more flexible or so diversified. They became shippers without the risks of shipowning, and acted as brokers or bankers to smaller traders in need of capital. They also started up as commission agents, buying and selling cargoes for others who discovered that the Sassoon turnover guaranteed them excellent cargo space at reasonable freight rates. Above all, they were warehousemen with an interest in some of the choicest wharves in the Far East.

Within five years the Sassoons had a solid footing along the whole China coast. They were also among the first to open branches in Japan after a new Treaty was negotiated in 1858. A lively Englishman named James Barnard made himself such an asset in Yokohama that he became one of the few gentiles to be given managerial status by the firm during the nineteenth century. Blessed by prosperity and a healthy influx of sons, the firm had become even less inclined to offer positions of trust to anyone outside the charmed family circle. By the time the Shanghai branch was opened, David Sassoon had added considerably to the four offspring of his first marriage. S. D. Sassoon* was born within a few weeks of the family's arrival in Bombay. Reuben opened his eyes in 1835 and Abraham five years later. In the bumper year of 1841, the patriarch simultaneously sired twin boys and became a grandfather!

Such a large clan demanded space, not to mention the pilgrims, holy men and supplicants who often came from afar and expected hospitality. David Sassoon began to consider following the rich Parsees up the cool heights of Malabar Hill, overlooking a palm-fringed coast. They lived in palatial bungalows with imposing façades and pillars wide enough apart to take two carriages abreast. He bought a site but seemed in no hurry to sink his capital into clearing the ground or furnishing the numerous rooms and servants' quarters which would be needed. He first built a smaller summer retreat, Garden Reach, among the shady trees in Poona, and only decided to complete his mansion when the city's sanitation became a menace to health. During the monsoon the foul slums became a network of sewage with rows of jerry-built tenements separated by gullies of filth.

The Sassoons were an exceptionally virile and robust tribe. It did not protect them from the hypochondria of a highly imaginative race. Reticent over business matters, they were far less so about health. Their letters fairly throb with exciting symptoms, and bulletins pour out on the latest pregnancy. Three generations of letter-writers, including women who rode to hounds with the best and husbands who won glory on the battlefield, would show the same terror of the microbe. 'L. is much more composed and quiet but she is not allowed to leave her room and is constantly watched by two nurses and her maid. .' 'Grandpapa is slightly better today and he intends taking the quinine according to your prescription. .' 'According to a letter in *The Times*, snuff is the great specific for influenza. .' 'She has been on a mild diet and today was allowed to take some chicken broth. .' While most sahibs asked for delicacies like hams and Stilton, the late-Victorian Sassoons kept imploring their London friends to send out Holloway's Ointment and other nostrums to repel the Bombay mosquito.

Abdullah, David's eldest son, married at twenty and at once moved to a house in the suburbs, quickly supplemented by a thatched holiday villa at Mahabaleshwar, 5,000 feet above the steaming miasmic island. His bride, Hannah Moses, came from a Baghdadi merchant family who settled in Bombay before David's arrival. Their marriage had every prospect of happiness, but Abdullah became alarmed when three baby girls arrived

---

* He was named Sassoon David, but will henceforth be referred to as 'S.D.' to avoid inevitable confusion with his father.

with maddening regularity. He would have to wait a full seventeen years for a son. Elias had also found his mate among pioneers, the Gubbays. His Leah bore him a son, already over nine years old before Abdullah at last had an heir. It partly consoled the younger brother for the discomforts of a lonely exile in China while the first-born remained at his father's right hand, snug in his villa and clubs.

Abdullah was less indolent than he looked. David Sassoon was permanently anchored in Bombay but kept all his sons on the move. Abdullah was quickly assigned to re-establish trade contacts with his birthplace, still considered more rewarding than the new branches in Hong Kong and Shanghai. In Baghdad he discovered several promising recruits to the various Sassoon offices in China where suitable personnel were thin on the ground in those early years. But even junior staff would be engaged with the cautious deliberation which had become almost ritual with David Sassoon. It made him hesitate when his sons pointed excitedly to the profits being made in cotton.

He declined to be hurried. He understood opium, but the Cotton Exchange was still alien territory. He therefore sat patiently on his hands when C. N. Davar opened Bombay's first mill in 1851. A dozen others soon followed him, but David Sassoon and the equally canny Parsee magnates up on Malabar Hill waited until the vanguard had painfully cut their wisdom teeth. The new mills were badly ventilated, with fire a chronic hazard. Native labour was casual and mostly too unskilled to handle even the old-fashioned machinery. Cleaning and ginning remained primitive, largely by hand and foot-rollers, while the yarn itself was unsuitable for the newly developed British looms. America found it easy to deliver better quality cotton more cheaply and faster. Before the opening of the Suez Canal, cargoes from Alabama would be unloading in England while Indian yarn was still puffing up the coast of Africa.

In Bombay the Sassoons were perfectly situated between England, the main exporter, and a China hungry for imports. The latter offered the fatter return on outlay and with fewer problems except distance, but ultimate success hinged on Elias's shrewdness in assessing risks. The Shanghai office demanded a man of dedication. Vital decisions had often to be made without waiting for the erratic monthly mail from Hong Kong. It was a solitary stint. Elias missed the companionship of his wife, but his natural self-discipline was reinforced by the stern moral precepts of the Torah. In a thriving foreign colony with few white women, several foreign traders took Chinese concubines or began to stammer in a hoarse opium voice like their own customers.

Elias was a quieter man who enjoyed study and meditation after the unceasing daily haggles with sea captains and the most corrupt customs service on earth. Like other prosperous merchants, he had soon built himself a two-storeyed house behind the high Settlement walls which were needed as much for sanitation as defence. It was modest compared with Garden Reach in Poona or Abdullah's picturesque showplace on the steep Ghats, but his charming little garden alongside the yellow Whangpoo was gay with peonies or flowering cherries.

This slightly stooping, short-sighted exile would never be at ease in Settlement drawing-rooms, but he liked to meet Englishmen and Americans and linger near some of the elegant French women who brought a spice of Paris from their Concession. He lent his patronage to the Shanghai Club which had opened soon after he started up in the port. On Sundays, if not occupied, he enjoyed watching the little Mongolian ponies race, but never joined other members in shooting pheasant or snipe. He much preferred to walk alone in the new park before going to evening service.

The tiny Sino–Jewish congregation had somehow survived for generations. They were mainly small traders with a sprinkling of ancient nobility who often held high office in the province. In quilted robes and with pigtails dangling over their prayer shawls, they had startled him before he acquired enough Mandarin to talk to them. He slowly came to understand their strange liturgical deviations which seemed to owe more to Confucius and Buddha than the Law of Moses. He was only at ease with a group of refugees who, like his own family, had fled from the pashas at the close of the century. They were joined by the office managers, clerks and warehousemen whom Abdullah or his father recruited from Bombay and Baghdad.

After his first long spell of duty, Elias returned to India to make the usual detailed report and, above all, to enjoy a little family life. His exile had meant a nine-year gap between the births of his two eldest sons. He was temporarily replaced in China by Abdullah, who felt more at home in Bombay or among his convivial sea captains on the Gulf. He loved the leisurely bargaining over coffee and a hookah but took less kindly to the thrusting competition in the Treaty Ports where his name was less familiar than in India or Persia. Moreover, he lacked the resignation and quiet philosophy which had helped Elias to survive his lonely years in Shanghai.

Abdullah was always impatient to hurry back to his wife and their comfortable bungalow in Poona, but even a short tour of the branches in Canton, Shanghai and Hong Kong left its mark. He had a flair for soothing people with a few genial words in the manner of visiting royalty. Clerks in some remote office often felt they knew him better than Elias who had moved quietly among them for years. It was an astonishing gift which paid dividends in a firm ruled by a respected, but almost legendary, patriarch whom few would ever see again after they were engaged and sent overseas.

David Sassoon followed an unchanging executive policy for twenty years. Each son would be thoroughly initiated into the routine procedures of Forbes Street before leaving for visits to Baghdad, Bushire and the other Gulf Ports. These short but intensive tours gave them confidence and experience, but there was a subtler purpose. Moral stamina had to be developed for the longer spells of duty in China. Apart from Abdullah, the first-born, none of the brothers enjoyed any special privileges. The married ones were packed off to Shanghai or Hong Kong like the bachelors. Not for some years would housing conditions in the Settlements attract one or two of the wives enough to accompany their husbands. Besides, they appreciated the comforts of a wealthy Bombay household too much to find alien China appealing.

David's wife, Farha, helped to comfort those left behind. She was a gentle matriarch and piously devoted to all the minutiae of household ritual. With a large family of her own and constant interludes for child-bearing, she was content to spend her time in Bombay or the summer retreat up at Poona. She rarely ventured out of doors except to attend the synagogue on Holy Days or to visit the Jewish poor. Her two step-daughters had married in their teens, one of them (Amam) producing ten children. Her own daughters, while strictly raised in the faith and pro-tected from worldly temptations, enjoyed a slightly less rigid purdah than she herself had known in Baghdad. Suitably escorted and chaperoned, they might occasionally visit a bazaar, but most of their hours were occupied in study or learning the social graces. Smallish, they had a grace and pride of carriage that hinted at a distant Spanish ancestry. The effect was enhanced by their attractive dark eyes, olive skins and glistening black braids.

Kate married into the Ezekiel clan of Calcutta when she was only fifteen. She was musical and overcame a clammy climate that so often put the family piano out of tune. She used to write long letters to her brothers in a newly-acquired, flowery English. In May 1859, she informs Reuben, then in Shanghai, that 'my brother Abdullah gave a very grand party inviting all his friends to supper in his new house which he has lately built'. She also reported fireworks and merriment which hardly consoled him in his temporary exile. He missed the Bombay clubs rather more than his wife whom he had married when he was only eighteen and alone in Hong Kong. His little Kate (yet another Ezekiel!) would soon grow tabby-fat and rarely joined her husband socially. She buried herself instead in her own nirvana of sweetmeats and novelettes.

Reuben would arrange matters so that his younger brother, Abraham, was usually in Bombay with him. Abraham had one experience which all the others envied him. At fifteen, he had been sent to London by his father, who was gradually overcoming his suspicions of western ways but took the precaution of entrusting him to the tutorship of Hermann Adler, son of the Chief Rabbi. He was coached in English and returned with a handy grasp of the language, apart from a secret nostalgia for the delights of Victorian England. It made his years in the Crown Colony of Hong Kong more tolerable.

Most people liked Reuben's jaunty style, although the more snobbish clubmen thought his taste in jewellery a shade flashy. He was short, thickset and as barrel-chested as Abdullah, but with more of the dandy about him. He puffed cigars specially imported from Manila and toyed with an elegant snuff-box, yet his languid clubman's pose camouflaged a very shrewd head. His feats of mental arithmetic became a party trick, but nobody in Bombay could dismantle and put together a column of figures with more finesse.

Closer in age than the others, he and Abraham were naturally drawn together, but they also formed a close attachment with Abdullah. He found them far more congenial than his full brother, Elias, in whom at times he detected a resentment and jealousy. But such rivalries remained well submerged and did not impair remarkable team-work. Often separated by entire continents, without telephones and cables and with letters clogged by slow or unreliable boats, all the brothers acted together by an educated instinct. They sensed infallibly how the others would respond to the prod of crisis. And by constantly shuffling the pack, David Sassoon made them almost interchangeable.

They were paid generously, and each was allowed to invest on his own so long as it did not conflict with the firm's ventures. For this reason, they speculated mainly in real estate and bought properties in Hong Kong and elsewhere, either alone or sometimes jointly, from their first savings. As expected, the quiet and secretive Elias was careful with his money and inclined to play a lone hand. Within a few years, he was able to pay over £2,000 for shares in the China Steam Navigation Company. He also snapped up sites on the Shanghai mud flats at agricultural prices, sometimes as low as £90 an acre. (It would soar to £300,000 an acre by the time his grandson, Sir Victor, came to develop the Bund!) He guessed that the port must grow, but was surprised by the influx of fifty thousand Chinese labourers who poured into the Settlement by 1855, eager to work and escape vicious taxation by the warlords. Elias would be among the first to invest in the housing estates that soon sprawled over the Chinese city.

By allowing his sons to amass small independent fortunes, David Sassoon showed generosity as well as an understanding of human frailty. Avarice was nipped before it could fester. Married sons with homes and families of their own might have been seduced from the parent firm had they – or their wives – felt too restricted. Individual enterprise could be a splendid safety-valve as well as proof of capacity. In the years to come, none would be admitted to partnership in the firm until he had made sizeable capital by his own efforts. David Sassoon remained the sole owner until 1852, when Abdullah joined him as a partner and Elias shortly afterwards. Only after their father's death, when the firm needed new blood at the top, would any of the younger brothers be given a place at the Board table.

By the time of the Indian Mutiny, a bare quarter-century since the rugs were laid on the first floor over the cramped counting-house and godown in Tamarind Lane, the firm was already one of the most powerful in the Orient. A contemporary observed, without the slightest acrimony, that 'silver and gold, silks, gums and spices, opium and cotton, wool and wheat – whatever moves over sea or land feels the hand or bears the mark of Sassoon & Co.'. The times were, of course, propitious. Labour was cheap and abundant, and taxation negligible. Trade had thrust ahead, powered by new industrial methods and lubricated by railways, ships and the telegraph.

The Sassoon firm had unique advantages. Few competitors were as closely integrated or enjoyed a more reliable information service. It preserved them from the fate which overtook so many others as a too eager alchemy went to work in mid-century Bombay. They resisted dazzling new prospectuses and preferred to buy up businesses wrecked by gamblers or badly run by indolent, near bankrupt owners.

They had no taste for pioneering. David Sassoon followed the Gubbays, Ezras and Ezekiels to India. He had only sent his son, Elias, to China after the Jardines and others had secured a foothold in the Treaty Ports. From the beginning and almost by instinct, he conformed to the classic tradition by launching his millions on the *second* wave.

Chapter Two

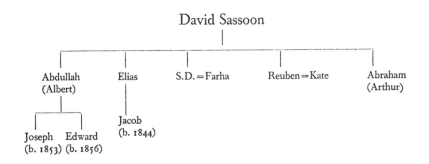

David Sassoon

Abdullah (Albert)	Elias	S.D. = Farha	Reuben = Kate	Abraham (Arthur)

Jacob (b. 1844)

Joseph (b. 1853)   Edward (b. 1856)

The cotton magnate and first Parsee baronet, Sir Jamsetjee Jejeebhoy, once declared emphatically that 'the chief cause of David Sassoon's success was the use he made of his sons'. He trained them to be chorus masters, with himself as conductor. Dressed in the flowing robes and turbans of Baghdad and always moving respectfully behind their parent, they looked hardly distinguishable. But differences in age and status were soon reflected in personality.

Abdullah remained at his father's side, deferential but watchful behind the sleek bonhomie. He seemed rather like an amiable sea lion who barked and performed jolly tricks but slid into the tank when one tried to touch him. Elias looked more the mandarin than a Baghdadi, with his spectacles and yellowing skin. He was businesslike and inclined to be abrupt at the meetings in Forbes Street. Reuben was always himself. He seemed to sparkle perpetually, from his gold teeth to the flashing diamond on his finger, but his lists of figures gave proof of long hours at his desk. Whatever he said, he was sure of support from genial Abraham who, unknown to his father, wore Western clothes when in Hong Kong and quietly encouraged his friends to call him 'Arthur'.

The odd man out was S.D., perched between Abdullah and Elias, and his younger, easier-going brothers from whom he was isolated even more by temperament. Tall and thin as a cheroot, with a glum day-dreaminess about him, he looked delicate and spoke with a slight lisp. After his counting-house apprenticeship, he found relief from business by helping to edit a new Hebrew–Arabic periodical. He was often so much more withdrawn than Reuben or Abraham that his father took pity and sent him to Baghdad for a course of study. There, at the age of eighteen, he met Farha Reuben, daughter of a devout and wealthy merchant.

She was four years younger, dark and petite like his sisters but far less submissive, as he soon discovered after they married. Hardly reaching to his beard, she was quick-tempered and had a waspish turn of phrase. He was sickly but uxorious, born to be the victim of her fitful changes of mood. During her first pregnancy she is said to have demanded a certain rare peach grown only in Kashmir. According to the story, he promptly went north and returned with the fruit after an exhausting journey. By that time his wife had lost interest and refused to touch it.* But even she could not persuade her father-in-law to make exceptions. Her husband was duly dispatched to the Shanghai branch while she fretted in Bombay and fussed over her baby son.

She lived on Malabar Hill in David's stately Palladian mansion whose verandas offered a panoramic view over the Bay. Sans Souci owed rather more to Persian fantasy than Potsdam. Tinkling fountains blended with the chatter of green parrots in the banyan trees as half a dozen gardeners tended the flowers and ferneries. Through the Moorish arches and across a marble courtyard trooped a retinue of coachmen, grooms and house servants, supplemented by such traditional local specialists as the lamp-trimmer, the tea-brewer and the *dhobi*, with his weekly pile of linen. The cooks were of course Jewish, a resident *shochet* ensuring that all meat was solemnly slaughtered. An outhouse was built for the ritual bath with its living spring of water. One special room was also filled with sacks of wheat from the previous year and kept strictly apart from everyday victuals and utensils. It would be used on the eve of Passover to bake the *matzos* or unleavened bread eaten during the eight days of the festival.

Like most other wealthy Jews of Persian or Mesopotamian origin, the Sassoons kept a number of slaves bought from Arabic-speaking tribes. Their rights were scrupulously respected according to the Torah, the more trustworthy being given early freedom. A letter of release, signed in 1843 by David Sassoon in the presence of witnesses, grants formal liberation to his slave, Salem, whom he had previously freed.

His unmarried twin sons and others in the household would rise at sun-up to join him in morning prayers. A carriage took him to Forbes Street where he was approachable to the most junior of his staff but saw few merchants in his later years. He drove home at two for tiffin and did not often return to the counting-house after his siesta. Leaving Sans

---

* Since a similar anecdote is told in other family histories, it is offered here with some reserve. Nevertheless, the episode is consistent with later impulses, like that described on page 73.

The head of the family with three of his eight sons, Elias, Abdullah and Sassoon David Sassoon. The photograph was taken shortly after the Indian Mutiny. A few months later, 'S.D.' left to open the firm's London branch. He was the first of the clan to wear western dress.

From his mansion on Malabar Hill, David Sassoon constantly issued advice and policy directives. This letter praised the work of his son, Solomon, in Shanghai. The letter heading, like the firm's cheques, was in English and Hebrew.

The Bund, Shanghai, in the 'nineties when the two rival Sassoon firms were among the leading traders, shippers and property-owners in the Treaty Port. (Reproduced with permission of Jardine, Matheson & Co. Ltd.)

Sir Albert (Abdullah) Sassoon.
(*Vanity Fair* cartoon by Spy)

Reuben Sassoon
(*Vanity Fair* cartoon by Spy)

Souci promptly at five o'clock, he liked to drive to the Bandstand or promenade gravely on the Esplanade, 'like Isaac at eventide', according to a contemporary. He looked older than his years with a heavy, snow-white beard framing the gentle but careworn face. He would often exchange visits with Dr John Wilson, a celebrated Biblical scholar and archaeologist, who had mastered Hebrew. They liked to debate matters of dogma and played long games of chess while David Sassoon smoked his hookah dripped in rose water. Sometimes he drove up to Mazagon to call on the Parsee banker–shipowner, Pestonjee, or his closer friend, Sir Jamsetjee Jejeebhoy. He conversed with them in their own tongue and much enjoyed the nostalgic Persian melodies which their servants plucked from the sitar.

More often he devoted his early evenings to talmudic study, receiving visitors and writing letters. Pleas for business advice, dowries, spiritual guidance and endowments came from the Gulf, the Holy Land, China, Japan and even beyond. A small community in New South Wales – one time refugees from Baghdad – might need prayer-books; the congregation in Tientsin required funds to open a new school; and from a dozen rabbis came desperate appeals for Sassoon, descendant of Princes of the Exilarch, to defend his brethren against some local oppressor. He weighed evidence, sifted genuine penury from professional begging letters, and poured out advice, together with his many lakhs of rupees. Every letter was answered in his own firm hand. Visitors who came from afar were given food hampers and clothing for their homeward journey, apart from the inevitable donations. Many stayed. From Baghdad, Aleppo and Damascus he brought over and resettled entire families. Most had to be fed, housed and given medical care. In his last years, no Jewish beggar would ever be seen in the streets of Bombay.

He spent over £100,000 on public benefactions alone, a significant pointer in itself to the wealth amassed by his firm even before the boom of the 'sixties. He built synagogues and Hebrew schools in Byculla and Poona and endowed almost a miniature 'welfare state' for his co-religionists. A scholarly traveller from Palestine, Jacob Saphir, spent six months in Bombay during 1859. He has left a vivid if rather fulsome account of David Sassoon and the fifty or so families from Baghdad who still spoke Arabic and wore the costume of their homeland.

'A single Prince is the head over them all. Every Sabbath and every Monday and Thursday, he comes early in the morning to the Synagogue in the town to say his prayers with the community, and on the other days of the week he goes with his coach far afield to the Synagogue which is in the suburbs, and where his elder sons and the other wealthy people who live in their gardened houses attend. In the afternoon, towards evening, I was many times in his office, and there they forgather to offer the after-noon and evening prayers in public. As evening approaches on Friday, the gates of his office are closed till Monday (for on Sunday they do not open according to the regulations of the Government). The table of the house of David is like the table of a king, and the whole courtyard down below is filled with a large multitude of poor people, who come every day from all countries, and what is dispensed to them is more than enough to still the hunger of those who forgather there. For the special and worthy poor who remain in the courtyard of the Synagogue or their house, they send them their portion with dignity.'

David Sassoon was, however, wise enough to see the dangers of be-coming too inward-looking and parochial. He endowed the Gothic-style Sassoon General Hospital at Poona for the benefit of all sects and creeds of Indians, as well as Jewish patients. Built on two floors with accom-modation for two hundred men and women, it was equipped on the most modern Western scale, together with a hostel for doctors and nurses. Separate buildings were put up for lepers and maternity cases. The usual massive clock tower was included in the architect's plans. Punctuality was the first unoriental habit David Sassoon picked up from the British.

He also gave generously towards an asylum in Poona for the relief of destitute invalids, aware that after-care might be desperately needed by those discharged from hospital, still crippled and unable to work. He once returned thoughtfully from visiting Abdullah's villa at Mahabalesh-war where European fruits and vegetables flourished in a red clay soil. He could not help contrasting its vivid flowers and the woods swarming with wild birds and game with the filth and flies he had just left below in Bombay. He soon bought a few acres and set them aside as camping grounds for the poor.

He was offered many public appointments but only accepted that of Justice of the Peace, often acting as sole magistrate in disputes between Jews. They were mainly law-abiding and lived according to a strict moral code, but many of their neighbours were bred to stealing or thuggery almost from the cradle. Years ahead of his time, he saw the danger signs of juvenile delinquency and took action. At Sewree on the eastern shore of the island, a former editor of the *Bombay Times*, Dr George Buist, had established the Bombay School of Industry in 1850. He rescued several young offenders from gaol and attempted to teach them a useful trade, but was chronically short of funds and hampered by apathetic officials. David Sassoon removed the school from its ramshackle premises to a new building off Grant Road and guaranteed a regular income for its upkeep. A former sergeant-major of the Bombay Horse Artillery was put in charge, assisted by his wife who ran the tailoring class. Several boys were given an apprenticeship as carpenters, turners and blacksmiths and placed in employment as far as possible from their vicious backgrounds. The Sassoon Industrial and Reformatory Institution, the first of its kind in the Orient, became the prototype of many others.

David Sassoon formally swore allegiance to Her Britannic Majesty in 1853, signing his naturalization certificate in Hebrew. He still spoke not a word of English, but none would prove more anglophile in act or sentiment. A flagpole with the Union Jack proudly aloft became his totem, and all pupils in the Sassoon schools were taught to sing 'God Save the Queen' in English, Hebrew and Arabic. When he was sixty-two years of age and his wife gave birth to a baby girl, their last child, a Bombay wag affected surprise that she had been named Mozelle instead of Victoria. But the dart was aimed more at Abdullah, who constantly invited fellow-clubmen and his Chamber of Commerce colleagues to address him as 'Albert'. He hesitated to make the change official while his father was alive, but unblushingly named his second son, Edward Albert.

The Sepoy Mutiny offered scope for more practical demonstrations of loyalty. It scarcely touched Bombay but there were some anxious moments. David Sassoon went off to Government House with a dramatic offer to assemble and equip a Jewish Legion in the event of civil war. The gesture was sincere, if of dubious military value; most of these untrained and stooping volunteers were hardly warlike potential. Fortunately, perhaps, they were not called upon. When the news improved, the family assembled with the whole community in the synagogue at Byculla. In the long prayer shawl which he had worn so long ago on the boat from Baghdad, David Sassoon read from the Psalms and offered thanksgiving. He then led a torchlight procession to the house of Albert-Abdullah, who provided food and drink for all. To celebrate the end of the Mutiny a few months later, they ordered every Jew in Bombay to light up his house and recite prayers and blessings for the Royal Family.

Soon afterwards, when the East India Company officially ceded all its political powers to the Crown, David Sassoon marked the occasion with a magnificent banquet and ball at Sans Souci. A triumphal arch in red, white and blue spanned the long avenue leading to the mansion. The gardens were brilliantly illuminated by coloured lights as five hundred of Bombay's leading citizens and neighbouring princelings awaited the Governor. He was greeted by a full military band who played the Anthem under the gateway, adorned with banners and flags. After a lengthy menu scrupulously arranged to avoid offence to Jewish and other caste palates, Lord Elphinstone proposed the host's health. He told his fellow-guests: 'We must not forget that at the time of the Mutiny, when threatened with danger and whilst some were panic-stricken, Mr Sassoon and his family were the first to come forward in support of the British Government.'

Some of the diners may have regretted not having followed his example, both patriotic and profitable, in buying so heavily in Government Stock while almost everyone else was selling. During the crisis he had made an even less expected gesture of loyalty. His family would henceforth be permitted to wear western clothes as often as they wished, 'so that it may be known on which side you are'. The patriarch himself would never abandon his traditional garb, while Albert and his brothers were also too tactful to do otherwise during his lifetime, except on very formal civic occasions. In a photograph taken shortly after the Mutiny (facing page 32), the third son is the only member of the group not wearing western dress. He had the best reasons, as he was leaving for England.

S.D. had returned thankfully from the moist heat of Shanghai which suited him far less than his more robust brothers. He had missed his wife and baby son, Joseph, and seized eagerly on the prospect of emigrating. His younger brother, Abraham (who now signed himself 'Arthur', except in his letters home), had volunteered, but was considered too young at eighteen. He could hardly oppose his formidable sister-in-law who was pregnant again and more determined than ever to break out of the chafing purdah-cum-ghetto of Bombay. London now seemed infinitely more tempting to her than any peach from Kashmir.

David Sassoon's decision was influenced by three main factors. The quickly expanding cotton trade made it desirable to send one of his sons to open an English branch. S.D. was the most easily spared and might benefit from a less extreme climate. Finally, there was reassuring evidence of a more liberal attitude in England towards Jews. Baron Lionel de Rothschild, allowed at last to swear an amended oath on the Old Testament with his head covered, had just taken his seat in the House of Commons. His brother, Mayer, was soon afterwards elected for the Hythe Division of Kent. One of his successors in that constituency would be Sir Edward Albert Sassoon, Bart., son of Abdullah.

Chapter Three

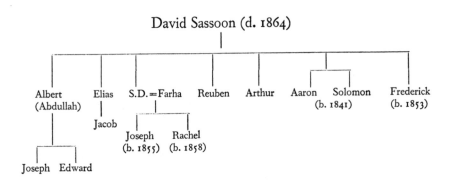

David Sassoon (d. 1864)

Albert (Abdullah) — Elias — S.D. = Farha — Reuben — Arthur — Aaron (b. 1841) — Solomon — Frederick (b. 1853)

Jacob (under Elias)

Joseph (b. 1855) — Rachel (b. 1858) (under S.D. = Farha)

Joseph — Edward (under Albert)

S. D. Sassoon arrived in England towards the end of 1858 and settled briefly into a charming Georgian house overlooking Regent's Park. He was joined a few months later by his wife and their two infants, Joseph and baby Rachel. Their first taste of a London 'pea-souper' made them eager for the broad acres craved by most socially conscious industrialists and merchants in mid-century Victorian England. The chosen land was Ashley Park in Surrey, only seventeen miles from London. David Sassoon readily agreed to buy his son this fifteenth-century estate where Cromwell was said to have resided during the trial of Charles I. It was annexed to the Manor of Hampton Court in Henry VIII's reign and later passed into the hands of the Fletchers, who had acquired their wealth and a baronetcy through directorships in the East India Company. With the Company's eclipse by private traders, it seemed almost symbolic that a Sassoon should now hold the title-deeds.

The gabled, rose-red brick Tudor mansion had numerous lofty rooms with mullioned windows and rich cornices, some a trifle chipped. A maze of underground passages and several 'haunted' chambers added to its romantic appeal. The ornately embossed staircase dominated a hall whose walls were hung with paintings of heraldic shields and emblems. The showpiece was a vast ballroom where Henry VIII's courtiers and their ladies had cavorted. The house itself was perched on a crest of the Thames with graceful swans visible by spy-glass from the terrace. It stood among some two hundred acres of wooded parkland, thick with lime and larch.

The long avenues were lined by elms and the stateliest cedars in the county. While modest compared with the Rothschilds' lakes and gardens at Gunnersbury Park or the 3,500 acres of Tring Manor, it was an agreeable enough place for a man of twenty-six who enjoyed solitude and liked best to retire to his library after a day in the City.

There was no shortage of funds to furnish the mansion with the finest Chippendale, while some of Kneller's imposing portraits looked down on ottomans and lacquered cabinets chosen by a more exotic hand. In her boudoir hung with satin, Mrs Sassoon was content with her prospect of English country life. The rich green turf was a delight to the eye; the woods sparkled with pheasants; and a dozen conservatories promised flowers and fresh vegetables for her children. The neighbours had been a little hesitant at first to accept an exotic newcomer whose Babu accent slightly confused them. They soon found that this vivacious and stylishly dressed foreigner could be charming, though quick to take offence. She was not easily patronized.

Life at Ashley Park was pleasant and leisurely for the first year or two. The little châtelaine had an entourage of servants who were devoted to her, although she rather bullied them during the bleak winters. She longed wistfully for the blandness of Poona when no number of beech blocks in the huge fireplaces could warm those vast apartments. Her husband was more adaptable. His light business duties gave him the leisure to add to his library of rare Hebrew manuscripts, and he spent many congenial hours on translations and writing scholarly papers for periodicals in India.

The Sassoons belonged to the Sephardic sect which comprised all oriental Jews, in addition to those refugees from Spain and Portugal who had originally settled in England after the Inquisition. They were far outnumbered by the Ashkenazim, many of whom had come from Germany, like the Rothschilds, and whose numbers would be considerably increased by future Russian pogroms. The smaller, proud community of Sephardim stood aloof from these Yiddish-gabbling children of the ghetto with their caftans and side curls. They were more prosperous, cultured and exclusive, rarely marrying outside their ranks. They also had their own liturgy and wrote and pronounced Hebrew in a manner often incomprehensible to others of the faith.

S. D. Sassoon automatically became a warden of the Spanish and Portuguese Synagogue in Bevis Marks, within walking distance of his office. Already fluent in several languages, he soon improved his English but never quite lost a Bombay fuzz. He established smooth relations with Lancashire's exporters of piece-goods and City houses demanding regular shipments of tea, dried fruit and metals. But he was only too happy to escape to his books and the pleasant glades of Ashley Park. Not one of his descendants followed him into the City.

He had been sent to open a branch then considered of far less importance than either Shanghai or Hong Kong. His cosy routine between humdrum Leadenhall Street and Ashley Park was shattered by the American Civil War which made the London office highly sensitive to a volatile cotton market. The staff now had to maintain an up-to-the-minute news service with Bombay, often under trying conditions. The speediest means of transmitting market prices and other information was by telegraph to Suez, at £3 5s. for twenty words, and on to Bombay by steamer. Every other week all mail went by boat from Suez to Galle in Ceylon. It was then telegraphed to a poky office at Colaba Point.

The frenzied demand for India's cotton transformed her economy and catapulted the Sassoons into an unprecedented prosperity and influence. Jacob Saphir had already noted by 1859 that 'they have arrived at great wealth, approximately five million sterling'. This could only have been guesswork since the firm was the last to make its accounts public, least of all to a chatty rabbi. Whatever the figure, it would be multiplied several times over during the next feverish five years when something like £80 million of new capital poured into Bombay.

Lancashire had felt the grip of unemployment immediately after Alabama's rebel ports came under blockade. Starved of American cotton, Manchester turned in panic to the Indian mills. New spinning and pressing companies were hurriedly formed, and empty factories began to change hands at exorbitant rents. From Apollo Bunder to the Wellington Fountain, the streets were jammed with bales awaiting shipment. Yellow-capped police on the wharves tried vainly to divert an endless tide of heavily-laden, tinkling bullock carts into the railway sidings. In every alley European brokers haggled feverishly with the up-country middle-men who stroked their gold-embroidered shawls and enjoyed having the whiphand. Any shed on the Colaba Causeway was snapped up and turned over to squads of coolies who arrived by the thousand from their paddy fields. Slightly dazed and unaccustomed to working as stevedores, they loafed cross-legged on the wharf walls or chattered with their wives while naked babies swarmed over the bursting bales and left a trail of stale urine.

The price of cotton shot up to inflationary prices which English mill-owners paid to avoid complete ruin. Under a spreading tamarind on the Esplanade sat brokers who bought and sold thousands of bales of the poor short-staple cotton, known as 'Surats' and universally dreaded in the trade. At the height of the famine when so many Lancashire mills were closing down, a Manchester cleric used to offer up a fervent prayer, 'Oh Lord,

send us cotton, much cotton in many bales, but, Lord, let it not be
Surats!'

The firm of David Sassoon & Sons was well placed to enjoy this yeasty
season. In the seven short years since a pioneer Parsee had turned his first
spindle, they had steadily expanded their trade in textiles until its turnover
was second only to opium. Already established as solid entrepreneurs for
the leading millowners and cotton growers, and backed by sizeable
capital reserves, they were ideally geared to step up supplies to Lancashire's
hungry mills. They had other advantages. Space, always limited on this
narrow and impossibly crowded island, was now at a premium. The
Sassoons had a generous share of the foreshore, dating from their first
trading days with the Gulf Ports. It saved them from having to rent rat-
ridden godowns which leaked like sieves during the rains.

David Sassoon cherished his lines of communication like any good
general. They were lengthy and diffuse but manageable, thanks to a
member of the clan at each end, from Manchester to Manchuria. Nearing
seventy, he was content to leave much to his sons, supported by a trusted
force of Jewish clerks, warehouse overseers and storemen with proven
loyalty to a firm which many had served from boyhood. The family
executives were smoothly deployed. Albert and Elias together directed
operations from Bombay, now more than ever the hub of their empire.
The elder brother kept goods flowing to the Persian Gulf which he knew
so well. He apportioned wharfages and handled the complicated transport
schedules by sea and land. He also visited England where his half-brother,
although hard-pressed and sorely missing the peace of Ashley Park, was
efficiently co-ordinating the busy branches in Liverpool and Manchester
with his head office in Leadenhall Street. Albert helped to tie up various
loose ends before hurrying back to India. He seemed unaware that S.D.'s
stamina was being sapped by all this unexpected pressure.

Elias, the China trade specialist, soon adapted himself to the frantic
atmosphere of Bombay. Of all the sons he had the widest mercantile
experience and was best equipped to maintain a delicate balance between
orders from East and West. He shrewdly assessed risks and avoided the
many ambushes laid by share-pushers and speculators for the Sassoon
rupees. With his son, Jacob, who was almost a replica of himself even to
the spectacles both wore, he virtually took over the day-to-day running
of the business. More than once, however, he was irritated by his father's
over-caution. For this he privately blamed his brother.

Albert might be short of inches, but he was already walking on the
stilts of the first-born. He was now his father's proxy in supervising the
schools, hospitals, synagogues and other Sassoon endowments. He signed
a £3,000 cheque to pay for an eight-foot statue in memory of the late

Prince Consort, one of the firm's many patriotic acts of piety. No pitched battle developed between the brothers, but Elias resented carrying a heavier responsibility which left little time for home life or the clubs where Albert was such a popular figure. He was perhaps less than just to his brother whose sociability worked as a useful lubricant in the business mechanism.

A similar, if smaller, patch of irritation was forming in the Far East where Reuben was based mainly in Hong Kong, with Arthur as his willing lieutenant. Solomon, one of the twin boys, was more serious and industrious. He made his headquarters in Shanghai but kept an eye on his brothers and also remained closely in touch with the firm's agent in Yokohama. He made many a holiday or business trip to Japan whose landscape and graceful people appealed to a poetic streak in his nature. A reserved and devout bachelor, he modelled himself on his father and found the Talmud a greater comfort than the card-tables and race-meetings which his brothers could not resist.

Reuben was respected in Hong Kong as a man of the world and a good judge of madeira. He seemed just as much at home when he went north to Shanghai. He did not win his 'pink' like a future Sassoon, but enjoyed the picturesque meets of the newly formed Paper Hunt Club. The foxes wore red cowls over head and shoulders to pick them out in the gloomy swamps. The coolies used to stop their blindfold oxen at the water-wheels, while the foreign devils jumped their Mongol ponies over fences and often landed in the Soochow Creek.

A round of gay Settlement parties in March 1863 toasted the health and happiness of the Prince of Wales and his bride, Princess Alexandra of Schleswig-Holstein. Reuben spent happy hours pasting pictures of the royal couple's new home, Marlborough House, into his album. He also found delight in an occasional day's shooting. The country air was cool and ideal for potting snipe, even if the Jewish dietary laws denied him the fruits of his bag. Such pleasures were not for the austere-minded Solomon, who still appreciated his brother's extraordinary talent for solving financial problems by making only a doodle or two on his starched cuff.

Any differences of temperament were submerged during these boom years when all David Sassoon's sons justified his patient training. At their Barmitzvah, each son attained not only his religious coming-of-age but a solemn responsibility as heir to vast riches. They paid the price in lost youth. Their family galleons sailed the Atlantic, the Indian Ocean, the Pacific and the China Seas, but none among them had ever launched paper boats.

No firm could fail to stay afloat during Bombay's four years of high tide, but the Sassoons escaped the disasters which later submerged many of their competitors. So much sudden wealth had led to commercial debauchery. A dozen new companies spawned every day, mostly bogus, and with nothing but paper assets to justify a mushroom rise in values. Gamblers became self-intoxicated and speculated in any share that came on the market. Coffee, furniture, steamers, hotels, jewellery, distilleries, livery stables – there was no shortage of rupees for a nimble turnover. The greatest frenzy of all was in land reclamation. With pier room so restricted, the most flamboyant schemes were launched for draining the swamps. Shares in the Back Bay Reclamation Company, 2,000 Rs. at par, soared to 50,000 in a few weeks. Every mud flat on the island was bought, sold and swiftly re-sold, some of the share-pushers having paid only a nominal deposit before issuing a dazzling prospectus. It became superfluous to reclaim a single foot during this wildcat delirium. The lemmings still raced headlong to the golden strip of foreshore.

Even the normally level-headed Parsees were caught up in this orgy of speculation. J. N. Tata, destined to become India's leading industrialist and social benefactor, was among the earliest victims. The son of a prosperous contractor, he had hastened back from China to join the textile boom. He became fascinated by an eager little broker, one Premchand Roychand, who had established agencies in several cotton-growing districts, and held court in Mazagon where his mansion became a miniature stock exchange, from dawn onwards. Friends, hangers-on, gamblers and share-pushers made their daily pilgrimage up the hill to wait patiently for a hint that could turn to gold. A pencilled note from Roychand would at once unlock the coffers of the Bank of Bombay in which the Government held shares. The directors had feverishly altered their Charter, doubled the capital reserve and were eager to offer almost unlimited advances to the wildest of speculators.

The Sassoons had no faith in Roychand and his hare-brained reclamation plans. They preferred to buy up godowns and wharves ready for the new steamer services. Through their Elphinstone Land and Press Company, they also invested quietly in property sites which would pay an enormous dividend when Bombay started to build office buildings and scores of tenements for the city's enlarging army of factory workers. The sons in the Far East were quietly urged to buy land for development while prices still remained economic.

Bombay's inflationary share values had become less and less tempting to those who foresaw a sudden end to the cotton boom. China seemed a far safer and more attractive outlet for capital. But a central banking unit was needed to discount bonds and keep commodities and currencies flowing evenly. The Hong Kong and Shanghai Banking Corporation was duly established by an international group of merchants with a capital of

$5 million. It would merge the requirements and interests of the established agency houses and thereby short-circuit delays in referring bills to houses in Bombay and faraway London.

Hong Kong was the headquarters, with premises in Queen's Road first rented from the Sassoons and purchased outright from them a year or two later. Arthur Sassoon and Thomas Sutherland of P. & O. were original members of the Board. A major branch was at once set up in Shanghai where the two majestic bronze lions outside the Bank became one of the city landmarks. They would often be touched for luck by passers-by on the Bund. A smaller office was soon established in Yokohama to handle the fattening trade with Japan.

Arthur's pleasure in his first directorship was soured by distressing news from India. Up in Poona, one November afternoon in 1864, the patriarch had walked for the last time among his foaming beds of hydrangea. He retired to write his daily letters to the Bombay office and must have fallen into a gentle sleep. A servant heard him cry out faintly, 'Abdullah, Abdullah', having forgotten that his son was in England. He died with the quill pen still in his hand.

He was buried in the grounds of his synagogue in Poona after a ceremony conducted according to the ancient customs of Baghdad Jewry. The family mourners slashed their garments as a sign of grief, the womenfolk loosening their hair and the sons tying handkerchiefs about their necks. Seven circuits were made round the grave before the coffin was removed and the bier overturned. A cloth was laid over the grave and all present threw coins upon it. For seven days afterwards, prayers were said at Sans Souci where the family sat together on hard low stools. The sons attended services – in Bombay, Shanghai, Hong Kong, London, and wherever else they might find themselves – to recite the sacred daily prayer for the soul of the departed during the eleven months of mourning.

There was an immediate response to Sir Bartle Frere's suggestion that the eminent merchant and philanthropist should be commemorated by a statue by Thomas Woolner, R.A., to stand in the new Sassoon Mechanics' Institute. So many wished to contribute, including the Parsees, that the Governor decided to head a public subscription list which would not be limited to India. All the Jewish communities in Persia and China responded, together with local traders of different faiths. The Rothschilds, Montagus and Moccattas sent liberal sums from England, as expected, but spontaneous offerings also came from Lancashire mill-workers, and even a five-guinea cheque from Mr Gladstone.

· · · · ·

Albert and Elias now had little time to indulge their private differences. As soon as the American Civil War ended, Lancashire had turned back to Alabama, anxious to shed the Surats which had clogged her spindles. Slump, panic and chaos gripped Bombay as the price of Indian cotton slipped from half a crown a pound to tenpence, and then even lower. The Bank of England's discount rate was raised to 10 per cent, and the air soon thickened with the odour of charred prospectuses and worthless share certificates. Hundreds of small bona fide investors and almost all the bogus promoters were swept away by the same ebb tide. The Bank of Bombay collapsed, bringing down Premchand Roychand, the Tatas and a host of others.

David Sassoon & Sons emerged intact, indeed more powerful. They had prudently avoided stock-piling and were therefore only slightly hit by the fall in cotton prices. Their profits from textiles, opium and other goods had been enormous. With strong capital reserves, they were insulated against crippling loan charges and sudden rises in the Bank of England rate. Above all, they could now buy heavily in a panic market. The slump in Indian cotton would be felt for some years, but it was partially balanced by a larger intake from Lancashire's mills. The firm, strongly represented on the Manchester Cotton Exchange, began to buy more piece-goods in bulk for resale to India, China and Japan. They also extended their range of merchandise and penetrated new markets. A branch in Singapore started importing Java sugar to appease India's sweet tooth. A representative went on to Rangoon and made contact with some of the larger paddy farmers to ensure supplies of rice, if harvests failed elsewhere. The firm had long imported tea from China, mostly for resale to England, but began to interest itself in local cultivation. Only a million pounds of Indian tea was exported to Britain in 1860; before the end of the century, it had increased tenfold and far exceeded the supply from China. The Sassoons would take a fairly generous share of this trade when their own experiments to grow coffee in Ceylon proved abortive.

There was no falling off in personal initiative after their father's death; quite the reverse. His counsel would be missed, but they could at last speak their minds, liberated from a sense of being pieces on a chessboard. Each son now had the stimulus of a solid personal holding in the business. Apart from estate in England valued at £160,000, their father had left 'upwards of two million sterling', according to the vague Press announcement. No precise figure was ever published, but it was generally assumed in Bombay that he had been worth over five million pounds.

He had provided substantial dowries for all his daughters, three of whom had married and were comfortably settled, and the inheritance would be divided equally among the eight sons whose holdings in the firm might reasonably be valued at some half a million pounds a head. Such an interest, when added to properties privately acquired over the years, would make them men of enormous wealth at a time when a good servant in Bombay was grateful for fifteen shillings a month and Shanghai's semi-skilled workers were being paid half a crown a week.

Wherever they now established themselves, the Sassoons followed a tradition set by the patriarch from his first days in Bombay. They were exacting about time-keeping and made few concessions to the Oriental's free and easy disposition. They had more than their share of Jewish litigiousness. The family archives bristle with disputes over excessive charges made by some tradesmen, often involving paltry sums. They never forgave disloyalty and showed no mercy to employees, Jew or gentile, who had embezzled funds. As employers, however, they paid the best wages and pioneered welfare schemes for workers and their families, including more and more non-Jews in the coming years of expansion. For the present, their head office in London and the various overseas branches were almost entirely manned by co-religionists recruited mainly from Baghdad and Persia. In addition to Sundays and the numerous local holidays of the East, they always kept their places of business closed on the Jewish Sabbath and all Holy Days, although never going so far as the Rothschilds, who decorated an office at New Court with the traditional citrons and palm branches during the Harvest Festival of Tabernacles.

The Bombay community and many distant beneficiaries had mourned the passing of David Sassoon with a natural apprehension for their future. They were quickly reassured. Albert (only his closest kin would henceforth call him Abdullah) honoured all existing endowments and even added to the family's list of pensioners. But he lacked his father's deep piety and found it difficult to concern himself with an orphan's education or pleas from clerks in Canton and Hong Kong to subsidize a daughter's dowry or place some promising lad on the firm's staff.

The new Chairman was showing much more energy than in the past. His brain hummed with plans for building docks and possibly moving into cotton manufacture. He became a leading member of the Chamber of Commerce which had once snubbed his father. He was among the first to buy a site on Elphinstone Circle where he planned to build the head offices of David Sassoon & Sons. He also hastened designs to complete and equip the Mechanics' Institute which his father had promised to endow shortly before his death.

All this activity placed inevitable strains on Elias, who missed his independence and the healthier climate of Shanghai. During the sticky summer months, he often dined with his trousers tucked into top-boots to keep out the mosquitoes, even on Malabar Hill. As second-in-command, he was permanently anchored in Bombay, while Albert and his family moved grandly between Sans Souci, Garden Reach in Poona and their delightful villa at Mahabaleshwar.

The pattern was becoming all too clear to Elias. His brother would remain the suave Chairman, although increasingly absorbed in civic affairs and his social life. He was playing host to the Governor, local officials, the Parsee magnates and any native princes who happened to be visiting the Presidency. He was being canvassed to accept nomination to the Bombay Legislative Council. His two sons had private tutors and would doubtless follow him into the business after completing their education in England. He was still in his prime, full of vigour and affable, if a touch pompous. He had lost his hair which gave a more patrician look to the longish face, framed by an almost white imperial beard.

Also bald, Reuben had grown very like him physically, but he was too active and spring-heeled to cultivate his brother's bourgeois corpulence. The old China hands thought him the cleverest and most congenial of the Sassoons. He attended his synagogue regularly but also enjoyed the company of pretty women. He shone at the card-table, and fellow-members of his clubs were fortunate to draw him as partner. Arthur was no less popular in Hong Kong where he had steadily moved up the social ladder, thanks to his recent entry into merchant banking circles. As a rich and personable bachelor of twenty-five, his mantelshelf was thick with cards.

Their brother, Solomon, was far more conscientious, and led an almost monastic life in the Settlement. He once wrote to James Barnard in Yokohama and asked him to send a couple of good dogs for his solitary walks. He posted a cheque for £35 to cover their cost, plus freight. It was one of his rare extravagances. Solomon impaired his health through over-work, and Elias had finally persuaded him to leave Shanghai for an ex-tended tour of some of the firm's branches, including Japan. After going south to confer with Arthur and other directors of the Shanghai and Hong Kong Bank, he sailed for Bombay in the winter of 1866. He reluct-antly agreed to Albert's suggestion to visit the London office and also investigate Manchester's latest spinning techniques.

As a result, Solomon narrowly missed an event which delighted the family. Wearing a smoothly ironed silk hat and a frock-coat cut by the best Parsee tailor in the city, Albert drove up to Government House in Poona where Sir Bartle Frere pinned the Order of the Star of India to his broad chest. He celebrated with an elaborate supper and ball at Sans Souci, where he attempted to please all tastes by introducing excerpts from

Italian opera between the customary Indian dances. The *Bombay Gazette* reported with approval that no 'natives' were among the three hundred guests and solemnly congratulated 'Mr Sassoon and his family on their evident wish to ally themselves with English society in Bombay'.

Albert's pleasure was wrecked by news from England. Woolner had made excellent progress on his statue of the patriarch. A site had already been roped off in Bombay's newly-opened Mechanics' Institute, but it would first be exhibited for some months in the North Court of the Victoria and Albert Museum in London. S. D. Sassoon travelled up from Surrey to see the scale model, although not feeling at his best during the abnormal heat of July 1867. He dropped dead while standing in the foyer of the Langham Hotel waiting for a cab to take him to South Kensington.

The Sassoons gathered at Sans Souci to discuss the vacancy in the London branch and generally to regroup. Their father's policy of rigidly excluding strangers from management had paid dividends in the early years, but there were disadvantages in this mutal pollination. The firm had thinned dangerously at executive level. S.D. had not been a business genius, but it seemed unthinkable to replace him by anyone outside the family. Reuben at once volunteered to take over in Leadenhall Street. He was bored by Bombay's synagogue society and looked forward excitedly to meeting epicures like the Rothschilds, who hunted in the Vale of Aylesbury and entertained so magnificently in their Mayfair mansions. His wife was pregnant with their first child and he hoped, without much conviction, that a change of scene might make her more tolerable. His widowed mother decided to sail with them. She had languished in Bombay since her husband's death and was anxious to meet her Ashley Park grandchildren.

Albert saw them off with little apprehension about the London office or indeed any of the other branches. All was set fair. Solomon, the devout bachelor, had no interest in 'godless' England and seemed relieved to return to his work and prayers in Shanghai, with an occasional trip to Japan for relaxation. The youngest brother, Frederick, was still in his teens, but surprisingly mature for his years. He would now be given an intensive business training in Elphinstone Circle before joining Solomon in China. Arthur was disappointed to lose Reuben's companionship and would dearly have loved to join him in Leadenhall Street. However, he was promised opportunities to pay more visits to London in the future. He went back to Hong Kong with a directorship in the firm.

Albert was now ready to go on the Bombay Legislative Council. He thought Elias would welcome fuller business responsibility and might perhaps send his son, Jacob, out to Shanghai, Hong Kong and the Gulf Ports as a kind of roving manager. Unhappily, Elias refused to fit into the neat jigsaw. During the three years since David Sassoon's death, the split had widened between his two eldest sons. With no crisis to clear the air, personal resentments had seethed and bubbled underground. Elias saw himself as a permanent deputy to his brother who would enjoy public life and the prestige of being Chairman until he was ready to hand over to his son.

Elias decided on a show of force which might bruise the others but would be more painful, if delayed. He had adequate working capital of his own, experience and, above all, twenty-three-year-old Jacob's proven ability. Nevertheless, the final step was only taken after many agonizing days of planning and prayer. His deep religious sense and a talmudic training made him question his own motives until he could hardly distinguish between self-interest and clan loyalty. He finally persuaded himself that the firm was too well established and prosperous to founder if he seceded. He guessed that Albert would be brought closer to Reuben and Arthur, both of whom were ambitious and might not altogether mourn his own departure from the hierarchy.

He announced his resignation in the autumn of 1867. It naturally caused a hubbub in trading circles, but without public sign of family discord. As the curtain fell, the two principals bowed stiffly to each other and went their own ways, rather like rival actors after an exhausting long run. Albert expected Elias to set up in a small way of business. He might compete inconspicuously, but could scarcely disturb the solid parent firm with its international reputation.

Elias behaved with good sense and dignity. He called his new firm, E. D. Sassoon & Co., and quietly formed long-term plans without making any move which might embarrass his brothers. He was absolutely confident of success. He loved Solomon and respected his character and ability; the others he dismissed as too casual, all brilliance and shallow hedonism. From past evidence, they would probably do little more than keep the business running steadily but without much creative imagination.

As it happened, he and Albert had almost completely misjudged and underrated each other.

Part Two (1867—1901)

Chapter Four

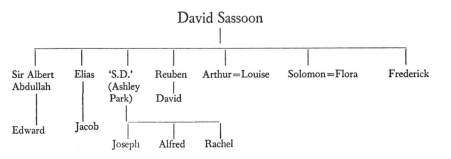

David Sassoon

| Sir Albert Abdullah | Elias | 'S.D.' (Ashley Park) | Reuben | Arthur=Louise | Solomon=Flora | Frederick |

Edward — Jacob

Reuben: David

'S.D.' (Ashley Park): Joseph, Alfred, Rachel

Elias lost no time in laying his broad policy lines. He planned to bite cautiously into the opium market, but would confine himself at first to traditional trading in dried fruits, nankeen, metals, tea, Chinese gold, silk, spices and camphor. With all these he was familiar; he would move more gingerly into cotton while continuing to develop his property holdings in China. He opened offices in Bombay and Shanghai, admittedly smaller than those of his old firm, yet imposing enough to encourage merchants and shipowners who already knew him by repute. He was scrupulous to avoid any suspicion of poaching. He made it plain that he did not intend to compete seriously with his brothers, although the new concern would be run on parallel lines. There was more than enough business to go round. Any residual bitterness felt in Forbes Street and Elphinstone Circle was tempered by the satisfactory turnover in all their branches, notably after the opening of the Suez Canal which boomed Bombay into an imperial port breathless to challenge Calcutta itself.

Elias knew every inch of the family empire, although so far lacking the personnel to operate on a major scale. With only one son of mature age, he would need to go outside for staff, perhaps a blessing in disguise after a lifetime of policy taboos imposed by his father. He had fewer inhibitions about employing non-Jewish branch managers to supplement the habitual intake of recruits from Bombay and Baghdad eager to work for any Sassoon. It was virtually the same story in China, once local traders had overcome their first bewilderment and a very natural sense of confusion. They soon distinguished them as *Kau* (Old) and *Sin* (New) Sassoon.

Before settling into offices on Bombay's Rampart Row, Elias had rapidly opened agencies in the Gulf Ports and Baghdad. Jacob was dispatched to Shanghai where he benefited from his father's long connection with that city and other Treaty Ports. He showed enterprise in rapidly engaging representatives throughout Japan. He also took the initiative in schemes that ranged from importing rice from Saigon to buying up more building sites in Shanghai. In Sassoon House, erected on land bought cheaply on the Bund by his father, he was soon being talked of as a commercial genius second to none in his family.

The relationship between Elias and his brothers became more strained with business competition. They remained outwardly polite to the rebel, but social contact virtually ceased after the secession, apart from letters about David Sassoon's benefactions and meetings at funerals or anniversary mourning services. For years to come, all the family births, Barmitzvahs and marriages would be acknowledged formally by letters and exchanges of gifts, rather in the fashion of distantly related kinsmen of royal blood.

The challenge had released unsuspected springs of energy in Albert. He served on the Bombay Legislative Council and became one of the Governor's inner ring of advisers on educational and building projects. His cheque-book was always open to endow a scholarship or two, but the courtier in him may have triumphed over the selfless educationalist when, in 1872, he donated £10,000 towards the reconstruction of the Elphinstone High School. It was a gesture of thanksgiving for the recovery of the Prince of Wales from typhoid, the disease which carried off the Consort.

The Sassoon name was becoming familiar and respected in England. Reuben applied himself effectively to affairs in 12 Leadenhall Street and the Manchester office, but still managed to enjoy every moment of a busy social programme. He was welcomed by the Rothschilds, and often seen in the homes and theatre boxes of other Anglo–Indian merchants. He kept a good, spicily oriental table at his house in Lancaster Gate where his dinner parties were being talked about in fashionable circles. However, his ego was sharply bruised when his youngest sister, Mozelle, visited him soon after his arrival in London. Still in her teens and fresh from the purdahed opulence of Sans Souci and Poona, she had returned one morning from her first carriage ride in the Park to discover that he occupied only one mansion, and not the whole of the stately crescent, as she had imagined!

Reuben dutifully attended the Spanish and Portuguese Synagogue. Faithful to family custom, he also maintained a chapel in his home for private worship. More with a collector's instinct, perhaps, than from any deep-seated devotion, he furnished it with imposing Scrolls of the Law and ancient appurtenances zealously acquired over the years.* He took an interest in the youngsters at Ashley Park and satisfied himself that they were imbibing the Torah despite the heathen temptations of country life. Joseph had celebrated his Barmitzvah without disgracing himself, and Alfred and his sister were receiving Hebrew instruction from a visiting rabbi. Resident non-Jewish tutors also gave them lessons in literature, painting, music and deportment, but Reuben thought his widowed sister-in-law was spoiling her children. She expressed open disdain for commerce. After Oxford University which had only recently opened its doors to Jews, so long barred from matriculation by religious tests, they would settle down as country gentlemen and scholars. Alfred, she was sure, would become a concert virtuoso. His violin-playing was promising, but Uncle Reuben thought the purchase of *two* Stradivariuses extravagant and slightly premature.

He reported all this to Albert who was now too busy to seek re-election to the Bombay Legislative Council. He had opened a branch in Calcutta and was expanding his interests in Persia where the Shah had at last promised the half-Jewish British Envoy, Sir Henry Drummond Wolff, a concession for control of his country's railways and mines. Baron Julius de Reuter was encouraged to put down £40,000 in caution money, which the Shah refused to return when the scheme fell through. The concession remained in abeyance, but the King of Kings signified his appreciation of Albert Sassoon's friendly, if cautious, interest in the affair by investing him with the Order of the Lion and the Sun. This was soon followed in 1872 by a knighthood. Queen Victoria was advised that the opening of the Suez Canal could make the chairman of David Sassoon & Sons an even more attractive figure to her own City merchants and bankers. His diplomatic gifts were also commended by British Government representatives who sometimes called on him for a quiet briefing before going on to the Courts of Teheran or Peking.

Albert simultaneously celebrated his knighthood and welcomed the new Viceroy, Lord Northbrook, by giving a ball at Sans Souci. From 10 p.m. onwards, over a thousand guests drove up to the mansion through an avenue of lamps and coloured flares which bathed the flower-beds and fountains in a glow visible for a clear mile from the top of Mount Road. A band played the National Anthem and other suitable airs. Bishops, nabobs and every mobile member of Bombay's *élite* had arrived by midnight, when a magnificent supper was laid in a huge lower room. The Viceroy sat beside Lady Sassoon, who was rather nervous and far less at

---

* His scrolls, amulets, lamps and Passover dishes were included in the Anglo–Jewish Historical Exhibition at the Royal Albert Hall in 1887. They are now part of Rabbi Sassoon's unique collection of sacred relics at Letchworth.

ease than her husband. He proposed the loyal toast with warmth and eloquence.

Soon afterwards, he paid a visit to England and was much taken with the elegance and liveliness of Louise, Arthur's bride of a few months. His brother had seemed a hardened bachelor when he set out from Hong Kong to make an overland semi-business tour of Europe, via Bombay. His itinerary included Vienna, where he met the twenty-year-old daughter of the Chevalier Achille Perugia. She was then staying with her distant kinsmen, the Rothschilds. A member of one of the oldest and most patrician Italo–Jewish families, her pedigree was faultless, but Arthur was equally excited by her beauty and a strong dash of Latin temperament. He was soon helplessly in love and determined to become the first of his house to break out of the narrow oriental marriage circle. He was hardly a romantic figure, with his sparse hair and a beard that aged him beyond his mid-thirties, but he had wealth and name. Besides, a brisk charm acquired in many cities gave him a useful lead over his rivals. The courtship was unusually brief for those days, but Arthur still had a pressing business tour ahead of him.

They were married in Trieste at the home of the bride's uncle. It was touch and go, as the bridegroom later discovered. The scales were tipped by his sister-in-law, of whom more would be heard. 'I would not have married my husband,' his wife privately told Lady Battersea, Sir Anthony de Rothschild's daughter, 'had not Marie, who was then only ten years old, approved of him.' Arthur, long anxious to join Reuben, quickly settled his affairs in Hong Kong, with Sir Albert's full approval. His departure might temporarily weaken the firm's managerial strength in China, but he would be an asset in the thriving Leadenhall Street office.

The newly-weds installed themselves at 2 Albert Gate to the south of Hyde Park and only a short carriage ride from 'Rothschild Row', the imposing line of mansions at the Apsley House end of Piccadilly. Sir Albert was fascinated by his sister-in-law's artistic taste. Her marble hall had a flowing elegance, with its graceful wrought-iron staircase and huge panels of silken damask tapestry set in the walls. The drawing-rooms would be painted white in the latest French style, and the mirrors framed in marble. Vivid brocades adorned all the chairs and sofas. The only evidence of Arthur's orientalism was a Chinese vase or two and some exquisite pieces of jade sent by friends as wedding presents.

Albert used their house as his headquarters for the series of agreeable engagements which opened with his first levée in full Court regalia in May 1873. Shortly afterwards, he and the Rothschilds were among the guests at a State Ball held at Buckingham Palace in honour of Nasr-ed-Din, the Shah of Persia, whom Queen Victoria detested although he had kissed her photograph at Windsor railway station and always addressed her as 'my auspicious sister of sublime nature'. She found an excuse not to attend, which disappointed Sir Albert but gave him an opportunity to meet the Prince of Wales and also to exchange civilities in Persian with the ugly and quite graceless potentate. The Prince welcomed any relief from this visitor, whom he had disliked almost from the moment he landed at Dover in his sky-blue frock-coat blazing with rows of rubies. At Windsor he had stubbornly declined to ride in the procession until his white horse had had its tail dyed pink.

Sir Albert left reluctantly for India, but not before visiting the Manchester office where he studied details of the newest cotton looms now being installed all over Lancashire. Before sailing home, he attended morning service at the London synagogue in Bevis Marks and then closeted himself with Reuben whom he promised to keep informed of his newest and most ambitious project. He had interested himself in the Bombay waterfront from his boyhood. Largely through his initiative, the firm had been favourably placed during the boom period when warehouse space was being snapped up at famine prices. He guessed that the Suez Canal would transform the port, but only if safe anchorage could be guaranteed for larger ships. Albert therefore bought a site on the south side of the Colaba Company's estate, with easy access to the Cotton Centre. An army of coolies began to clear the foreshore for the first wet dock on that coast.

The municipal authorities showed little enthusiasm, and several of his business rivals prophesied disaster for this white elephant slowly being hacked out of the rock. By June 1875 the 200,000-square-foot Sassoon Dock was ready to take shipping. Rates were kept down, but the volume of traffic soon led to a demand for public ownership. The family enjoyed four years of handsome dues before agreeing to sell for seventy-five lakhs (about £750,000), a sum met by the issue of 4 per cent Government Debentures.

The Dock was an emphatic success but quickly became too small to take the port's ever-growing traffic. Within a few months of its opening, the citizens of Bombay were already canvassing plans for a larger one to be financed by public money. The Prince of Wales was invited to lay the foundation stone when he arrived that November to start his tour. He disembarked to a salute of guns from a dozen men-of-war at anchor in the harbour. Through streets lit by gas flares, oil lamps and Chinese lanterns, rolled scores of gilded carriages carrying all the nawabs and rajahs, several in gold tunics flashing with jewels. Alas, on this day of days, Sir Albert Sassoon and his brother, Elias, were praying side by side in the synagogue to mark the anniversary of their father's death. Albert was represented at the ceremony by his second son, Edward, since his first-born, Joseph, had recently married and was in Calcutta with his bride. (He died not long afterwards.)

Sir Albert was among many who showered invitations on the Prince. He arranged a small and exclusive luncheon at Sans Souci in his honour and further commemorated the royal visit by a ten-foot high equestrian statue outside the Town Hall. The sculptor, J. E. Boehm, was given a £10,000 commission, no longer a significant sum to the millionaire head of a trading empire which seemed to flourish with every new branch.

He had nevertheless become more restless for the delights of England where the Prince of Wales, who evidently liked Jews, was showing such marked favour to the Rothschilds. Reuben continued to send him exciting titbits about this clan and his own very congenial life in London. The Duchess of Buccleuch and Mrs Gladstone attended his musical soirées, and once or twice he had played cards at the Marlborough Club in Pall Mall, a haunt of H.R.H. and his friends. He reported with enthusiasm on his new corner mansion at 1 Belgrave Square. It was even larger than the one in Lancaster Gate but so oddly built that his carriages and horses had to be carried up by lift to stables on the roof. There was a spacious conservatory of exotic plants and ferns which made a pleasing framework for buffet parties in the summer months. He had a finely appointed billiard-cum-smoking-room, and informed his brother that he was laying down some excellent port. He enjoyed attending sales of promising clarets, burgundies and madeiras but was specially careful to select only the finest pink champagnes which the Prince of Wales was making fashionable.

His only son, David, born in England soon after their arrival in 1867, was already entered for Eton but continued his Hebrew studies and joined the family at daily prayers. Reuben had little to say about his wife. She had grown even fatter and pointedly retired to her separate suite when his sporting friends arrived. Albert could sympathize. His Hannah was active in visiting Bombay's Jewish schools, but an uninspired hostess at his many dinner parties and receptions. She pleaded ill-health to avoid accompanying him on his English visits, and showed no interest in the bracing bulletins from Brighton, where David Sassoon's widow had settled near Reuben's pleasant weekend house at 7 Queen's Gardens. He hinted repeatedly that Albert's bronchitis might benefit from the sea air, not to mention the social amenities of Thackeray's 'London-super-Mare', now a popular retreat for City stockbrokers, bankers and merchants.

Sir Albert had begun to read his English mail with a touch of envy. To judge from his brothers' letters and the swathe of flattering newspaper clippings, the Arthur Sassoons were making a strong impact. Margot Tennant, herself a brilliant débutante and never one to flatter her own sex, had endorsed Louise publicly as 'one of the most delightful women I have known!' She would confess that the rarest compliment ever paid to her was when she visited Ascot for the first time and temporarily 'mislaid' her escort. Making her way to the station in a heavy downpour of rain, she was mistakenly greeted as 'Mrs Sassoon' by a distinguished young stranger who carved his way through the crowd to find her a railway carriage.

Louise, still childless, promised to act as Sir Albert's hostess if he decided to take up residence in London. His wife, with head shaved and the unbecoming wig of an orthodox Jewish matron clamped to her skull, would scarcely feel comfortable in a Mayfair household or at the formal dinner parties to which his brothers were now inviting so many non-Jews. Reuben was told to keep his eyes open for a suitable mansion where his brother might spend several months a year, though he would still maintain Sans Souci and his villas in Poona and Mahabaleshwar.

Albert was now approaching his sixtieth year. A rich but rather lonely man, he missed the society of Reuben and Arthur and secretly grieved over the defection of the brother with whom he had shared his boyhood. E. D. Sassoon & Co. had started to compete significantly in opium and Indian yarn. According to reports from Shanghai, they were also investing heavily in real estate. In Fenchurch Street, London, they had quickly opened an office, first managed by Jacob and then by his younger brothers who each served his time in China in the traditional fashion.

Sir Albert's main hopes centred on his second son, Edward, who had had his statutory two years in China. He was a good-looking youth who might not as yet rival his cousin Jacob in business drive, but his father set a higher value on his obvious good sense and charm. In due time he would surely make an admirable Chairman. Other appointments to the firm were made from within the family. Sir Albert found a place for a nephew, Charles Moses, and a brother-in-law, S. Shellim. One of the few to break the safe patriarchal policy was a non-relative, Silas A. Hardoon. He owed his chance to Arthur Sassoon's marriage. The Hardoons had left Baghdad during the Daud Pasha régime and were happy to work in the Sassoon offices and wharves. Silas, a bright-eyed boy and eager as a squirrel, had an urchin wit which made people laugh. He could prattle in half a dozen dialects and became night-watchman in one of the warehouses, making himself popular with the cosmopolitan traders and sea captains who did business with the firm. His quick brain picked up details of merchandise and bills of lading. When he climbed on to a stool, he showed an aptitude for figures which recalled Reuben. He was soon moving nimbly between the various wharves and offices as a kind of roving major-domo, although still among the lower-paid staff.

When Arthur and his wife settled in England, a replacement had to be found for Hong Kong. The youngest of the brothers, Frederick, was the obvious choice, but he was still in his early twenties and lacked the hard core of experience for such a key branch. He was sent off under the wing of Silas Hardoon, who was only a little older, but resilient enough to carry the dual roles of tutor and office sub-manager. The arrangement worked so well that, after a year or two, it was considered safe to send Hardoon north and leave Frederick to manage the Hong Kong branch.

The Chairman's half-formed strategy for moving to England was most unexpectedly finalized for him. Solomon was on a visit to the head office in Bombay when he met Sir Albert's grand-daughter. She was seventeen, half his age, but unusually mature and voluptuous even for the Orient. She spoke and wrote English, French and German almost as fluently as Hebrew, Arabic and Hindustani. She could quote Shakespeare by the page and had studied the Torah with the most learned rabbis. However, she had too much charm to be a blue stocking. Once he had overcome his shyness, Solomon found her irresistible.

When Sir Albert had recovered from his first surprise (even in a family so inbred, it was rare to bless a grand-daughter's union with one's own half-brother!), he welcomed a match which must clearly benefit them all. Solomon might not dazzle Government House with his badinage, and he would never shuffle a pack of cards or a balance-sheet like Reuben, but his trade returns for the Chinese branches were proof enough of industry and clear thinking. He would make an excellent successor to himself in the Bombay office. Besides, with such an earnest and devout wife at his side, who better to lead the local Jewish community after similar labours in the Shanghai vineyard?

This was harvest time for David Sassoon & Sons. The Yangtse mud glinted with gold as soon as they laid a brick on it. It was the same in all the Treaty Ports where land values bounded from year to year. Their wharves and godowns were bursting with opium, cotton goods, silks, spices, tea and metals. In the mid-seventies, when the rupee began to drop from its fairly stable value of two shillings through the demonetization of silver in various European countries, they could hedge or withstand any shock by swiftly moving goods to less sensitive areas. Conversely, in later years they would buy heavily in silver when it soared in price, thus offsetting their heavy losses from a critical glut in piece-goods. As soon as opium sales dropped, the firm promptly scored compensatory gains in silver, sugar and dyes.

Scores of junk masters along the China coast were now more or less permanently on their payroll. Few ocean-going freighters announced sailings before checking with the Sassoon branch managers in their teak-panelled offices. They were able to charter fleets of tramp steamers at short notice. More important, the P. & O. and other major companies, long spoilt by an easy monopoly of mail and passenger traffic, quickly discovered after the opening of the Suez Canal that most traders were unwilling to pay luxury freight charges like £20 a ton for silk or cotton at £15. Cut-throat competition with big French ships and the swarming little tramps of all nations had made the old-time aristocrats toe the Plimsoll line. By 1883, Sutherland of P. & O. agreed to carry cotton for as little as 20s. a ton.

The Sassoons enjoyed the benefits of this slump in freight charges but took a long-term view in supporting the big liner companies. The smaller traders would then hint bitterly of 'a most-favoured firm' clause and complain that high freight was driving them out of business. In this period of ruthless competition, when 'private arrangements' became standard practice, few shed tears over the casualties. Many among them had cheerfully fallen on China in the rough and tumble after the Opium Wars. They were now left to doze and die on its mudbanks, like exhausted crocodiles. As shippers of bulk cargoes, both Sassoon firms not only survived the freight war but emerged even stronger.

Sir Albert did not hesitate too long after Solomon's marriage. He had title and wealth, and his firm seemed impregnable throughout Asia and the Levant. His decision to settle in England was welcomed by Reuben and Arthur whose status could only be improved by having the Chairman among them. Solomon would take over in Bombay as managing partner, but London automatically became the firm's nerve-centre, with all major policy decisions and directives originating from Leadenhall Street.

Authority was now heavily weighted at the English end, an ideal platform for launching a brilliant social programme but remote from the firm's traditional strongholds in India and China. In taking this step, the three brothers became in effect absentee landlords. By contrast, E. D. Sassoon & Co. entrenched itself still deeper in Bombay. It was the natural supply base of a house looking towards Europe for its imports but eager to service the hungry consumer markets, both at home and in the Far East.

Chapter Five

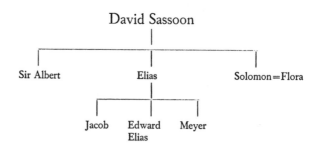

David Sassoon

Sir Albert   Elias   Solomon=Flora

Jacob   Edward   Meyer
Elias

After only ten years of independent trading, Elias and his sons felt equipped, both psychologically and financially, to give a lead to the more complacent parent firm. Cotton manufacture was an obvious outlet, but Sassoon caution made Elias hesitate until a Parsee had again shown the way. J. N. Tata recovered from his misadventures with Premchand Roychand and indirectly profited by his experiences in the false boom. During the ill-starred attempt to open an Indian Bank in England, he hurried to Lancashire to develop the brokerage side of their business. He interested himself in machinery and the workings of the Manchester Cotton Exchange. On his return, he thought much about the possibilities of manufacturing cotton locally instead of relying on Lancashire's piece-goods. Fourteen mills were now operating in Bombay with about half a million spindles, but many more had closed down through lack of money or bad management.

To rebuild his capital Tata had first gone to Hong Kong, exchanging silk goods for the opium his brother shipped out from Bombay. Profits were satisfactory, but he saw little chance of breaking either the Sassoons' hold on this two-way traffic or the handsome rebates and discounts which they and others enjoyed in the freight market. He returned to India in 1869, investing his limited funds in a disused oil-pressing plant which he rapidly converted into a small cotton mill. The output was insignificant and not of good quality, but he familiarized himself with machinery and day-to-day administration. He recovered his whole outlay in two years and sold the plant at a respectable profit. After a rather disappointing sales tour of the Middle East, he decided to concentrate instead on the Chinese market which wanted something better than Bombay's coarse cloth and low-count yarns. Against the advice of friends who thought it madness to start manufacturing anywhere but in Bombay, he bought ten acres cheaply from the Rajah of Nagpur. The site was some three hundred miles inland but close to a railway station and local labour. More important, he would also be at the heart of his raw material.

Both Sassoon firms betrayed only the mildest interest. Several Parsee millowners had bankrupted themselves of late, and Tata's former indiscretions with Roychand seemed a poor enough prospectus. They watched his scramble for investors with some amusement. They would be ready to profit by his mistakes if he failed through lack of capital and the greedy, inefficient Management Agencies. His greatest hazard, they guessed, would come from unskilled and migrant workers who moved seasonally to the cities in their thousands.

Albert Sassoon had now pitched his tent at 25 Kensington Gore, a spanking mansion worthy of a millionaire knight. He felt excusably remote from Tata's ramshackle sheds in Nagpur. The two white and gold drawing-rooms were furnished and decorated in different styles, mainly Louis XVI, but with several hints of his Japanese and Chinese tastes. Other exhibits were an oaken cabinet ordered for the Empress Eugénie before the disaster of Sedan, and some exquisite pottery formerly owned by the Empress of Germany. Queen Victoria was represented by a tapestry portrait over the vast fireplace in the Jacobean dining-room. This room on the ground floor was the showplace. The woodwork, carved and inlaid with ebony and ivory, had been salvaged intact from the Prince of Wales's Pavilion at the Paris Exhibition. At night, the lamps in bronze gilt brought out the full splendour of six immense tapestries depicting scenes from *The Merry Wives of Windsor*.

The size and décor of the house had a suitably embassy grandeur. Sir Albert had found it sound policy to cultivate the Chinese Ambassador, commercial attachés from Persia and the Levant, and any Indian princes who might be visiting the capital. He spent his mornings at the head office, attending to correspondence or in conference with his brothers. They studied reports from Bombay where Solomon appeared to be taking the Empress Mills altogether too seriously. Tata had at last issued all his shares and equipped the factory with 15,500 throstles, 14,000 mule spindles and 450 looms. They were driven by a pair of engines capable of developing 800 h.p., a sensation in Nagpur but unlikely to make the London and Manchester Cotton Exchanges throb with apprehension. The

London trio shrugged this off as pioneer's fever, but noted with surprise that E. D. Sassoon & Co. were quietly prospecting for factory sites in and around Bombay.

Leadenhall Street still teetered between apathy and counter-action. The firm's profits had mounted despite a famine in the Presidency, the jumpy rupee and renewed Russian activity on the Afghan border, which could threaten Anglo–Indian trade interests in both Persia and China. In such a context, this £200 a year provincial Parsee could hardly stampede them into sinking substantial capital into speculative new mills and equipment. However, they alerted the Manchester office to watch for any new moves by E. D. Sassoon. It was soon confirmed that Elias's sons, Edward and Meyer, commuted regularly between their headquarters in Fenchurch Street and the Cotton Exchange, while Tata, looking rather like a light walnut Jorrocks with his side whiskers, was also becoming a familiar figure in Manchester. He was reported to have engaged two clever engineers, James Brooksby and Jeremiah Lyon, to act as consultants and efficiency experts at the Empress Mills. And he was also tendering for new machinery.

A waiting game now opened. It demanded a sense of timing as well as tactical subtlety. The rival Sassoon firms would continue to watch each other, both vigilant for any sign that Tata would either crash or survive. Judging from the first two or three years at the Empress Mills, Sir Albert was being proved right. The stocky Parsee had made the beginner's error of buying inferior looms. His cloth was poor in quality, with production figures even lower than those of his Bombay competitors. His Company stock slumped to half its issue value, and several shareholders started to panic. He hurried back to Lancashire and sank most of his remaining cash in better and more up-to-date plant, scrapping the old machinery. Within a very short time, his bales became saleable and output shot up. He could soon pay stockholders a 16 per cent dividend, but continued to plough every spare rupee back into the business.

E. D. Sassoon & Co. had now learned enough. They quickly bought land for factory sites and began looking around for any badly-run mills which might be taken over at cost or even below and put on a paying basis. Their branches had long handled Lancashire piece-goods and would find it comparatively simple to distribute cloth manufactured in Bombay. Tata lacked capital and was buried in the interior, while they had superior shipping facilities as well as warehouses ideally sited on Bombay's splendid harbour and docks. Moreover, immigrant Jews from Baghdad would make a reliable home-based labour force, far less prone to absenteeism than the migrants of Nagpur.

The prospects seemed so exciting that Elias recalled Jacob from the Far

East, and temporarily replaced him with two sons-in-law. Father and son were soon in conference at Rampart Row until the small hours. Jacob even postponed his forthcoming marriage to a kinswoman, Rachel Isaacs, the daughter of a wealthy Calcutta merchant. Instead, he went ahead recruiting staff and setting up machinery for a mill they had just bought. It was to be named after the Princess of Wales. All was going smoothly to plan by 1880, when Elias was taken ill and died suddenly while visiting some tea plantations in Ceylon. He was only fifty-nine.

The Alexandra Mill began to operate later that year and quickly showed a profit. Jacob had adequate capital, organizing flair and the supreme asset of plentiful labour. In the steaming paddy fields he had to rely on Indian workers, but his fellow-Jews adapted themselves better to mill work. Several earned rapid promotion as overseers and managers, and shiploads of eager recruits soon began to arrive from Baghdad. They were promised full employment and the now standard Sassoon guarantees of Hebrew schools, trade apprenticeship for their children, synagogues, medical care and holy burial grounds.

Jacob did not repeat Tata's early mistake of cheeseparing on machinery. After the Alexandra had more than paid for itself, he built his new E. D. Sassoon Mill and spent lavishly on the latest equipment. His brothers periodically sent out experts from Manchester to instruct local factory managers on inspection and maintenance. Others showed them how to list materials and check returns, while a number of Englishmen stayed on to start a trainee scheme. Jacob was particularly keen to improve factory techniques and packaging. From the first, he set aside considerable sums for research into better assembly lines and a smoother transit of goods between factory and ship.

The other Sassoon firm was feeling the pressure. Solomon was a most conscientious man of business but lacked Albert's solid presence and *savoir-faire*. Deeply religious, he always read a whole Book of Psalms before leaving for his office each morning at eleven sharp. He was so modest that he used to enter the synagogue by the back door and slip quietly into his seat. After Flora had borne him three children, he reluctantly agreed to build an imposing mansion, Nepean Lodge, not far from Sans Souci. It was also of Moorish design, with marble floors and filigree panelling. Typically, he soon approved blue prints for a smaller, elegant villa to be put up in the grounds. It would be his home when, as he hoped, his son took over from him, while he devoted himself to his Hebraic studies and community affairs. Such was the programme, and it seemed foolproof at the time.

The firm was strongly established and thriving. In addition to his share of his father's estate and his income as managing partner of the Bombay office, Solomon had steadily added to his own property holdings in Shanghai and Hong Kong. They were being converted into bungalows, shops and apartments to yield a very satisfactory return. Unlike his brothers, however, he had no interest in splendour and seemed perfectly content to spend the rest of his life in Bombay. He was happiest studying the Talmud or meditating in the garden of his Poona villa, Rose Bank. Here they always celebrated the Holy Festivals with their children, worshipping at the synagogue built by David Sassoon. Their small son, David, proudly carried a miniature Scroll of the Law, tinkling with silver bells and replicas of the traditional gilt mantles. He was a solemn but alert youngster who, at the age of six, astonished his parents by giving a school-mate his kite in exchange for an Arabic translation of the Book of Ruth, first printed in Bombay in 1859!

Solomon often returned with regret from the peace of Rose Bank or the shady verandas of the Yacht Club, to which he had been elected, to grapple with the problems that harassed him in Elphinstone Circle. Flora would sometimes accompany him to the office which rather shocked colleagues who had never seen a woman in a counting-house, let alone consulted on policy. It was her first breach in India's purdahed fortress and one which she soon helped to widen by giving parties for forward-looking women, Hindu, Moslem, Parsee and European.

Solomon had excellent support from various relatives. There was A. M. Gubbay, a man as quietly unostentatious as himself; S. E. Shellim; and the explosively volatile Charles Moses, whom Hardoon had lately replaced as manager in Shanghai. The firm would have been happier with a member of the family in charge of that important branch, but Hardoon's business turnover was a strong argument in his favour. However, he was not easy to control and became impatient at the firm's inertia over cotton. He kept reminding Solomon that every other ship steaming into Shanghai seemed to be stuffed to the gunwales with piece-goods. The neighbouring godowns of Tata & Sons and *Sin* Sassoon were now handling practically nothing but bales, while he continued to sell chests of opium and other routine merchandise at diminishing profits.

David Sassoon & Sons only took action when Jacob's Alexandra Mill was already in full operation. They bought a piece of ground in Bombay for half a crown per square yard from the Frere Land Reclamation Company. It would treble in value within twenty years. The first mill of the Sassoon Spinning and Weaving Company was built on this site, two others following swiftly. They also began to manufacture wool, but the country's annual clip had to be supplemented by heavy imports from Australia. The first Indian woollen mill had been set up in 1876 in Cawnpore which was near the sheep country and fairly accessible to the coal of Damodar. It turned out rough cloth for the Army, both Sassoon firms taking their share of this trade. It was a useful sideline but almost insignificant in the realm of King Cotton. By the end of the century, one-third of India's half million factory workers were in cotton, with the Sassoon mills or their associated concerns among the largest employers.

E. D. Sassoon & Company had several thousand hands on their pay-roll with an output, man for man, far higher than that of any other plant in Bombay and even several in Lancashire. Jacob had shown foresight in briefing his brothers in London to explore ways and means of stream-lining cotton manufacture. He was eager to replace the old chaotic factory layout by a planned co-ordination which would save space and revitalize output. Spectacular results were achieved. He became the first millowner in India to install a conveyor-belt. It was crude and suffered many an early breakdown through careless operators, but for a time he alone was feed-ing raw cotton to his looms and seeing the finished yarn emerge, ripe for the bale and quickly on its way to the Bombay docks. With a minimum of delay, massive shipments of yarn could be dispatched not only to the Persian Gulf but to the Japanese ports beyond China.

Production remained a key problem in all the Sassoon mills. The manu-facturing boom had stimulated such a demand that it was not always practical to wait for new factories to be built and equipped. Semi-derelict businesses – one of them had been wound up four times in the past twenty years – were therefore bought up cheaply. Ancient plant operated by steam engines and wheezy boilers was scrapped, and the latest machinery imported from England at whatever the cost. Efficient planning by Man-chester experts was backed by dedicated Jewish overseers who gradually overcame the endless frictions and chaos of the old Managing Agency system. Working on similar and parallel lines, the two Sassoon firms soon went ahead of all their rivals, including Tata himself, who might have given them much severer competition had he not turned his attention to the richer fields of iron and steel. Even so, his early supporters had no cause to complain. The original £50 Empress Mill shares would be worth £700 by 1914!

Silas Hardoon was gripped by the cotton fever and decided to chance his arm. He resigned from David Sassoon & Sons in the summer of 1882, certain that he could succeed on his own. His capital was still relatively limited, but he had enormous faith in his local contacts and experience to see him through the early years. He was mistaken. Shipowners did not favour credit for a possible competitor to their better-placed clients, while local officials expected their full 'squeeze' in cash.

He had to admit defeat after only three years. With typical realism, he then joined E. D. Sassoon as their branch manager in Shanghai. This switch in loyalties did not shatter the calm of Leadenhall Street, but it seemed more significant to the old China hands. They took it as a public vote of confidence in the younger firm and a snub by implication for David Sassoon & Sons.

They were proved right, but not even Hardoon could have predicted that he would die richer by far than any of his masters.

Chapter Six

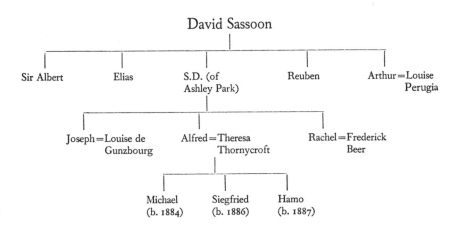

Throughout the last two decades of the century, the Court Circular was rarely without some daily reference to the Sassoons. Sir Albert had entertained the Duke and Duchess of Fife at his home in Brighton or held some lavish reception at 25 Kensington Gore for members of the Diplomatic Corps. Reuben had sipped the waters at Marienbad with his friend, the Heir Apparent, who then returned to spend a week in September with the Arthur Sassoons at Tulchan Lodge, Inverness-shire.

The London-based clan had quickly entered the beau-monde. It was not altogether surprising. Leisured, wealthy and pleasure-loving, they were obvious candidates for the new aristocracy of commerce and banking as represented by the Rothschilds, the Rand magnates, prosperous tradesmen like Sir Blundell Maple and Sir Thomas Lipton and, finally, the Prince's financial advisers, Baron Maurice de Hirsch and Sir Ernest Cassel. More remarkable, perhaps, was the ease with which Reuben and Arthur penetrated the charmed circle to develop a closer personal relationship with the Prince of Wales than almost any of the other Jewish sportsmen and financiers in his circle. They started as quite minor figures on the regal periphery, but soon matriculated as courtiers before graduating to the full intimacy of friendship.

The Marlborough House 'set', which so painlessly absorbed David Sassoon's sons, was the natural creation of a prince bored with a feudal hierarchy and eager to amuse himself with rich, affable and congenial men, whatever their genealogy. His own income of £100,000 a year – appreciably smaller than that of the great ducal landlords – would never quite accommodate his tastes. All his new friends were generous in emergency. Moreover, they guaranteed him a round of gay house parties, grouse-shooting, yachting and card games. He was the first of the royal blood to dine out in private houses and showed a frank preference for those with the finest cuisine, wines and cigars. He turned to cosmopolitan, quick-witted Jews like the Rothschilds who spent their money with such panache. He relished their spicy food, the Yiddish jokes and City gossip. Among them he could shoot, hunt, sail, guzzle and gamble in the grandest style without the gloomy protocol of royal castles or some of the draughtier stately homes. They were men of the world whose lively table talk was equally informed about the turf, orchids or such mysteries as the bullion market.

Reuben Sassoon might pride himself on his cellars, but he would never emulate a family who had bought a château in the Médoc to nurture their own vineyards. They bred Derby winners and the finest pedigree cattle in Europe; they maintained their own symphony orchestras and private zoos; and it seemed perfectly normal for the massed bands of the Household Cavalry and the Brigade of Guards to play at their village fêtes. One could almost credit the story of the guest at Alfred's palatial Halton House who chose milk with his tea in preference to lemon, at which a powdered flunkey had imperturbably inquired, 'Jersey, Hereford or Shorthorn, sir?'

The Sassoons were more formal and far less expansive. Seldom in the public eye and indeed almost inconspicuous during their early years in London, they were spared the disapproval shown by the Queen towards some of her son's other raffish friends. She condemned the Rothschilds as indolent and pleasure-loving men who had led her heir into a life of frivolity. Not until the early 'nineties would she overcome her early prejudice sufficiently to pay private visits to Baron Ferdy and his sister, Alice. Even so, she never quite forgot that the family was still only one generation from the Frankfurt ghetto and had enriched itself by speculation and floating foreign loans. (It was convenient to exclude the timely purchase of the Suez Canal shares from this context!)

The Sassoons had an easier passage to royal favour. They were admirably poised to make the best of both worlds. They profited by their friendship with the Rothschilds, yet enjoyed more immunity from the snobbery and racial prejudice that persisted towards that clan in certain quarters. Opium trading was still considered unexceptionable and apparently less noxious socially than vulgar profit-making on the Stock Exchange. Besides, their mercantile eminence in India and the Treaty

Ports lent them a semi-imperial cachet among the guardians of protocol at Buckingham Palace.

A subtle aura of exotic prestige seemed to linger over them. They might not own country estates or racing studs, and no person of taste could compare the Rothschilds' art treasures with Albert's bibelots and orientalia, yet he and his family slid smoothly into the niche usually reserved for visiting nabobs or the lesser rajahs. When the Sultan of Zanzibar arrived in London to seek closer affiliations with the Crown, he was entertained at Kensington Gore before going off to Brighton to enjoy Albert Sassoon's hospitality and counsel. In the years ahead, many other potentates and ambassadors automatically included his mansion at 1 Eastern Terrace, Kemp Town on their visiting lists.

The brothers would no doubt have reached Marlborough House and Sandringham through their own social talents, but the route was smoothly paved and shortened by the Rothschild clan. The first step was taken through Hannah, Baron Mayer's daughter, and followed by Sassoon marriages to two of her cousins, Leo and Aline. The baron had died in 1874, leaving nearly £3 million to his wife and daughter, in addition to the finest racing stud in the land and his mansion at 107 Piccadilly. When her mother died three years later, Hannah found herself alone and somewhat bewildered by her enormous inheritance. She had brains and charm but was no beauty. She soon fell under the spell of Louise Sassoon whose poise and elegance had made her one of London's most exciting hostesses. She could always be relied upon for original touches, novel at the time. At a ball for which Johann Strauss and his Orchestra provided waltz music, she defied convention by serving superb hot and cold soups at a buffet instead of a formal supper.

She also gave elegant and cosmopolitan dinner parties. Even haughty dowagers like the Duchess of Devonshire, 'Millie' Sutherland and Lady de Grey had to take note when the awnings were bright outside 2 Albert Gate. Mrs Arthur Sassoon's butler directed a dozen white-gloved footmen, imposing in livery and as tall as any in the Rothschild houses, where wages were reputedly graded by inches. Her French chef created an opulent cuisine which few gastronomes could resist. They could expect paté-stuffed quails, terrines of turtle, ortolans, wood strawberries from France and the first Tay salmon. Rare eastern fruits became as familiar a Sassoon hallmark as their coffee cake, soaked in cognac and served *flambé* with ice-cream and hot stewed cherries. It was a gastronomic riposte to the Rothschilds' celebrated chocolate gateau.

Louise always made a striking figure as she waited to receive her guests at the top of the staircase. Her magnolia complexion was set off by chestnut curls and a Persian aigrette. Her magnificent diamonds and a tiny waist nipped in over Worth's swirl of satin and brocade fascinated London's men-about-town almost as much as her accented English. Arthur, bald and swarthy, inevitably looked drab beside her, and he could not compete with Reuben who often made a slightly theatrical entrance in a crimson-lined evening cloak or his overcoat with the chinchilla collar. His heavy cuff-links, diamond rings and over-sized pearl shirt-studs were soon as recognizable as his shiny walnut dome.

The Earl of Rosebery was the most eligible of the young men at these exclusive dinner parties and soirées. He had first met Hannah de Rothschild at Newmarket and became her regular table partner at Albert Gate. When they married in March 1878, the Prince of Wales signed the register and proposed the health of the couple.

Hannah Rosebery and Louise Sassoon drew even closer together through an inspired piece of matchmaking. Hannah's cousin, Leopold de Roths-child, was likeable as well as immensely rich. He had inherited Gunnersbury Park and also bought himself an estate, Ascott Wing in Buckingham-shire. His London mansion at 5 Hamilton Place was up to the family's Medici standard. It seemed to Hannah that he had everything, except a wife! He used to protest half seriously that he would never marry until he had found someone 'as beautiful and accomplished as Mrs Arthur Sassoon'. Hannah Rosebery at last took this literally and went into conference with her cousin, Constance Battersea. They discovered that Louise had a younger sister, Marie, who happened to have just arrived at Albert Gate on a visit from Italy. She was then seventeen, a petite and olive-skinned beauty with a quick sense of humour. Her only handicap was a lack of enthusiasm for horses and hunting about which Leo was fanatical. She had to be coaxed into taking riding lessons. One day, when she was fairly safe in the saddle and wore a particularly fetching dark green habit, Lady Battersea introduced her very 'casually' to Leo at a meet near Leighton Buzzard. He was fascinated and invited her to Ascott Wing where he showed her over his fine stables and lent her a hunter. They began to ride together every day. Before very long, he had proposed and was accepted.

On 16 January 1881, three days before the marriage, the Arthur Sassoons gave a magnificent ball attended by the Prince of Wales and a strong force of Rothschilds, who arrived in state from their various Mayfair mansions. Many other guests were held up on the wedding day by one of the worst blizzards in years. A very frail but determined Disraeli was finally able to reach Albert Gate for the reception, but missed the religious ceremony when his carriage became snowbound.

The Prince was paying his first visit to a synagogue, the Central in Great Portland Street, and sat between Lord Rosebery and Louise. He followed the service from a translation while the couple stood side by side under the sacred canopy. When they were blessed by the rabbi and the bridegroom had stamped a wine glass with his heel, the Prince was among those who signed the register before driving off to the Arthur Sassoons' for the wedding breakfast. A weary Disraeli was waiting impatiently, his face a wizened mask with the celebrated dyed curl plastered snail-like on his forehead. He sipped a glass of champagne, which momentarily revived him, and toasted the Prince who in turn proposed the health and happiness of the couple. Among their treasures was a letter, written by Disraeli in a noticeably shaky hand, in which he congratulated the bridegroom on his choice and confessed, 'I have always been of the opinion that there cannot be too many Rothschilds'.

H.R.H. was evidently of the same mind. In Paris he was constantly entertained by the Baron Gustave at his mansion in the Avénue Marigny. After one pleasant visit he decided to call his new 200-ton yacht *Aline*, as a compliment to the Baron's daughter, soon to marry Sir Albert Sassoon's son and heir. Shortly after his return from France, the Prince accepted an invitation to a ball in his honour at 25 Kensington Gore. The Sassoons were not yet in his entourage, but he recalled Sir Albert's hospitality at Sans Souci during his last Indian tour and was perfectly aware of the family's close affiliations with the Rothschilds. He had seen Reuben and Arthur in the Marlborough Club and at race-meetings with Leo and Rosebery.

The ball was a glittering London début for Albert Sassoon. His hall had been transformed into a grotto, with the water-lilies sprayed by coloured fountains. Bowls of ferns and roses adorned the drawing-rooms, while guests on the terrace admired an arcadia created by fairy lights and the host's ample cheque-book. The Prince was conducted to an opulent buffet of his favourite dishes. At his usual high speed he consumed grilled oysters and snipe, stuffed with *foie gras*, washing them down with a jug of pink champagne, decanted and iced exactly to his taste. And Reuben was at hand with a casket of his finest cedar-wrapped Havanas. Finally, there was the delectable Mrs Arthur Sassoon herself, acting as hostess. She was a delight to the connoisseur's eye.

It was altogether a most enjoyable party and soothed the host after a blistering quatrain in *The Pink 'Un'*:

> Sir Albert Abdullah Sassoon
> That Indian auriferous coon,
> Has bought an estate called Queen's Gate
> And will enter upon it in June.

That summer the Prince and Princess of Wales opened the Children's

Hospital at Brighton and went on to lunch in Eastern Terrace. Uniformed police and detectives in mufti almost spoilt the occasion because an anonymous letter had warned of a plot to blow up the house. The Prince did not take it seriously. 'My dear Sir Albert,' he chuckled, 'this is the 21st of July, not the 1st of April.' He then sat down to do cheerful justice to a six-course meal, with several Jewish dishes on the menu.

Albert's rambling house was only a short carriage-ride from his brothers' smaller and rather more attractive villas in Hove, facing the Parade. Reuben was at 7 Queen's Gardens, which he had painted a gay mazarine blue, while Arthur and his wife had settled nearby in King's Gardens. So many other members of the clan had by now installed themselves in the resort that Henry Labouchère understated the case when he sardonically defined Brighton as 'a sea-coast town, three miles long and three yards broad, with a Sassoon at each end and one in the middle'.

From 1884 onwards, the seaside colony was joined by formidable little Mrs Sassoon from Ashley Park, who often dined with Reuben and chatted entertainingly about books and the theatre when in one of her summer moods. As a guest, she was variable in temper and seemed unimpressed by the royal seal which her brothers-in-law were patiently acquiring. She was also less than tactful about their friends, the Rothschilds, whom she and her children privately called 'the hairy-heeled ones'. Too proud for commerce, her branch was naturally deprived of the handsome dividends which Sir Albert and his brothers enjoyed. S. D. Sassoon had left a considerable fortune, together with several properties in Shanghai and Hong Kong which yielded a pleasant income, but Ashley Park was an extravagant *ménage*. Huge and crumbling, it needed numerous servants and a more or less permanent building staff to keep it habitable. The ball-room was large enough for an entire village fête to be held there in bad weather, but an indoor bicycle race ended in a heavy bill for repairs when one of the sons later put his foot through the weakened floor.

The widow could be craggy, but she also had a sentimental side. She bought a piece of land in the High Street at Walton-on-Thames and built a Public Hall which the Council used for meetings, Christmas Fairs and local recreations. A park in Hove, known as St Ann's Well Gardens, bears a plaque recording another of her generous gestures. She was walking one afternoon near the seafront with Reuben's daughter, later Lady Boyle, when two waifs scurried across their path like frightened mice. Mrs Sassoon caught them by the collar and asked why they were running away. 'Because we ain't allowed 'ere,' they stammered. She promptly bought a plot large enough for two croquet lawns and opened it to the public. Discovering that the children's father was out of work, she had him taken on as gardener in the new park.

She became a familiar figure on her promenades. Small, elegant and dressed in black, she was never without an ornate umbrella-parasol carried in all weathers. She noticed a bulky constable on traffic duty near the Hove Parade one midsummer afternoon. He was evidently feeling the heat. 'You need a melon,' she said firmly. 'There is nothing quite so good for cooling you down.' She went briskly on her way but stopped at the police station to ask the strength of the local force. Six dozen of the best melons in Sussex were delivered next day, with her compliments. But her temper could be less sunny, and the familiar umbrella then became an instrument of displeasure. It would snap open to shield her face if she happened to run into someone she was anxious to cut. More often than not, the victim would be a devoted friend who had innocently offended her.

A snobbish nostalgia for the past began to absorb her soon after her husband's death. Her grandson, Siegfried, recalls that the very first time he saw his name in print was when she solemnly unfurled a parchment to point out his lineage. Isolated alike from the business world and the more fashionable circles in which other Sassoons frolicked, Ashley Park took refuge in romantic pretensions to culture and gentility. With no father to restrain them, the children were particularly vulnerable to an over-indulgent but very determined matriarch.

Her eldest son, Joseph, born in Bombay shortly before his parents came to England, went to Christ Church, Oxford, where he led a shy and studious life. He inherited something of his father's withdrawn personality and never appeared to be listening, but had sudden bursts of dry humour. With his secretary, Arthur Read, who also tutored his sons, he would retire to the spacious library and spend long hours studying catalogues of first editions and antique furniture on both of which he spent lavishly. He collected rare Hebrew books and took an interest in the Spanish and Portuguese Synagogue, although his devotions were mainly limited to fasts and feasts. He was broad-minded enough to send £5 cheques from time to time to Walton's Church Restoration Fund. He also did his duty in local affairs and became a J.P. which drew him a little out of his shell, particularly when he developed an enthusiasm for bridge and golf.

His secretary's brother, W. W. Read, was a county cricketer who once brought a strong eleven, including Dr W. G. Grace, to play against a selected fifteen from Walton-on-Thames. The park, fringed by lofty oaks, was large enough to accommodate a first-class pitch which was always kept in immaculate condition. The charming thatched pavilion was another attraction for local players when they entertained visiting sides. At cricket matches, tennis parties or dances given for his daughters, Joseph could be charming, but his carriage always picked up speed when unexpected visitors were seen heading for Ashley Park. He became fanatical about languages and mastered Persian so as to read the original *Rubaiyat* of Omar Khayyám. He even acquired a working knowledge of Welsh specially to converse with one of the Ashley Park nursemaids in her own tongue!

His sister, Rachel, was small in build like himself, with lustrous Jewish eyes and an ivory skin envied by her sallower kinswomen. She did not encourage the beefy young men who paid her compliments at Hunt Balls and escaped to London, whenever possible, for plays, concerts and art exhibitions. She would shut herself in her room to scribble descriptions of scenes or piquant situations which had taken her fancy. Gentle by nature, she was intensely moved by all human suffering and dissatisfied with the cheque-book philanthropy of her uncles. Her mother hoped she would soon meet a suitable young Jew and settle into respectable domesticity, but consented reluctantly to her taking up unpaid hospital nursing.

Mrs Sassoon's dreams and ambitions were fiercely trained on her younger son, Alfred, who was only six when his father dropped dead in the Langham Hotel. She had always pampered him outrageously. He grew up to be a little under middle height and slender, with a dimpled chin, dark hair and a fashionably thick moustache. He had an easy languid charm with the right hint of caddish insouciance to make him fascinating to many women. He was devoted to his mother, but this did not prevent him from siding with Rachel when the matriarch grew tiresome. Such amiable diplomacy, like everything else, came naturally to him. He played the violin delightfully, even if his talent scarcely demanded the two Stradivariuses or a long series of lessons from the great Sarasate. He painted and etched with more than an amateur's flair. In common with so many other Sassoons, he was graceful in the saddle and might have become a first-class point-to-point rider but for his dislike of horsy society. He had the eye and wrists of a natural cricketer, and few could match him in the ball-room as dancer or lady's man. To underwrite all these gifts, he had a liberal allowance which he seemed feverishly eager to spend. He was determined never to set foot in a counting-house, still less to bury himself at Ashley Park.

After a few gay undergraduate terms at Exeter College, Oxford, he decided that a degree was surplus to his requirements. He convinced his mother that no gentleman's education could possibly be complete without the Grand Tour of Europe. It stopped short in Paris where he took an elegant house and began to haunt the *coulisses* of the Comédie Française. His romantic looks and a becoming touch of youthful cynicism made him popular in many artistic and semi-bohemian salons. There was no lack of cocottes and flatterers to enjoy the open-handed generosity of 'the rich nabob, Alfred Sassoon', as Sarah Bernhardt described him in her Memoirs. At his house she reports losing a bracelet from which hung a single diamond drop presented to her by Victor Hugo after her opening night as Doña Sol in *Hernani*. Enclosed with the box was a tender note saying, 'This tear which you caused me to shed is yours, and I place myself at your feet.' Alfred had volunteered to make good her loss but, according to her own account, she refused. It suited her to record dramatically that 'he could not give me back the tear of Victor Hugo'. The episode is not mentioned again, but it seems that she had only mislaid the bracelet. She was still wearing it on stage, forty-five years later, during the third act of her last play, *Régine Armand*.

Soon after his return from Paris, Alfred broke his mother's heart by marrying out of the faith, the first of his clan to do so. His eldest son, Michael, now over eighty, can still recall his horror on first being told that his grandmother had rushed frenziedly to the synagogue to curse any offspring of this unholy union. She said funeral prayers and even sat the ritual period of mourning for her 'dead' son. His name was never again mentioned in her presence, and her other children were strictly forbidden to have any further contact with him.

Socially, Alfred's marriage to Theresa Georgina Thornycroft was hardly a *mésalliance*. Her family had never worn cloth of gold or enjoyed a retinue of horsemen at the courts of medieval caliphs, but there was nothing shameful in their pedigree. They could trace themselves back to Cheshire gentry and prosperous farmers of the thirteenth century. A branch of the family later farmed rich estates and occupied Moreton Hall, near Congleton. Thomas, who was born just after Waterloo, sculpted busts for the new House of Lords and an equestrian statue of the Queen which was shown in the Great Exhibition. He was also interested in mechanics and put together one of the first threshing machines to be worked by steam. He made model boats for his sons and later turned to building ships in sections in his studio.

His wife, a gifted sculptress and painter, executed many portraits of the Royal Family and used to work for several months of the year at Windsor or Osborne. Their children all inherited considerable artistic gifts. John was sent to Jarrow to learn draughtsmanship and became a distinguished naval architect. He developed a leading boat-building concern at Chiswick Wharf and constructed torpedo-boats and destroyers for the Government. He also found time to build a yacht, the *Waterlily*, which became a family delight. Between commissions for groups like 'Commerce' at the base of the Albert Memorial, Thomas Thornycroft enjoyed cruising on the

Thames and encouraged his children and grandchildren to make sketches of the winding backwaters from the deck. His three daughters all grew proficient at sculpture and painting, but his second son, William Hamo, showed the most promise. After a brilliant career at the Royal Academy School, he went on to a knighthood (like his brother), became an R.A., and sculpted numerous bronzes, including Cromwell's statue at Westminster and the Gladstone Memorial.

Alfred Sassoon shared artistic tastes with Theresa Thornycroft who was herself talented enough to exhibit several times at the Academy. But apart from this and the sexual attraction of opposites, the marriage had little promise of success. He was twenty-two and Theresa five years older, although far less mature in the worldly sense. She was particularly vulnerable at the time, not having fully recovered from her infatuation with a Congleton farmer, Jack Walker, who had callously jilted her for a barmaid.

She was gentle, but needed more than gentleness to control a volatile and quick-tempered Jew, over-indulged from infancy. He had little need to work and even less inclination. He had considerable gifts and could handle a violin or a lathe with equal skill, but grew bored too quickly. Only a miracle could have made him settle placidly into the Weald of Kent. On the other hand, life at Weirleigh was a delight for country-bred Theresa. The house commanded a superb view of the gauzy hills twenty miles away, rising above the hop gardens, the orchards and marshes which melted into sleepy Channel ports. It was perched enchantingly over a carpet of pastures, studded by Norman churches and half-timbered, cobbled villages through which hay carts rumbled at a pace set by some of the sleekest cattle in England.

This ill-matched couple were only briefly at peace with each other in the house recalled with so much affection by their son, Siegfried.* Theresa had a studio at the top where she painted her Ruisdael-like skyscapes and tried to capture the tranquillity of low mists and dew-soaked grass. She had a ringing happy laugh that came naturally to one so good-natured. An excellent swimmer and one of the most fearless horsewomen in the county, she also loved skating on the frozen ponds or playing tennis with Alfred and their neighbours on the two courts behind the house. They had stable-room for a couple of hunters and room for the ponies which their sons would ride almost before they could walk. Weirleigh still preserves the cedars, the walnut tree and the well where they played as children.

* *The Weald of Youth* and *The Old Century* (Faber) are less well known than some of his other volumes of autobiography, but they offer many glimpses of a sensitive talent developing from earliest childhood.

Michael was born in 1884 and Siegfried two years later. Hamo, named after his uncle, followed in 1887 and was only four when his father grew bored with domesticity and the restrictions of peaceful Kent. The break finally came when he ran off with Theresa's 'best friend', and set up house with her in Pembridge Gardens. His wife put a brave face on the affair and spent solitary hours on horseback or painting religious subjects in her quiet studio. Siegfried Sassoon long treasured one of her fine Nativity studies for which he posed as the infant Jesus. 'I've never been so good since,' he wryly confessed to the present writer.

As a boy he was tallish for his years, thin and delicate-looking, with rather prominent ears. He had Theresa's blue-grey eyes but more deeply set, a cleft chin like his father, and a patrician aquiline nose not unlike that of old David Sassoon. His slight hesitancy of speech was matched by oddly jerky movements as if he sometimes found it difficult to co-ordinate mind and muscle. Even so, he sat his pony beautifully and was a natural batsman. His mother, solicitous for his health, kept him at home during his early years when Michael and Hamo went off to preparatory schools. He soon learned to play the piano and began gorging himself on books, particularly poetry, afterwards stammering snatches of verse that kept ringing in his head. By the time he was eleven, he was scribbling rhymes of his own ('I had mermaids on the brain'), and his mother had convinced herself that he would become a poet.

His brothers were more down to earth. Michael was stocky in build, and Hamo, with a footballer's back, obviously heading for six foot. Both were true Thornycrofts and useful with their hands. As boys they learned to use tools and were soon able to make models of the beloved *Waterlily*. It was always their mother's proud boast that she had banged in its very last rivet.

Michael was encouraged by his father to take up the violin and practised doggedly to please him. While at Malvern he was sent across to the cottage of a Mr Edward Elgar, who was then conducting school choirs and supplemented a precarious livelihood as a composer by giving lessons. He was honest enough to turn down this particular pupil. After Michael had scraped away during an interminable audition, Elgar announced that a course of lessons would be a waste of time for all concerned. Michael could hardly camouflage his delight at this reprieve. 'I was born with a spanner in my mouth,' he recalls, and never had the slightest doubt that he would one day become an engineer and not a concert violinist. It was much more fun to be solemnly piped aboard *Waterlily* by their uncle who used to serve a delicious strawberries and cream tea on the magic run up to Maidenhead.

Michael still remembers those gay cruises along the Thames and the red-letter day in high summer when their mother took them to the ship-yard to see Princess May (afterwards Queen Mary) launch a torpedo-boat built by their Uncle John. He can never forget their father who used to come to Weirleigh most Sundays until his coughing made it difficult for him to undertake even the short journey from London. In *The Old Century* Siegfried has vividly recalled 'Pappy' as a merry brown-eyed man with his family signet ring on one finger and a large diamond on another. Under his splendid moustache he usually smoked a fragrant cheroot in an amber holder. Before tuberculosis ravaged his body, Alfred Sassoon would make the villagers roar at his witticisms and practical jokes after hitting several sixes on Matfield Green. He romped with his sons and trundled them on breakneck rides in the gardener's wheelbarrow. He would suddenly seize Michael's violin and play wild czardas while they sat wide-eyed at his feet, munching the preserved fruits he often brought them. Their mother always stayed in her studio until his cab had rolled away to the station, when she would emerge red-eyed but with a brave smile.

Alfred had found little rapture in adultery, and coughed the long and lonely nights away. He mocked the pretensions of his uncles who had peddled their opium for the incense of Marlborough House, but felt pity for his elder brother, Joseph, who had timidly refused to see him. His mother's unforgiveness bit more deeply, although he laughed at her solemn synagogue curse on himself and his children.

She too was suffering, but remained implacable. She was briefly con-soled when Joseph married a few months after his brother's fall from grace. His bride possessed every quality she had found lacking in Theresa Thornycroft. She was young, beautiful and cradled in the strictest Jewish orthodoxy. Her father, the Baron Horace de Gunzbourg, came of a Bavarian line of financiers who had settled in St Petersburg, where they founded a vast fortune by selling vodka to the troops in the Crimean War and soon established themselves as bankers to the nobility. Louise de Gunzbourg had led a pampered life. She was fussed over in the nursery by the mighty, including Turgenev. The family salons in St Petersburg and Paris saw the débuts of Patti and many others, while their mansion in the Rue de Tilsit was famed for musical soirées graced by such quartets as Sarasate, Joachim, Saint-Saëns and Rubinstein. As a young belle, she had worn her first Court dress at the Tsar's Coronation.

Like her mother-in-law, she was excited by Ashley Park's semi-feudal grandeur but found the cold less endurable than in St Petersburg. She suffered agonies in the severe winter of 1886, when all the windows were solidly snow-banked by blizzards that sent piercing draughts through the candlelit rooms with their fishtail burners. Joseph was more than anxious to humour his wife, but his budget would not run to costly renovations. There were heavy demands on his purse after the arrival of five sons (including a brace of twins) who would all be sent to Eton. A fairly effective hot water system was only installed when one of the boys came down late for dinner and pleaded in excuse that it had been impossible to do up his cuff-links with frozen fingertips.

Such discomforts apart, the younger Mrs Sassoon had taken to village life and began to entertain generously. She gave elaborate garden parties and organized river fêtes with professional thoroughness. In time, she would become something of a household dragon through her passion for perfection and *bon ton*. She was always served first at meals and her family had to follow suit when she put down her own knife and fork. As a result, neither Eton nor the most fastidious of army messes ever quite cured some of her sons of eating too fast.

After a few early skirmishes, there was no dispute about who would rule as châtelaine of Ashley Park. At the smallest hint of friction, Joseph would slip away to his library to catalogue his folios and write letters. As it happened, the dowager capitulated with a good grace that surprised them all. Alfred's marriage had left her much shaken, and in her daughter-in-law she was quick to recognize a toughness more than equal to her own. With Alfred lost to her, she could no longer afford to alienate Joseph or the series of sons his wife was producing with such efficiency. She had therefore retreated with dignity to Brighton, first extracting a promise that Joseph would never admit Alfred to Ashley Park or have any contact with the renegade's family.

Rachel ignored this embargo and made secret visits to Weirleigh. Finally, she followed her brother's example by marrying out of the faith. She was nearly thirty and apparently doomed to spinsterhood when she announced her engagement to Frederick Arthur Beer in 1887. Her mother thundered an edict of 'excommunication', but without any effect. They were married at Chelsea Parish Church, with Mr and Mrs Gladstone among the signatories to the register.

After the stuffy atmosphere of Ashley Park, where Rachel could only find relief by composing melancholy piano sonatas, Frederick seemed almost heaven-sent. Indeed, his wispy gentle smile had an ethereal quality. He was small and dapper, with a brownish beard curling silkily over his cravat. Spaniel eyes reflected a timid and over-sensitive nature, and Rachel was not surprised to discover that his father had always treated him with contempt.

Julius Beer hailed from Frankfurt, like the Rothschilds, and had made a quick fortune on the London Stock Exchange. He had bought *The Observer* in 1870, more as a rich man's toy and an occasional mouthpiece for his views on foreign affairs than a profit-making investment. It was one of his many avenues to polite society which at first cold-shouldered him for his pushfulness. He entertained in some style at his mansion in Portland Place and spent his winters on the Riviera. As a self-made man, he was disappointed at having sired a weakling, and became even more bullying on hearing whispers about Frederick's illegitimacy. Few were surprised when he died suddenly in Mentone, at the age of forty-three, after an attack of apoplexy.

Rachel had comfortable means, but felt relief that Frederick was not another suitor who found her good looks and private fortune equally irresistible. Julius Beer had left his son *The Observer* and *The Electrician*, an income of £20,000 a year, and horses, carriages and plate suited to a fashionable *ménage*. They installed themselves in an elegant house at 7 Chesterfield Gardens, with one of the most imposing Adam staircases in Mayfair. Frederick was free at last from his father's reproaches. Now he could recline peacefully on a huge sofa with bromides and bottles of ether at hand to relieve his 'migraine'. The curtains were always drawn as light seemed to dazzle him, but no oculist could discover any defect in vision.

Rachel's training as a nurse showed quick benefits. She dismissed the more obvious quacks and rallied her husband, at least in the early years, by giving lavish dinner parties. They helped temporarily to relieve his tensions and self-absorption. It seems that the doctors all failed to detect or understand the early symptoms of general paralysis of the insane. No masseur could disperse these strange 'headaches' which suddenly made this mild man so irritable or, at times, feverishly gay.

Rachel had a touching confidence in her own powers. She soothed him by playing Chopin when the sleeping draughts failed, although poor Frederick might have benefited more from mercury. He began to show all the signs of incipient *folie de grandeur*, but his wife had no suspicion of the truth. She humoured him cheerfully even when he insisted on having the Beer family crest clipped out on his black poodle's back.

Chapter Seven

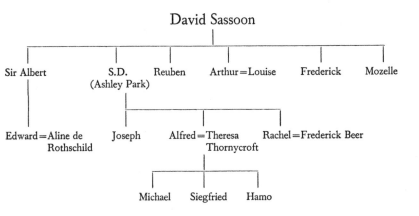

David Sassoon

Sir Albert — S.D. (Ashley Park) — Reuben — Arthur=Louise — Frederick — Mozelle

Edward=Aline de Rothschild — Joseph — Alfred=Theresa Thornycroft — Rachel=Frederick Beer

Michael — Siegfried — Hamo

Mr Gladstone had been a guest at Rachel Beer's wedding breakfast, but this was a minor junket compared with the splendour of the Sassoon–Rothschild union a few months later. Sir Albert's son and heir, Edward, who was born in Bombay and served his time in China, had quickly become anglicized. He was slim and spruce, wore a clipped military moustache and looked the complete Volunteer in his captain's uniform of the Middlesex Yeomanry. He went about his City duties with a nonchalant good nature which suggested he would one day make an easygoing Chairman. He enjoyed fishing, ice-skating and, for self-improvement, read the works of Tolstoy. Most of all, however, he liked potting grouse at Tulchan Lodge, Speyside, which his Uncle Arthur had rented from the Dowager Lady Seafield.

He was over thirty when he met the Baron Gustave de Rothschild's second daughter, Aline. She was ten years younger than himself but had a subtler taste and intellect. Her life had already spanned two brilliant worlds; the châteaux of France's leading bankers and statesmen, and the salons where she had met some of the most distinguished artists, writers and composers in Europe. It was a sophisticated, mainly non-Jewish milieu, and few would have shown surprise had she followed Hannah and other kinswomen in marrying a gentile. As it happened, a current wave of French anti-semitism was causing the Rothschilds to close their ranks. It showed itself in practical sympathy for the early colonists in Palestine together with a benevolent paternalism towards refugees from Tsarist persecution. Their enemies became more malicious. The Dreyfus Affair, in which Rachel Beer would take such an unexpected rôle, was not far off. It was already commonplace to open any morning newspaper in France and see some cartoon ridiculing the family. A typical one showed Aline's young cousin sitting by himself in a vast carriage with two coachmen in front wearing the family livery. 'That's the little Baron taking the air,' remarks a passing tramp. 'So young – and already a Rothschild!' sneers his friend.

Edward thought Mlle de Rothschild as pretty and elegant as his own Aunt Louise. He fell just as helplessly in love as Arthur had in Vienna. Aline could ride better than most women, skated with grace and even shared his taste for fishing. He thought it perfectly natural for the Prince of Wales to name a yacht in her honour and considered himself the luckiest man on earth when she accepted him. He spent days searching Paris for a wedding gift before he found a superb pearl necklace which cost him £9,000.

Sir Albert was delighted with the match which he announced in advance to the Prince of Wales, the Duke of Connaught and the Shah of Persia. Each sent gifts before the wedding day, 14 October 1887, when the Chief Rabbi of France officiated, with a choir from the Opéra, at the synagogue in the Rue de la Victoire. Twelve hundred guests attended the reception afterwards at Baron Gustave's mansion in the Avénue Marigny. The streets of the Faubourg were clogged for several hours with the most imposing cavalcade of carriages seen in Paris since Napoleon III's wedding. Ancient names hung like banners over the Regency chiffoniers and tortoiseshell cabinets. It seemed that a score of private collections had been ransacked for exquisite *objets de vertu* to supplement the bridegroom's gift of pearls, Sir Albert's diamond necklace and a spate of brilliants from the Rothschilds. The Prince of Wales sent a rather tasteless silver ewer and basin of *repoussé* design, representing Hercules vanquished by a nymph.

The newly-weds moved into 25 Kensington Gore, Sir Albert having tactfully retreated to Brighton which also suited his now chronic asthma and bronchitis. He would become even more of a recluse in his last years, rarely coming up to London except to confer with his brothers or to stay with Edward and Aline when they gave some special dinner party. One of these was rounded off with a performance by the Comédie Française company who were applauded by the Prince of Wales, the Duke of York,

Lady Randolph Churchill and Margot Tennant, with whom Aline had developed a close friendship. Before long she was admitted to 'The Souls', a coterie of wits and statesmen recently formed at the Tennants' home in Grosvenor Square to offset the raffish Marlborough House circle and a rich but vulgar bourgeoisie. The founder members were the philosopher-statesman, Arthur James Balfour, and Margot Tennant whom some thought he might marry. He denied the rumour with the dry aside, 'I rather think of having a career of my own.'

The group earned their nickname because they talked so much about each other's souls, but their unwritten articles of association also stressed that wit, gaiety and political distinction would be rated higher than mere good looks and such frivolities as baccarat. The set was described in a contemporary newspaper as composed of 'personages distinguished for their breeding, beauty, delicacy and discrimination of mind', qualifications which were no bar to Aline Sassoon who had begun to despair of finding any substitute for her Parisian intelligentsia. She was very much at home in this floating salon which met in Mayfair or Belgravia and, even more congenially, at country houses like Cliveden, Hatfield and the Wyndham home, Clouds. 'Etty' Grenfell was among the most quick-witted and entertaining members of the set. She had married Willy Grenfell (later Lord Desborough), an intellectual, but also a famed athlete who had twice swum the rapids below Niagara Falls. Taplow Court, their Thames-side house, was only one of several delightful haunts favoured by The Souls. Aline Sassoon spent many pleasant hours with the Grenfells whose boys would later become close friends of her own son. A deeper friendship developed with Lady Horner, the confidante of Burne-Jones and Ruskin. Mells Park, her home near Frome, had been the mecca and inspirational font of the pre-Raphaelites and Aline found herself powerfully drawn to sensitive Frances Horner, whose many talents included superb needlework and painting. Through her encouragement, Aline also took up art and fitted out a small studio at the top of the house in Kensington Gore.

Apart from their intellectual after-dinner charades, The Souls appropriately discussed spiritualism and the occult. Professor Oliver Lodge always had a respectful hearing, and Balfour later became President of the Society for Psychical Research. He was displeased when, after inquiring gravely if any of the group believed in ghosts, Margot declared with a laugh that 'appearances were in their favour'. On this subject, at least, Aline Sassoon did not see eye to eye with her cynical friend. After her beloved elder sister, the Baroness Léonino, was killed in a hunting accident, she began to take spiritualism with the utmost seriousness.

Edward found these moral aesthetes and proconsuls a little beyond him and swam genially in the background when they gathered at Kensington

Gore for philosophical argument. He was more interested in their political
agenda and liked listening to George Nathaniel Curzon's lofty discourses.
He could not help being impressed by a group who could bring Gladstone
and Lord Randolph Churchill together for an almost friendly luncheon.
It was rather more embarrassing when The Souls took a high moral tone
about the ruinous stakes reported from the Marlborough Club. Edward
Sassoon, who had no interest in racing or gambling in any form, could
only nurse his moustache and sigh for Uncle Reuben.

His uncle had now become so addicted to bridge that he never travelled
without his own folding card-table. One of his first gifts to the Prince of
Wales was a set of ivory baccarat counters embossed with the fleur-de-lis.
The Heir always tucked it into his crocodile dressing-case before going
on his travels. He used this set for the celebrated party at Tranby Croft in
St Leger Week, 1890, when Sir William Gordon-Cumming was caught
cheating. The scandal was meat and drink to the righteous Souls who
gleefully suggested 'Ich Deal' as an apter motto for the Heir to the Throne.
Reuben Sassoon had been a member of that gaming party and was, in fact,
responsible for issuing the baccarat chips. He had also witnessed the document in which Gordon-Cumming had solemnly pledged himself never
again to play cards for money.

Edward Sassoon kept his usual discreet silence. He had often to steer
diplomatically between his wife's rather awesome patricians and the very
different world which dazzled his uncles. He was himself developing
political ambitions, but meantime had to be trained to take over as
Chairman. His father was in poor health and semi-retired to his mansion
in Eastern Terrace, where he had gloomily started building a family
mausoleum, forty-foot square, with high brick walls and an Islamic-type
dome cut into starry patterns.

His uncles' regency was not too exacting, and business generally seemed
to chime with pleasure in Leadenhall Street. Arthur took it all very
genially: 'We went to the office (i.e. Reuben and I) yesterday at 11
and remained till 1, while he signed the Hebrew and Arabic letters. While
we were there, Bishop called and offered some Persian opium and he said
there was a margin of more than $100 between the price here and that in
Hong Kong, so we thought we might as well buy a small lot and make a
little money. (Five days later they bought 67 chests.) We went afterwards
to Sandown with the Prince and Rosebery in a special and were grieved
to see Ladas beaten. I had a plunge on him £40 to win £70. Better luck
next time!'

Arthur relished his mild bet or two and occasionally pulled off a
pleasant coup on horses bred by 'little Bob' Rosebery or Leo de Rothschild. But he was far less addicted to speculation than his brother who

could rarely resist a flutter on the Stock Exchange, usually with such good returns that his flair was often a little exaggerated by rumour. His coups inevitably came to the receptive ears of Marlborough House where they did him no disservice. He was never the Prince's adviser-cum-banker like Hirsch or his successor, Cassel, but his shrewd touch with investments was valued by a patron whose Privy Purse often wore thin. When the subject of an ideal government was once jokingly discussed after a private luncheon, the Prince unhesitatingly nominated Lord Esher for Prime Minister and Reuben Sassoon as his Chancellor of the Exchequer.

The royal acquaintance had begun with quite casual encounters at race-meetings and sundry Rothschild house parties. It ripened when the Prince found the Arthur Sassoons as entertaining as any in his circle. He could fault neither the cuisine nor the company at Albert Gate, and Louise was a hostess who rarely bored him. He disliked women who talked serious politics and was enchanted by her piquantly accented chatter. Riding side-saddle in the Row or watching the inter-regimental polo at Ranelagh, she seemed to glow like an orchid from the gnarled trunk of Anglo-Saxon dowagers. She waltzed coquettishly, yet with perfect decorum, at Windsor Castle during Ascot Week, and made witty smalltalk when the men returned from decimating the partridges and pheasants at Leighton Buzzard. Her sister, Marie de Rothschild, was equally elegant and never wore the same pair of gloves twice. She had become a passionate huntswoman and one of London's most brilliant bridge-players, but Louise had the more natural gift for entertainment. She was almost incomparable in anticipating every whim of a favoured guest like the Prince of Wales.

Nobody retired at Tulchan, even in the smallest hours, if he craved another Scottish reel or a final rubber while he smoked the last of Reuben's Havanas. He could always be sure his mattress would not be turned on a Friday — a superstitious terror of his — and that his favourite ginger biscuits would be at his bedside, together with light literature about the Turf or yachting. Louise could *never* be guilty of a solecism like that of the duchess who thoughtfully provided another royal guest with a bed-side copy of *The Lord's Prayer*, exquisitely bound and inscribed, 'With the Author's compliments'.

Tulchan was only a smallish rented place beside the Duke of Richmond's forests or Lady Seafield's magnificent Castle Grant, but H.R.H. found it more congenial. He once complained laughingly of not being asked there of late for the grouse-shooting. A flustered Arthur explained that the Lodge was not equipped to accommodate a royal suite, and the Prince had promised at once to come with only two or three servants. On that next visit he shot snipe and brought them back for his dinner.

There was no longer any embarrassment over old-fashioned dietary laws. David Sassoon's son might tempt some guests with novel Jewish dishes, but his chef also provided the choicest of black Bradenham ham, haggis and other forbidden delights. Since the grouse-shooting season often irritatingly overlapped Yom Kippur, arrangements had to be made to keep the sacred and profane apart. Arthur, a slightly implausible figure in tweed knickerbockers, would change into sober black and unpack his prayer shawl before retiring to fast on the holiest of all days in the Jewish calendar. His guests continued their sport, but the Prince periodically sent a servant to the games-room, where his host was confined for the day, to inquire tenderly after his health.

Reuben was closer to the Prince of Wales in the decade before his Accession. From the late 'eighties onwards, he was ideally placed to play courtier. Albert had to have his legs massaged daily and stayed in Kemp Town, where he kept open house only on Sundays. However, even as part-time Chairman, he was conscientious in dealing with business matters. Arthur enjoyed his shooting and the sporting weekends at Leo's or Sir Ernest Cassel's place near Newmarket, and also had to keep riding on his wife's ceaseless roundabout. Edward spent most mornings at the head office, while Aline's dinner parties or her circuit of 'soulful' country houses absorbed the rest of his time.

Reuben alone seemed to have all the leisure essential for a place in the royal retinue. He gave occasional parties at Queen's Gardens and enjoyed his weekends by the sea, but his wife had become even less congenial. After one dinner, his niece (later Lady Ezra) reported in her diary: 'We went up to Aunt Kate's regions – where she lives – quite a separate establishment. She is enormous with a very pink and white face, light hair, and a mantilla – puffing away at the hookah from which she is inseparable. Her rooms are full of pretty flowers and odds and ends, and she is always carried up and down stairs.'

Reuben felt far more at home in Belgrave Square, where he coddled his best wines and cigars. He arranged elegant musical soirées and could muster the most accomplished bridge-players in Europe for a rubber when he needed a change from the Turf Club or the Marlborough. His advance to the innermost royal circle surprised even those aware of the Prince's philosemitism. He kept a generous table, yet had no yachts and stables or even a modest shooting-box like his brother. However, he was a travelled man and lively, with an eye for a pretty woman and just the right touch of flamboyance to amuse the Prince. His white waistcoats were admirably cut, and he had a sprightly taste in jewellery. His favourite diamond scarfpin was shaped like a horse and jockey and he always wore it with a pair of cuff-links adorned by the royal cipher.

Reuben was in his element at Sandringham weekend shoots. During one house party in November 1887, he gave his sister-in-law, Louise, an almost hour by hour account of his bliss. 'This morning being the Prince's birthday, he received a great many presents, amongst them was my cigarette case, and there were 5 other similar cases, but mine was more appreciated as being uncommon.' He minutely reported the rubbers of whist and bridge, the bags of pheasant, and a billiards lesson he had given one of the maharajahs who was over for the Queen's Golden Jubilee.

It had been a dizzily exciting year for him. He spent most of August in Homburg where the Prince had hopefully taken up lawn-tennis for his figure. Reuben was host at a huge picnic party, so successful that he repeated it soon afterwards for another seventy guests. Arthur could not be there, but thoughtfully sent the Prince some grouse from Tulchan. Reuben regurgitated his triumphs in detail. 'H.R.H. thanked me over and over again for the treats I gave him. He left this afternoon after making me dine with him last night to meet the Grand Duke of Mecklenberg-Strelitz and the Duke of Cambridge and today I lunched with him. I never saw him in greater spirits.' His young brother, Frederick, who had left Hong Kong on a pleasure tour of Europe, changed his itinerary specially to lunch at Homburg. He shirked the picnic at the last minute, pleading in excuse that he was hardly presentable with a half-grown beard. He was possibly intimidated by the guest list.

It soon became almost ritual for Reuben to accompany the Prince on a month-long cure at one or other of the foreign watering-places. He endured a weight reducing diet which he did not need, and also went on long penitential walks after the Prince had eaten some tremendous meal. They took mud baths together at Marienbad and drank the bitter waters thrice daily. They found some relief from austerity. Maud Allen danced for them one night, wearing only two oyster shells and a tantalizing five-franc piece.

Only a sharp attack of gout prevented Reuben from joining the Prince on a visit to the Baron de Hirsch's estate in Hungary during October 1890, when the party had included Lady Randolph Churchill and the Arthur Sassoons. Crippled and forlorn in Belgrave Square, he had to content himself with his brother's mouth-watering descriptions of the chamois-hunting, the gigantic hauls of partridge and a series of banquets with the local nobility.

Reuben was valued by the Prince as an amusing travelling companion, but even more for his interest in the turf. He was knowledgeable about bloodstock and regularly visited the Sandringham Stud and Egerton House, Newmarket, where Richard Marsh trained the Prince's horses. Dressed in a brown suit and matching bowler hat like his friend, he watched the gallops on the Heath and enjoyed sipping his madeira in the private room of the Jockey Club. In time he budded into the Prince's semi-official turf accountant, in the most literal sense. He knew his friend's winnings and losses almost to a sovereign. He also kept tally of all his purchases at yearling sales and even, it was said, the stable lads' wages. When one malicious gossip referred to Arthur Sassoon as 'a Jew page-boy, jumping up after each course to make bets for his master', he was probably mistaking him for his brother. But Reuben's main function was to serve his royal patron as a kind of racing ready-reckoner. His own bets were not heavy and he often won by closely studying breeding and acting on 'information'.

Value for money became a passion with him. He might spend liberally on his cigars and wines but considered them social investments, like his parties, which were infrequent but never niggardly. His sense of economy was outraged by the smallest hint of unnecessary waste. When Edward was staying at Eastern Terrace with his father, Reuben thought he was being overcharged for a hired landau and pair. 'I have always paid £16 16s. for the 3 days to Silverthorn's of Brighton,' he commented rather sharply.

This taste for correspondence had been indulged from David Sassoon's earliest days in Bombay when his sons were dispersed over wide areas. Appetite increased with addiction, and the social titbits would pass like trays of *petits fours*. 'We go tomorrow to "Penn", Amersham till Friday,' Arthur reports chattily. 'On that day we sleep in London and on Saturday go to Synagogue to hear Lionel (Leo's son) read the Torah.' Before the weekend is out, he is writing again. 'We had a magnificent shoot today about 800 pheasants, 8 guns – but they were beautiful birds. Curzon came for the day . . . I wonder what was decided about the Chinese loan. I think it is hardly worth the risk.'*

Letters were usually written in English, but often in Hebrew and Arabic if intimate or confidential. No matter where the brothers found themselves, whether abroad, at Sandringham or on remote Speyside, a flurry of notes shot between them, either to entertain each other or to request comments on business matters. Documents calling for a decision or signature went first to Eastern Terrace and then shuttled between Arthur, Reuben and Edward. Relevant extracts would later be dispatched to Bombay or Frederick's office in Hong Kong.

The family correspondence in the 'eighties contrasts strongly with the acrimony of the following decade. It shows a growing absorption in splendour. The three brothers took naturally to an oriental hedonism once they had loosened their ties with fellow-Jews. There was cash and to spare for living in the most opulent style. In 1890, despite fairly substantial losses in opium and quicksilver, David Sassoon & Sons showed a profit

* The background to this loan is discussed more fully in chapter eight.

of £111,395 17s. 5d. Edward was paid £9,543 0s. 11d., while Frederick, who did not go on the Board for some years, received £7,987 9s. 4d. The Chairman with Reuben and Arthur, now senior directors, would certainly have drawn a good deal more.

During these years of plenty, the London partners had no cause for alarm. It was still possible to combine a demanding social life with the overall direction of financial policy. They had, of course, to keep an even balance of capital, in itself a complex operation with trade covering India, China, the Middle East and a sensitive Manchester Cotton Exchange. The entire top floor in Leadenhall Street was occupied by a staff of translators who dealt with bills of lading, marine insurance and a ceaseless flow of mail in Hebrew, Arabic, Persian, Chinese and Hindustani. Their letters, written in flawless copperplate, became a prestige hallmark for the firm. It always flattered overseas correspondents to be addressed in their own language. The translators were a polyglot and sometimes volatile team who worked together in a clublike atmosphere. They gave little trouble until a certain morning, when one of the few Armenian clerks was shot and slightly wounded by a jealous husband.

Office administration was smoothly handled by the manager and major-domo, Henry Coke, who dealt with the reports from abroad and settled routine queries. The various import and export managers each had specialists under them for different commodities and territories. Coke acted as co-ordinator-in-chief, thus sparing the brothers and 'Mr Edward' all minor irritations. They would arrive by carriage or hansom to sign cheques and any important letters, but their main function was to keep a day-to-day scrutiny on world currencies, particularly the state of the wayward rupee, so liable to disruption by a failure of the monsoon or unexpected changes in fiscal policy. There had been several anxious moments since 1879 when Lord Lytton, the Viceroy, had forced through the abolition of the revenue tariff which gave Lancashire an unfair and much resented advantage over Indian cotton goods.

The firm needed to keep its substantial capital reserves fluid against any emergency. Here Reuben was invaluable with his acute brain which chipped off figures like a circular saw. He watched all currency fluctuations and skilfully analysed the accounts from Solomon, in Bombay, and Frederick, who was being kept mobile between the Treaty Ports.

Sir Albert's varied contacts were an asset which few other trading firms could command. When his health allowed, he always made a point of attending diplomatic receptions and often entertained the Chinese Ambassador, a close personal friend, and other influential members of the Corps. By the late 'eighties, his soundings at the Persian Embassy were being echoed in the City of London. The Shah was again in deep water and might shortly welcome artificial respiration. The sympathy of the British Government, already nervous of Russia's renewed interest in the Gulf, could be relied on for any responsible counter-initiative. A golden opportunity presented itself in the summer of 1889, when the Shah arrived on another State Visit.

The previous tour had sorely tried the Prince of Wales, who now expected the Rothschilds and other hospitable friends to come to his rescue. He made it known that Sir Albert's fluency in Persian and his firm's trading interests in the Gulf might together relieve the strain of a visit which filled the whole Court with alarm and despondency. Nobody seemed over-eager to meet the boorish potentate. This visit, however, proved less of a strain than that sixteen years earlier, although one or two unsavoury moments were unavoidable. The Shah, a devoted fruitarian, was so plainly relishing a vast bowl of cherries during one banquet at Windsor Castle that the carpet around his chair was studded with the stones he had spat out. Suddenly noting that other guests were rejecting theirs in the more orthodox fashion, the King of Kings at once went down on his knees to recover his discards.

He was generally good-humoured on this visit, thanks largely to Sir Albert Sassoon. Although a sick man and shaky on his legs, he had responded heroically to the call of duty. He was favoured by a natural *bonhomie*. Serene and smiling, he commentated and patiently interpreted for the visitor who often took him warmly by the arm. Not everyone, however, could stomach such pleasantries. Many of the Bevis Marks congregation were shocked by this homage to a ruler whose extortions and ruthless persecution of his Jewish subjects recalled Daud Pasha's infamous régime. But Sir Albert was a master hand at gentle diplomacy, and his family's benefactions were a most powerful argument.

He hardly missed an engagement. He went to Kempton Park races with the Prince and the Shah and then joined them for dinner at Lord Rosebery's in Berkeley Square. He also accompanied the Shah to Halton House, Alfred de Rothschild's château in the Vale of Aylesbury, before staying overnight with Baron 'Ferdy' at neighbouring Waddesdon Manor. On July 4, Sir Albert took over the entire Empire Theatre for an entertainment which made a brilliant climax to the tour. After dining at Buckingham Palace, the Shah drove to the theatre with the Prince and Princess of Wales and other members of the Royal Family. Several hundred guests, including a cluster of foreign royals and every ambassador in London, were greeted by a guard of honour from the Coldstreams. They took their places in an auditorium elegantly decorated with flowers and satins. A ballet *divertissement* was then performed with a taste and style which many compared favourably with the Royal Command Performance at Covent

Garden. The lights finally went down at 1.30 a.m. after the entire audience had been served with a full-course supper under the gleaming lustres.

The Shah had gladly accepted Sir Albert's invitation for a bracing week-end at Brighton. They drove together from the station to Eastern Terrace, while the crowd cheered and waved Persian flags or Union Jacks. Next day their carriage made its way slowly through the decorated esplanades and along the Lower Cliff. Suddenly the Shah insisted on getting out and going to the water's edge where some lady bathers were taking a decorous dip. He explained through a blushing interpreter that it would please him to see them disrobe completely. They fled in some panic, leaving unhappy Sir Albert to excuse such remarkable prudishness. His guest only recovered from this discourtesy over a banquet which continued into the small hours. Feeling a little jaded next morning, he agreed that a visit to the Turkish Baths in West Street might prove beneficial. It was an inspiration, even if the muscular masseurs did not turn out to be the nubile houris expected. Now refreshed and beaming with good humour, the Shah thanked his host for an enjoyable visit and pinned a hard-earned Order to his frock-coat.

Sir Albert was soon afterwards created First Baronet of Kensington Gore. The title was more than a recognition of his hospitality. It impliedly acknowledged his help in securing a Concession which could block Russian designs on Persia. Other practical benefits soon became clear. Baron de Reuter had almost given up hope of ever seeing his caution money back. He was now repaid his £40,000, plus a bonus of £2 per share when a capital issue of £2 million sterling was made for a new Imperial Bank of Persia. The cash was put up mainly by Glyn Mills, J. Henry Schroder and David Sassoon & Sons, whom Sir Albert represented on the Board. The Shah also gave a sixty-year Concession to finance and exploit his country's mineral wealth and other resources.

Apart from such tangible benefits, the State Visit had been a decisive social coup for the House of Sassoon. Yet it had not brought unalloyed pleasure to Sir Albert. The carriages, with their flunkeys, crests and cockades, had flowed daily back and forth along Kensington Gore, with always a crowd of onlookers to watch the foreign notabilities arrive at Number 25. It was therefore astonishing to see a distinctly moth-eaten cortège draw up there one evening. Some villainous-looking Arabs in dusty robes and the filthiest of *djellabas* swore viciously at three sad camels who sank to their knees while several bulging sacks were unloaded at the *front* door. The caravan drivers departed in a fury of curses, having quite failed to make the butler and footmen understand that they brought gifts from the Shah's devoted followers in England. The vile-smelling sacks were then found to contain nothing but old newspapers and rags.

A few inquiries quickly disclosed the culprit as Sir Albert's own nephew, Alfred, who had never forgiven the clan's stuffiness over his marriage to Theresa Thornycroft. He had hired the camels from a circus and engaged half a dozen unemployed actors for this special performance. The Shah's visit seemed to him a perfect opportunity to remind his family 'where it had all started', as he told a friend afterwards.

Alfred had not long to live. His sons' sharp-tongued nurse, Mrs Mitchell, took them to see him for the last time in a flat at Grand Parade, Eastbourne. Whether by her husband's orders or his mother's Theresa would never know, but it did not lessen her anguish at being turned from the door. The boys made a brave effort to smile when their father, flushed and pitifully emaciated, cracked jokes until he fell back on his pillow. Their grandmother, a smallish and still elegant woman despite her wizened parchment skin, arrived from Brighton with a huge bouquet and a basket of peaches. She greeted them kindly and began asking numerous questions in an oddly accented, sing-song voice without appearing to listen to their answers.* She then showed them the family tree and ran a jewelled index finger from David Sassoon's name down to their own at the very base.

Little Uncle Joe from Ashley Park stood silently by the frost-covered window, tugging his moustache and obviously finding it difficult to fight back his tears when his brother was racked by a fit of coughing which left his handkerchief bloodstained. The boys put their arms round 'Pappy's' neck but were forbidden to kiss him goodbye for fear of infection. He told Mrs Mitchell to treat them to a shrimp tea at Beachy Head, but it failed to cheer them. They returned home with icy fingers and eyes red-rimmed from the clod and their helpless tears.

Alfred Ezra Sassoon died a few weeks later in March 1895. Siegfried was too upset to go to the funeral. At his grandmother's insistence, it took place at the Sephardic cemetery in London's Mile End, although Theresa had timidly pleaded that the body might rest under the yews at Brenchley near Weirleigh. Michael and Hamo recognized their Uncle Joseph but none of the other relatives who shook them solemnly by the hand. They were shocked by the stark austerity of the ceremony; the hearse without a single flower or wreath, in accordance with Jewish ritual; the sad-eyed, sallow strangers wearing black felt hats or skullcaps; and the lamentations intoned with such awesome intensity. They arrived back at Weirleigh with heavy hearts. For some days they could not bring themselves to tell Siegfried or their mother of their distress at not being able to join in

---

* This became a Sassoon characteristic, according to Siegfried, who told the author: 'They always seemed to be asking questions, such as "How old is Galsworthy? Is he a clever man?" Rather tiring!'

the 'jabber-jabber', as Michael called it, when their 'Pappy' was lowered into his grave while the snowflakes spattered the bleak and alien cemetery.

Their father had not left them in want, but his private income had been heavily reduced when his mother cut off his allowance after the marriage. Each would have about £600 a year at twenty-one, and provision was also made for their education. Michael and Hamo would go to Malvern, and Siegfried to Marlborough, with Cambridge to follow if they decided to go up, as their Uncle Hamo advised. It caused them no heartache to be denied Eton and other luxuries which their Sassoon cousins would enjoy, but Theresa still had to budget with some care. Within a few years she sold her jewellery and most of the family's best cutlery to buy a couple of hunters for herself and a pony for 'Sig', who already rode with confidence. Dressed in velveteen with a jockey cap, he rarely missed a day out with the groom, Richardson. The two tennis courts were also kept going, and there would be no skimping on sports gear, books and music for Siegfried, with a lathe and tool kits for his more practical brothers. They had care-free days on the *Waterlily*, and it was a treat to go over to Tunbridge Wells and hear celebrities like Paderewski or Sarasate. The latter kindly asked them to his dressing-room and talked about their father whom he well remembered as a promising pupil. For days afterwards, Siegfried practised his scales religiously but soon went back to scribbling verse or memorizing whole passages from Alfred's quarto edition of the *Rubaiyat*, bound in pink damask, which he found one day in his mother's studio.

Theresa had the boys to comfort her in the holidays, and she turned slowly back to her painting and the joy of riding to hounds or swimming in the Medway before it froze over. Her wounds healed, but left scars. She could forgive Alfred, if not his mother, whom she held mainly responsible for keeping her from his bedside. She had as little sympathy with the former Louise de Gunzbourg of Ashley Park or the other relatives. In a moment of bitterness she once declared roundly that 'the Sassoon women are like lacquer and absorb rather than reflect'. From this indictment she could only exclude her sister-in-law, Rachel Beer, and the boys' kindly great-aunt, Mozelle (Mrs Hyeem of Brighton), whom they had nicknamed, 'Aunt Brazil Nut'.

They were irritated at school, and finally bored, at being asked if they were related to 'the Royal Sassoons', who had entertained the Shah of Persia and were such close friends of the Prince of Wales. They preferred to think of themselves as Thornycrofts, but warmed nevertheless to Auntie Rachel who showed their mother genuine affection and drew even closer to Weirleigh after her brother's death. They always looked forward to visiting her in London. At Charing Cross, as Siegfried has recalled in

The Old Century, they used to be met by a brougham complete with coachman and attendant footman on the box, each dressed in the chocolate-brown livery of the Beers and with elegant cockades stuck in their hats. The stately butler, Drew, led them up the marble staircase in Chesterfield Gardens to a drawing-room stuffed with gilt chinoiserie, assorted Dresden, mounted butterflies and lacquered cabinets, all adorned with the inescapable family crest. Mr Beer himself would materialize from a shadowy corner and proffer a limp hand, but he soon retired to his ottoman after a friendly-sounding mumble. Their aunt would explain superfluously that he was 'not very well'. The phrase blended with that airless and overheated room, with the windows closed or muffled by heavy brocade curtains, and a permanent sickly-sweet odour of perfume and medicaments.

It was a relief to troop into luncheon along a mirror-walled corridor, Rachel leading the way in a feathery hat, her silk dress rustling and a Burmese fan clicking like castanets to her breathless smalltalk. As always, says Siegfried, she gave out a delicious smell of violets. The dining-room was a splendour of Chippendale and Corot, brightly lit by electricity, still a novelty to them after the oil lamps of Weirleigh. They would probably have preferred a little sunlight and fresh air, but soon forgot such discomforts when Aunt Rachel's French chef served up his admirable curries. Convinced that her poor orphan nephews were in a permanent state of malnutrition, she insisted on providing banquets with double portions of curry, quails in aspic, macédoine and pâtisserie. They would afterwards be taken to a matinée, usually Maskelyne and Cooke's Mysteries at the Egyptian Hall, where the mechanically-minded Michael recalls going on stage and holding up the whole performance to find out 'how it's done.'

The exciting day's outing, so rich in both novelty and cuisine, would usually end in their being sick long before they arrived home, but it was worth the discomfort. They loved Auntie Rachel and came to understand her idiosyncrasies. She used to talk excitably about books or music, her brown eyes flashing like 'Pappy's'. Suddenly, and quite without warning, she would break off and go into an absentminded trance. 'She always gave an impression of having slept badly the night before,' writes Siegfried. Her distrait manner was mainly due to taking heavy sleeping draughts when the strain of nursing her husband overwhelmed her. He was losing the power of speech, and paralysis had slowly crept into his limbs. Their mother had explained rather vaguely that 'Uncle Beer' had no relations and suffered from 'a bad heredity', but she usually became embarrassed and would change the subject when they asked too many questions. Rachel used to come down to Weirleigh from time to time, laden with boxes of fruit and sweetmeats. She would sit and chat with Theresa for a while but soon grew distraught about Frederick who might have forgotten to take his pills or perhaps been seized by a 'migraine'. She then departed in a flurry of kisses, leaving behind parcels of children's books and annuals which had been hopefully sent to her for review.

In the intervals between nursing her husband, she had turned eagerly to journalism. Frederick had inherited *The Observer* but was too ill to take any practical interest himself. Rachel began to write features and leading articles before finally assuming the editorship. She quickly grew more ambitious and was encouraged by the example of a Miss Alice Cornwall, who bought the *Sunday Times* after making a fortune in the Australian goldfields. Rachel decided to buy it in October 1893, when its fortunes were none too bright. She thought its rather formal liberalism might be revitalized and planned to edit it. The eight-page penny paper offered limited scope for her writing talents, but she impressed the need for an objective political approach, a novel contribution to those doctrinaire days. She considered her £11,000 well spent, although several harassed sub-editors would be driven to near distraction by leaders written in an indecipherable hand and usually delivered at the last minute by a footman. Proofs were brought to her from St Clement's Press by a messenger, Gus Wingrove, who later became the paper's head printer. He would wait patiently below stairs at Chesterfield Gardens and was often sent back in her carriage.

The eccentricities of 'Madame Midas', as journalists called her, became so well known that nobody showed much surprise when she took specials at £25 a time to go down to Weirleigh or visit some friend in the suburbs if she happened to miss the regular train. She was nevertheless appreciated in Fleet Street for her occasional flair and business-like decisions. One of her wisest impulses was to persuade George Augustus Sala to contribute a gossip column to the *Sunday Times*. He would personally deliver his 'Echoes of the Town' each week, dressed in his usual regalia of dazzling white waistcoat and a chocolate-coloured frock-coat worn with Blucher boots.

Rachel was, of course, working under appalling personal difficulties. To own and edit two newspapers simultaneously, as well as writing leaders, book reviews and occasional feature articles, would have taxed a woman with the most serene domestic background. Exposed to continuous physical and mental strain, it became impossible. When T. P. O'Connor, M.P., himself a brilliant editor, called one evening to discuss a business scheme, probably the raising of capital for the *Sun* which was then losing £30,000 a year, he was shocked and infinitely depressed by his reception in Chesterfield Gardens. It coincided with one of Frederick's worst periods, but 'T.P.' knew nothing of this as he followed Drew into the dimly lit drawing-room and picked his way round piles of unopened parcels of review copies almost reaching the crystal chandeliers. Through the gloom he could barely make out 'two shrunken, pitiful and pathetic figures', huddled over the fireplace and speaking nervously in whispers. He soon crept away, as from a house of mourning.

Only a few months later, just before Christmas 1896, he saw a very different Rachel Beer at the Hotel Cecil. She looked cool and elegant as she curtsied to the Princess of Wales who opened the Press Bazaar and complimented her on *The Observer*'s admirably arranged stall. Rachel had invited the boys to come up from Kent and act as pages. Wearing silk breeches and frilly white blouses, they stood behind her while she chatted easily to the Princess and the Duke of Cambridge. Although very nervous, they were alert for her signal to advance, bow gracefully and sweep off their plumed hats. This much-rehearsed operation was wrecked by ten-year-old Siegfried, who managed to trip over his two left feet and skittle his brothers' hats.

Rachel braved the disaster like a Boadicea. To console Siegfried for his *gaffe*, he tells us that she gave him a new copy of *The Time Machine*, autographed by the author. She also bought him a splendid cricket bat at Wisden's when he and his brothers next came up to London. At the same time, she ordered an entire set of cricket equipment, nets included, for the garden of the Beer house at Richmond which was rarely used. She explained cheerfully that it might do their uncle good to have the footmen bowl to him. Since Frederick was by then half paralysed, the crate remained unopened.

Chapter Eight

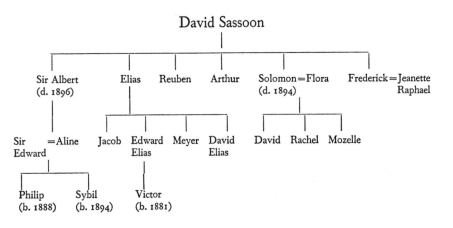

The Imperial Bank of Persia at first yielded more prestige than profit. For a firm long established in Baghdad and the Gulf Ports, it was obviously an asset to have high-level merchant banking interests in Teheran, but the country was backward, officials corrupt and grasping, and the people had grown suspicious of all foreign investors. In its opening five years, the Bank's capital was reduced to £650,000, and the directors had difficulty in collecting any revenues. The Sassoon office files would make constant wry references to a chaotic state of affairs. 'The Shah gave a peremptory order that the money was to be paid – upon which satisfactory arrangements were made and the recalcitrant Moolah was brought to book. A proposal also came that the Bank should pay the allowance of the Persian Cossack Army recovering the amounts from the local Govts by order from the Teheran Treasury, to show the Persians that the Bank *is* the Bank of the Persian Government.' The Shah was soon afterwards shot dead in a mosque, leaving a semi-bankrupt treasury. His government secured a further loan by pledging the customs of Bushire where David Sassoon, as an almost penniless refugee, had once been roughly searched by port officials when he stepped ashore. Sixty years later, his grandson, Edward, casually signed his approval of the loan on behalf of the Imperial Bank.

It was a relatively small investment for a firm whose portfolios covered varied enterprises like the British South African Co., the Persian Gulf Steamship Co. and Chicago and N.W. Granaries. Cotton and the now less important opium still formed the backbone, but the range of merchandise also took in cloves, morphia, indigo, quicksilver, copper, yellow metals, Scotch pig-iron, dates and pearls. In India the firm's mills had flourished, but other interests were steadily being developed through a network of insurance companies, land development concerns and paper mills. Leadenhall Street rarely interfered with Bombay while the balance sheets remained plump. Sir Albert would sometimes pay a brief visit and hurry back to England after seeing his wife and attending a few official receptions, but Reuben and Arthur scarcely set foot on Indian soil after their departure.

On the surface there seemed little to choose between the London-based directors of the two Sassoon houses. To a cynical eye the founder firm simply sent its sons to Eton, while the E. D. Sassoons favoured Harrow. Jacob's younger brother, Edward Elias, had married Leontine Levy, the stylish and cultured daughter of a leading Cairo merchant. He had a fashionable address in Grosvenor Place and a weekend villa in Third Avenue, West Brighton. His brother Meyer's bride was one of Sir Albert's grand-daughters, which made it rather difficult to maintain the old bitter vendetta. When Edward Elias's son, Victor, celebrated his Barmitzvah, Sir Albert sent him a handsome writing desk.

The E. D. Sassoon brothers might not be quite so close to the royal purple, but they and their wives also entertained duchesses and held elegant soirées. Their Old Masters, rare porcelain and Aubussons were worthy of their neighbours. Meyer lived in Hamilton Place, the Rothschild corner of Park Lane, and belonged to the Cavalry Club. He and his wife spent lavishly on pictures which in years to come would prove their taste and a sure business instinct.*

Yet the firms differed in one vitally significant detail. Sir Albert ruled, at least nominally, from Leadenhall Street. His nephew, Jacob, was far more active as Chairman of the rival firm and remained emphatically based on Bombay. He could also rely on firmer backing at the European end. His brothers relished their social life but were never permitted to follow the easier pattern set by Sir Albert. Meyer was a sound business man with a civilized sense of relaxation. He might have preferred to collect his pictures and snuff-boxes, but had to keep reasonable hours in Fenchurch Street. His brother, Edward Elias, moved energetically between London and Lancashire and often went overseas to visit branches. It was not surprising that his son and heir, Victor, had been born in Naples in 1881 while his parents were *en route* to India. Unlike Reuben and Arthur

---

* Their daughter, Mrs Derek FitzGerald, would later sell Lagillière's 'La Belle Strasbourgeoise' for £145,000. Her parents had originally bought it for £14,000.

in the parent firm, Edward Elias frequently sailed to Bombay to consult with his brother, Jacob, who was still busily opening mills and dyeworks and had started flourishing branches in Calcutta and Karachi.

Their youngest brother, David, had proved a disappointment. After dabbling in the London office, he was hopefully sent out to Shanghai. Silas Hardoon found him far more difficult to handle than Frederick in the old Hong Kong days. He was already a gay libertine at twenty when he arrived at Sassoon House and rapidly made a local reputation as racing man and philanderer. He joined the Shanghai Volunteers – the semi-police force which helped to keep order in the Settlement – the Paper Hunt Club and a Masonic Lodge, but yawned openly at Hardoon's business homilies. He used to retreat behind his racing paper at the faintest stirring of a company balance-sheet.

This David was named after his grandfather without inheriting his character or looks. He was tiny, with a swarthy face and a beak of a nose, but had an animal magnetism which made him dwarf and often cuckold taller and better favoured men. As an accomplished ballroom dancer and a bachelor, he was in demand at Settlement parties but gave chaperones some nasty moments. After one of Hardoon's desperate reports, the firm at last decided to settle a large capital sum on David, plus a handsome director's income. He was given a roving commission as a sinecure. It enabled him to spend half a year in London and the winter months in Shanghai.

Jacob, somewhat prim and a model of piety himself, lacked the patience to handle a wastrel who left many a trail of scandal. His only son had died in infancy and his wife had since become a chronic invalid. His eyes, weak like his father's, had troubled him from childhood, and he would only leave India to consult European oculists and ophthalmic surgeons. The threat of blindness did not limit his working hours. In a few years his companies had expanded to make him the largest single employer of factory labour in and around Bombay, the mill named after him operating seventy-five thousand spindles. He lived at luxurious Braganza Hall, but had villas besides in Poona and Mahabaleshwar, each with its semi-permanent complement of rabbis and pensioners. Being a Sassoon and sociable, he used to take parties of guests to the regattas at the Yacht Club or the show-jumping in Poona.

Even his opposite number, the serious-minded Solomon, relaxed a little during the palmy 'eighties. He once ordered 'a fashionable new Victoria phaeton', which was shipped out to him from England at a cost of £234 3s., and Coke was soon told to send him a new £110 dinner service and damask linen. He was clearly being mellowed by his wife, who had now become a prominent hostess. With Lady Cowasji Jehangier, a member of the great Parsee family of philanthropists, she was actively leading an anti-purdah movement that was no longer a suffragette joke in the drawing-rooms. She found another willing ally and a lifelong friend in the Governor's wife, Fanny Reay, whom she met or wrote to almost daily.

David Sassoon & Sons naturally gained in prestige by such personal ties with Government House. Flora's dinner parties were tasteful, and the company would be chosen with the meticulous care she gave to her strict Jewish cuisine. She was splendidly gowned and usually wore her seven-roped pearl necklace, each pearl of which had been lovingly added, year after year, by her husband. Her animated manner often hid a nagging anxiety about Solomon who sapped his health to maintain the firm's turnover. Lacking Jacob's financial wizardry and his remarkable reflexes to business trends, he applied himself almost fanatically to office routine.

It was still not enough to prevent E. D. Sassoon & Co. from increasing their early lead in cotton manufacturing and the new dyeing processes. Jacob accurately foresaw that Japan might soon develop her own mills and could become a formidable competitor in both the Chinese and Indian markets. He was therefore quicker off the mark in producing higher-quality goods. At the same time, he encouraged Hardoon to buy up small property lots in the Chinese quarter of fast-growing Shanghai.

Foreign capital was now being poured into China. Sites were snapped up for office buildings, new factory plants and tenements for workers. This enabled Hardoon to serve his employers and also enrich himself. He continued to worship at the synagogue but was taking an interest in Buddhism which gave him an intimacy with prominent Chinese merchants denied to most outside businessmen. He served simultaneously on municipal councils in the British Settlement and the French Concession. Such flexibility deserved a reward. Hardoon would often buy something on his own account if the firm's larger investment seemed almost certain of success. Thus he neatly eliminated risk from speculation. With little capital he would steadily acquire several pieces of property which yielded him good rents for re-investment in other lots.

The two Sassoon houses had been too profitably engaged in manufacturing and shipping cotton yarn, as well as consolidating their import and export business with Britain and the Far East, to pay overmuch attention to their old rival, J. N. Tata, who was planning to create a mighty generating plant out of the jungle swamp of Jamshedpur. The Sassoons were merchants by instinct and training rather than industrialists. They tended to nurse their holdings, content to operate for a safe margin of profit. Yet over-caution would turn out to be quite as dangerous in the long run. Tata showed more enterprise and founded his huge fortune by branching into real estate, chemicals, cement and rolling stock. He was always alert and mobile. While the Sassoons were slowly adding mill to mill in the already overcrowded island of Bombay, he spent several months touring Alabama and Georgia to buy cotton and study modern techniques. He then went north to Pittsburgh, visiting iron and steel plants for pointers to his dream of supplying Indian cities with all their light and power.

Tata remained friendly with the Sassoons whose interests did not encroach on his own except in textiles. The only collision came about through his objection to the high freightage charged by the leading steamship companies sailing between India, China and Japan. It gnawed so deeply into his bones that he committed one of his few errors of judgement since the misadventure with Roychand.

P. & O. and other leviathans of the seven seas were undercut by tramp steamers from the very opening of the Suez Canal. Their overheads were heavier than those of the seasonal and more flexible smaller fleets who could therefore charge less for freight. To check this 'irresponsible competition', the big companies came to private understandings which would avoid poaching and protect them against price-cutting. A series of Conference agreements settled tariff rates, spheres of operation, tonnage to be carried and kindred matters of mutual interest. Handsome 'rebates' or discounts were offered to all who would agree to use their vessels exclusively for fixed periods.

By 1890 the P. & O. had begun to earn far more from freight than passage money. The system plainly suited the Sassoons and other bulk shippers who took their rebates while benefiting from a speedy and regular cargo service. Tata was less enthusiastic. He denounced these Conference 'arrangements' as a thinly disguised monopoly to keep charges up to a profiteering level.

David Sassoon & Sons saw no reason to join in the freight war which caused so much bitterness during the last quarter of the century. Their relations with the major lines had been cordial from the first years in the export trade. They had known and liked P. & O.'s Superintendent, Thomas Sutherland, almost from the day he sailed by opium clipper from Hong Kong to Nagasaki to explore the opening of a mail service with Japan. They had taken a major initiative with him in founding the Hong Kong and Shanghai Banking Corporation, and Arthur and his successors served by his side on the Board. It was no disadvantage to have a friend at court like Sutherland, who later became a Suez Canal director. Similarly, the firm valued its good relations with the British India Steam Navigation Co. (soon to be merged with P. & O.) through the busy coasting trade with the Gulf.

They stayed on the touchlines when Tata entered into independent

agreements with the Austrian Lloyd Line and the Italian concern, Rub-
batino. When these allies decided against such a long-term risk, the Parsee
bantam promptly arranged with a Japanese line to carry his cotton at a
cheaper rate than the 'ring' was asking. He quickly became intoxicated by
his vision of an all-Indian steamship service but was misled by vague
promises of support from various Bombay millowners and shippers. He
decided to go ahead and form his own Line with two new ships and some
others taken over from his Japanese associate, Nippon Yusen Kaisha. His
advertised freight charge was only 12 Rs. per ton of 40 cubic feet against
the P. & O.'s 19 Rs., but Tata again found himself in choppy waters when
his competitors lowered their own rates. His personal motives began to
be questioned when he offered generous rates to the Japanese Cotton
Buyers' Association to use his ships exclusively. It was rumoured that he
was himself planning a cartel. When the Parsee millowners finally with-
drew their backing, it was the end of Tata's dream.

He took his losses philosophically and soon made his own peace with the
shipping lines. He established excellent relations with his old 'enemy',
P. & O., and gave enthusiastic support to their cold-storage plants for
shipping fruit and other perishables. Before very long, his hydro-electric
schemes and mighty expansion in iron and steel had more than compensated him for a brave defeat.

The Sassoons would prove rather less resilient when things went against
them. They had enjoyed unbroken prosperity since the Civil War cotton
boom. During a full quarter-century their holdings had proliferated,
fertilized by a shrewdness in spreading risks, from building sites on the
Shanghai Bund to running coastal vessels on the Persian Gulf and investing
in the granaries of the American Middle West. Both firms began to feel
the sharp pinch of crisis in the 'nineties. The rupee became so unsteady by
1893 that the mints had to be closed to the free coinage of silver. Fluctuations in its price hit trade, especially with China, but the Sassoons were
able to hedge on currencies, thanks to their deeply penetrating interests
and banking facilities.

Opium was more difficult. The House of Commons had condemned
the traffic in 1891, and traders could not ignore other signs. The Chinese
were not only growing it themselves but taxing every chest imported. To
compensate for this prospective loss of revenue, the Government of India
imposed a 5 per cent general tariff on all imports. Lancashire protested
and had this quickly reduced to $3\frac{1}{2}$ per cent. A heavier excise was then
placed on Indian cotton. This naturally caused resentment among Bombay's millowners who complained bitterly of discrimination. Several
had to close down, crippled simultaneously by the excise, successive
failures of the monsoon and the accompanying catastrophes of famine and

bubonic plague. The Sassoons suffered, but they were among the few to survive.

The Far Eastern situation was no less disruptive. The Japanese again became militant over Korea, and showed clear designs on Formosa and Manchuria. With their substantial holdings in China, neither of the Sassoon firms could be complacent about such a potentially dangerous competitor. Furthermore, the Russians and the Germans were plainly interested in developing commercial 'spheres of influence' at the expense of a weakened China. In this context, everyone in the West suddenly grew eager to lend money to Peking in return for concessions of one kind or another.

David Sassoon & Sons were quick to propose sterling loans for railways and other enterprises. Sir Albert turned instinctively to the Rothschilds, but New Court chanced to be in an ultra-cautious mood at this time. They had recently gone to the rescue of the Barings whose ill-judged adventures in the Argentine almost precipitated a panic in the City of London. For this reason, coupled with the family's anxiety not to offend traditional German connections, they politely excused themselves. Sir Albert, who was then in his mid-seventies and not too robust, lacked the energy to push ahead on his own initiative or to oppose Reuben and Arthur. Both were strongly against further capital expenditure in China or indeed anywhere else. They were distressed by the poor returns from the Imperial Bank and reminded the Chairman of the firm's heavy losses in silver and the steady depreciation in their stocks and shares. These arguments reinforced a go-slow policy, followed by a gradual reduction of staff in the Hong Kong and Shanghai branches.

Sir Albert's Chinese Loan might have paid enormous dividends had it gone through before China's humiliating defeat by the Japanese in March 1895. It would certainly have given Britain and the Sassoons a useful vantage point. As it was, a Franco-Russian loan was floated to help Peking pay the huge war indemnity in exchange for valuable rights and concessions. Some months later, a Russo-Chinese bank was hastily formed to finance railway construction in Manchuria.

The founder firm was now paying dearly for a tribal policy which depended on a continuous male succession. It was no consolation that the quintet of boys at Ashley Park were destined, almost from birth, for Eton and the Army. At the partnership level, David Sassoon and his eight sons had formed such a strong team that it survived the defection of Elias with comparative ease. Having so long excluded strangers, the firm's weakness in management was dramatically exposed. Leadenhall Street's buoyant atmosphere had evaporated with the now regular losses in opium and silver. The brothers also showed painful scars from the over-production of Indian cotton and a punishing excise. Unfortunately, they found it difficult to adapt themselves. Sir Albert could not so often leave Eastern Terrace where he was cared for by Mead, his personal attendant, and a small retinue of servants. Reuben's worsening gout had compelled him to move from Belgrave Square to a service flat in Pall Mall which was more accessible to his clubs and Marlborough House. He was wealthy enough not to exert himself except at the card-tables or an occasional day's racing. Arthur was also disinclined to give up his shooting and entertaining. He read every line of *The Times* daily and could rarely be faulted on aristocratic lineage or the sporting calendar, but these were doubtful assets in times of commercial trial. Their nephew, Edward, had never been a desk man or enthusiastic to travel abroad on company business. He became even more domesticated and keener to pursue a political career after Aline had given birth in Paris to his son and heir, Philip, in 1888. Sybil arrived six years later.

The year 1894 was one of mixed fortunes for this branch. Frederick married and Solomon died. The former, the youngest of David Sassoon's sons, had done well in Hong Kong but seemed anxious to settle in London after his long stint. His bride was Jeanette Raphael, a member of the same wealthy banking family into which one of Reuben's daughters had married. Reuben was particularly delighted and confided to Arthur that 'the father will probably settle £100,000 on the girl with the prospect of a great deal more in future as he is supposed to be worth two millions'. They expected much of Frederick, but his plans for moving into an elegant house in Knightsbridge and joining the head office were dashed by the sudden death of his brother, Solomon, in Bombay. Within a few weeks his potential successor, Sir Albert's son-in-law, A. M. Gubbay, also died.

These two heavy blows had fallen precisely when the Indian branch needed a firm hand. To the surprise of her brothers-in-law, and something like horror in Bombay's business community, Flora Sassoon announced her decision to take over from her husband. She confided briskly to Lady Reay and other anti-purdah intimates that she had no intention of sitting back to draw dividends. She was only thirty-five and would keep a grip on affairs until her son was ready to sit in his father's chair.

Young David seemed so far more interested in his collection of Hebraica. It had grown steadily since he first exchanged his kite for that still-treasured copy of the Book of Ruth. Unfortunately, he was so delicate that the doctors prescribed an open-air life well away from the city's heat. He spent most of the year at the villas in Poona or Mahabaleshwar, taking lessons in Persian from a *munshi* and of course studying the Torah. For healthier recreation, his mother made him join the Bombay Light Horse. It was a success. He had the family's good hands and was soon breaking in difficult mounts for fellow-cadets.

Flora had two other children; Rachel, already a lively girl of marriageable age, and the gentle, soft-spoken Mozelle, who was condemned to years of helpless suffering. She was dropped as a baby by her nurse and sustained an incurable spinal injury. Flora nursed her devotedly, but there were times when only faith helped her to endure Mozelle's sufferings and the chill of widowhood. 'Il Palazzo' was completed but she let it stand unoccupied for years, almost like a monument to her husband. She spent many hours in the little synagogue at Nepean Lodge where they had so often prayed together.

During his lifetime she had partly familiarized herself with business matters in order to understand and share his burdens. She visited the office infrequently in the months of mourning. Instead, she studied the account books and overseas mail at Nepean Lodge where she usually received Charles Moses, a grandson of David Sassoon.* He was ambitious and, like the London partners, treated her at first like some over-enthusiastic shareholder at an Annual General Meeting.

Flora was always a most patient listener, with a gift for unobtrusively extracting useful information. The fact that she was a woman made her doubly wary of giving offence, but her grasp of detail became plain when documents and accounts were formally presented for her signature or approval. She could be unexpectedly stubborn over quite minor points and reacted sharply to the smallest hint of cheating or disloyalty. Among her private papers is a bulky dossier concerning litigation with a Bombay garage-owner who had sold her a motor car with a breach of warranty. The amount involved was mouselike compared with the mountainous correspondence which followed. Flora wrote relentlessly, sometimes twice a day, to her solicitors, witnesses and scores of others until she extracted full satisfaction.

Once the Bombay merchants and brokers had grown used to a woman Sassoon in authority, many found it pleasant to deal with her. The salon atmosphere had returned to the Bombay branch for the first time since Sir Albert's departure, but it demanded a harsh desk routine in those critical days. Flora used to spend her mornings at home, seated in her high-backed chair at a card table neatly stacked with queries and correspondence from China, Japan and the Persian Gulf. She answered all letters promptly, following David Sassoon's lifelong practice, and gave the head

* His mother was Amam, the patriarch's second daughter. Another link with the firm was his marriage to Flora Sassoon's sister.

office curt reminders if they were slow in replying. In the late afternoons, she normally drove to one or other of the mills on her way to Elphinstone Circle where she consulted with Moses and Shellim, but no longer as a nervous business débutante. She was painstakingly methodical and had an often disconcerting memory. Her talmudic training helped, and some of the veteran book-keepers began to compare her with old David Sassoon. It invigorated a branch so long resigned to the hegemony of remote Leadenhall Street.

At formal receptions in Nepean Lodge or Government House she carried herself like a Vicereine. Her proud bosom and deportment gave an impression of stateliness, enhanced by the celebrated pearl necklace and a diamond tiara which she wore over her thickly braided tresses. But her manner was never dowagerish. She was extremely feminine, although some quickly discovered her toughness of fibre.

Her co-feminists were delighted when she breached the Royal Bombay Yacht Club who invited her 'to make use of the Club's facilities as a token of appreciation of the meritorious services rendered by her husband'. She thus became the first woman to be given the right to stroll, with her friends, on the hallowed lawns. It was whispered at the time that the gesture had less to do with Solomon's memory than the Committee's anxiety to extend the Club premises over part of her estate. In any event, Flora secured her honorary membership. The yachtsmen built on, and Bombay's suffragettes celebrated another hole in the prickly hedge of purdah.

Sir Albert, delighted with her efficient handling of affairs, soon confirmed her appointment as managing partner, with the same powers as her late husband. She was too womanlike not to appreciate the honeyed words of praise that reached her from London. At the same time, she was secretly convinced that Solomon's brothers had helped to drive him to an early grave while they were taking their ease at race-meetings or, worse, serving pork chops to the Prince of Wales. She made up her mind to keep the initiative, although it was becoming less easy.

The cotton trade with the United Kingdom had dwindled through the Government's vicious tariff policy. Bumper crops in India also proved a mixed blessing. The improved and fast-working looms were spawning a mammoth glut of yarn which not even the faithful Chinese market could absorb. The Bombay branch, already hit by the decline in opium exports, now had to concentrate on other merchandise like copper, tea, hides and skins, spices, yellow metals and the traditional products of the Gulf, while local properties and other investments needed the closest supervision.

Flora still managed to produce almost spectacular results. Sir Albert and his brothers approved her efforts, although their letters occasionally sounded a note of warning about tricky speculations in silver, usually after some unwelcome investment loss. However, the wires hummed with compliments to 'our dearest sister' during the first two or three years of her régime. Advice was offered, but only with great tact. They became anxious at one point about the abnormally large shipments of pearls arriving in London after the customary inspection by the Bombay office. 'Pearls should be sent to reach us from October to April,' she was reminded. 'From then until the end of May are the best times for selling. June, July and August are generally very dull months and it would be well not to advance during these months.'

To help her or perhaps to keep a closer eye on things, Frederick was sent out to spend some months in Bombay. He had become a director on New Year's Day 1896, but was careful not to show any brash interference. He was often closeted with Charles Moses, who soon departed on a visit to London, probably to make his own private report. If there was any coalition between them, Flora seemed unaware of it.

Frederick exerted sympathetic charm when the pressure became heavy. He sat at her right hand while she presided crisply, but with courtesy, at Board meetings. Together they supervised the many associated concerns, including the Sassoon and Alliance Silk Manufacturing Company, the various spinning, weaving and dyeing plants, the Port Canning Company and a number of insurance offices in which the firm had a considerable stake. Frederick's experience of the Far East was also helpful after Japan secured admission to the exclusive most-favoured-nation 'club'. It could not be long before she started manufacturing piece-goods and undercut Lancashire's millowners and exporters, like the Sassoons, in the Chinese market. Nevertheless, the treaty of commerce allowing the Japanese to manufacture on Chinese soil also granted other foreigners a licence to set up industries of every kind. The two Sassoon firms, solidly established from Shanghai to Hong Kong, had personnel, sites and shipping facilities which assured them a promising start. Both houses lost no time in prospecting spinning and weaving plants, apart from rice, paper and flour mills.

All this touched a responsive chord in Sir Albert. He sensed that the new agencies to be set up in China could speedily compensate his firm for any losses in opium or cotton exports, but it would take capital and the most careful planning. All tempting speculation would be resisted, as in the Bombay boom days, but fierce competition was expected from the Japanese and German newcomers. And he no longer underrated E. D. Sassoon who enlarged their plants in Shanghai under Hardoon's stimulus and quickly opened a branch in Kobe.

Their flourishing warehouses in Calcutta and Karachi already supplemented Bombay's massive shipments of wheat, linseed and cotton yarn, while they were also interesting themselves in the latest processes for extracting oil from cotton seeds and beans. By now they had smashed the older firm's solid monopoly in Gulf business and were represented in Baghdad and Bushire by vigorous agents who sent gums, dried fruits and precious stones in bulk to London. The staff in Fenchurch Street always welcomed these shipments which often included samples of almonds and a sweetmeat called 'Manna'. It did not live up to its biblical fame, but was tasty enough for nougat fanciers.

Sir Albert, now nearly eighty and frail, could still snuff the spice of challenge. In mid-October 1896, he made his last social-cum-business trip to London. He called on the Chinese Ambassador who had often visited him at Eastern Terrace. A few days later he had a final heart seizure in his lonely mansion. Edward was away in Paris with Aline. Reuben and Arthur, who both happened to be in Brighton at the time, raced over from their houses but were too late.

The baronet was buried in his vast mausoleum. All the firm's mills and offices, and those of E. D. Sassoon & Co., closed for the day. Scores of Jewish and Parsee bazaars followed suit throughout India. In Shanghai the flags flew at half-mast on all the opium ships and from the roof of the P. & O. building.

Sir Albert's personal estate was valued at only £385,000, but he had previously provided for his son. Edward succeeded automatically to the baronetcy and the chairmanship of the firm. He would maintain the house in Kemp Town mainly for the family mausoleum, but was not too en-chanted with Brighton and preferred to take a shooting-box, Alvie Lodge, near his Uncle Arthur's place. He had long concealed his distaste for the baroque establishment in Kensington Gore. Within a few months of Sir Albert's death, Reuben scented an ideal property not too far from 'Rothschild Row'. The ebullient and unstable Rand millionaire, Barney Barnato, had built an imposing mansion at 25 Park Lane, overlooking Stanhope Gate. He and his very nervous wife were swung aloft in a crane to cement photographs of themselves under a corner-stone. Londoners speculated on the significance of a series of hideous figures on the roof which, according to Labouchère, were some of the owner's creditors, turned to stone while awaiting settlement! After Barnato's suicide, Reuben sounded out the executors who were asking something in the neighbour-hood of £35,000. Edward and Aline agreed, and soon made drastic plans to undo some of Barnato's architectural crimes.

They first tore down the figures and found them a home in Preston Park, Brighton. Lalique glass chandeliers were then purchased, together with some exquisite eighteenth-century furniture. Several of the Baron

Gustave's tasteful works of art were crated and shipped over from the Avénue Marigny, while Aline toured European galleries and private collections for other suitable paintings. The new baronet was content to rely on her admirable taste and cheerfully paid out large sums for treasures which included some rococo panelling from a palace in Vienna. In the library he installed a unique armchair made to his own design. It had six legs and a long body sloping backwards, which offered sofa-like relaxation and was much coveted by A. J. Balfour. He and other friends often stopped their carriages in Park Lane to inspect the work in progress. It would take a full three years before the mansion was rebuilt and furnished to the new owners' satisfaction.

The wonders of Number 25 were duly reported to Bombay where the failure of the monsoon in 1896 had left a trail of famine and death. By the following spring, bubonic plague had broken out in the slums where most of the population lived in one-room hovels without light or ventilation. Vermin bred freely in the damp mud floors. The unprofitable grain crop put 300,000 on relief in the Presidency alone, but disease was much harder to control. Although houses were lime-washed and all rubbish burned, some 18,000 victims died in a year. Trade slowly came to a standstill. Huge stocks of goods piled up and were left to rot in the quarantined port, and several cotton factories had to close down. Mill workers were fleeing the city at the rate of over 10,000 a week. Others rioted or took to looting. Bubonic plague was bad enough, but the ultimate horror was a wave of Asiatic cholera which swept the relief camps. When the rains came at last, malaria killed off thousands whose resistance had been sapped by malnutrition.

Flora Sassoon took positive action. She accepted personal responsibility for her mill-hands, but felt a wider duty to the sick and destitute masses who were being too hastily evacuated to famine-hit villages, often remote from medical care. Although herself under intolerable strain, she kept her head and at once joined the Plague Committee set up to arrest panic and segregate infected cases. She had more confidence than most in the anti-cholera prophylactic which a young Jewish bacteriologist, Professor Waldemar Haffkine, had developed and was now being officially encouraged to use. He would have preferred more time, but this was an emergency.

Haffkine was a blond, Aryan-looking man from Odessa who had studied under Pasteur. The ex-Viceroy Lord Dufferin, then Ambassador in Paris, had heard reports of his work and persuaded him to go out to plague-ridden India. The Government gladly offered him a bungalow on Malabar Hill, part of it for use as a laboratory. A shy man and deeply religious, he naturally turned to his neighbour, Flora Sassoon. She had grasped the significance of his experiments but others blocked the way, especially official fence-sitters. Fanaticism, fanned by politics, was even more dangerous. Anti-inoculation riots were being sparked off by agitators who had already caused bloodshed between Moslems and Hindus. They combined to denounce the prophylactic as unclean and an offence against their religion.

Flora and her 'Purdah Club' now showed their mettle. They spread the Haffkine gospel among Jews, Parsees and other communities, patiently rounding up half-terrified recruits for the needle. Flora was one of the first to be inoculated. Next day the whole of Bombay rang with the news, and many followed her example. Haffkine was now almost a daily visitor at Nepean Lodge, and some whispered that he had hopes of marrying Rachel to whom he was obviously attracted. It came to nothing, although they remained devoted friends. Throughout his stay in Bombay, he used their house as his second home, turning to Flora for comfort when his clinic was being boycotted and the cart-loads of corpses still rolled by on their way to the burning grounds. She was herself only a few months older than Haffkine, but developed a strong maternal feeling for the dedicated and quiet-spoken scientist who reminded her of Solomon.

Against this background of famine, disease and communal rioting, it was not easy to run the mills. Several closed, and the rest operated at only half strength. The offices of David Sassoon seemed to be invested with a gloom which only lifted a little when the letters arrived from China like a bright bundle of joss sticks. Business was improving in the Settlements, although the branch managers were embarrassingly eager to refer all major decisions to Bombay.

Flora remained calm in crisis. Her hair was now thickly streaked with white, her eyes showing signs of sleepless nights spent at her desk or by Mozelle's bedside. She grew more impatient with a head office which re-acted to her troubles with apathy or often hostility. Her temper was not softened by reports of grouse-shooting on Speyside and the wonders of the new Chairman's mansion in Park Lane. A change in the old patriarchal attitude had been felt almost from the moment of Sir Albert's death. Edward still addressed her respectfully and in his usual affable way, but he had clearly become a figurehead. He was rumoured to be seeking a seat in the House of Commons which would make him even more remote from business. Reuben had his gout and Marlborough House to occupy him, while Arthur was moving still closer to the Prince of Wales. Both brothers, accustomed to affluent ease, were showing petulance over the crisis in India and began to express open dissatisfaction as their profits began to slump. The oriental resentment of a woman in charge, and one who moreover knew her mind, had remained dormant during the first spell of prosperity, but her brother-in-law, Charles Moses, was showing far less deference. In any policy disagreement he could always be sure of support from Frederick, who was now permanently based in London and tasting his authority.

Ambition was Frederick's driving force, together with a strong tribal feeling. He was loyal to Sir Edward's nominal chieftainship and wrote him long memoranda which proved good sense and conscientiousness. He could not always resist sniping at Flora, an easy enough target. She resented being criticized for not selling silver for forward delivery at a time when another poor monsoon had brought the second great famine of the 'nineties. Scarcely a blade of grass sprouted from the once rich soil of Gujarat. At Godhra in the Presidency fifteen hundred people were killed off by cholera in three days. Draught bullocks were dying by the thousand, nursed to the end by peasants who were themselves so weak from hunger that they had to be carried to the emergency soup kitchens.

The family archivist, David Solomon Sassoon, had a nice sense of irony. Without further comment, he closes his scrapbook for this period by placing his mother's certificate of inoculation, signed by Professor Haffkine, beside a London theatre programme to commemorate a Command Performance in honour of the German Emperor and Empress. It is painted on silk, with 'Reuben Sassoon, Esquire' most elegantly engraved upon the cover.

Chapter Nine

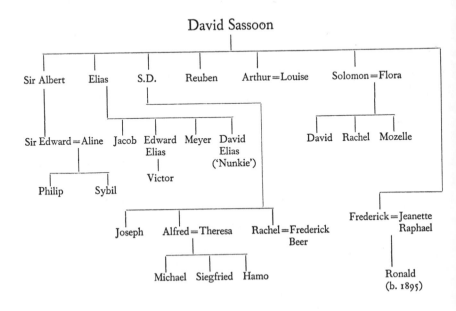

David Sassoon

Sir Albert — Elias — S.D. — Reuben — Arthur = Louise — Solomon = Flora

Sir Edward = Aline   Jacob   Edward Elias   Meyer   David Elias ('Nunkie')

David   Rachel   Mozelle

Victor

Philip   Sybil

Joseph   Alfred = Theresa   Rachel = Frederick Beer

Frederick = Jeanette Raphael

Michael   Siegfried   Hamo

Ronald (b. 1895)

Queen Victoria's Diamond Jubilee was celebrated by the Sassoons according to their very different tastes and circumstances. Jacob led prayers of thanksgiving in the Bombay synagogue, but the flags and bunting seemed almost macabre in a city which reeked of lime and death. Soon after Flora had driven from a reception at Government House, Poona, two other guests were shot dead by rioters as they entered their carriage. However, London's sunshine lent a gala touch to that memorable day in June 1897, when the tiny figure drove through the streets in an open landau with her white-feathered bonnet bobbing under a parasol of Chantilly lace. As the procession swung by on its way to St Paul's, young Victor Sassoon gave a special cheer for the Harrow contingent in the march past of Volunteers from the public schools.

Reuben, Arthur and Sir Edward were prominent in support of Lord Rothschild, who greeted the Queen at Hyde Park Corner with a loyal address from her Jewish subjects, some of whom, particularly the pioneer Zionists, had become more cynical about these London Sassoons.

Mrs Arthur Sassoon, a noted beauty, and her husband, at the Duchess of Devonshire's Fancy Dress Ball in honour of Queen Victoria's Diamond Jubilee.
They became close friends of King Edward VII.

Louise Sassoon

Joseph Sassoon, with his wife, in the spacious grounds of their country house, Ashley Park, near Walton-on-Thames. He and his sons took no part in the family business. Louise was the daughter of Baron de Gunzbourg, a millionaire banker in Tsarist circles.

Rachel Beer owned and simultaneously edited both the *Sunday Times* and *The Observer*. This portrait of his favourite aunt by H. Thadeus Jones had the place of honour in Siegfried Sassoon's library at Heytesbury House.

Alfred Sassoon shortly before his death at 34, with his sons, Siegfried, Michael and Hamo. The last-named, killed at Gallipoli, is commemorated by Siegfried in the poem 'To My Brother'.

Ashley Park, dating from the 15th century, was one of Surrey's show places. It housed a golf course and a cricket ground where Dr W. G. Grace often played in friendly matches. It was sold and broken up into a housing estate after the First World War.

Once the Rothschilds had overcome their first suspicions of Palestine, they gave generous support, but Dr Chaim Weizmann could not forgive what he called the 'indifference or hostility' of a dynasty, respected for centuries as defenders of the faith. The Sephardim in Britain were split in loyalties. Insistent reports came from Bevis Marks that Rabbi Gaster and other pro-Zionists in his congregation were actually under pressure from the powerful Sassoon elders to oppose a movement which, in their view, devalued their patriotic identification with the Empire. They were equally unsympathetic towards the immigrant ghetto refugees who escaped from the Tsarist pogroms. 'They might as well have lived in another world,' Weizmann still wrote bitterly about them and other rich Jewish families long after the National Home was won.*

Ashley Park celebrated the Diamond Jubilee with a party for neighbours and local dignitaries. Miss V. M. E. Conolly, then a small child, can well remember being welcomed into the oak-panelled hall. Guests were served 'a really remarkable buffet supper' and entertained by a concert party from London. 'Mrs Sassoon moved beautifully and held her head well,' she recalls. 'Her voice was low and musical. That night she was in red velvet and diamonds. She was definitely plump and only slightly taller than her husband who was, I think, about five foot five and very slight in build. He had black hair and eyes, which seemed half-closed, but his skin was light with a yellowish tinge. I had previously glimpsed him once or twice, huddled into a corner of his carriage, as if he suffered from the cold. On this particular evening, he walked very erectly and moved genially among his guests with two of his children. He smoked cheroots all the time and passed them around to the men. For once he talked to the guests. Ordinarily, I was told, he was a man of few words and rather forbidding.'

His sister, Rachel Beer, became less inhibited once she had liberated herself from Ashley Park. Although the *Sunday Times* and *The Observer* both declined in circulation during her régime, not surprisingly in view of her determination both to edit and write while trying to nurse a mentally sick husband, she had flashes of incisive and independent thought. She showed courage over the Dreyfus Affair. She could never be considered an inspired editor or leader-writer, but her handling of Esterhazy's confession earned her an honoured place in journalistic history.

In September 1898 *The Observer*'s correspondent in Paris, Rowland Strong, was approached by Major Esterhazy, whose 'evidence' convicted

---

* Flora's descendants all gave warm support to Palestine but were always puzzled by Weizmann's coolness whenever they met. Not until his autobiography, *Trial and Error*, was published in 1949, would this branch appreciate the depth of his resentment or the never-forgotten reasons for it.

the Jewish officer, Dreyfus, of treason and condemned him to life imprisonment on Devil's Island. When Colonel Henry of French counter-espionage later committed suicide to avoid exposure, Esterhazy panicked and admitted to Strong that he had forged the infamous *bordereau*, setting out the secrets which Dreyfus was alleged to have spied out for Germany. Evidently he hoped to save his own skin by pleading that he had acted under military orders.

Quite apart from her natural reaction to anti-semitism, Rachel's sympathies were automatically engaged by any cruelty and social injustice. She was also enough of a journalist to recognize all the signs of a 'scoop'. She listened attentively to Strong but decided not to print anything before she had personally cross-examined Esterhazy about his story of the forged *bordereau*.

Esterhazy shaved off his moustache and arrived in London some days later, having got over the frontier to Belgium without being recognized. He was hidden out in a flat in St James's Street where he gave Strong an expanded version of his previous interview. Strong then arranged a meeting between Esterhazy and Rachel Beer in a private room at the Hotel Previtali. Esterhazy repeated his confession, explaining almost off-handedly that he had felt compelled to forge the additional evidence because, until then, there was only 'moral' proof. It says much for Rachel's self-control – and Strong's diplomacy – that the interview went off so smoothly. She listened politely to Esterhazy who must have been perfectly aware, from her appearance, that she was a Jewess. Quite unabashed, he told his story as if admitting some minor and rather tiresome disciplinary offence. 'I am one of those men who are soldiers by profession, and who cling to the old medieval traditions of military discipline . . . It is nearly always necessary to manufacture the material evidence against spies, because otherwise they would never be punished . . . The *bordereau*, having been written by me, it became necessary to give it the indispensable air of an authentic document . . .' The meeting lasted a full hour. Rachel and Strong then hurried back to the office to dictate notes and prepare articles which appeared in two successive issues.

The articles created a stir throughout the world, several newspapers reprinting them in full. However, Esterhazy had second thoughts and recanted, aided and abetted by Arthur Newton, a shady London solicitor who specialized in blackmailing actions against newspapers and was later struck off the rolls. They threatened a libel suit, and *The Observer* settled out of court for £500 and costs. Rachel did not regret publication of the articles even when the newspaper was savagely vilified by anti-Dreyfusards who made a special target of the Jewish owner. Her courage was further vindicated when *Le Matin* printed, in 1899, a positive admission by Esterhazy that he had written the *bordereau*. It gave Rachel and her paper some satisfaction at having helped to end Dreyfus's long martyrdom.

Her own nightmare did not end when Frederick Beer died in 1903. She broke down and at first refused hysterically to have him buried. The little party from Weirleigh was among the few who followed the coffin to Highgate Cemetery. Frederick was laid to rest in the Beer family mausoleum which Rachel had submerged under several dozen enormous lilies. She returned distraught to Chesterfield Gardens where she locked herself in her room for some days, refusing to touch the trays of food which Drew left outside the door. The doctors had to send for Theresa who managed to break the hunger strike and persuade poor Rachel to emerge. It was months before she accepted the fact of her husband's death.

She became even more erratic and absent-minded. She continued to harass her newspapers by writing strange leaders on any subject that took her fancy, including one on the advantages of cannibalism. Her appetite remained insatiable for review copies which were rarely unpacked, let alone read. Siegfried was astonished one Christmas to be presented with a fat copy of *Bibliography of the World's Municipal Literature*, an odd choice for a poetically-minded boy of thirteen.

His aunt's reason finally crumbled in 1904 when she broke off an editorial for *The Observer* half-way through the second paragraph with a pathetic 'to be continued in our next'. Soon afterwards, she was certified and placed in the care of the Commissioners of Lunacy. She was not violent and would be able to end her days happily, under supervision. Two women, Daisy Moss and Norah Howard, nursed her devotedly at Chancellor House in Tunbridge Wells. This was an imposing mansion originally built, it was said, for Judge Jeffreys. The doctors considered it ideal and approved a *ménage* more or less on the previous scale. Rachel was still, of course, an extremely wealthy woman, although her two newspapers fetched very little.*

Her faithful butler, Drew, agreed to serve in Tunbridge Wells, taking with him several of the staff from the two London houses. The carriage was also kept on, together with the two footmen in livery, and the Beer paintings looked even more impressive on the high walls of Chancellor House.

* Both *The Observer* and the *Sunday Times* had slumped so badly that in 1904 the solicitor, Hawksley, acting for Rachel's trustees, approached R. D. Blumenfeld who was in England to wind up the London edition of the *New York Herald*. He asked £5,000 for *The Observer*, but Blumenfeld declined. Hawksley then offered to 'throw in' the *Sunday Times* as well. This was also rejected. A few months later, Lord Northcliffe bought the *Observer* for £5,000 and, in 1911, sold it to Viscount (Waldorf) Astor for £40,000. In 1904, the *Sunday Times* was sold to George Schmidt, a German, who amalgamated it with his *Sunday Special*. It was bought by the Berry family in 1915.

Encouraged by her two nurses, Rachel slowly recovered her interest in the world. When she was too ill to see people, she invited local charities to make use of the house and hold fêtes in the grounds. She had a splendid organ installed and often gave recitals for one or two friends in her drawing-room. She was always pleased to see Theresa and the boys during those twilight years.

Flora was meantime under such strain in Bombay that a less resolute woman would have suffered a nervous collapse. Famine, the rupee and a continuing slump in cotton had led to further depreciation in the firm's Indian holdings. It made the head office over-critical of any investments which did not turn out well. Flora became more oppressed by a sense of isolation. Sir Edward was good-natured but preoccupied with Park Lane and now the House of Commons. The Unionist Party officials thought him both safe and highly eligible when a by-election cropped up in the Hythe and Folkestone Division. He had wealth; his friends included the Prince of Wales and Arthur James Balfour; and the Carlton was his favourite club. His wife was an elegant hostess and, more important, a Rothschild. The Baron Mayer had represented the same constituency for fifteen years.

Sir Edward was elected in 1899 and at once became a true-blue supporter of imperialist policies. He established himself as an authority on currency and fiscal questions, particularly over India. He wanted to see a stable rupee and approved Lord Curzon's land reforms. As a director of the Imperial Bank of Persia, he nimbly caught the Speaker's eye to warn the House that Russia was stalking the Middle East and the hills of Afghanistan, and he was among the keenest supporters of Sir Francis Younghusband's high-handed action in Lhasa. He spoke vigorously, if a little excitably, on half a dozen other subjects close to his heart, notably Tariff Reform and the iniquitous death duties. He was also dedicated to the benefits of Imperial Telegraphy.

He was a spruce man with a charming manner which made him welcome on several House Committees even if some found him verbose and his English a trifle idiosyncratic. His energy was appreciated by Hythe, but Aline was the thundering success. She was always superbly groomed, her natural kindliness singling her out from other constituency wives and routine bazaar-openers. She persuaded her husband to endow orphanages for the sons of soldiers and sailors and took a personal interest in the welfare of fishermen and their families who were going through hard times. She also busied herself with local hospitals and clinics which she equipped with the latest X-ray apparatus.

Sir Edward bought Shorncliffe Lodge, a well-appointed weekend place at Sandgate and convenient for his constituency. There was swimming and sailing for Philip and Sybil, both growing up to be merry and attractive children, although the boy seemed delicate. He was rather coddled by his mother who herself had a premonition of early death and often dashed off to Italy and Egypt for warmth. However, Philip would soon be going to Eton where plenty of exercise might do him good, although Aline was perhaps a little apprehensive about reports of cold baths and other austerities.

There was no lack of variety and amusement for the Edward Sassoons and their children. Uncle Reuben gladly gave up his afternoon's bridge at the Marlborough Club to take Philip to hear Patti, while little Sybil had the run of every nursery in Belgravia and Mayfair. From the beaches and sun lounges of Sandgate they made their way up to the family's new hunting lodge at Kincraig for grouse-shooting and fishing. At Christmas, there were parties in the Park Lane mansion and a round of visits to Leo and Marie Rothschild, Lady Horner at Mells and the gay house parties at Taplow Court. It was particularly amusing for Philip since Edward Horner and the Grenfell brothers would be new boys with him at Eton. Before the House of Commons reassembled, Sir Edward usually found time to visit the Avénue Marigny *en route* to St Moritz for skating and the bob-sleigh runs which he was still athletic enough to enjoy.

Flora could expect no more than a kindly neutrality from the second baronet, but even less from the senior partners. Arthur was now much taken up with Albert Gate, Tulchan Lodge and entertaining the Prince of Wales at Brighton, where local confectioners and pastry-cooks used to exhibit appreciative notes from Louise in their shop windows. They were prized as the next best accolades to a full Warrant. Reuben's gout was causing him to take second place to his brother as a royal provider. They frequently joined forces, not always with happy results. In the summer of 1899, A. J. Balfour wrote with some acrimony to Lady Elcho, one of Aline's closest confidantes among The Souls, about the Prince of Wales's recent visit to open a hospital in Brighton. 'We discovered to our deep indignation that we had been brought down under false pretences,' he reported feelingly. H.R.H. had gone to stay with Reuben, leaving the other members of his party, including Lord Rosebery and the Duke of Devonshire, to spend the weekend with Arthur and Louise. Their hospitality was every bit as lavish as Reuben's, but Balfour did not like being shunted into the family annexe. 'We were dragged *both* nights to a long, hot and pompous dinner (at the Reuben Sassoons) – peopled with endless Sassoon girls— I believe the Hebrews were in an actual majority – and tho' I have no prejudices against the race (quite the contrary), I began to understand the point of view of those who object to alien immigration!'

Others were also showing surprise, and sometimes jealousy, at the Sassoons' social prominence. London gossips reported that a visitor from overseas was so impressed by the style of a dignified gentleman in Hyde Park that he inquired about him. It was Lady Sassoon's butler taking a constitutional. Parisian *boulevardiers* repeated another story about Aline, who was said to have asked an acquaintance of the Faubourg St Germain to recommend some deserving old nobleman. 'I've a vacancy for a hall-porter,' she explained. The source of this malicious anecdote was Robert de Montesquiou, the royalist snob and dandy who modelled for Proust's Baron Charlus. He was not perhaps the most reliable of reporters. An anti-Dreyfusard, his rabid hatred of the Rothschilds dated from the time when he asked Baron Alphonse, Aline's uncle, to lend him some jewels for a costume ball. The Baron had excused himself, explaining that they belonged to the family. 'I knew you had jewels but was unaware that you had a family,' sneered the Comte.

Such stories and the incessant chatty references to Eton and the Sandringham shoots did not comfort Flora, who was often being sharply reminded to curb expenditure at her end. Where a steadying touch from the top might have helped, she had to submit to needling reproaches. In a characteristic note at this time, Frederick writes: '*Bar Silver*. The Banks have shipped large shipments both last and this week. With a rising exchange, you should have tried to send us offers for forward. The result of our small shipment this week of £2,500 will leave us a small profit, but it should have been ten or twenty times this amount. We do not wish to be out of this market.'

His attitude was a little harsh, but understandable. He had shown a taste for leadership from his first days in Hong Kong. He was now very much in his prime and more self-reliant, with wealth of his own and a rich wife who had recently presented him with an heir, doubtless a future entry to the House of Sassoon. He liked his sister-in-law and respected her for holding the fort, but believed sincerely that a woman with three children, one a helpless invalid, was no longer the ideal managing partner for Bombay. He and his brothers, backed by a Chairman who liked to compromise and would rarely oppose the others on a major issue, were waiting for the right moment to take action.

Flora guessed that some reorganization was in the offing, but she was kept in the dark. Her temper had suffered. She was sleeping too little and often worked far into the night rather than delegate. She sensed and possibly exaggerated hostility among her staff. The atmosphere had become almost impossibly unnerving when she was peremptorily told that there would be no place for her in a new private Company to be incorporated from 24 December 1901. The capital was £500,000 in £100 shares, £200,000 in Ordinary and the balance in 5 per cent Preference. There would be no public issue. Sir Edward remained as Chairman, with Reuben, Arthur and Frederick as directors. The non-Jewish, rather austere Cecil A. Longcroft, who had started as a junior clerk in the head office and seemed to live only for business, was to be a shareholder. Another was the grandson of Sir Albert, David Gubbay, who stood barely five foot but was already a giant in the counting-house. His shrewd mastery of figures invited comparison with Reuben at his best. They would make an excellent supporting force for Frederick, who now became the effective administrative head at 12 Leadenhall Street. His old ally, Charles Moses, replaced Flora in Bombay.

In the City of London and on the Bund, but more specially on the Bombay Cotton Exchange, the incorporation of such a highly personalized and old-established business caused astonishment. However, the family had a reputation for infallible timing. The new company was soon talked of as a bid for breathing-space rather than any sign of cautious retrenchment. In cold fact, the firm needed to consolidate and re-group to meet intensified competition in both India and China, and above all the coming challenge from Japanese manufacturers.

The company's Articles of Association were wide. It acquired the business of bankers and commission agents previously carried on by David Sassoon & Co., and would continue 'as dealers in any kind of goods and produce, wharfingers, warehousemen, bankers, general merchants, importers, exporters, and charterers of ships and vessels, ship and insurance brokers, carriers, forwarding agents, planters, growers, farmers, stockowners and breeders, etc.'

Rumours were soon flying about Calcutta and Bombay that Flora would form her own company. She had no such intention. She was too sick at heart, and eager to leave for Europe where she hoped that some miracle of surgery might help poor Mozelle. Her attitude to the whole unhappy business was summed up in a note to her dear friend, Lady Reay. 'I am retiring from the firm tomorrow, as I do not think I can any longer drudge all day while the others take a superficial interest only, doing more harm than good when they suddenly awake.'

Charles Moses moved into her office and gave orders that the local newspapers should not be forwarded to her overseas. A ledger clerk insisted on paying the postage from his own pocket. Another wrote to deplore Flora's 'catastrophic' departure, while a veteran employee lamented 'one pleasure less in this sordid world of ours'.

Flora put on a good face at Ballard Pier where she and her family were seen off by a crowd of officials, tearful servants and well-wishers of all creeds. Her stateroom was choked with bouquets and gifts. Just before sailing-time, a Parsee girl ran forward to place a garland round her neck, inscribed to 'Her Majesty, the Queen of Bombay and Empress of Malabar Hill'. Flora sailed away with a small retinue, including a rabbi to conduct daily prayers.

They broke the voyage to spend a few days in Paris where Aline and Edward took them to the Opéra to hear Jean de Reszke. In the Avénue Marigny, the Baron Gustave gave receptions in their honour. Flora took two suites at Claridge's in London but soon departed for a rented flat when the hotel manager objected to the highly-spiced *kosher* food which her own cooks prepared in the private rooms. Otherwise, it was almost a triumphal tour which coincided pleasantly with King Edward's postponed Coronation. Flora and her elder daughter attended the service in Westminster Abbey, while her son rode in the procession with a contingent of the Bombay Light Horse and later attended his first levee.

Flora had a joyful reunion with Lady Reay and another old friend from Bombay days, the Duchess of Connaught. They went to Henley together and were welcomed in the Royal Enclosure at Ascot. After Gold Cup Day, Flora's daughter noted in her diary that 'Uncle Reuben is very feeble and misses running errands for the King very keenly'. He was consoled by the M.V.O. which his old friend conferred on him – and Arthur – in the first of the Coronation Honours. Soon afterwards, Winston Churchill wrote satirically to his mother, 'I am curious to know about the King. Will it entirely revolutionize his way of life? Will he sell his horses and scatter his Jews or will Reuben Sassoon be enshrined among the crown jewels and other regalia?'

There is no spectacle more pathetic or ludicrous than that of the ageing courtier, too rheumatic to bow with comfort and less agile than his master. This was to be Reuben's fate. He was now increasingly confined to Hove, but eager as always to receive the King and old friends from the Marlborough House days.

Flora was enjoying herself too much to show any deep resentment of her treatment by the firm. It made the clan even more openly anxious to shower salaams and hospitality upon her and her children. At Aline's glittering Coronation reception, Flora was very much at home among the rajahs. She talked wittily to a dozen old friends, and seemed like a vivid Boldini bursting from its canvas. Flanked by her daughter and Lady Reay, she chatted and laughed while all the duchesses swooped to kiss her. Balfour, now Prime Minister, Rosebery and others waited patiently to offer their respects. It was a triumph, repeated soon afterwards in Louise Sassoon's box at Covent Garden where 'she was the centre of all eyes', according to the *Pall Mall Gazette*. 'Her remarkable constellation – in diamonds, *bien entendu* – put the stars to shame.' The Duchess of Marlborough and Lady de Grey left cards. A visit to Lansdowne House was followed by tea with the Duchess of Devonshire and Mrs George Keppel. Then came lunch with the Arthur Sassoons and dinner with 'the other branch', the Meyer Sassoons in Hamilton Place, where Indian fish and egg curries were served. Flora, however, declined to eat a morsel, suspecting with good reason that the kitchen was not strictly *kosher*.* Allowing for such dietary scruples, the Rothschilds found her delightfully stimulating. Leo entertained her royally at Gunnersbury Park, while Alfred arranged a concert in her honour at Seamore Place where Caruso, Melba and Kubelik were afterwards presented to her.

Mozelle was benefiting from her stream of visitors and an exciting list of engagements. She was wheeled up to the Strangers' Gallery to hear a speech from Sir Edward, who invited them to the Eton and Harrow cricket match at Lord's. Through a garden-party gauze of parasols, filmy hats and silk toppers, lushed and brushed to perfection, they saw a good half dozen of David Sassoon's great grandsons sauntering towards them with the statutory Etonian nonchalance. Plump Mrs Sassoon from Ashley Park, tightly laced into a confection of Worth tulle, was smoothly convoyed by her five sons, including twins known as 'Teddie' and 'Fweddie'. Flora nodded approval on being told that the Headmaster of Eton always gave them leave of absence for the Jewish holidays. She would, however, have been more impressed had these young Sassoons followed the example of other families, like the Waley-Cohens, and gone to the Jewish House at Clifton where they could still observe their faith at a public school. But Clifton was not Eton.

She left the Ashley Park contingent to talk with the E. D. Sassoons, whom she could meet with less constraint now that her business career was over. She was greeted warmly by Jacob's brother, Edward Elias, who often came out to Bombay. He and his wife, Leontine, seemed to her less haughty and far more relaxed than her own side of the family. They presented their Old Harrovian, Victor, who had just come of age and was at Trinity College, Cambridge. He seemed a personable youth with a quick turn of phrase, but his mother seemed to worry about him and deprecated the influence of her brother-in-law, David, the bachelor roué. 'Nunkie', however, was not present that day. Reuben hobbled towards them, leaning heavily on the arm of his Old Etonian son who had reluctantly

---

* When Flora's son, accompanied by Haffkine, later attended the Delhi Durbar to celebrate King Edward's Accession, they lived for a week on specially-prepared sandwiches and raw cauliflower to avoid non-*kosher* food. Virtue had its reward. Both were spared the gastro-enteritis which claimed many victims.

come up from Brighton, his mother having excused herself at the last minute.

Aline and Louise presided jointly over a gay, patrician group. Flora did not take to her sister-in-law, Mrs Arthur Sassoon, who seemed almost too exquisite and enamelled to be quite real. She was very much at home under this ceaseless confetti of nicknames and badinage about grouse butts, the Jockey Club and recent house parties. Aline, strikingly beautiful under her picture hat and parasol, held court with the same charming gaiety, but Flora found her gentler and more sympathetic than the older woman.

She shook the languid hand of Aline's son and later noted in her diary that 'Philip looks delicate and so much like his mother'. He seemed ill-at-ease, and she rightly guessed that a boy sensitive about his heavy-lidded, oriental eyes and strong traces of a French accent might not have had too easy a first Half at Eton.

Part Three (1901–1919)

Chapter Ten

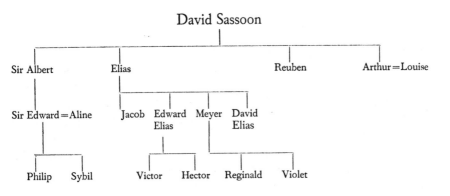

Philip Sassoon was barely fourteen when he entered Tatham's House in May 1902. He soon discovered that 'exotic' looks were no serious handicap to the exceptionally well-connected. Eton was a mirror which faithfully reflected Edwardian self-indulgence and caste snobbery. Her sons were heirs to a rich-living, materialist heaven, whether they sprang from the landed aristocracy or the equally class-conscious industrial empires. They might value 'effortless superiority' as the only possible flower to wear in one's lapel, but few were above sneaking looks at the Court Circular. The flag on the Round Tower reminded them that young Sassoon's people dined often at the Castle. He might be an odd little Oriental with a funny lisp and that curiously guttural accent, but his father was a baronet M.P. who entertained celebrated O.E.s, like the Prime Minister and Lord Rosebery, in his Park Lane mansion. And the social columns regularly confirmed that Lady Sassoon was on the warmest visiting terms with the Ribblesdales, Desboroughs and Horners whose offspring were at the school and friendly with her son.

Eton became a microcosm of all Philip's future virtues and failings. Sensitive about his Jewish name and sallow skin, he was shy at first, but the school's climate was favourable to an intelligent, precocious boy who could carry off a slightly theatrical rôle. He was born into the feverish aestheticism of the 'nineties and instinctively preferred Beardsley's arabesques to algebra. A natural elegance, backed by his fluent command of

French, soon developed into a dandyism of manner and dress not un-attractive to many who still practised *fin de siècle* poses.

This graceful, highly impressionable boy might have been bullied more and perhaps toughened with benefit, had he not enjoyed a most liberal allowance and royal connections. The social climbers and snobs whis-pered that he always read the Court column of *The Times* before chapel. He drifted easily into the company of sophisticates, but took care to stay close to athletic swells like the Grenfells, despite a professed dislike of team sports. He preferred to take up beagling, fives and tennis but some-times, it was said, presented new cricket bats to the Captain of Games and selected senior dry-bobs. It was not entirely self-interest. He was genuinely warm-hearted and loved to order cakes and sausages from Little Brown's shop for tea parties which the House Dame, Miss Skey, arranged in his room.

'M'Dame' was a redheaded, freckled woman who helped to protect him from Eton's tapioca and chilblains. She knew how deeply he missed his mother and was the first of a number of older women to understudy for the part. She may have suspected that his rather feverish gaiety concealed a deeper malaise than the normal schoolboyish homesickness. It made her even more sympathetic, and he never forgot her kindness.

Osbert Sitwell, who fagged for him, was also sensitive to Philip's complex nature. His own unhappiness at Eton was tempered by the con-sideration of the older boy who might be affected but was incapable of malice or the ritual bullying expected from one's fagmaster. He recalls him as 'very grown-up for his age, at times exuberant, and at others melancholy and preoccupied, but always unlike anyone else. He was extremely considerate and kind in all his dealings, as he remained, I am thankful to say, all his life.'

Both boys were abnormally shy and artistic, and they shared a fear of the herd. Sitwell disliked games and choir-practice so much that he used to pray to catch cold in order to read peacefully in bed for a few days. He was grateful to Philip who excused him from the more menial fagging chores and even humoured such odd hobbies as collecting hundreds of pen nibs. He was always delighted when his friend came to spend part of the holidays at pinnacled Renishaw Hall, near Chesterfield, a baroque delight of ivy-coloured splendour, with its Chippendale and Adam treasures and the magnificent Brussels tapestries.

Philip nourished a taste for beautiful things from boyhood. It formed part of a premature *savoir-faire* which compensated for his lack of dis-tinction at games. He had a witty eye for the grotesque and developed into a gifted mimic. He read quickly and in bursts, memorizing quips which helped to make his chatter gay and amusing. His background helped. Few of his contemporaries were in a position to speak with such authority on Rumpelmayer's *marrons glacés* or to mention casually that Sargent was painting his mother. Expert bridge was only one of his worldly gifts. While staying with family friends, he once suggested a rubber. An older boy commented sarcastically that it was not a game for children. Philip played brilliantly and had sweet revenge at the 'inquest' when he dissected the tactics of his partner who had been so rude to him. Reuben Sassoon would have approved!

Philip missed his great-uncle who had always spoilt him a little and used to give him occasional holiday treats, like a good lunch at the Savoy, followed by a matinée. Nearing seventy, Reuben had all but retired to his house in Hove. He huddled into a quilted dressing-gown and would hobble wistfully to his cigar cabinet to examine his collection of over three thousand Havanas which he could no longer savour with any pleasure. But he still enjoyed passing his fingers over the ciphered cuff-links given him by his royal master and the many trays of keyless watches, rings and diamond scarfpins. He died in 1905, leaving more than half a million, part of which was to go to Philip after the death of his own son, David. He did not live to see two of his daughters marry Christians, but might have found it difficult to resist the attractions of a son-in-law like Sir Charles Boyle, a former Governor of Mauritius.

Philip saw little of his five Ashley Park cousins who were at Eton with him, but remained most respectful to his 'dearest Aunt Flora' who was now making annual visits from Bombay, accompanied by her children and the usual corps of rabbis, cooks and attendants. She was Presented at Court in 1907 by the Countess of Crewe and in turn presented her own daughter, Rachel.

The Arthur Sassoons were the most impressive of all Philip's relatives. They had grown much closer to the King who rarely missed a day or two grouse-shooting with them during his annual autumn tour of Speyside. The bag might be bigger on some of the neighbouring estates, but he found himself more at home at Tulchan. He was mellower in his last years and offered the childless, ageing couple an affection which sometimes surprised his entourage. One day, while out on the Countess of Seafield's moors, he dozed off in the back of his brake and awoke to see his friend trudging ahead. 'Come up here with me, dear Arthur,' he called out anxiously. 'You and I are getting on in years.' Arthur was also spared the cruel practical jokes which Reuben and others had endured.

The King's habitual informality at Tulchan was flattering to his host, but once caused him some embarrassment. They were out on the moors when one of the stalkies, who had had a cheering nip and was misled by the lack of royal pomp, suddenly shouted at the Monarch, 'You stop wheer y'are!' He then beckoned to the Heir and snapped, 'And ye git oot here wi' me.' The Prince of Wales obeyed meekly, while his father treated it as a joke.

The atmosphere was even more cordial and relaxed at 8 King's Gardens, Hove, which King Edward infinitely preferred to the house of his daughter, the Duchess of Fife, in Sussex Square. In the early winter months when his bronchitis was often troublesome, he took to spending weekends with 'dear Arthur'. Louise fussed him deliciously when he became peevish at having to cut down on his cigars. She was never an 'intimate' in the scandalous sense, but as he grew older, it was agreeable to flirt harmlessly with this elegant and cosmopolitan woman whose prattle always took him out of himself.

When he began to wheeze from catarrh, she watched his symptoms but also spoilt him with delicacies. Since one unfortunate episode early in February 1904, she took elaborate safeguards to protect any distinguished guest under her roof. Mr Balfour was suffering from a sharp attack of influenza at that time. The Hove breezes and Sassoon hospitality proved so beneficial that he did not object when Arthur told him that the Duke of Devonshire, then a touchy Cobdenite rebel in the Cabinet, was also planning to come down for the weekend. The famed cellar and cuisine induced a welcome euphoria, but proximity had its dangers. The Duke departed on the Monday morning in an explosion of sneezes. He had picked up a cold from the Prime Minister, who returned to London now fully recovered and all smiles.

The King might be tempted to gluttony in King's Gardens, but he would never be exposed to chilly draughts or any risk of infection. He luxuriated in a hot-house warmth and was dissuaded from going out except on fine days when he would stroll arm-in-arm with Arthur and Louise on the Promenade or across The Lawns opposite their house. Often they drove to Worthing where the King liked to sit on the pier, well wrapped-up, to read his newspapers. He was bored by punctilio and preferred to walk unannounced into local shops with Mrs Sassoon who had an admirable taste in cameos and antiques. Before leaving for London in his maroon Daimler with the unnumbered plate, his hosts would thoughtfully fill the boot with the rest of the mangoes and Elvas plums which he had so obviously enjoyed.

Philip could only relish these royal visits at secondhand, but they nourished his repertoire of anecdotes. His head had buzzed with famous names almost from the nursery. His mother, who had maintained her enthusiasm for politics and the arts, preferred intimate little dinner parties to the more glittering receptions *chez* Louise. Statesmen and politicians came to Park Lane for serious discussion on the lines of the former quorums of Souls. ('So we went off to Lady Sassoon's, where we had a little party of five – those two, Winston, myself and Arthur Balfour – with whom we talked on "decadence" and other depressing topics,' recalled the Anglo-Catholic Liberal, Charles Masterman, who had recently been elected for West Ham.)

Margot Asquith could be relied on for a fire-cracker or two when the talk became too pompous. Conan Doyle was also a welcome guest. He was good company even if he laughed rather too often at his own jokes. Aline was perhaps less interested in Holmes than the author's views on spiritualism. Another writer, H. G. Wells, was bagged for her table soon after he published *Kipps*.

Art was usually represented by Sargent, bearded and pink-faced, his eyes popping when he tried to splutter some remark. His superb portrait of Lady Sassoon was the Academy's outstanding picture in the 1907 Exhibition. The painter did not need his usual gauze of flattery. Aline wore a rose with her black silk dress which brought out the full beauty of her ivory skin, sensitive hands and the sad Jewish eyes.

In the Parliamentary recess, Philip saw the gay side of his father who was a polished billiards-player, a good shot and more than a match for the youngsters at tennis. Bob-sleighing was now too dangerous, but he could still show his children an enviable artistry at skating. Although closer to his adored mother, Philip took after Sir Edward in his careless generosity with money. The baronet might be over-earnest in the House about the bugbear of death duties, but he earned a reputation outside for being good-natured and sometimes downright unbusinesslike when his sympathy or sense of humour was touched. Edgar Wallace was one of many who did not leave 25 Park Lane empty-handed. He very easily persuaded Sir Edward to invest £1,000 in his new *Evening Times* which he was certain could compete successfully with the *Evening News*. Sir Edward flicked over the cheque and said cheerfully, 'I don't expect to see it back again.' He was right. The paper lasted only fifteen months.

After a few days in St Moritz or at the shooting-lodge, Kincraig, Philip often spent part of the school holidays with his friends, the Grenfell brothers, at Taplow Court, and specially looked forward to visiting Mells Park, the gabled home of the Horners. Their son, Edward, was at Eton with him and they went shooting and played tennis or skated together. Lady Horner listened to his amusing gossip and was sympathetic during his darker moments of introspection. When Philip carried off the King's Prize at Eton for French two years running, nobody was more delighted than his mother's closest friend.

These little academic triumphs helped to give him a more genuine self-confidence. After the bleakness and confusion of Lower School, life was more like a nicely-folded napkin with one's own silver ring. Eton could offer much to a boy heavily dosed with both snobbery and sensibility. There was the matchless elegance of the Fourth of June when lordly wet-bobs threw the traditional bouquets into the river while the Guards Band played. And there were other delicious and more languid rhythms; the swans gliding below Fellows Eyot, or enchanting walks with Osbert Sitwell over frozen meadows touched with the magic of a Dutch landscape.

He was more secure as an Upper Boy but would never entirely overcome his nagging sense of being alien and Jewish. His dual nationality, French and British, legally came to an end at nineteen. He made his choice without hesitation. It would be far less easy to shed his other skin, even though his formal synagogue-going was long since past.

His father endowed beds at the Home for Jewish Incurables and opened an occasional soup kitchen, while Aline gave up many evenings to girls' clubs in London's ghetto, but this was traditional philanthropy. Philip could not be expected to lose any sleep over brutal pogroms or the squalid East End tailors' dens. He raced after beagles and obeyed school rules by keeping out of the side streets of Eton and Windsor to avoid brushing shoulders with the public. His friends seemed just as untroubled by the sufferings of the non-Jewish masses. They saw little wrong with hunting pink and powdered flunkeys; and everyone had approved of the young patrician who missed his train and told the stationmaster to 'bwing me another'. If anything, they thought the lower orders were being pampered now that income tax had risen to a disgraceful 11*d.* in the pound.

There were exceptions like Charles Lister, Lord Ribblesdale's ungainly son, who gave impassioned support to hunger marches and joined the Independent Labour Party while still at school. Few of Philip's contemporaries were so politically conscious. Patrick Shaw-Stewart, a general's son, was less moneyed than the others and a brilliant scholar. The brothers, Julian and Billy Grenfell, were laughing blond giants who excelled at athletics, classics and almost anything else they touched. The three won Open Scholarships to Balliol, while Philip went up to Christ Church, the traditional finishing school for Etonians. He would miss his Dame, Miss Skey, and promised solemnly to keep in touch with her.

He would be among many school friends at Oxford, yet it would never be quite the same. 'The New Elizabethans', as the unique Balliol set came to be called, mixed brains and brawn and added a touch of Etonian insolence. Handsome as Greek gods and blessed with splendid physiques, they excelled as boxers, horsemen and crack shots, picking up 'Blues' almost as effortlessly as their prizes for poetry or mathematics. Their table-talk was dazzling, but they could be rowdy and liked to blow coach horns in the Quad long after midnight. Julian Grenfell, Lord Desborough's son, strutted about Oxford with his greyhounds and used to flick a stock-whip. He looked and acted the Regency buck but also wrote sensitive poetry and often discussed religion with his undergraduate friend, Ronald Knox. His brother, Billy, could flatten anyone with a blow, but he was gentle underneath and a true scholar. Patrick Shaw-Stewart had blossomed into a witty, cynical sophisticate who would gain an effortless First and a Fellowship at All Souls. Charles Lister remained an unrepentant Socialist and spent his time among Fabian friends and trade union 'agitators' at Ruskin College. He fomented a strike among girl workers at the Clarendon Press and joined every leftist demonstration. He was 'rusticated' for a term after offending some pompous don. His friends gave him a full-dress mock funeral all the way to the station.

Philip Sassoon could not compete with this circle, either intellectually or as an athlete, but was 'co-opted' because of Eton and his party-giving talents. Another point of contact was the Bullingdon Club, rendezvous of the fox-hunting and point-to-point set which they had all joined to-gether, but being at different colleges was something he regretted deeply. Other gaps opened between himself and the gifted Balliol coterie. They were better talkers than himself and enriched their intellects from genuine scholarship. He had to make a new reputation as a mimic, parodist and spinner of epigrams.

He was reading for the Honours School in Modern History but at his own pace and with a casual dilettantism which would not have satisfied the Balliol dons. Christ Church had lately taken on a raffish and *nouveau riche* flavour, but he could still enjoy the framed names of earls and viscounts on every staircase. He felt at home with his fellow-undergraduates and was shrewd enough to know his own limitations. Oxford was bigger and more competitive than Eton. Without a Blue, he could not hope to penetrate Vincent's, but still managed to flit gracefully between the slightly decadent poseurs in Christ Church and Balliol's intellectual bloods.

His romantic-looking pallor matched his exotic name and air of in-scrutability. Little Miss Skey had gone, but his scout filled his tub with hot scented water and laid out his clothes. They were perfectly cut to a lithe figure kept slender by exercises and a sparing appetite. He could afford brocaded waistcoats, with evening coats for a Commem. Ball, and some with claret and other coloured lapels for his various clubs. The bootmakers came from the Turl to measure his feet and, according to unfriendly gossip, fitted him with built-up heels. For a day with the Hey-throp or the Bicester, he wore elegant buckskin breeches, hunting pink from Savile Row and his bowler with the proud blue Bullingdon ribbon. There was nothing of the aesthete about the way he took fences or played opponents into the ground at tennis or fives. Whatever the whispers that floated around him, the Grenfells, Horner and Lister liked him for his sense of mischief and bubbling spirits.

Between the full-blooded Bullingdons and his set of exquisites in the House, Oxford satisfied most of his social needs. He kept well clear of the Union where he could not hope to compete with virtuoso talents like Raymond Asquith, Philip Guedalla and Ronald Knox. He showed no interest in politics and was far too nervous to make an effective public speaker. His delivery was hesitant, even when he had memorized a speech, and the accented lisp was not to be ventured at the Union. The private and intimate salon, with himself as generous host, became his true stage.

He was half-way through Oxford, which he was enjoying so richly that four years seemed none too long for a degree, when he learned of his mother's illness. Only her husband and a few intimates knew that Aline Sassoon was bravely enduring the slow agonies of incurable cancer. While home for the Long Vacation of 1909, Philip learned that the end was near. He crossed the Channel and raced to his mother's bedside in the Avénue Marigny. Before she died, still only in her mid-forties, she commended her children to the love and care of her dearest friends, Margot Asquith and Lady Horner. She left £240,000 to be divided between Philip and Sybil, after a few bequests, together with her collection of jewels. The magnificent pearl necklace, her husband's wedding present, was left to Philip in the hope that he would give it to his bride when he married.

He was only twenty-one and not perhaps as emotionally mature as his worldly manner suggested. Sybil, although six years younger, was in some ways more poised and better able to absorb the tragedy and comfort their father. Philip turned for sympathy to his late mother's friends who welcomed him to their homes and accompanied him to the theatre or on shopping excursions. Once the months of mourning had passed, he was as amusing as ever, telling stories of his travels or acquaintances with a delightful sense of absurdity that just missed caricature. He remained friendly with the Balliol Etonians whom he still met on the hunting field, but they became less available in their last year once they had started reading seriously for Schools. Lonely and still vulnerable to melancholia, he communed more with the lazy, gilded youth in his own college. If he was too exotic for some, others welcomed the elaborate dinner parties which he would personally supervise down to the last petal. He came to disdain the House's celebrated wild fowl and mulled claret and had a seven-course banquet specially prepared by a London restaurant for a party in his rooms. It was kept hot on the train and served promptly at seven by a relay of college scouts.

This extravagant style of living did not endear him to the 'hearties' or even the Old Etonian crowd who were finding his mannerisms less amusing. He now rolled his guttural r's with a relish, while the lisp had become more pronounced, perhaps deliberately. He fussed over the flowers, the curtains and the décor of his rooms which Charles Lister, fresh from his tours of the slums, thought absurdly opulent. He was too good-natured to make it a personal issue, but Julian Grenfell was less forbearing. After one party in Christ Church, he turned viciously on Philip and drove him round Tom Quad with his big Australian stockwhip, double-cracking it 'within inches of Sassoon's sleek head', according to an eye-witness. No doubt he could have hit him with perfect accuracy. It did not lessen his victim's humiliation.

The country cousins from Weirleigh enjoyed a less exalted, but far more serene, education. At school and later at Cambridge, Michael and Hamo were better at games than textbooks, although both had a strong technical bent quite untraceable to their Sassoon blood. Michael put in his three years' apprenticeship at the Thornycroft works before sailing for Canada. He made his way to British Columbia where he worked on the railways for a time and did a variety of odd jobs before finally joining a fish cannery on the maintenance staff. His brother, Hamo, was even taller than Siegfried but strong as a heifer. His gentleness and grave courtesy charmed everyone he met. He had a first-class mathematical brain with a natural flair for anything mechanical or scientific. It was thought that he might develop into an outstanding architect, which would certainly have delighted his Thornycroft uncles, but a taste for adventure attracted him to civil engineering. After taking his degree at Clare College, he went out to the Argentine and worked with a construction firm building breakwaters and bridges until the outbreak of the 1914 war.

Siegfried's time at Marlborough was uneventful. His physique improved and he won his House Colours for cricket and rugger. He read a good deal of romantic verse and surprised himself, if not his mother, by winning a half-crown prize awarded by one of the masters for a poetry competition. He played the school organ with average talent but creditably, considering that he was practically self-taught.

At Clare, Cambridge, he was a good enough cricketer to keep himself fit and in the college swim without making his shyness too conspicuous. He was still hesitant in speech, which rather discouraged Uncle Hamo who had hoped he might read for the Bar. He tackled the Law Tripos dutifully, but his attention soon strayed from Blackstone to Mallory. For want of anything better, he changed to History which gave him little more satisfaction. He was now seeing his Tripos in terms of heroes and villains, dressed in blank verse. He lost himself in dreams to the accompaniment of

Chopin which he played on his pianola, only emerging for a cricket match or a round of golf. In the vacations, back at Weirleigh with his brothers, he renewed his love of the countryside. He now saw it with the poet's eye, sensitive and rather sentimental, without losing his zest for village cricket or the smell of hay wagons. He loved hacking over the fields with his mother who, he recalls, would sometimes jog twenty miles to visit an old crony for a bit of lively gossip.

Siegfried went down from Cambridge without a degree, in the noble cause of poetry. He had unsuccessfully attempted a blank verse poem on Edward I for the Chancellor's Prize, but consoled himself with a slender volume of poems which he published anonymously, paying out £7 towards the printer's bill. His mother read it with pride and poor Aunt Rachel would surely have been just as appreciative. Uncle Hamo had exploded over his nephew's decision to leave Cambridge, but may have unwittingly contributed to his destiny. Siegfried went one day to his studio where Mr Thornycroft was making sketches for a statue of Tennyson. He good-humouredly invited him to try on the poet's faded cloak and an old wide-brimmed black hat which fell over his nose. But it had been an unforgettable moment of elation.

He was twenty, content to read and day-dream in his ivory tower at Weirleigh where he smoked a briar and composed sonnets which he had issued in pamphlet form for private circulation. They seemed to him so banal in cold print that he threw all but four copies on the fire. These lyrical juvenilia, the product of so much anguish and exaltation, hardly reflected the tweedy extrovert who rode to hounds with his mother, won point-to-points and carried many a match for the Blue Mantles cricket eleven, although he would always describe himself as a 'hopeful pre-interval bowler'.

He liked to talk to the Matfield villagers who remembered his father's cricketing days. He felt at home with them, but rather less so with some of the young women he met in the Queen Anne country-houses. He usually became tongue-tied or tripped over himself at dances. To Mrs Leeds, a friend of the family, he writes cheerfully at Christmas 1906: 'Ain't it seasonable, but cold? We got back last night from Melbury Rd . . . but O, Lor, in 2 hrs. to creep off 7 miles in a local train, 3rd class for economy, with a blue nose, to stay for a dance and tonight on the prancings of my flabby feet – O the tumultuous heavings of my unimpeachable white weskit . . . Haslemere seems a whirl of festivity. Visions of Mrs Howard Leeds tripping to her carriage over red baize, between lanes of menials, the whole swathed in a shimmering cloak . . .'

.　　.　　.　　.　　.

His cousin, Ellice Victor Sassoon, had come down from Cambridge just as Siegfried arrived for his first year. They would have had little in common except a love of horses. Victor had been expensively educated at Harrow, but his schooldays were far different from Philip's. Although his father was born in Bombay and his mother in Cairo, he was surprisingly unoriental in appearance. His nose was slightly aquiline without being semitic, and only the dark handsome eyes gave a hint of alien origin. But at Harrow he had his first taste of anti-semitism. Unlike Philip whose means permitted every little luxury, he was not helped by being kept on a below-average schoolboy's allowance. His father had a sound theory that too much pocket-money might draw attention to his son, but went to the other extreme. However, his Uncle David, the family's black sheep, could always be counted on for a sovereign or two. It was something Victor would never forget. Unfortunately, he was not the best model for an impressionable boy who thought his father unsympathetic.

Jacob, the head of E. D. Sassoon, had long since written off his youngest brother as one of his firm's permanent debentures. The jaunty man-about-town showed no intention of marrying or reforming. He had given up his rooms near Victoria Station for a handier suite of chambers in Pall Mall which he shared with a Gubbay cousin of similar tastes. His landlord was Mr Justice Charles, who remained blissfully ignorant of the scandalous goings-on under his roof. His tenant's tastes became so notorious that one of London's best-known procuresses once wrote to offer him a virgin for £25. David Sassoon declined with mock hauteur, reminding her that he was a *Freemason*.

Nunkie, as he was affectionately known alike to his nephews and a succession of adopted 'nieces' from the chorus, dispensed gay hospitality at hours which shocked his neighbours. He spent most mornings studying racing papers and form books until eleven, when his valet served an admirably chilled half-bottle of 'bubbly'. To improve his ballroom technique, he then practised steps before a long mirror and emerged in silk hat and frock-coat to visit his wine-merchant or tailor before lunching at the Constitutional. He never missed a day's racing in the Home Counties; otherwise, he would drive down to Brighton with a girl, quite unabashed by any frozen Sassoon glances on the promenade. Almost every evening, he would take a party of friends and their women to Murray's Club for supper and dancing which often continued in his rooms until dawn.

Nunkie liked nothing better than to run up to Trinity, Cambridge, where his nephew was enjoying life far more than he had at Harrow. Victor was nicknamed 'Eve', from his initials, E.V., and became a popular member of his college. Tall and well-built, he was a strong swimmer, played a sound game of tennis and was useful with his fists. He loved amateur theatricals, but there was nothing of the aesthete about him. His only touch of foppishness was a monocle which he sported now and then because his left eye was slightly weak. Besides, it suited a gently mocking manner.

He could be brusque when bored, and developed a cynical style that made him amusing at parties. He was light on his feet and almost as accomplished a ballroom dancer as Nunkie, whose success with women he envied. He began to flirt with every pretty girl he met at May Week Balls or in the holidays. Worldlier and more assured than most of his friends, he was usually the ring-leader in any wild undergraduate rag. One night he formed a club for bachelors and took the pledge at a riotous ceremony. 'After studying my pedigree,' he explained, 'I am convinced that I would either produce a genius or an idiot. It's a risk I'm not prepared to take.'

Few knew that he was not being wholly flippant. His first serious love affair had been with a Christian. It ended in heartbreak for both because of racial opposition by their families. He then began to read industriously for his History Tripos. He took Second Class Honours in 1903 and was practical enough to have his degree quickly conferred. (It was just as characteristic of Philip not to bother to collect his B.A. until 1930!) In the library at 46 Grosvenor Place, Victor accepted his father's congratulations but remained unrepentant about his fast friends or his Cambridge bills, mainly for clothes and wines. He often wished his father had a little of Nunkie's gaiety or the more easygoing outlook of Uncle Meyer, who relaxed from office duty and entertained lavishly in Hamilton Place or the luxurious villa he had built himself near Dinard.

Victor had never found it easy to talk to his father, who obviously preferred his younger son, Hector. He therefore showed more interest in the prospect of going out to India and on to Shanghai for his business training. Until then he had secretly dreaded a vista of endless days in the Fenchurch Street office or tedious rounds of the Manchester Cotton Exchange. He was bluntly told that his finances would only improve if he applied himself to business and settled down with a suitable bride among the distinguished Anglo–Jewish families whom they met socially. Both parents, while not ultra-orthodox in observance, dreaded that he would marry out of the faith or become involved with one of his uncle's troupe of chorus girls.

He would lose the London music-halls, riding in the Row, and watching the balloon-races at Ranelagh. Most of all he hated to leave Nunkie who, however, promised to see him during his annual tour of the East. Bombay excited him. Until that first visit, he knew little about Jacob Sassoon's character or the scope of the family business. The firm had six flourishing mills but was now feeling severe competition from Japan who, by 1903, had nearly three million spindles and was turning out 650 million lb. of cotton yarn a year, much of it for export to the Chinese market. However, the war with Russia in 1904–5 temporarily halted her production of yarn and also sent up the price of silver which Manchuria wanted. Bombay thrived again and in Jacob's mills, as well as the three main plants owned by the David Sassoons, millions of spindles were soon in full production.

Victor had only been in India a few weeks before Jacob came to understand him better than his father had ever done. He did not approve of his nephew's frequent visits to the Taj Mahal Hotel, presumably to drink or worse, or his round of the clubs where gambling and *burra pegs* were ritual with the members, but an austere upbringing had not made him intolerant. With no children of his own and fearing blindness, he warmed to this gay young man who had so much poise and obviously a good head on his shoulders. He tinkered with spindles and took an interest in the newest-type throstles from Manchester and the United States, always asking intelligent questions of the maintenance staff. He liked to watch a loom being dismantled, but it was more difficult to make him spend a morning in the counting-house.

To escape the city's moist heat, he drove in his uncle's carriage over the bright red roads up to Mahabaleshwar where one could breathe and play golf. He was welcomed at Viceregal Lodge, Delhi, and not only for his name. Harrow and Trinity had added a smooth gloss to a naturally sociable personality. He was comfortable enough in his uncle's villa in Poona, Ashley House, but preferred to slip away to the bungalows of gay cavalry officers whom he could join for hunting and a chukka of polo.

He felt even more excited by cosmopolitan Shanghai where he developed a passion for the jade and ivories which he came across in Bubbling Well Road. He often went off to the Paper Hunt Club for dinner and joined in their sing-songs, adding a few from his Cambridge repertoire. At the Settlement parties he was in demand and enjoyed himself, thanks to Nunkie who had 'marked his card' in advance!

He was a little bored by Silas Hardoon's warnings about Japanese competition, but did not ignore the threat from powerful concerns like Mitsui and Mitsubishi, with their huge reservoirs of cheap labour. However, E. D. Sassoon had a useful start. Apart from textiles, the firm was shipping a considerable tonnage of wheat and oilseeds to China, together with yellow metal ingots and Batavian sugar. They were also spreading their interests in Shanghai and Hong Kong through subsidiaries in public tramways, insurance, laundries and breweries. Above all, they had the invaluable advantage of owning some of the best property sites in the Settlement.

Victor was stimulated by all this excitement and competition, but could not be dissuaded from returning to England. He would miss his kindly uncle who showed his confidence by appointing him to a junior partnership in 1906. It seemed to Jacob's brothers, including Victor's own father, that this was a premature accolade for a young fellow of twenty-five who had promptly celebrated by buying a couple of jumpers which he trained and rode in a few races in Bombay. They were not particularly good, and he gave one of them away after it finished last in a selling hurdle.

But Jacob never ceased to believe that his nephew might one day become a more valuable asset than any of the others. Nunkie was only a nominal director and not to be trusted with anything more serious than a one-step. Edward and Meyer were still in their mid-fifties, but settled in their ways and readier to execute, than initiate, policy decisions. There were few other candidates from within the family circle. Meyer's only son, Reginald, was still at Eton, a rather nervous, short-sighted boy. Edward's younger son, Hector, had recently celebrated his twentieth birthday but seemed determined to imitate his brother's more frivolous habits. Victor therefore seemed the only hopeful prospect among the fourth generation.

His father was not so sanguine. His heir's directorship and improved finances only seemed to encourage the familiar rake's progress of fast women and slow horses for which Nunkie was blamed, as usual. Victor went to the same tailor for his wardrobe, which now included motoring coats for the noisy car he drove so recklessly with a hat over one eye. When he should have been at his desk in Fenchurch Street, he would be bowling down to Brighton or watching the 'balloonatics' at Ranelagh.

In top-hat, morning coat and carnation, with his monocle squeezed into a supercilious eye and the inevitable chorus belle on his arm, he looked a typical 'masher', yet nobody took more passionate note of aerial demonstrations at Brooklands. He was a founder member of the Royal Aero Club when it started in 1909, and began to take lessons at Wisley. He followed the flights of birdmen like Frank Hedges Butler, Claude Grahame White and Moore-Brabazon, and went almost crazy with excitement when Blériot first flew the Channel. It almost eclipsed the news from Bombay that his uncle had been honoured with a baronetcy for his philanthropies and civic service.

Jacob Sassoon was delighted, but not for himself. He had only accepted the title because it would go by remainder to his brother, Edward, thereby making Victor his eventual heir.

Chapter Eleven

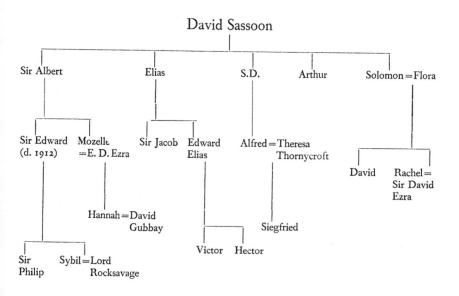

Soon after receiving his baronetcy in 1909, Sir Jacob played a prominent part in forming the Eastern Bank Ltd. with a capital of £2 million. The registered Head Office was in London but its policy guide-lines would be laid down by Bombay. Branches were speedily opened in other Indian cities, as well as Baghdad and Singapore. The sixty-five-year-old baronet was its powerful driving force. He foresaw the advantages of an exchange bank which could be used to transfer sums to countries needing short-term loans for industrial expansion. Both the Hong Kong and Shanghai Exchanges now actively welcomed speculators. There was no limit to investment in this heyday of the Joint Stock Company. The Bank could capitalize any number of new enterprises in the Treaty Ports, either by forming subsidiary companies or investing in firms requiring loans for tools and machinery from Europe. The rapid industrialization of the Far East had also led to a boom in marine and fire insurance companies, but there were many other outlets. Java was growing more sugar, while Malaya's tin mines and rubber plantations also invited capital. In a dozen cities, from Shanghai down to Singapore, sites were snapped up for shops, factories, workers' tenements and warehouses. These could be built and then serviced through a network of allied concerns partly or wholly responsible for bricks and mortar, insurance, light and power. The central holding company thus had an open basket into which its subsidiaries poured a golden rain of wealth in every known currency.

The Eastern Bank, operating in the days before exchange controls, seemed an inevitable development for a house with extensive overseas interests. E. D. Sassoon continued to trade independently, but they could now use banking facilities by raising short-term loans for themselves and guaranteeing overdrafts to plantation owners in Malaya or Shanghai's building contractors. As a result, the firm would be far less vulnerable to violent fluctuations in the rupee or a temporary drying-up of liquid gold reserves when the India Office was caught on the wrong foot before the First World War. A cotton slump caused vast unsold stocks of piece-goods to accumulate in Hong Kong and Shanghai, but they were able to offset their own losses by buying heavily in silver which quickly soared from two shillings an ounce to six. A sudden inflation in the price of rubber also meant a useful killing for the Hong Kong branch which, at that time, settled quarterly for all share-dealings.

David Sassoon & Co. made no attempt to follow Sir Jacob into merchant banking. They stuck rigidly, perhaps too rigidly for those inviting times, to their Articles of Association. They expanded with prudence inside the framework of what would become mainly a holding operation. This policy was possibly ultra-cautious, but it could be justified. Undercutting by Tokyo had resulted in heavy losses in India, while the whole Chinese investment field became highly volatile when the Manchu dynasty was finally blasted out in 1911. But Leadenhall Street's strategy had deeper and more personal roots. The Chairman was broken in spirit after Aline's death. His business rôle, never over-active, now become titular. Frederick might have been competent to take a more progressive line, but he would not chance his arm while still junior to Sir Edward and Arthur. He would have to wait some years before his own son, Ronald, left Eton to become his powerful right-hand.

He had good backing from dapper little David Gubbay and the rather forbidding bachelor, Cecil Longcroft. These two faced each other across a big double desk and made an excellent team, although completely different in temperament. Gubbay knew every inch of the export and import business, but his position was mainly that of an accountant-treasurer. His financial genius was banked down by the firm's anxiety to avoid 'speculation'. Longcroft, the first non-Jew to become a Sassoon director, was efficient, but a rather puritanical view of life had narrowed his business thinking. His punctiliousness over routine made him deskbound and too insular. He found it an effort even to go up to Manchester, and nobody could persuade him to tour the overseas branches. He had an intimidating way of sticking his thumbs into his waistcoat and then giving wretched juniors sermons which always ended with, 'Watch your money and your health'. He had no patience with City men who spent long weekends playing golf or left early to gamble and drink in their clubs.

Whatever their faults, Sir Albert and his brothers had won many a battle in their salons and at diplomatic parties. Their personal touch was being missed. Arthur, the only surviving member of the trio, now rarely made even a token visit to the head office. He was himself a tired worn-out man of seventy when King Edward came to stay with them for the last time. He arrived in Hove on 10 February 1910, coughing more than usual and very low in spirits. Louise tried to rally him, but he could not be tempted by his favourite dishes. Muffled in scarves and a heavy raglan, and with his homburg no longer at an angle, he linked arms with them and walked slowly along the front. Both noticed how quickly he tired. He refused to stay in bed and became irritable when Louise suggested timidly that his cigars might be causing shortness of breath. The Sussex air failed for once to brace him. He was worried over Lloyd George's determination to force through his 'People's Budget' and abolish the House of Lords' veto over Money Bills.

Mr Asquith appeared at the Arthur Sassoons' two days later, the 12th, to discuss the Speech from the Throne. He found the King highly irascible. It was rumoured that he might even show his displeasure by staying away altogether from the Opening of Parliament. Mr Asquith was relieved of this particular nightmare, but spent a restless night awaiting comments on the drafted Speech. In a distinctly frozen atmosphere, King Edward made a number of alterations which grudgingly accepted the the need to clip the Lords' authority over finance.

Asquith's visit had made him more prickly. He cut short his stay to return to London and see his advisers. Arthur and his wife bade him farewell. As it happened, they were the last of his subjects to entertain him in a private house. Yielding to his doctors who wanted him out of chilly England as quickly as possible, he contracted a severe cold while on his way to Biarritz and died in Buckingham Palace on May 6.

The blinds were drawn at King's Cliff where he was deeply mourned as a friend. Arthur wore a black tie and did not visit a theatre for months. Now ailing and despondent, he had little heart for the celebrations that Coronation summer, the hottest for years. But Philip, just down from Oxford, enjoyed the brilliant round of dances, dinners and fancy-dress balls. He was perfectly happy with his Second in History after four years at Oxford, and in no hurry to sit at a desk in Leadenhall Street. In addition to Number Ten, where Margot Asquith made him welcome, he was dining at the best tables in London, with Mells and several other country houses always open to him. He travelled frequently abroad and in style, often staying *en route* in the Avénue Marigny where he catalogued the exquisite pictures, tapestries, snuff-boxes and pottery recently bequeathed by his grandfather, Baron Gustave. They would adorn 25 Park Lane rather more artistically than some of Sir Albert's relics.

At dances and dinner parties he squired his pretty and vivacious sister, Sybil, who was to be presented next season. His only regret was the dispersal of so many old friends. He had long forgiven Julian Grenfell, who had joined the First Royal Dragoons and was serving in the East where he had quietened down and now wrote serious poetry in off-duty spells. Edward Horner was 'devilling' in the chambers of F. E. Smith, who predicted a bright future for him at the Bar.

Philip kept in touch with them all. He was rather amused by the political 'conversion' of Charles Lister, who would never lose his sympathy with the poor and under-privileged but had grown disillusioned with the tactics of his fellow-Socialists. After taking his First in Greats, he had entered diplomacy and was stationed in Constantinople. The cleverest and most ambitious of the 'New Elizabethans' was probably Patrick Shaw-Stewart, who had left an All Souls' Fellowship to make his fortune in merchant banking. He soon went on the Board of Baring Brothers.

Philip showed no eagerness to begin a career. He kept himself trim by playing polo at Ranelagh and Hurlingham. He was enchanted by the London début of Diaghilev's Russian Ballet and rarely missed a first night or the opening of an art exhibition. He also found a new interest in the country house which Sir Edward had recently bought at Cockfosters, only twelve miles from London. Trent Park had a romantic history. Built in 1750, it was popularly supposed to have been one of Dick Turpin's hiding-places. The 1,000-acre park lay on the southern border of Enfield Chase, a corner of the royal forest which George III had presented to his physician, Sir Richard Jebb.

Sir Edward saw it as a pleasant weekend retreat and more accessible than the house at Sandgate, which he now used only to entertain local party workers and constituents. Since his wife's death he had lost his zest for sport and hardly ever went up to the shooting-box in Scotland. The old sparkle had gone out of him. He often went abroad for the sun's warmth and to revisit places where he had spent happy times with Aline. While at Cannes in the winter of 1911, he was involved in a car collision on the Croisette which shook him up severely. He returned to England more melancholy than ever, and rapidly declined in health.

The following March he was distressed by his Uncle Arthur's sudden death while staying with the Leo de Rothschilds at Leighton Buzzard. Apart from family mourners, the funeral was attended by Rosebery, Derby and many other members of the aristocracy. King George V sent a wreath 'as a token of friendship and in remembrance of many happy days spent at Tulchan'. An obituarist could find little to say about the deceased except that Arthur 'knew the Bible perfectly and read *The Times* through from beginning to end every day'. He left £650,000, exclusive of substantial real estate in China. The property went to his widow, after a legacy of £100,000 for Reuben's children and various bequests to other relatives.

Two months later, Sir Edward died at his home in Park Lane. He was only fifty-six. His remains were buried in the family mausoleum at Eastern Terrace. One of the mourners was Sir Jacob who had arrived in London a few days previously, after consultations with eye specialists in Wiesbaden. Before leaving home, he gave £20,000 towards building a pavilion on the Apollo Bunder to commemorate George V's landing for the Coronation Durbar.

He called to condole with Philip and Sybil and then visited Flora who had now settled into a Mayfair mansion at 32 Bruton Street. She still refused to sell Il Palazzo, her husband's 'shrine', although the Gaekwar of Baroda had offered to buy it for nearly £70,000. Her farewell voyage from India was memorable. It is recorded in detail by Flora's daughter, Rachel, who soon afterwards married her cousin, David Ezra, a member of the pioneer family of merchants and philanthropists who had first settled in Calcutta in 1821.

Flora had travelled with sixty pieces of baggage and her mahogany 'thunder-box' together with the customary escort of rabbis and servants. All quarantine regulations were waived in their favour at Basra. The Pasha placed a suite in his palace at their disposal. They stayed three months in Baghdad where they were received like visiting royalty by the Vali and city dignitaries. 'The British Consul-General, Mr Lorimer, cannot do too much for us,' reported Rachel. Among the Jewish community, which included many kinsfolk descended from those who had stayed behind after David Sassoon's flight, Flora was honoured as much for her piety and scholarship as her name. She was given the rare privilege of reading from the Torah in the synagogue. No woman had for centuries been allowed to leave the curtained gallery during service. Flora read from the very Scrolls dedicated long ago by the Sheikh Sason.

Sir Jacob thought very highly of 'the little mother of Eastern Jewry', as she was called by the Sephardic community in London. During his visit, he saw her often at Bevis Marks where both his brothers were elders. They gave elaborate dinner parties for him, but he had become less sociable since his wife's recent death. His poor sight also made it difficult for him to appreciate Meyer's rare snuff-boxes or the delicate studies by Manet and Degas which would one day fetch enormous sums. He was more interested to talk with his favourite nephew, Victor, who showed a grasp of business affairs but was still enjoying himself rather freely for a working director. He seemed to be spending altogether too much time and money on flying. This incensed his father and gave his mother nightmares whenever an airman was reported killed. Fortunately for Sir Jacob's peace of mind, he returned to India without being told that his nephew had entered for the Grand Prix organized by the Aero Club de France. It was to be held three weeks hence, and Victor found it impossible to think about office matters.

He had become fanatical about military aviation after first reading H. G. Wells's *War in the Air*. Now that the Government had created a Royal Flying Corps and was sending experts to report on Germany's airships, he was determined to qualify as a pilot while his reflexes were still reasonably brisk at thirty. On 24 June 1911, he was given the Royal Aero Club's Certificate, number 52, after a test flight at Brooklands in a Sommer bi-plane.

For the Grand Prix race a year later, he flew as an observer in the two-seater Blériot monoplane powered by a 70-h.p. Gnome engine. With the other thirty-four machines competing for the £2,000 prize, he took off with the pilot, Hamel, from Angers on the cross-country Anjou circuit. The plane was soon caught by a terrific gust of wind. Hamel became air-sick and Victor, thrown several times out of his seat, had some difficulty in remaining on board. They landed at Cholet, bruised and shaken, with their chassis smashed and one cylinder out of action, but scored the second best time in the first round of the race.

Victor heard a few days later that Cousin Philip had a splendid chance of getting into the House of Commons. He was not in the least envious and much more excited at having at last squeezed enough money from his father to buy himself a small monoplane. Even with his director's fees, it was not easy to maintain a plane as well as a roadster. He had reluctantly given up all thoughts of starting a small racing stable of his own.

Philip's financial position was very different. Sir Edward had left over a million pounds in trust for his children. Sybil received one-quarter of the estate, out of which an annuity of £6,000 would be paid to her whilst a spinster under thirty years of age. Philip inherited most of the remainder, including all his father's properties and his shares in the family company. Sir Edward's will expressed the hope that his son would attend to the interests of the firm, 'so that its reputation and standing so laboriously

Flora Sassoon, scholar, philanthropist and famed hostess, was for many years managing partner of the firm's Bombay office.

Theresa Thornycroft Sassoon in her garden at Weirleigh in Kent, Siegfried's birthplace, recalled in many of his writings.

The future author of *Memoirs of a Fox-Hunting Man* takes a fence. An early drawing by his mother, herself a fine horsewoman.

Sir Edward Sassoon, 2nd Bt. and M.P. for Hythe.
(*Vanity Fair* cartoon by Spy)

Sir Edward Sassoon's wife, Aline, daughter of the Baron Gustave de Rothschild. From a portrait by Sargent. She was herself a talented artist and had her own studio at 25 Park Lane.

built up by his ancestors for close on a century may not be tarnished or impaired by the possible neglect or mismanagement of outsiders'. It was rather a pious wish since Philip had shown no symptoms of any appetite for commerce. He accepted a directorship which would never be anything but nominal, and Frederick automatically succeeded as Chairman.

Sir Edward had hoped that his children would 'devote some part of their time and money to objects of benevolence'. He went on: 'I enjoin on my son and daughter in the strongest possible manner my desire and hope that they will, until one or other marries, live together ... this being their mother's wish as well as my own.' No mention was made of religious observance or marriage within the faith. It did not surprise the Anglo–Jewish community.

Sir Edward had died of cancer which also killed his wife, and his last public benefaction was to endow a bed at the Home for Jewish Incurables. Otherwise, he departed from family practice by making no provision for charities, explaining with some asperity that the Liberals' increase of death duties had discouraged him. Finally, he hoped that his son and heir would maintain the link with the Hythe constituency.

Philip found this easier than to give allegiance to the firm. His inheritance from both parents, supplemented by legacies from the Baron Gustave and other relatives, made him a millionaire at twenty-three. He owned a Park Lane mansion, weekend houses at Trent Park and Sandgate, and the shooting-lodge on Strathside. He saw little prospect of occupying either over-ornate Sans Souci in Bombay or the Poona villa, but would temporarily maintain them out of family sentiment.

His father's hint about Hythe was taken, although he had not previously contemplated a political career. However, having lived from boyhood in an atmosphere of salons, he could see the social advantages in being a rich young M.P. If he could win a seat without too much effort, it would be a tribute to his father's memory and an agreeable exemption from Leadenhall Street.

He sauntered into Parliament with quite remarkable ease. He was unanimously adopted as Unionist candidate for his father's old constituency, cheerfully accepting the Party's unexceptionable slogans, 'Empire United in Trade and Affection' and 'Fair Play for Ulster and the Church of Wales'. A graceful bearing charmed the few waverers. His electioneering speeches were a trifle awkward and showed a fondness for the mannered aphorism, but Leo de Rothschild led a battery of bigwigs to his rescue and carried every meeting.

He was elected by a clear majority over the Liberal to become the youngest Member at Westminster. It did him no harm in his constituency to refuse the newly voted £400 a year salary which several other wealthy

Members accepted readily enough. It was certainly no bid for cheap popularity. For the rest of his public life he would decline any pay for his services.

His natural impulse to self-dramatization now had fuller scope. The Oxonian mask of aesthetic elegance was replaced by a half-conscious imitation of the Disraeli mystique. If he lacked the flashing brilliance of his model, he cultivated a similar nonchalant style and was considered the best-dressed man in the House. The flawless tailcoat, white waistcoat and the diamond in his shirtfront became his armour as well as a provocation to the Opposition who jeered at his lisp and exotic mannerisms. If his hesitant maiden speech was not quite worthy of 'a new Disraeli', well-wishers and sycophants responded as if he had handed down the Tablets from Sinai.

In Park Lane he and his sister entertained a procession of names as glittering as any during Aline's régime. The faithful complement of Rothschilds, Balfour, Rosebery and Sargent was expanded and enriched by a younger leavening of artists, writers, polo-players and sybarites. Before banquets were served, a dignified major-domo ritually lit the wax candles in their high chandeliers with his slender brass wand. The room was 'too big for less than a thousand diners', Max Beerbohm commented dryly after his first visit. He was among those who could not resist the French cuisine, but confessed that he had come away with some relief from 'the chatter and clatter and hustle and guzzle'. However, he adored such touches of style as crystal bowls with pink carnations floating inside them.

Philip had also bought himself a property, he later renamed Port Lympne, set among the hills on the Kent–Sussex border and looking out over Romney Marshes. It would be convenient for his constituency and a delightful *pied-à-terre* for entertaining his friends away from London. The old manor house could be adapted to the more exotic architecture he had in mind. It was to be a slow and costly business which would not be completed until after the war. Meanwhile, he was enjoying life to the full, although Osbert Sitwell and a few other intimates were finding him too restless. He seemed to bubble with high spirits as he dashed about London in his small two-seater, hunting down pictures or some porphyry table earmarked for a corner of 25 Park Lane. He had endless charm, but many accused him of being affected and over-precious. Hilaire Belloc's sister, Mrs Belloc Lowndes, was one of several middle-aged matrons who defended him. When she teased him about remaining a bachelor, he had replied cheerfully, 'I shall only marry when I find someone as lovely and perfect as my sister.' It would become a standard evasion.

Sybil was remarkably poised for her age. She was not only witty and well-read, but an all-round sportswoman who shone at swimming and tennis. She was a crack shot like her father. All this did not make her any less feminine. Presented a few months after Sir Edward's death, she was the leading débutante of the 1912 Season. Of the many suitors buzzing about her, the favoured one seemed to be Lord Rocksavage, whom Philip had first met on the polo field. 'Rock', a curly-haired Adonis, was considered the handsomest male in England. The men of fashion all copied his polo shirts and breeches, the cut of his dress-clothes and such innovations as the pleated trousers with a polished waistbelt which he favoured for tennis. He had served gallantly in the Boer War with the 9th Lancers, acting later as A.D.C. to the Viceroy of India, Lord Minto.

He was an outstanding polo player and big game hunter, but had other claims to being the most eligible bachelor of his day. He was the son and heir of the fourth Marquess of Cholmondeley, holder of seven peerages, several dating back for centuries. The marquisate carried with it one of the highest hereditary offices in the land, that of Lord Great Chamberlain in alternate reigns. The holder had jurisdiction over the Royal Palace of Westminster with responsibility for certain ceremonial duties at Coronations, royal funerals and the State Opening of Parliament.

The family seat, Houghton Hall, bordered on Royal Sandringham. Originally built for Sir Robert Walpole, whose daughter married the third Earl of Cholmondeley, it was a mansion in the grand manner, standing in 30,000 ample acres. Although Walpole's most valuable paintings were later sold to Catherine the Great, the bronze group of Laocoon given him by the Pope was preserved. Other masterpieces included the celebrated Mortlake tapestries, woven in 1672, and some remarkable carvings attributed to Grinling Gibbons. Many exquisite pieces would later come from the Avénue Marigny and Philip's private collection.

Lord Rocksavage was thirty, eleven years older than Sybil Sassoon, when he proposed. Public imagination was touched by this union of a beautiful young heiress, the daughter of a Sassoon and a Rothschild, with a nobleman whose classic profile was always being reproduced by the magazines. Many felt cheated that the marriage would not be solemnized with full pageantry in one of London's fashionable churches. Sybil did not choose to follow Hannah Rothschild's example. After an engagement of only a few weeks, the couple were quietly married on 6 August 1913 at a registry office near Buckingham Palace Road.

Philip gave his sister away and was obviously delighted with a match for which he rightly prophesied success. Others in the Sassoon clan were far less enthusiastic. Flora disapproved of the marriage on religious grounds, but also resented the fact that a substantial portion of Sir Albert's wealth, to which she and her husband had contributed so much hard work and sacrifice in the troubled 'nineties, would now pass out of the family and, even worse, into non-Jewish hands.

As Sir Edward's successor, Philip had nominally become head of the family, but Flora remained sceptical of his goodwill. She discounted his occasional sorties from the flunkeyism of Park Lane to open some soup kitchen in the East End of London. He wrote her charming notes in which he mentioned her 'Bruton Street court' with the gentle flattery that came so easily to his pen, but 'dearest Aunt Flora' was vexed by his indifference to community problems. He had displayed a thoughtless lack of tact in escorting Mrs Arthur Sassoon to a dinner given by the Russian Ambassador. This was in 1913, during an ugly rash of pogroms against which the Rothschilds had protested vigorously. The British community ignored Philip's *gaffe* in contemptuous silence, but a Warsaw newspaper recalled that his surname meant 'joy', in Hebrew. He was reminded that the situation was anything but joyful in their country.

He had followed his father into the Yeomanry and took a commission in the East Kents. Summer camp and polo kept him fit for his strenuous round. The House of Commons was seeing less of him, but he often ran down to his constituency to listen to local troubles. He was more at ease in Park Lane where favoured guests were entertained to banquets, followed by concerts in his music room or the private theatre where he put on operettas and playlets. Nobody denied his skill in organization, backed by his vivacious sister who played hostess for the big occasions, but the lavish food and entertainment sometimes led to overmuch 'hustle and guzzle' for fastidious tastes. In June 1913, after a sumptuous dinner with the usual phalanx of duchesses, diplomats and politicians, the company trooped out to witness a special performance of Maeterlinck's *Death of Tintagiles*. So many other guests arrived before curtain rise that several had to stand. The luckier ones stayed near the windows, although heavy plush curtains kept out the air. Edward Marsh fled from what he called 'the Black Hole of Calcutta'. The heat and the dazzle of tiaras and medals had combined to give him a blinding headache.

Marsh might sneer, but he was too inveterate a man-about-town-and-country-houses to resist dining *chez* Philip. He could always be sure of bridge, snobbish tittle-tattle and jokes to be passed on to Winston Churchill, whom he had served as private secretary and confidant since 1907. 'Eddie' seemed to have all the qualifications for Philip Sassoon's graceful and rather decadent inner circle. He was sexually impotent and made no secret of it. He talked in falsetto, and a nervous giggle suited his birdlike manner and the uptilted eyebrow. He gave elegant dinners, followed by accomplished bridge or bézique, but his own frivolous chatter and anecdotes were the major attractions. Using a cigarette-holder to stab home his *obiter dicta* on pictures, books, fashion and politics, he would only pause to reclaim the monocle which tinkled on to his stiff shirtfront. Marsh often dined in Park Lane, but he was rather more taken with another Sassoon, whom the third baronet had then barely heard of, and would certainly have excluded from his circle. A few weeks before escaping from the Maeterlinck play, Marsh read a poem called *The Daffodil Murderer* which Edmund Gosse had sent him. It was written as a parody of Masefield's *The Everlasting Mercy*, but showed such narrative feeling and rhythm that 'Eddie' sent Siegfried Sassoon a note of friendly praise. It came at a time when the poet was tasting the first wine of being published at someone else's expense. T. W. H. Crosland had already printed some of his sonnets on Villon in *The Academy*, but he was very unsure of himself and his talent. He needed a less gruff and kindlier patron than Crosland. Marsh filled the bill to perfection.

Siegfried had hesitated long before sending his poem to Gosse, the author and literary pundit who gave celebrated 'Sunday Afternoons' at his house in Hanover Terrace. He was touchy and self-important, and the poet was rather awed at meeting him in the House of Lords where he presided over the Library. But Gosse, a distant kinsman of the Thornycrofts and Uncle Hamo's best man, turned out less crusty than expected. Quite apart from the family connection, he seemed genuinely to approve of Siegfried's verses and invited him to tea with his wife and their two golden-haired daughters. He was soon asked again and listened in fascination while Gosse argued with Arnold Bennett, George Moore and others in his circle. But he remained ill-at-ease and could only mumble self-consciously when someone addressed a remark to him. It was an eccentric, if endearing household in which even Sir Edmund took second place to the family tyrant, Buchanan, the huge black and white cat who would not eat unless Lady Gosse fed him personally. The spoilt monster even had his own writing paper and stationery for dealing with correspondence.

Siegfried felt far more comfortable talking *à deux* with Marsh, who helpfully analysed his poems and pointed out certain defects in style. He thought the young poet too out of touch with life and in need of fresh experience to enlarge his vision. He therefore persuaded him to rent chambers in Raymond Buildings, Gray's Inn, near his own. With his small but adequate private income, Siegfried would be able to write his poems there, practically under his mentor's eye, and still enjoy the artistic and literary delights of the capital.*

* In *The Weald of Youth* (Faber), Siegfried Sassoon has reconstructed these pre-war years with great charm. Published in the gloom of 1942, it perhaps over-idealizes in retrospect, but offers many delightful touches of self-irony.

It was sound advice. Marsh, an insatiable first-nighter, took him to the ballet and the opera and once introduced him at breakfast to Rupert Brooke, who had known his brother, Hamo, and used to go rock-climbing with him. Brooke was boyishly unkempt in old flannel bags and sandals, his long tawny hair falling over the collar of an open shirt. Siegfried admired him but had done too little himself to venture more than nervous small talk.

Marsh and the Gosses were kindly, but it was always a relief to be back at Weirleigh reading his poems to his mother or playing Debussy on the piano. He lounged in the garden where he used to romp with his brothers, both now across the Atlantic, and rarely missed a chance of seeing the Kent cricket eleven in action. He was not far off county standard himself and turned out for several good club sides, more than once bowling against Edmund Blunden, a fellow-poet and neighbour who became his lasting friend. He also won several point-to-points on his sturdy hunter, Cockbird. It seemed more difficult than ever to write verse on crispy mornings when the chalk downs invited one out for a day with the hounds.

He was still keen on golf and went off to watch Harry Vardon play in the Open. Cycling between the blossoming orchards for a few holes at Rye during that cloudless summer of 1914, or jogging home in a dog-cart with his cricket bag under the seat, the Kaiser's dark threats seemed as remote as the Wars of the Roses. Even when the lamps of Europe started to go out, they shed a glow on the dream of chivalry shared by all the gay, golden subalterns of his class. The only difference was that he enlisted in the Sussex Yeomanry as a private and cantered blithely to war on Cockbird, now promoted to troophorse.

None of David Sassoon's dozen great-grandsons in uniform seemed less likely to become a legendary and highly controversial figure.

Chapter Twelve

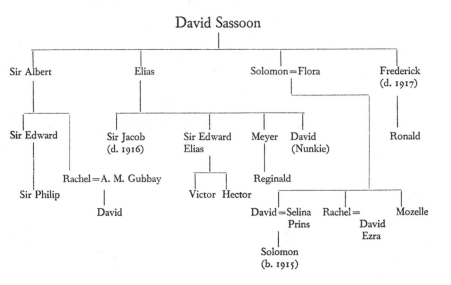

David Sassoon
- Sir Albert
- Elias
- Solomon = Flora
- Frederick (d. 1917)
- Sir Edward
- Sir Jacob (d. 1916)
- Sir Edward Elias
- Meyer
- David (Nunkie)
- Ronald
- Rachel = A. M. Gubbay
- Reginald
- Sir Philip
- David
- Victor Hector
- David = Selina Prins
- Rachel = David Ezra
- Mozelle
- Solomon (b. 1915)

Victor, senior member of the fourth generation Sassoons, was its first war casualty. He enlisted for flying duties with the R.N.V.R. and was commissioned as Sub-Lieutenant. He joined a squadron of the newly formed Royal Naval Air Service in November 1914. Although he had often flown solo, he was then thirty-three and failed to meet the stiff medical standard required of a wartime pilot. He hid his disappointment and volunteered as an Observer.

He was posted to Dover and quickly became a popular figure in the Mess. They nicknamed him 'Daddy', but nobody showed more enthusiasm for his duties. Their machines were 80 h.p. rotary-engined tractor biplanes, manned by a pilot in the rear open cockpit with his Observer out in front. The Unit was billeted in transit, with every pilot, mechanic and rigger at key pitch to get over to Dunkirk, ahead of the R.F.C. stationed across the valley.

In the early morning of 6 February 1915, Victor and his young but experienced pilot, Flt. Lieut. John Babington, were standing by for an anti-aircraft practice run on a fixed course near the harbour. Their machine was still in its shed with the doors closed, since these lightly loaded biplanes were apt to tip over in the 30-m.p.h. wind that had sprung up. Two Naval Staff officers drove up to the aerodrome a few minutes before scheduled take-off. Leaning on their walking-sticks, they glanced derisively at the closed shed-doors. One murmured, 'Too rough, I suppose?' Victor polished his monocle and drawled back, 'Still ten minutes to go, by *my* watch.'

The machine was wheeled out. A mechanic swung the propeller, Babington revved up and taxied out, with a man at each wingtip to steady the machine in the strong wind. Without throttle, the engine was kept running slow by 'blipping' it on and off with a thumb switch. They had only moved a few yards when a gust heeled them over on to port wingtip skid, buckling the wheel. Babington kept the engine going by 'blips' while a light hand-trolley came alongside, removed the damaged landing wheel and briskly slapped on a spare.

Pilot and Observer exchanged grins when the machine began to climb. They turned downwind at about a thousand feet to steady themselves for the first 'run'. Victor looked up from his map in the front cockpit and gave the signal to turn. The wind was behind them as Babington banked sharply and started to swing round. The engine faltered, spluttered and died away. In seconds the crank-shaft began to spit flames and oil between Victor's shins. He seemed quite unperturbed as he shifted his legs, without even troubling to look round at his pilot. Both guessed that a spring must have broken in one of the automatic inlet valves. They would have to land in an open field.

Babington switched off the ignition, relying on his speed to finish the turn and head upwind. But the aircraft did not straighten out or respond to the controls even when he had the stick pulled right up against his body. They went into a slow spin with only five hundred feet in hand. Babington tugged savagely at the control stick but the machine, with its nose well down, stubbornly refused to flatten out. It continued to spiral downwards like a bent corkscrew, while the wind shrieked in the struts and bracing wires.

'She won't come up,' he shouted. 'Turn off the petrol.' Victor nodded and switched off the main tap in his cockpit. Straightening up, he smiled over his shoulder and gave a casual 'thumbs up' signal. It must have taken remarkable self-control. An airman, in the next room the night before, had heard Victor shout in his sleep, 'Pull her up! For God's sake, pull her up.' Neither had mentioned the incident in the squadron, where taboos and premonitions were severely discouraged.

Victor recalled his nightmare as the plane began to lose height, but stayed 'methodical and precise, cool as a cucumber', the pilot later reported. They were now sure to crash, although Babington still hoped desperately to flatten into a horizontal glide. Each ridge and brown furrow in the ploughed field became almost clear enough to be counted. He had just time to shout 'windscreen', a reminder to his Observer to press down the little hinged sheet in his cockpit. Victor's upturned thumb was the last thing he remembered.

Babington must have been insensible for some minutes before coming to in the wreckage. The control stick was jammed into his chest. He pushed it aside, released his safety-belt and tried to move towards what was left of the forward fuselage. His right leg had caught in the rigging and the left ankle was out of action. 'Are you all right?' he called out anxiously. He heard a faint groan, followed by a long silence.

Babington was hurt, but not as severely as Victor who had two broken legs and a badly smashed thigh. He was given a shot of morphia and taken off by stretcher to a hospital in Dover. 'The machine was a write-off and would be reduced to scrap,' recalls the pilot. 'In later editions of this particular type, the tail units were modified in order to give easy recovery from a spin. Indeed, it is even probable that this particular accident served a useful purpose and contributed to the avoidance of other similar – and worse – crashes.'

Victor stayed in a plaster cast for eight months. A room in his home at Grosvenor Place was converted into a small operating theatre where his bones were set and re-set. He underwent an intensive series of exercises and massage treatment while his mother watched his diet and read to him when the nights were long and the pain kept him awake. He guessed, but was not told, that he might never walk again or, at best, with a distinct limp. His right leg would always be slightly shorter than the other. To comfort his mother, he made light of the news from France when she worried about her younger son, Hector, who was serving with the Grenadier Guards.

The war seemed very close when Reggie, Meyer's son, came home on sick leave in September 1915. He had been wounded by a rifle bullet in the Battle of Loos while his company was trying to hold Chalk Pit Wood under heavy shellfire. Sitting in his wheelchair, Victor felt a pang of envy as Reggie's wound quickly healed. Cursing his own cage, he could understand his cousin's exhilaration at going back to the comradeship of waterlogged trenches and no-man's-land. It was still difficult to believe that this awkward-looking, myopic chap was actually a subaltern in the Irish Guards. Everyone knew that he was so short-sighted that he had to wear glasses for hunting, yet he had passed his medical by some miracle of ingenuity and finesse.

Reggie was a slightly comic figure, shy and gauche, and quite unlike his nattier brother-officers. He took their jokes with good humour and soon won a reputation for being incredibly fearless. Wearing a uniform sloppy by Caterham standards, and with his puttees often soggy with blood and mud, he used to laugh or hum to himself when under fire, 'as if it were the Eton Wall Game and not a machine-gun barrage', to quote a fellow-Guardsman.

Victor shook Reggie's hand, wished him luck and promised cheerfully to 'drop in' on him one day. He was still optimistic about flying again. In fact, he was luckier than he knew not to be invalided out altogether. His jaunty manner and determination somehow persuaded a sporting board to give him another chance. He was out of his wheelchair at last but still limped heavily and often suffered considerable pain. He brushed aside his father's suggestion that he should go to Uncle Jacob's villa in Poona where he would have had every comfort and attention.

As soon as he was fit, he put on his uniform and hobbled into the Admiralty. He could not convince a Medical Board that he was airworthy, but was now reporting for administrative duties, thanks to Babington who had pulled some strings. The pilot had recovered from the crash and was posted to the Admiralty for Experimental and Test Flying. 'Not being admirals,' he recalls, 'we had no secretaries; and the Admiral's typist-pool, or whatever it was called, was hopelessly at sea when it came to dealing with the subject of "flying machines", and perhaps couldn't be expected to follow the technicalities and jargon of our trade. We could not fly all the new machines, keep in touch with outside progress and development, and at the same time organize a reference library and a clerical registry. Victor had all the necessary background flying knowledge, and he had brains. As soon as he became fit for light duties while still on sticks and under treatment, we got him posted to the Experimental Section. Our troubles were over.'

A few months after the crash, he acted as best man at his old pilot's wedding. 'My Observer was there – limping but as alert as ever – to superintend the take-off,' says Air Marshal Sir John Tremayne (who renounced the surname of Babington for family reasons, in 1945). They remained the best of friends and often flew together again after the war, but never in another two-seater. 'Perhaps that would have been asking a lot of the Observer. However, I don't think for a moment that he would have hesitated!'

Victor never ceased to complain that being deskbound was bad for his thigh and infinitely less useful to the country than sitting in an Observer's cockpit. However, he was not quite out of things. He had never taken to office routine with the firm, but now showed a zest for organizing paperwork. He would earn the gratitude of operational personnel by cutting corners when they became ensnarled in red tape.

He was now heir to a baronetcy. Sir Jacob had died suddenly in 1916, leaving his fortune to be divided between his three brothers. Edward Elias succeeded to the title. Victor, who had long regarded his uncle as a kind of father-substitute, mourned him deeply.

Both Sassoon houses, amply capitalized and enjoying strong international links, were able to adapt themselves smoothly when Bombay was transformed overnight into a huge port of embarkation. Mills and factories had been converted to turn out tents, boots, saddlery, gunnies and clothing for the military. From long experience of shipping, the two firms also increased their tonnage of wheat, tea and foodstuffs of all kinds to the United Kingdom. E. D. Sassoon, always more prominent in the oilseed business, now took an active part in supplying Henry Van den Bergh with the right kind of raw materials for his attempts to find a pure and edible margarine substitute for butter.

India was soon showing distinct war strain. The overseas casualty figures were heavy, and the Muslim population grew resentful at Allied operations against Turkey whose Caliph was revered as head of the Islamic brotherhood. Gandhi now arrived back from South Africa, where he had organized a passive resistance movement which could readily be adapted to Congress's growing demand for self-government. From his hermitage at Ahmedabad he began his campaign to relieve poverty and over-taxation among the peasants, even offering hope to the Untouchables. His activities, combined with those of Mrs Annie Besant and Tilak, who brought Hindus and Moslems together at Lucknow in a home rule programme, soon led to serious labour difficulties for the Sassoons and other factory-owners. The first outburst of patriotic loyalty had been succeeded by disillusionment as more and more men were sent overseas. Those who remained behind became openly bitter over food shortages and high prices.

The Sassoons were being forced to retrench in the Far East. The Manchu dynasty was succeeded by squabbling generals who offered little stability to western traders. China's millions, now over-taxed and famine-stricken, had grown far less attractive, either as workers or customers. The Great War had temporarily halted investment by the Allied nations, but Japan was quick to seize the advantage while Britain, France and Russia were fighting. Neutral but hopelessly disunited, China was therefore in no position to resist Tokyo's infamous Twenty-One Demands in 1915. Shantung and Kiaochow, previously held by the Germans, were handed over, together with valuable mining concessions in Manchuria. Japanese 'advisers' then attached themselves to the Government and claimed exclusive rights to invest capital in China. This was partially baulked by the Americans, who reminded Tokyo of the 'Open Door' principle, but the West had inevitably lost face by their apathy over Japanese aggression. Even in the Treaty Ports, traditional bastions of foreign trade, there were few serious attempts to boycott the Japanese when they started to pour manufactured goods across the narrow sea. They would henceforth finance the warlords in exchange for coal and steel works, factory sites and slices of customs revenue.

Sir Jacob was being missed even more in Shanghai than in Bombay itself. Silas Hardoon had never been easy to control, but his respect for the Chairman had ensured a kind of loyalty which would not be so readily given to others. He was now rich through property deals and planned to start on his own, once the Treaty Ports returned to normal. For some years he had seen little of Edward, the new baronet, and even less of Meyer. He envied them as directors who had drawn huge incomes for what he considered little effort.

When Sir Jacob died, his brother, Edward Elias, was sixty-three. He had long been more active in the firm than Meyer, but the routine tours of overseas branches became infrequent as his health declined. But for the war, he would probably have retired from the business altogether, remaining as nominal Chairman while his heir took over as Managing Director. His son's crash made such a plan unpractical, but he could not help dismissing Victor's duties at the Admiralty as mainly clerical and trivial. As head of the Bombay office with a turnover of several million a year, his son could surely make a more valuable contribution to the Allied effort. Besides, the doctors confirmed that bones healed faster in a dry climate.

Victor took not the slightest notice of these hints and arguments. With his brother, Hector, and Cousin Reggie both fighting in France, he had no intention of shedding his uniform and sitting out the war in the Taj Mahal Hotel or one of his late uncle's villas up in the hills. Although often in pain, his Service records show scarcely a day's sick leave. He was promoted to Flight-Commander in 1917, and then served for a year in Paris on Air Liaison with the Americans, when their first units arrived in Europe.

A few months after Sir Jacob's death, David Sassoon & Sons had also lost its Chairman. Frederick, the last surviving son of David Sassoon, died in May 1917. Leadership passed to Sir Albert's grandson, little David Gubbay. Frederick left £700,000 to his widow and two children, Muriel and Ronald. The latter also inherited his father's charm and remained unspoilt despite Eton. He was a high-standard club cricketer, tall and powerfully built. With his crinkly black hair and rather prominent nose, he was the most Jewish-looking of all the Sassoons, but did not share Philip's tortured psychosis on that account. He laughed a great deal and seemed altogether an intelligent, good-natured boy who, if he survived, might one day succeed David Gubbay. He was hit in the foot by shrapnel at Hill 60, and limped badly for the rest of his days.

One direct result of the war was a truce in old rivalries. For the first time since Abdullah and his brother had gone their separate ways in 1867, the Sassoons gave signs of unity through the freemasonry of suffering. As the casualty lists came through, branches long separated by ancient feuds and suspicions began to exchange messages of sympathy. Between London, Paris, Baghdad, Bombay, Shanghai and Hong Kong, a flow of letters kept everyone abreast of family tidings.

Sir Edward Elias Sassoon and his fellow-directors expressed sympathy when a Zeppelin bomb fell in Leadenhall Street and practically wrecked the offices of the other firm who had to move to King William Street. Mrs Arthur Sassoon's drawing-room in Albert Gate, where so many glittering receptions had been held in the 'nineties, was converted into a workshop and showroom for disabled officers and their families. Many were fitted out with clothes she had bought or collected. Even Rachel Beer found an outlet for her energies by arranging entertainments on behalf of the Rusthall V.A.D. Hospital. She equipped and endowed a ward named in her honour. Her good friend, Ben Greet, also presented pastorals every year in the grounds of Chancellor House for deserving causes.

At 32 Bruton Street, Flora was extending her philanthropies beyond refugees from Russia, Poland and devastated Belgium. She was surrounded by the usual complement of rabbis, scholars and community welfare officials, but many non-Jewish institutions also sought her help. Unlike her brothers-in-law, she refused to join the anti-Zionists and offered thanksgiving when Balfour made his historic Declaration in 1917, pledging government support for the establishment of a Jewish National Home in Palestine.

These had not been easy times for Flora, despite her wealth and social position. She would never remarry, but the years of widowhood were long and oppressive. She felt even more isolated after her daughter married David Ezra and settled permanently in Calcutta. They had been more like sisters than mother and daughter. The younger girl, Mozelle, was now completely bed-ridden but suffered her martyrdom with nobility. She wrote poetry and sketched between visits from her mother's corps of friends. She was enduring almost incessant agony from her spinal injury and could not easily be moved. She controlled her terror when the

Zeppelin engines throbbed overhead and London's anti-aircraft guns barked out almost before the shrill police whistles had died away.

Her brother, David, occupied a separate flat in the house with his young wife and two babies. He had married Selina Prins, the daughter of an Amsterdam diamond merchant, whose family pedigree included several distinguished scholars. His zeal for book-collecting had grown into an absorbing passion. His library of scrolls and rare Bibles now included manuscripts hunted down by his agents in the remotest corners of the Near East and Asia. Flora could deny him nothing, once paying £600 for a folio which he had set his heart on but could not afford. But his sister, Rachel Ezra, was even more helpful in keeping him posted about liturgical treasures in India, North Africa and China when the war halted his own travels.

They wrote to each other almost every day. He told her of his visit to a silent, almost deserted Ashley Park. All the five sons were in the Army. The only non-Regular among them, another David, had left Eton with an enlarged heart and studied under Professor Tonks at the Slade, where Augustus John was a contemporary and became his very close friend. He was turned down several times for military service but finally joined a Labour Corps and won his commission.

Joseph became even more of a recluse and had to be coaxed out of his library for his wife's Red Cross fêtes in the grounds. He died early in 1918. 'I had regard for him,' Flora's son reported feelingly to Bombay. 'As I know, he was the *only* member of the family who did not talk about *money* and had a liking for knowledge, education and literature. I was much struck, when he came to see my books, with his knowledge of Jewish things.'

He always felt closer in spirit to those who cherished the ancient traditions. British soldiers, who liberated Baghdad, also discovered that the Old Testament atmosphere had been preserved among the leading families. Stanley Rowland of the Devon Regiment recalls being billeted in the old Sassoon home, 'a fortress-like, flat-roofed building with strong outer walls without windows. There was a garden in the centre with an inside balcony extending along the four walls.' Some of the Sheikh Sason's descendants were still living in that house in 1918. They were kind to the soldiers and cooked them sweetmeats and other delicacies. The daughters mended their clothes but remained in semi-purdah behind shuttered windows above the courtyard garden. The army returned their hospitality by lending the Sassoons an Indian batman to heat their milk on the Sabbath.

Flora's daughter and son-in-law, David Ezra, welcomed numerous servicemen to 3 Kyd Street, Calcutta, where they were generously entertained, after a conducted tour of the private zoo with its leopards, cranes, zebras and golden turkeys. Apart from the baby bears who sported on the lawn, the star attraction was a well-stocked aviary. The mynahs were trained to croak 'God Save the King' and 'Three Cheers for the Prince of Wales'.

Flora's son was far too reserved to train a chorus of patriotic mynahs. He was intensely loyal and would always treasure the memory of riding in King Edward's Coronation Procession, but the war caused him a deep anguish of spirit. As a cadet in Bombay, he had learned to use a rifle, although without thought of ever going into battle. It would have been impossible for him to hurt, let alone kill, another human being. His poor health spared him this dilemma of conscience. Instead, he was found congenial work with the Admiralty Censors for whom he translated Hebrew and Arabic documents and helped to decode messages intercepted in the Middle East. He was later called in by the Ministry of Information to prepare a Judaeo–Arabic Proclamation which was distributed in Jerusalem as part of a propaganda drive against the enemy.

He became even more austere, living for the day when he could again withdraw to his Hebraic manuscripts. Meantime, he became openly contemptuous of those who, in his view, had betrayed their heritage. When Sybil married Lord Rocksavage, he wrote bitterly to his sister, 'I see all the Sassoons, one by one, going away from the pale. Another nail in the coffin.'

Flora was equally distressed but maintained some show of friendliness towards Philip, the David Gubbays and several of the E. D. Sassoon branch. Her son found them too worldly and superficial and, in the end, shut himself away whenever they were asked to dinner or some reception in Bruton Street. 'I told Mamma,' he wrote to his sister, 'that I never want to sit near these people – they make me feel quite ill for days. They follow in the steps of Esau.'

Unlike Philip, Victor and the Ashley Park youngsters, his own children would be given a strict religious education. They learned to speak Hebrew and Arabic, as well as English, from their cradle days. The boy would *not* be sent to Eton, but to a Jewish seminary in North London to study for the rabbinate. Their father discouraged any snobbish pride of ancestry.

During the war, when Rachel Ezra sent her little nephew an elegant pair of pyjamas for his birthday, her brother thought it necessary to chide her. 'I do not think it right that he should sleep in silk suits – much too extravagant – and, after all, what is he?' Unconsciously, he was almost echoing the remark made long ago by Alfred Sassoon when he sent his disreputable camels along to Kensington Gore!

Chapter Thirteen

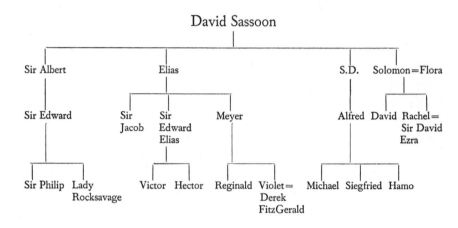

Since a subaltern's expectation of life in the trenches was said to be only about three weeks, the Sassoons were remarkably fortunate in suffering only one fatal casualty. Siegfried's brother, Hamo, had hurried back from the Argentine to enlist with the Royal Engineers. He was hit by a sniper's bullet at Gallipoli and died after having his leg amputated. Siegfried found some relief from his grief by composing a commemorative poem, 'To My Brother'. The verses express the nobility of martyrdom and selfless courage without the savage protest yet to come. While in training at Liverpool for his commission, he wrote to a family friend, Mrs Leeds, in May 1915, 'I shall never forget the beauty of the country as I saw it from the train between London and Wrexham a week ago. It seemed nothing but golden-green powdered with gold with splashes of white hawthorn. Is it that one never appreciated these things to the full, until their existence is threatened? Here it is all chimneys and drill book and sore feet, but the world is laid away with all its cheery little worries!'

He was posted to the First Battalion of the Royal Welch Fusiliers and, after the battle of Loos, found himself billeted with Robert Graves, whose war poems he liked but considered, at that time, unnecessarily raw in flavour! They became friendly. The other member of the trio was David Thomas, a former rugger-player, who died painfully soon afterwards from a bullet through the throat. It grieved Siegfried whose mood quickly turned to anger. 'He went out on patrol looking for Germans to kill', Graves has written in *Goodbye to All That*. That evocative little classic, together with the memoirs, poems and letters of Blunden, Owen, Osbert Sitwell and many others, all recall the young self-tortured subaltern with kindly affection. For generations of readers, however, his own verse and the sensitive Sherston trilogy remain the best guides to Sassoon's progress. Through them one can follow the happy-go-lucky idealist who gave the Germans 'every chance to pot him', as he later told Arnold Bennett, and finally became the angry satirist whose poems were like gobbets of flesh impaled on barbed wire.

The salient facts of his war career are now very familiar and need only be recalled in brief. In his early fighting days he was still very much the wild steeplechaser. His men in the Battalion nicknamed him 'Mad Jack' for his courage and utter disregard of rule-of-thumb tactics. On the eve of the Somme offensive, he took a few grenades and made a solo attack by daylight on a German trench which was holding a copse on the edge of Mametz Wood. The enemy rushed off and Siegfried then sat down and calmly read a book of verse in their trench. He did not bother to report to his C.O. when he got back.

War was still an exciting, if sometimes dangerous, game for him. Wire-cutting by day was 'rather like going out to weed a neglected garden after being warned that there might be a tiger among the gooseberry bushes', as he wrote afterwards in *Memoirs of an Infantry Officer*. Another of his delights was to throw accurate hand-grenades at close range. 'He was always a fine fieldsman at cover point,' comments his brother, Michael. With equal coolness he brought in a badly wounded lance-corporal under intense enemy fire. It won him his Military Cross.

He was always brimming with a cheerful dare-devilry which gave him no time for self-questioning. The carnage only began to seem hopeless and tragic after the raids, when he was back among the corpses and the shell-shocked zombies. His depression, festering worse than any attack of trench mouth, deepened after a bout of gastric fever. A high temperature suggested lung trouble, and he was sent home for treatment and observation. He was visited in hospital by his old friend, Robbie Ross, who introduced him to the Morrells, a couple disenchanted by the war and actively preaching pacifism.

Lady Ottoline, a half-sister of the Duke of Portland, lived with her husband Philip, the Liberal M.P. for Burnley, at Garsington near Oxford. In their grey-stoned Tudor manor house overlooking a superb lawn framed by ilex trees and purpling elms, with a lily pond to lend a dreamy touch of escapism, they nursed many a wounded rebel spirit. The art critic, Clive Bell, was given a job on their farm because his conscience would not allow him to fight. Many other pacifists found sanctuary at Garsington, including the Jewish painter, Mark Gertler, Lytton Strachey and Bertrand Russell.

Their gracious mansion, with its Samarkand rugs, lacquer cabinets and refectory tables, seemed almost a mirage to Siegfried Sassoon after the charred battlefields. There was always a smell of incense in that house, and croquet on the lawns outside. Lady Ottoline herself was vivid and at first overpowering, but he came to appreciate her warmth. Tall and plumpish, she sported exotic clothes, baggy pantaloons with an oriental caftan, ropes of pearls and scarab knuckle-dusters. Her bobbed marmalade hair was usually crammed into a vast hat over flashing greenish eyes.

Siegfried was gauche and shyer than her more articulate pets, 'Bertie' Russell and Strachey, but she drew him out and tried to persuade him that his poetry could do much to rouse the people against the endless slaughter. His attitude, however, was far less clear-cut than that of the Morrell band of conscientious objectors. He shared their bitterness, but they had not wallowed in the trenches with dead horses and doomed men.

Garsington was soothing for a time. Siegfried bathed in Lady Ottoline's well-intentioned flattery but soon grew restless. Neither his horror nor his outraged idealism would ever quite leave him after the Somme. It might suit Clive Bell to milk cows at Garsington, and one respected Russell's readiness to go to prison for his articles, but Siegfried felt that his place was with his men.

> When I'm asleep, dreaming and lulled and warm—
> They come, the homeless ones, the noiseless dead.

After several weeks of inactivity in the frozen mud, the bells of hell suddenly went ting-a-ling. The Company was sent to reinforce the Cameronians who had been driven out of some hard-won trenches on the Hindenburg Line. Siegfried's platoon went over the top but was turned back with heavy losses by a strong machine-gun team. When his lance-corporal was shot dead by his side, he threw off his tin hat and equipment, took a couple of grenades and again went out, this time with only six men. He got near enough to see the faces of the enemy in field-grey before a bullet hit him in the neck, but he was still able to crawl forward and fling his grenades. He was recommended for the D.S.O., but his platoon hoped for a V.C. He went unrewarded, as the Highlanders were soon afterwards driven out of the recaptured trench.

He was in no mood to worry about decorations as he lay in an English hospital bed. His neck wound was slight, but he also had trench fever. Worse, a black desperation had settled over him. There seemed no end to the massacre. Verses yet unwritten were now revolving in a brain almost unhinged by indignation and his sense of impotence. Wandering along Piccadilly, he was haunted by visions of corpses. Friends became alarmed and pulled strings, hoping that he would take some snug billet at home. *The Old Huntsman* volume of poems had meantime appeared, dedicated to Thomas Hardy. It shocked readers who would have preferred a more romanticized picture of the Front. The bitter jokes and down-to-earth similes were specially condemned by women nurtured on Rupert Brooke. Armchair warriors and jingoists were spared no more than the generals who had flung thousands of men into the Battle of Arras.

Yet the collection was snapped up in the shops and had to be reprinted several times. It was quoted, recited and debated by many who disagreed violently with the author's views. Among them was the Minister of Munitions, Winston Churchill, who soon memorized most of the poems. This gave 'Eddie' Marsh a flash of inspiration. He persuaded his master to meet the soldier-poet whose verses he admired even if he did not approve their sentiments. Siegfried could not guess why the Minister wished to see him, but was curious to meet a man whose personal qualities he respected more than his political philosophy.

Marsh relished his own kindly machiavellianism. He sensed that Churchill was a shrewd enough politician to appreciate hidden benefits in Sassoon's poems. They had infuriated the generals but might have a propaganda value in reminding civilians, particularly slacking factory workers, of what the men at the Front were enduring. Marsh misled himself, however, into imagining that his chief could ever take a pacifist under his wing, still less that the poet would accept work from the Ministry of Munitions.

Siegfried spent an hour with Churchill while Admiral Fisher kicked his heels outside, furious at being kept waiting for some neurotic verse-spinner who was upsetting Service morale. Within a few minutes, Marsh knew that his little scheme had no hope of success. He sat back to enjoy the Minister's performance, although a little sorry for Siegfried who had no hope of checking the torrential monologue.

Churchill had started off genially enough. He chatted about fox-hunting and praised the poetic qualities of *The Old Huntsman*. He quoted from it aptly and accurately, smiling in a friendly way as he recited a well-phrased couplet. But the mood changed just as abruptly. With a cigar clamped in his jaws, he began marching up and down the room while he harangued his visitor on the glories of fighting a just war. He stopped only to glare at Marsh, whose monocle kept popping into his lap as his master's voice grew more rasping. The 'interview' ended with a characteristic curtain line. Churchill pulled up in front of Siegfried's chair and barked angrily, 'War is the normal occupation of Man.' He then paused to add with a grin, 'War, *and* gardening.'

Siegfried escaped with relief to Garsington where his volume of poems was being passed from hand to hand. Lady Ottoline smothered him with kindness and reminded him of his duty to write even stronger verse when he was well again. It would not be easy. The 'booby-trapped idealist', as he ironically called himself, was racked by an almost hopeless dilemma. 'Siegfried's unconquerable idealism changed direction with his environment,' Robert Graves later wrote perceptively in *Goodbye to All That*. 'He varied between happy warrior and bitter pacifist.' To continue his holy war on War through his poems, he would have been forced either to masquerade as a desk soldier or, even more repulsively, as an instructor training others for the slaughter. These subterfuges seemed to him as distasteful as laying down one's arms, which many would have misinterpreted as cowardice. While he paced the orchard at Weirleigh, the clear sounds of gunfire from across the Channel seemed to call him back to his companions.

He had to make his position clear. In July 1917, he addressed 'A Soldier's Declaration' to his commanding officer and sent a copy to the *Bradford Pioneer*. 'I am making this statement as an act of wilful defiance of military authority, because I believe that the war is being deliberately prolonged by those who have the power to end it. I am a soldier, convinced that I am acting on behalf of soldiers. I believe that this war, upon which I entered as a war of defence and liberation, may now become a war of aggression and conquest. I have seen and endured the sufferings of the troops, and I can no longer be a party to prolong these sufferings for ends which I believe to be evil and unjust. I am not protesting against the conduct of the war, but against the political errors and insincerities for which the fighting men are being sacrificed.'

He then reported to his Battalion H.Q. at Litherland and waited for the storm to burst. His letter was published, but *nothing* happened. Driven almost out of his mind by an aching sense of futility, he flung his Military Cross ribbon into the Mersey. He did not know that a question was about to be asked in the House which would probably lead to his court-martial and imprisonment.

Graves saw the pity and futility of it all. His own admirable account does only modest justice to his selfless initiative in the affair. He guessed that his friend was now facing great personal anguish and almost certain punishment for a brave deed which had made less impact than a single blistering sonnet. Aided by Marsh, he began a campaign to 'rig' a medical board for Siegfried who, they pleaded, was mentally overwrought and not responsible for his actions. As a result, he was treated as the victim of psychological shell-shock and sent to a convalescent home near Edinburgh, Craiglockhart, which he promptly renamed 'Dottyville'. Under the care of a distinguished neurologist, W. H. R. Rivers, who urged him to resume his poetry as part of the therapy, he began slowly to calm down but without changing his attitude to the war. It also helped him to meet another patient, Wilfred Owen, whom he encouraged to write poetry.

They were good for each other. Owen was lapsing into a bitter melancholia about the war ('teaching Christ to lift his cross by numbers'), but Siegfried made him sit down and write verse for *The Hydra*, the hospital magazine to which he was also contributing. 'He had the profile of an Egyptian King,' Owen wrote to a friend, but no Pharaoh was more cruel in the poems he composed at Craiglockhart. Soon to be collected under the title *Counter-Attack*, they show contempt for civilian apathy and war fever alike, but his most savage indictments were reserved for brasshats, both in Whitehall and at G.H.Q. He despised the 'Scarlet Majors at the Base' with a special loathing after an experience at the Hotel de la Poste in Rouen. Eager for a hot bath and a meal, he found that it had been put out of bounds to troops from the line so that the Staff might not sully themselves. He could never forget the haughty young red tabs in shiny leather boots and tinkling spurs who were supplementing the hotel menu with hampers from Fortnum and Mason.

It eased a little of the poison out of his system to contrast their 'puffy petulant faces' with the ghosts who never left him at Craiglockhart.

> I see them in foul dug-outs, gnawed by rats,
> And in the ruined trenches, lashed with rain,
> Dreaming of things they did with balls and bats
> And mocked by hopeless longing to regain
> Bank-holidays, and picture-shows, and spats,
> And going to the office in the train.

As soon as he felt better, he called on his publisher, William Heinemann, and persuaded him to send a copy of *The Old Huntsman* with his compliments, to the Commander-in-Chief of the B.E.F. He was of course perfectly aware that it would go through the hands of his cousin, Haig's vigilant secretary, Sir Philip Sassoon.

Philip's advance to Haig's side had been almost as smooth as his election to Parliament. Many thought it odd at first that this taciturn and abrupt professional should appoint a rather foppish chocolate soldier as his equerry. But as the war went on, their qualities would become more and more complementary until each was able to read the other's mind with considerable accuracy. Both were former members of the Bullingdon at

Oxford and also shared a passion for polo. Haig had served as a subaltern with the 17th Hussars in India and returned there as Inspector of Cavalry when the Sassoon name was at its zenith in Bombay and Poona. He later became A.D.C. to King Edward and was one of the few commoners ever to be married in the private chapel at Buckingham Palace. His snobbish streak made him specially affable towards those close to the Throne.

He was perfectly aware of Philip's past family connections with the Court, not only because of his uncles and his parents but through Leo de Rothschild, whom Haig had met at a Swiss spa when both were nursing sick livers. They became close personal friends. When Haig was appointed C.-in-C. in December 1915, it was from Leo that he first heard the news, a full day before Mr Asquith informed him officially. That Christmas, Leo sent over fifty pairs of fur-lined gloves to be distributed among the Staff.

Haig, who did not like politicians, found his secretary useful in his wrangles with the War Office and Number Ten. Philip was tactful and had an oriental gift for keeping secrets. Besides, he had valuable ties with the political *élite*. Mrs Asquith, the P.M.'s wife, had been his mother's dearest friend and never forgot the death-bed promise to look after his welfare. The Foreign Secretary, Sir Edward Grey, was another old family connection, while Balfour, First Lord of the Admiralty, had known Philip from the cradle.

Haig's temperament needed the very emollient which his private secretary was able to apply at all hours. His soothing manner and flow of chatter rallied him from the dour moods which often terrified his Staff. Even senior officers began to use Philip as a go-between when the Chief was gruff and almost unapproachable. Moreover, Haig became so meticulous over detail that military critics put down many of his misjudgements to a railway time-table complex. Philip Sassoon, who had never previously needed to work by the clock, soon developed an orderliness that came to be valued by his master.

Philip loathed the stench and ugliness of war, but his isolation from the others at G.H.Q. made him bottle his emotions even when he grieved over the casualty lists. All the gay 'New Elizabethans' had in turn fallen in battle. Julian Grenfell was killed near the Ypres and Menin Road, and laughing Billy only a mile away. Charles Lister and Patrick Shaw-Stewart had served together in the celebrated Hood Battalion of the Royal Naval Division. The former died in Salonika, after being thrice wounded, and Shaw-Stewart survived Gallipoli, only to fall at Cambrai. Another casualty was gentle Edward Horner with whom Philip had played so many sets of tennis at drowsy Mells, where bearded Sir John loped after a stray ball and his wife called them in to tea and muffins.

He turned to books for relief and kept urging Mrs Beresford, his London secretary, and the faithful Mrs Belloc Lowndes to send out novels and biographies to distract him from the dead horses, mud and butchery. He found delicious oblivion in Proust whose *Du Côté de Chez Swann*, published only a few months before the war, he read and re-read in French. He was fascinated by the author's personality and impatient to meet him.

More pressing anxieties accumulated as soon as Lloyd George ousted Asquith and began to criticize Haig's strategy. It was now Philip's thankless and often uncongenial duty to maintain some facade of peace between his crusty master and a P.M. who used every devious method to by-pass him. The first clash came over strategy. Lloyd George, supported by Churchill, was eager to concentrate on the Middle East, while Haig advocated an all-out offensive on the Western Front. It became impossible to reconcile two men with such contempt and personal hatred for each other. From their very first meeting in January 1916, Haig had dismissed his enemy as 'astute and cunning, with much energy and push, but I should think unreliable'. After the Passchendaele disaster, Lloyd George used to assure his confidants that 'we could beat the Germans if only we could get Haig to lead them'.

A stickler for punctuality himself, Haig could not tolerate the P.M.'s notorious casualness over appointments and accused him of only respecting the feelings of friendly journalists or newsreel cameramen. Philip had to arrange his chief's secret journeys back and forth across the Channel, ensuring that there was no breach of security or the slightest hitch which might further upset the delicate balance essential for these meetings with the War Cabinet. After one stormy crossing from Boulogne in June 1916, they had stepped ashore at Dover where Philip was handed a telegram addressed to Sir Douglas. It stated that Kitchener and most of the crew had drowned when the cruiser H.M.S. *Hampshire* struck a mine off the Orkneys.

Apart from meeting boat trains and acting as a glorified traffic control officer at H.Q., Philip had to lobby continuously. His master had friends in high places, notably the King, who had openly snubbed Lloyd George by making Haig a Field-Marshal on New Year's Day 1917. But the C.-in-C. was aware that he could never be entirely safe while his enemy was at Number Ten and bent on assuming supreme command of the war. He therefore found it prudent to canvass a powerful mouthpiece, Lord Northcliffe. The proprietor of *The Times* and the *Daily Mail* had at first supported Lloyd George against Asquith and exposed the scandalous lack of shells, but his enthusiasm for the Welshman was fading fast. After a visit to G.H.Q. in 1916, his newspapers started to snipe at Whitehall's 'shirt-sleeved politicians' whom he accused of hampering the hardworked commanders in the field. Haig, delighted with an ally who might counter the P.M.'s staunch propagandists, Beaverbrook and Riddell, made much of him. They attended the Scottish Church together, and Haig afterwards allowed Northcliffe to air his views freely, with Philip supplying all the right cues.

The 'enemy' was not deceived. David Davies, the wealthy Welsh squire who served as Lloyd George's wartime P.P.S., used to keep his chief primed with gossip. He soon warned him that Haig was 'trying to get at the Press through that little blighter, Sassoon'. Philip had proved an inspired choice for the delicate rôle of intermediary between two such sharply opposed temperaments as Haig and Northcliffe. Even in his undergraduate days he had shown a flair for expressing himself in the witty little innuendoes that made him a valued gossip. He had since developed a remarkable talent for dropping hints with diplomatic finesse while playing the courtier to perfection. He encouraged Northcliffe to write down his private thoughts and suggestions for winning the war, promising to pass them on to the C.-in-C. Northcliffe, flattered, began to produce what he described coyly as his 'Jottings from the Home Front'. He was critical of Lloyd George's plan for creating a diversion in Salonika and praised Haig's steadfastness in keeping to his frontal-assault strategy in Flanders. He also deprecated the 'subtle poison' which Churchill was pouring into the Prime Minister's ear.

It became Philip's congenial task to act as postman in this exchange of pleasantries. He kept reminding Northcliffe of the C.-in-C.'s gratitude for his support and understanding, adding a gloss or two of his own. 'You cannot write enough,' he assured the Press Lord, who rarely failed him. After one of Northcliffe's tours of the Front, Haig reports to his wife that 'Lord N. was much pleased with his visit and asked me to let Sassoon send him a line should anything appear in *The Times* which was not altogether to my liking.'

The French generals and politicians were harder nuts. Aware that they could count on the British Prime Minister, they became more obstructive when Haig pressed his views on Allied strategy. In this atmosphere of prickly suspicion, it often fell to Philip Sassoon to keep the peace with the Quai d'Orsay and the French High Command. He spoke their language with idiomatic grace and had an inborn instinct for the sophisticated niceties of protocol. He was naturally Francophile, and it was no disadvantage to have had a French Rothschild mother. It gave him kinship with the banking barons as well as other influential figures in the *Almanach de Gotha*. He was, moreover, a rich English 'milord' who served enchanting dinners even during the asperities of war. The French showed their appreciation by giving him several decorations. If his style struck them as a little too exquisite and *fin de siècle* for a soldier, they preferred it to the brusqueness of most British staff officers who plainly resented being treated as subordinates by their allies. Le Capitaine Sassoon, although *snob enfin*, as one of his own Rothschild cousins described him, was not a career soldier and rather less touchy about such matters.

His brother-officers were not so tolerant. Robert Blake echoes the views of most war historians in his introduction to Haig's private papers: 'Aesthete, politician, millionaire, that semi-Oriental figure flitted like some exotic bird of paradise against the sober background of G.H.Q. He was not liked by the others in Haig's entourage but he amused Haig and helped him in his relations with the political world.' It was a slightly unfair judgement. Regular soldiers were naturally envious of a rich amateur, but he deflected part of Haig's unpopularity to himself when the politicians and military critics began to take pot-shots at his chief. In the final analysis, his rôle was perhaps more influential and often less easygoing than that of a mere 'Scarlet Major at the Base'.

He worked strenuously behind the scenes. When Haig had to meet Painlevé for a series of conferences, Philip arranged the dinners and time-tables. None was more adept in working out the smallest details of transport, protocol and precedence. He was equally gifted at assembling facts and presenting them concisely to his busy master. It would be Philip, rather than a senior officer, whom Haig chose to sound out Clemenceau on an early offensive.

While the French were being butchered at Verdun, Joffre motored over to G.H.Q. He pleaded with Haig to extend the British share of the line and advance the date of the coming offensive on the Somme. They finally decided on the strategy that would slaughter a million men on both sides for precious little military gain. During the discussions, Joffre took time off to present Sir Philip Sassoon and Lt.-Col. Alan Fletcher, Haig's A.D.C., with the Legion of Honour.

The British C.-in-C. was equally appreciative. In the last of three highly complimentary dispatches, he paid special tribute to Philip, 'by whose loyal and devoted assistance a great burden of work has been lifted from my shoulders'. There was some resentment, however, when he also recommended him for a C.M.G. The War Office at once protested that precedent excluded anyone below Major receiving this decoration. Haig promptly raised his secretary to the qualifying rank.

Several staff officers had suffered frozen feet and trench fever on the Somme. They naturally failed to appreciate such rewards for what they considered the comfortable duties of a civilian in uniform. It seemed even more incongruous to them that the impeccably breeched and booted Sassoon should be chosen to hand out Haig's Order of the Day on April 19

1918: 'With our backs to the wall and believing in the justice of our cause, each one of us must fight to the end.' Haig saw so little wrong with this procedure that he afterwards presented his secretary with the historic document as a war souvenir.

The Commander-in-Chief's attitude was understandable. A lonely man with terrifying responsibilities, he was being harassed by his French allies and shot at by the politicians at home. He needed to be constantly reassured and entertained. His war diaries reveal a remarkable quota of prattle and social trivia. In April 1917, a month when a million tons of British and neutral shipping had been lost and Allied morale on land was at a low ebb, he writes cheerfully: 'I walked with General Davidson and Philip Sassoon in the Bois. On return to the hotel about 7 p.m. I find an invitation to dine with the Minister of War. So Philip saw Painlevé's A.D.C. at once and made my excuses, and we dined quietly at the hotel.' (General Sir John Davidson, an old Sandhurst product and Boer War veteran, was Director of Military Operations in France. He attended most of Haig's conferences with the French political and military leaders, working closely with Philip Sassoon. They had a regard for each other's qualities which would have unexpected results after the war.)

During 1917, a fateful and anxious year, Philip was crossing the Channel so often that he flew whenever an aircraft was handy. The speed and convenience exhilarated him so much that he made up his mind to have his own plane after the war. Most of his leaves were shared with his chief, and Haig had the use of the Park Lane mansion for seeing various members of the War Cabinet. To cheer him up after a depressing conference with Lloyd George at Number Ten, often over an early breakfast in the small panelled room on the first floor, Philip would arrange tasteful luncheons at which the C.-in-C. could exchange views with Balfour, Jellicoe, Smuts and others. He would then withdraw discreetly to accompany Lady Haig on afternoon shopping expeditions or go off to tea with his sister, Sybil, and Leo de Rothschild.

Philip's leaves were not often spent in frivolity. He was always on call, but had the support of his sister who acted as hostess in Park Lane when she could escape from her own duties in the Women's Royal Naval Service. Her drive and organizing ability earned her promotion to Assistant Principal. It was not a sinecure. 'She was one of the most delightful and amusing people I have ever met,' said Dame Katharine Furse, the Director. Between them, they helped to raise the morale and prestige of a Service constantly exposed to prejudice.

Haig, once the idol of the Press, suffered bad publicity as soon as the tide of war turned against him. He had even fallen out with Northcliffe, who was hoping to become War Secretary, which Haig considered a terrifying prospect for both Army and Empire. An efficient system of public relations became more vital. Major Sir Philip Sassoon was given the task of conducting V.I.P.s round the battlefields. He had few equals as a cicerone. The Editor of *The Times*, Wickham Steed, the King of Montenegro, Balfour and the Prince of Monaco were among the many tourists he escorted round the 'sights'. These always included selected stretcher-cases, with the distant rumble of guns lending a picturesque accompaniment before the parties were taken off to dine in some château. Haig's old brandy usually rounded off the meal, but he was so sparing with it that the gesture only added to his reputation for being a 'dour, high-minded Scot', in the words of the Prince of Wales. The latter was serving with the Guards Division and thus often came into friendly contact with the C.-in-C.'s elegant secretary.

Philip needed all his charm to handle V.I.P.s and the awkward situations from which Haig recoiled. In February 1916 the Attorney-General, F. E. Smith, visited Headquarters but carelessly neglected to carry the pass compulsory in a military zone. He was stopped by a sentry and taken to the Hotel du Commerce at St Omer where he was locked up for the night. Philip sent the pass, but it was not smoothed over until he managed to persuade Haig to apologize over a convivial luncheon.

He found it more congenial to arrange tours by war artists like Professor Henry Tonks, 'Will' Rothenstein and, in particular, Sargent. He met his old family friend at Boulogne and motored him over to G.H.Q. where he was installed in an austere, tin-roofed hut which Philip made habitable with some gay scraps of curtain material and a hard-won electric heater. 'Philip Sassoon has been awfully keen and useful,' the painter reported back to his friend and biographer, Evan Charteris. Florid and bearded, with eyes that bulged in his angrier moments, he became a familiar figure in the Mess, where he was often joined by the cadaverous Tonks. Both kept serious working hours, but some thought, a little uncharitably, that Sargent selected his military subjects with all the discrimination of a fashionable painter. Sitting under an umbrella and invariably chain-smoking, he sketched an endless variety of high-ranking sitters, starting with General O'Ryan of New York. He also went round the trenches by tank in the foulest weather, 'looping the loop generally', as Philip after-wards recalled. More often, he could be seen wheeling a barrow-load of canvases amid the ruins of Ypres and Arras where he was busily making sketches for several realistic studies. 'Gassed' much impressed Haig who thought it conveyed the full horror of Germany's poison weapon.

Philip enjoyed the unconsciously comic meetings between his chief and the painter. Sargent used to splutter rather than converse, heaving like a stricken rhino before painfully chopping out a sentence, while

Haig was rarely articulate enough to make a final point without waving a helpless hand. The result, according to Philip, was 'a series of little pantomimes'. They became his favourite party pieces in later years.

His war had not been too uncomfortable until one leave in Park Lane when he fell victim to the Spanish influenza epidemic of 1918 which killed so many of the civilian population. He heard that Siegfried had left Craiglockhart and was back in the line, but gave no sign of any personal interest in him and refused to be drawn into any argument about his poetry.

He even hid his feelings behind an imperial calm when *The Old Huntsman* arrived at G.H.Q. His outward indifference to that hotly discussed volume confirmed an impression that he was not related to the poet. His general attitude made some question whether he was, in fact, a Jew.* Early in 1917 he had made a speech at the Folkestone Town Hall in which he assured his constituents that 'we have got the finest army our race has yet produced'. Nobody in the hall or among the Anglo–Jewish community beyond had much doubt of his meaning.

Siegfried had finally convinced Dr Rivers and himself that he could only recover his sanity and self-respect by going back into action. It might be futile, but would at least have more reality than his life at 'Dottyville'. He was posted to Palestine with the 25th Battalion of the Royal Welch Fusiliers. They were recalled to France in the summer of 1918.

His war closed with an appropriate act of quixotic bravery. Within a few hours of arriving in the line near St Vinant, he could not resist making another of his solitary forays into no-man's-land, this time to make a sketch of the enemy's dispositions! On his return, he was sharply rebuked by his brigadier for going outside the wire without permission. Typically, he ignored this and risked a court-martial to go out again and fill in a small point which he had overlooked in his earlier sketch.

He had almost crawled back when a sniper's bullet hit him in the head. Only his tin hat deflected the bullet from penetrating the brain, but the wound was still bad enough to end his fighting days.

He was sent home to the luxurious comfort of the American Women's Hospital in Lancaster Gate, only a few yards from Reuben Sassoon's old home. He was visited by the Morrells and petted by Lady Randolph Churchill who acted as a sort of honorary head matron. It did not stop him from writing more passionately about the war. He wept bitterly over the death of Wilfred Owen who had died only a few days before the

* The historian of 601 Squadron of which Philip later became Commodore, still described him as a Parsee in 1964.

Armistice when, as Siegfried wrote ironically, 'everybody suddenly burst out singing'.

One can appreciate Philip's embarrassment at having this wildly pacifist poet for a kinsman, but less easy to understand his seeming lack of interest in another heroic cousin, Reggie Sassoon, Meyer's son. On a particularly foul day in 1917, with a cold October wind blistering the cheeks of men just out of the mud at Boesinghe, Field-Marshal Sir Douglas Haig had inspected the Second Battalion, Irish Guards. Behind him rode Sir Philip Sassoon. Among those on parade was Captain R. Sassoon, M.C., whose uniform hung on a scarecrow frame. He peered at the inspecting cavalcade without, of course, giving any sign of recognizing his cousin who trotted by with parade-ground elegance. When asked about him afterwards, he simply murmured, 'Major Sassoon is a highly polished soldier.'

Reggie's war service had been almost as painful as Siegfried's. They were not dissimilar in temperament. Each was a passionate horse-lover and fond of steeplechasing. Both were shy and ill-at-ease in company, but possessed outstanding physical courage. In Reggie's case, however, this was uncomplicated by subtleties of conscience. It was 'Mad Jack' all over again, but without the pacifist verse. Nobody laughed louder than Reggie when he short-sightedly fell into shell-holes. After being wounded at Loos, he was always in the thick of the bloodiest fighting of the war. In his *Irish Guards in the Great War*, Kipling rightly said that 'when an officer dropped and could not get up again without help, he was assumed to be unfit for work – but not before'.

Captain Sassoon symbolized that spirit. He became ill in 1917, and fretted miserably in the Entrenching Battalion, 'where his heart was not', in Kipling's words. He kept sending his C.O. pitiful letters of protest, repeatedly urging his fitness to return to the Front. Col. Greer finally took pity on his 'stout-hearted savage' and rescued him from inactive service behind the lines.

On August 20 he was back commanding No. 3 Company at Boesinghe, a sector which the Brigade was trying to hold with the help of the Scots Guards. A stubborn machine-gun post was inflicting such heavy damage that Reggie decided to make a flank attack by Lewis-gun fire. He went over the top with only a small party and captured the post, killing seven Germans and taking five others prisoner. This made it possible for the Scots to advance and overwhelm a concrete emplacement which had defied them for days. He was awarded the Military Cross 'for conspicuous gallantry and devotion to duty . . . His dash and initiative at a critical moment were worthy of the highest praise'.

A fortnight later, he was badly burned and blistered by the new mustard-gas shells, but his colonel knew better than to take him out of the line. He was promoted Assistant Adjutant. Nobody now ragged and joked about the ugly duckling, short-sighted and reserved, who used to sit by himself in the Mess. He made friends with another Guards Captain, Derek Barrington FitzGerald, who had been transferred from the First to the Second Battalion and was badly wounded in the savage fighting of March 1918. FitzGerald, a member of an old Irish family and grandson of a Lord Justice of Appeal, was a personable and intelligent young man with much charm. On one of his leaves he met Reggie's sister, Violet, whom he married before the end of the war. It proved a remarkably long-lived and happy union, although the announcement was greeted with disfavour in Bruton Street. Already irritated by Sybil's marriage, Flora's son was even more disturbed that Meyer should allow his daughter to marry a non-Jew. He had little doubt that the pious Sir Jacob would never have given his consent. He reported as much to his sister, Mrs Ezra, adding piously, 'May God protect us from temptations.'

Siegfried had ridden to war as a happy-go-lucky steeplechaser. He emerged a poet. His future seemed predictable, if less glamorous than that of his cousins, Victor and Philip, who would evidently enjoy the frivolous life of rich young men. In November 1918 nobody could foresee that the crippled, but easygoing, Victor would raise his firm to a pinnacle of world power and influence. It seemed even more improbable that Philip would become the first Sassoon to make a mark in British politics.

This came about by transferring his allegiance from Haig to Lloyd George.

Part Four (1919–1931)

Chapter Fourteen

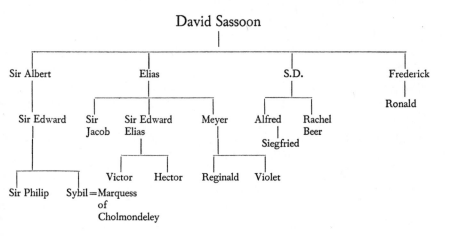

David Sassoon

Philip developed a sweet tooth for celebrities during his war service. It had made him feel a part of history, if only in elegant parenthesis. With his approaching demobilization in March 1919, it seemed that he would become merely another M.P. He had prudently presented himself to Hythe as a Coalition Unionist candidate in the November General Election. He was returned with a spanking majority after an embarrassing rumour that his cousin might put up against him. It was complete non-sense. A family brawl was the last thing to appeal to Siegfried. He had only joined in the 'Hang the Kaiser' Election because he was sceptical of Lloyd George's pledge to make 'a fit country for heroes to live in'. He stayed for a while with the Morrells who fed his Armistice fever of idealism and stimulated him to soldier on for social justice. Needing a fresh no-man's-land, he discovered one at Blackburn where Philip Snowden was fighting on the pacifist ticket. He had not given a second thought to standing for any constituency, least of all Hythe. He was not only a hesitant speaker who tripped over slogans and dried up when he became emotional, but would have been hopeless at shaking hands with electors or patting babies' heads. It was misery enough chasing about the Black-burn slums in his corduroy trousers, check shirt and flaming red tie. Voters jeered openly at pacifism and hailed Lloyd George as the man who won the war. To get a hearing at all, Siegfried had reluctantly put on his uniform and battle ribbons. As it was, he narrowly escaped being man-handled.

It was more fun to join the Reform Club and go about town with Eddie Marsh who knew everyone. They lunched at the Savoy with T. E. Lawrence who looked every inch the romantic colonel but talked seriously about literature. He wrote afterwards to Robert Graves that 'if any of my generation has earned harbour after storm, it is Siegfried Sassoon'. The poet also found sympathetic company at Osbert Sitwell's delightful house in Chelsea where he spent long hours discussing the collected edition of Wilfred Owen's verse which Edith was helping him to prepare. This was no easy task since several of the manuscripts were hardly decipherable and still bore traces of Flanders mud.

He was welcomed like a homecoming hero in Hanover Terrace, even though Sir Edmund Gosse could still be cantankerous. 'What are *you* doing here?' he snapped at him one afternoon. 'We don't want *you*, I'm sure! We're not talking about horses.' He had then taken Edith Sitwell aside for a *tête-à-tête*.

Siegfried grew resigned to such rudeness which he accepted with the gentle good humour that had survived the war. He was less tolerant of new rich grandees and never ceased to poke fun at the pompous. In years to come, his friends would be mystified by the odd-sounding pseudonym, 'Tak Yussuf Hoff', which he used for his poem about Blickley Hall. Soon after the war, he had gone to look over the place which had recently been let. A footman took one glance at the tall, rather unkempt visitor in hairy tweeds and said haughtily, 'Take yourself off.'

He was delighted when Gerald Gould suddenly offered him the literary editorship of the *Daily Herald*. This former trade union strike-sheet had emerged under George Lansbury as a socialist paper to which radical intellectuals like G. D. H. Cole, Osbert Sitwell and W. J. Turner con-tributed. The pay was only £5 a week, but Siegfried enjoyed coming up from Weirleigh on Tuesdays and Fridays, ignoring his mother's plain contempt for 'that rabid and pestilential rag'. He wrote literary notes or 'appreciations' and commissioned reviews and articles from Walter de la Mare, E. M. Forster, Robert Graves, H. M. T mlinson and other friends. The paper would finally be handed over to the T.U.C. and the Labour Party, but by then he would have tired of journalistic routine. Little by little, he had also grown wary of militant trade-unionism and rather less confident of the millennium.

His temperament had found an outlet in writing poetry and lobbing hand-grenades at the Germans. The Armistice left him in a vacuum which could only be filled temporarily by scribbling pieces for the *Daily*

Herald and collecting his war verse for publication. The foul slums of Blackburn had stirred his pity and indignation, but his values had become even more muddled as heart and head moved into open conflict.

While this confusion was churning within him, he received an invitation in the spring of 1920 to lecture in America under the auspices of the Fight the Famine Committee. It was thought that his poetry readings might win support for European food relief but, looking back years later in *Siegfried's Journey*, he admitted a deeper twofold purpose in accepting the invitation: 'In the first place I had pledged myself to expose war in every way I could; and here was my opportunity for an active campaign. I may even have told myself that it was a solemn duty to open the eyes of the Americans to those realities of which they needed to be made aware. My second reason emerged in a sudden impulse and longing to escape from the post-war complexities of my existence.' His own brief account of the tour is marked by a wry self-irony between the lines. Contemporary reports and the memoirs of people who met him at this time give a clearer picture of why the visit disappointed his audiences and himself.

He could not complain of his welcome. Dutton had just published his collection of poems, *Picture-Show*, which the critics greeted with rapture. Carl Sandburg acclaimed him 'Prime Minister of living English poets', while the Untermeyers and other literati offered him genuine warmth and hospitality. All went well at first. At Cornell, Columbia and Vassar he captivated the young in heart with his own shy charm. Many of them already knew his poetry and were intoxicated by newspaper accounts of his heroism and suffering. A minority possibly felt betrayed by this angular Englishman of six foot two with a long face, aquiline nose and the deep-set eyes that seemed to look through people. His sinewy body suggested the athlete, but the limbs co-ordinated in such jerky movements that the whole effect was gangling and slightly comic. It was a let-down for those who had expected a blend of Lord Byron and Rupert Brooke. Instead of romantic curls, he could only offer his mousy mane cropped close to an austere-looking Assyrian head. His readings were also anything but fluent. They suffered from a hesitant diction which made him sound abrupt even when he was reciting passages of great lyrical beauty. But everyone liked his naturalness and the way he laughed out loud at his periodic slips. Few could resist a lecturer who made no apology for breaking off his own poems in favour of Thomas Hardy.

He was less comfortable making smalltalk in the bookshops or signing copies, and suffered acutely when a New York photographer exhibited a huge blown-up portrait in his window. Before passers-by could identify the figure in sports jacket and Oxford bags, he would be loping along Fifth Avenue with legs held high like a stork as though, in the words of a friend, 'he was walking through a bed of bullrushes eighteen inches high'. When he did some window-shopping, a natural asceticism prevailed. He returned to his modest apartment on West 44th Street with only a new straw hat and some badly needed pipe-cleaners.

His telephone never stopped shrilling. He did his duty to his sponsors, even if the huge banquets terrified him far more than any minefield. A record crowd of two hundred and fifty guests arrived at the Astor for the Poetry Society of America's Dinner when he was announced as the joint guest of honour with W. B. Yeats. Before he could slip away, he was penned by a crush of diners waving menus to be autographed. At their head was the slender and very pretty poet, Edna St Vincent Millay, who had memorized many of his verses and kept pumping his hand in vigorous adoration.

Other friendly souls were Louis Untermeyer and his wife, Jean, who also wrote poetry and was a gifted singer of *lieder*. She saw that he was worn out by the strenuous tour and had the kindly thought of giving him a weekend airing in the country. He accepted with enthusiasm. As soon as they reached Milford, Pennsylvania, he was like a boy again. His hostess recalls him, 'riding the branch of a willow to let himself down on the opposite side of a stream, or leaping a fence into a field where a horse was grazing, to mount him bareback, and gallop around the enclosure'.

It was only a brief escape from an inner darkness which occasionally flickered into quite startling violence. He had addressed the National Council of Jewish Women and made such a pleasing impression that someone, evidently misled by his ancient name but hazy about the family history, had a disastrous inspiration. It had seemed a splendid idea to invite the great-grandson of David Sassoon to lecture at the Free Synagogue service in Carnegie Hall.

A congregation of two thousand mustered to hear the poet who was most amiably introduced by Rabbi Stephen Wise. After a few innocuous opening remarks, Siegfried began to stammer with pent-up irritation. The gathering sat frozen and startled as he accused them of knowing nothing about the realities of war and looking altogether too prosperous and too complacent for a religious service. Rabbi Wise was much distressed and tried to cover up. One can only surmise that some atavistic impulse had suddenly released a dormant Thornycroft resentment which turned against his unfortunate audience.

It betrayed a strong inner tension. There was not the slightest anti-Semitism, in the usual sense, in his outlook. The Untermeyers remained his friends for many years. Mrs Untermeyer still remembers his kindness when she gave a recital of Schubert songs at London's Aeolian Hall in

1924. He sent her a posy of violets so large that she could hardly pin it into her corsage. Owing to recent dental trouble, her performance was sadly below par, and Siegfried had hurried backstage to comfort her. 'I don't know whether or not your voice is beautiful,' he stammered, 'but it was art – *and* you carried my violets!'

He had an agreeable stay with Harold Laski after addressing the Harvard Poetry Club. He took every chance to lunch and talk with the stimulating Jewish professor whose witty paradoxes concealed a passionate love of the under-privileged. Another cherished companion was Sam Behrman who, in a very few years, would have his first play staged on Broadway by the Lunts. He was then on the *New York Times* and was making a name as writer and talker. Nothing gave Siegfried more pleasure, after a round of golf at the Westchester Country Club, than to lunch at the Algonquin with Behrman. But the latter would never forget an experience which rivalled any of the slapstick in his future plays. They were dining and laughing on the balcony at the Claridge when Siegfried unconsciously shot out a long leg and tipped a big pot of flowers over a dinner party below. In the uproar, they hastily paid their bill and took to the hills.

Back in London in the autumn of 1920, he felt infinitely pessimistic about the future of his country and the rest of Europe. The post-war boom was bursting like an overripe melon. Reparations had released a flood of German goods and raw materials which seriously upset the British economy. Industry had thrived briefly in taking up the backlog of war, but prices were already collapsing and unemployment had soared. The miners, dockers and railwaymen were soon threatening strike action. Siegfried saw the ghosts of Arras and Ypres on every street corner. They carried trays of matches, but nearly all of them were still straight backed and wore boots that shone under their frayed turn-ups. He passed them with a sense of helpless shame.

He learned that Ashley Park had been pulled down when his cousin died suddenly soon after the war. The estate would soon be broken up and redeveloped for attractive houses and shops. Meantime, Siegfried read about the junketings and conferences at Philip's palatial home, Port Lympne, which was now being used by Lloyd George as his semi-official headquarters. It seemed incredible to the bitter author of *The General* that a vast financial grant should now be canvassed for Sir Douglas Haig while thousands of ex-soldiers faced unemployment and near starvation. By one of those little ironies then commonplace in topsy-turvy Britain, it had fallen to Philip Sassoon to act as intermediary between Prime Minister and Field-Marshal, recently such sworn foes.

The newspapers were demanding that Haig should be given a peerage, but he had hinted that this might embarrass him without the hard cash to maintain it. Moreover, he disliked drawing attention to himself at a time when the Disabled Officers' Fund was in low water. He greatly needed the services of a skilled lobbyist and go-between, and his former military secretary was again at hand. Philip's only fault would be an understandable lack of proportion about money. He had grandly suggested £250,000, but the Prime Minister steered him firmly into more realistic channels. In the end, Haig was granted an earldom, an ancestral home and a State grant of £100,000.

Philip's energetic part in the negotiations had impressed Lloyd George who found him more congenial now that the old War Cabinet intrigues were behind them. He had already served the Minister of Transport, Sir Eric Geddes, as his Parliamentary Private Secretary for a year when Lloyd George took him over in February 1920. He was ineffectual in the House – his delivery was nervous and that sing-song, accented voice an incurable handicap – but he painstakingly memorized all his speeches. As Haig had discovered, he also had a natural gift for potting information in a hurry, as well as a magpie ear for gossip. With the country already unsettled by half a million jobless and his own position constantly under threat from within the Government, Lloyd George needed the very kind of listening-post which the C.-in-C. had found so indispensable behind the lines.

Philip Sassoon quickly became invaluable to a chief who hated reading papers and memoranda and was known to stuff them into his pocket or any handy drawer. He arrived on the scene just when Lloyd George was openly posing on his pedestal as Prime Minister of Europe. It made him even more neglectful of his parliamentary duties, despite urgent problems like rapidly increasing unemployment, lock-outs and strikes, the Irish 'troubles' and a growing discontent among his Coalition colleagues.

The Welshman had a magical gift for improvisation, but he relied more than most people knew on a P.P.S. who was always on cue with a note or a list of statistics. When the P.M. was abroad or engaged on one of his frequent amours, Philip made it his business to do some assiduous lobbying in the House. He lunched frequently on the terrace in summer and gave excellent little dinners in the Harcourt Room. He would take the political temperature very carefully before hurrying back to his private room at Number Ten to prepare a note on his findings. He had a sharply developed sense of danger and did not share his master's complacency about Curzon, the Foreign Secretary, and other Cabinet dissidents. 'The fiery Welsh particle' refused to take alarm. In times of crisis he simply needed to be amused and flattered, and Philip Sassoon did not fail him.

He came to be considered almost one of the family. There were even absurd rumours that he might soon marry Megan, who benefited from his taste and guidance when she acted as hostess for her father. Her name was not the first, although one of the least likely, to be linked 'romantically' with that of the richest bachelor in England. Those closest to him now smiled cynically when he trotted out the standard excuse that he would not marry until he had met someone as charming and gifted as his sister. It came to be accepted that the lovely women at his parties were chosen mainly as table decorations. They were rarely unmarried. He was turning more and more to matrons like Mrs Belloc Lowndes and Margot Asquith for motherly tenderness. He also paid regular visits to Cheddar where little Miss Skey had settled since leaving Eton.

He was not amused by some doggerel which someone had jotted down on the back of a menu at one stag dinner in the House of Commons:

> Sir Philip Sassoon is the member for Hythe:
> He is opulent, swarthy, jejune and lithe.
> Beneficent angels announced at his birth
> That Sir Philip Sassoon would inherit the earth . . .
> And the daughters of Britain will wish they were dead
> Once Philip Sassoon has decided to wed.

Some found it puzzling that Lloyd George, the tough and down-to-earth careerist, should find any use for this rather dilettantish lightweight. It seemed even more incongruous than his wartime appointment by Haig. Lord Beaverbrook thought he knew the answer. 'Sir Philip Sassoon was a brilliant gossip and a habitual flatterer,' he once declared. 'He had many houses and most capable chefs.' This was perhaps an over-simplification and stemmed from a dislike that had grown steadily from unforgotten days when Philip was conspiring with Northcliffe in Haig's interest. During one party at Beaverbrook's house, Cherkley, someone asked suddenly, 'Where's Philip?' 'Flattering somebody, somewhere,' suggested the host. Sassoon then emerged from behind a pillar, looking uncannily like a Velasquez portrait. 'Not *you*, Max!' he murmured.

As an exceedingly rich Jewish bachelor and aesthete, he was exposed to attack from many directions. Having been spoilt from childhood, he lacked the self-criticism which might have saved him. He was not helped by being an unpaid but privileged amateur in the harsh world of politics. The professionals grew watchful for the smallest lapse, as in the days with Haig. Loud was the rejoicing in May 1922, when he was caught out in a rare parliamentary indiscretion. While addressing some women constituents on Budget Day, he had casually disclosed that the tea duty would be reduced by 4*d*. It was said only a few minutes before the Chancellor's Speech, but made a good enough reason for an enemy to pen and circulate a verse:

> A hasty young Bart. at Folkestone
> Forecasted the Chancellor's boom;
> Being rapped on the knuckles,
> No longer he chuckles
> And wishes he'd not been Sassoon.

It was Philip's special misfortune to come into public life at a time of seething uncertainty, both at home and abroad. Few of the aggressive and ambitious men then in politics would have much patience with an exotic young hidalgo apparently left over from the decadent 'nineties. They showed even less charity as he climbed steadily into the Prime Minister's favour and confidence.

Lord Birkenhead had become Lord Chancellor after a spectacular, self-made career. Himself a man of abnormally robust appetites, he did not take to exquisites. He had never forgotten his humiliation at St Omer for which apparently he thought Philip indirectly responsible. A splendid opportunity for 'revenge' arrived while Philip and others were being entertained to dinner aboard his 80-ton yacht *Mairi*. It was steel-built and schooner-rigged but rolled a bit. This never worried 'F.E.' who used to follow a meal of pork chops and several brandies with a vast Havana when all the other passengers, except Churchill, had become sea-green corruptibles. Philip, however, was a poor sailor and only accepted the invitation after being assured that they would not put to sea. The engines turned while the entrée was being served. Philip shot to his feet and hurdled over two chairs and a table in his eagerness to reach the gangway. He discovered on deck that the yacht was still at anchor. F.E. had given instructions for the engines to be started, entirely for Philip's benefit.

The Lord Chancellor dined soon afterwards at Lord Balfour's home, Whittingehame, with Lloyd George and Sir Robert Horne as fellow-guests. It was a gay party, lubricated by some excellent brandy, and the talk soon turned to personalities. Lloyd George gored poor Curzon with a hilarious piece of mimicry. When someone remarked that L. S. Amery much resented the calumny that his father was a Jew from Salonika, F.E. pretended to consider the question. 'This isn't libellous,' he pronounced judicially. 'Can it be a libel to call a man one of a nation that has produced Jesus Christ and Philip Sassoon?'

Lloyd George joined in the laughter, but his own philo-semitism was well known. He had always been an admirer of the race and gave his fullest support to implementing the Balfour Declaration. He also defied snobbish precedent by sending Lord Reading, a Jew, to India as Viceroy after an unbroken sequence of aristocratic proconsuls. Although Philip took no pride in his ancestry and remained completely apathetic towards

Zionism, Lloyd George was perfectly aware that his enemies were making capital out of his appointment of a Jewish P.P.S. He ignored them. He was enough of a realist to value a wealthy and well-connected third baronet on his staff. Personally, he had little interest in society and once showed his dislike of royal protocol by declining to carry the State Sword at the Opening of Parliament. It suited him nevertheless that Philip regularly played polo with the Prince of Wales.

In the coming negotiations with foreign statesmen over war reparations and the new frontiers of Europe, it would be quite invaluable to have a cosmopolitan linguist as secretary, herald and courier. Moreover, Sir Philip was able to offer three charming houses, each admirably equipped for specialized entertainment. Few Prime Ministers could press a button for a little oriental genie to materialize gracefully and conjure up a private aeroplane, a nine-hole golf course and relays of flunkeys. When Winston Churchill was once asked why Sir Philip Sassoon was given so many Parliamentary jobs, he had replied cynically, 'When you are leaving on an unknown destination it is a good plan to attach a restaurant car at the tail of the train.' None of Philip's patrons would make better use of his hospitality than Lloyd George, but he showed more gratitude than many others who dined, wined and sneered. He found Philip particularly useful in a period of major conferences which could best be held in luxurious semi-privacy.

The Prime Minister felt uncomfortable at Chequers which had recently been presented to the nation. 'It is full of the ghosts of dull people,' he said gloomily. He loved the country and set about building a home of his own near Churt in Surrey. Unfortunately, it would not be ready until the summer of 1922. Port Lympne, Philip's home near his constituency, was most convenient for visitors from the Continent, while Trent Park was perfectly appointed for off-duty weekends. 25 Park Lane would also be available for the more formal dinners and receptions.

The three houses on which Philip lavished so much money and taste epitomized the varied strains in a restless personality. Park Lane, with its art treasures, eighteenth-century furniture, Aubusson carpets and tapestries, reflected the connoisseur and man of fashion. The pictures, lit with a stage manager's eye, were hung to blend perfectly with the architecture and furnishings. The collection itself was discriminating, although not outstanding by Rothschild standards. It included a Reynolds, a Velasquez and several Gainsboroughs. An entire room was devoted to Sargent, who overflowed to the columned marble staircase with his painting of Lady Sassoon and another of Sybil, the Royal Academy success of 1922, who was portrayed as a bejewelled Elizabethan. The true star of the Park Lane collection, however, was Zoffany, whose graceful conversation pieces may well have inspired Philip's own zest for collecting and grouping celebrities.

The new glass-walled ballroom was the talk of Europe. José-Maria Sert, the Catalan painter who decorated many of Diaghilev's ballets, had worked on it for two years, apart from some interludes at Port Lympne. Philip had lured him to Park Lane from his well-patronized studio in the Faubourg St Germain, giving him an unlimited budget. The mirrored walls recalled a vision of the lost Orient, with turbaned rajahs, mosques, pagodas, caparisoned elephants, palm trees and a baroque jungle of parrots and monkeys. In this bizarre, fancy-dress world of blue and silver, Philip gave dances for as many as four hundred guests, usually including the Prince of Wales and his younger brother, George. His friends could also spend a quiet evening in the charming little theatre, enjoying film shows or song recitals by artists like Chaliapin. Lady Oxford was often present, but became rather a trial. She was no respecter of genius and would hold forth in a piercing monologue even while Paderewski and Rubinstein were playing.

Philip himself preferred small stag dinners, followed by excellent brandy and a couple of rubbers of bridge. Winston Churchill always played an uninhibited game and re-doubled recklessly, to Edward Marsh's intense horror. If Lloyd George were present, a sing-song would usually follow, with Winston rendering old Boer War songs in his off-key bass. The Prime Minister then sang Welsh hymns or recited favourite quotations from the Bible. He would fix Philip with an evangelical eye and declaim in mock reproof, 'Go to now, ye rich men, weep and howl for your miseries that shall come upon you.'

It seemed that Philip sometimes took the injunction seriously. Soon after the war, he was having tea one afternoon in Park Lane with Lord Riddell, Lloyd George's confidant and owner of the *News of the World*. Suddenly he went glum. 'In this huge house I occupy only four rooms,' he sighed. 'Sometimes I ask myself whether the State ought not to take the rest for those who cannot otherwise secure homes.' But the mood passed as the house quickly filled with visitors. That night Riddell noted in his diary that Philip was 'flitting from room to room and person to person, like a bee in search of honey'.

Philip was himself an avid reader, snatching at every new book which might make amusing table-talk or possibly rope the author into his enclosure of celebrities. He had to wait some years before netting T. E. Lawrence, but was meantime compensated by his private edition of *Seven Pillars of Wisdom*. He was one of the original subscribers of thirty guineas for copies which were soon fetching £800 each. He was not, of course, tempted to sell, unlike Augustus John who sacrificed his presentation copy for £400 to buy a new car. Philip also held on to his three copies of *A La Recherche* which he had implored Proust to autograph for him. He was even prouder of the bits of flowery nonsense which the author had written to him soon after Sert brought them together.

In his last days, Proust sometimes used to hold court among his acolytes at the Paris Ritz where Philip often stayed. During one visit, Proust had sent him a note: 'For a long time I have heard nothing of you except the murmur of the water running into your bath. I was dining at the Ritz (where I often take a room for a few hours) and, believing I had no neighbours, I was telling a waiter who had learned the part of Sosie for the Conservatoire of what Molière's play consisted (the Conservatoire having rejected him and thus sent him back to his old profession at the Ritz). Suddenly threatening noises were heard from next door and the sound of a perfect deluge; I did not doubt that, in punishment for my irreverent explanations, Jupiter was letting loose his thunder. But no, I was told that Sir Philip Sassoon was taking his bath.'

The acquaintance had not developed. Proust died in November 1922 before he could make his first visit to England where he had many admirers. Otherwise, he would surely have been stitched into the social embroidery of Park Lane or Trent Park. Philip had therefore to content himself with reading the letters out to his guests at every opportunity, unaware of any meaningful glances which might be passing behind his back.

That Paris visit of 1921 was not entirely without profit. Chaplin had just completed 'The Kid' and took the opportunity to make a sentimental journey back to Europe while publicizing the film. Philip was feverishly anxious to meet him and prevailed upon Georges Carpentier, a mutual friend, to introduce him. It was not easy. 'Charlot' was mobbed wherever he went, and even Carpentier had difficulty in battling his way through the secretaries and bodyguards. Philip persisted, and the film star was cornered at last in his bathroom at Claridge's. He dined that evening with Philip and Sybil, promising to visit them in London when he returned from his trip to Berlin. It was the beginning of a long friendship, but Chaplin remains a touch hazy on detail. In his autobiography he mentions that Philip was official secretary to Lloyd George *during* the war and represented Brighton and Hove in Parliament!

When Chaplin hinted in Paris that the colour of the walls had depressed him at Claridge's, a suite at Port Lympne was quickly redecorated in his favourite yellow and gold. A whisper that he liked treacle pudding and missed his American wheat-cakes was at once relayed to Philip's chefs. Chaplin discovered that even William Randolph Hearst could not compete with a kitchen that baked four different kinds of bread for breakfast. Guests at Trent Park enjoyed a similar Arabian Nights service. The flowers were dyed to match the curtains in every room. Orchids were sent up for the ladies before dinner, while male guests always found a clove carnation and a beaker of cocktails waiting on their dressing-tables.

Park Lane was the more formal town home, but Trent satisfied Philip's need for a sophisticated weekend retreat near London, without the stuffiness of the usual country seat. He had the drain-pipes gilded over because they offended his eye and once ordered a footman to haul down the national flag and find 'something less garish', as it clashed with the sunset. The gardens and orangery were showpieces, like the lawns sloping down to a lake ornamented by rare black and white swans, duck and coot of every species, pink flamingoes and gay pelicans from distant parts of the world. Followed by a retinue of gardeners, Philip would proceed each morning and evening to feed his two king penguins. Nobody else was ever allowed to do this while he was in residence.

His guests bathed in a heated blue swimming pool, heavy with the scent from surrounding shrubs and flower-beds. Resident professionals, caddies and ball-boys attended seven days a week, from breakfast onwards, for any guests who felt like tennis or a round on the private nine-hole course. He played golf at high speed, sometimes whipping through eighteen holes in ninety minutes, and always attended by two caddies. One of them did nothing but mark his drives, since he preferred to lose a hole rather than spend time searching for his ball. For such an impatient and whirlwind golfer, it was a trial playing at Walton Heath with Lloyd George who made a habit of holding a 'conference' or a private talk with Lord Riddell and Philip on the green or even in the middle of a fairway while others waited impatiently to follow. The P.M. started playing more often at Trent Park where he could be a law unto himself.

He was perhaps happiest of all at Port Lympne which Philip began rebuilding soon after the war. The white marble terraces and loggia were italianate in style and inspiration, while the patio with its marble columns was graced by a gallery of blue glazed tiles imported from Spain. It was roofless, which suited his passion for eating out-of-doors in the hot sun, a habit that could be a trial to lighter-skinned visitors. Not that he was inconsiderate. He had first built a broad flight of a hundred marble steps leading to the house from one of the terraces, but decided that they were perhaps too dangerous for the elderly. They were demolished and replaced by a less steep stairway of one hundred and thirty steps.

In the Moorish-type courtyard, six fountains threw so much spray above rooftop level that his neighbours sometimes accused him good-humouredly of causing a county drought during abnormally hot summers. He had his own pumping station for supplying fresh water for the household and a heated marble swimming pool, designed on Roman lines. He preferred sea-bathing and used to drive at speed to his private beach off the Dymchurch road after an early morning round of golf at Hythe. A vast cabin, equipped with showers and warm towel-racks, offered his guests a varied collection of new and fashionable costumes in all sizes.

The house had over a hundred rooms and slept forty guests with comfort. The number of bathrooms was liberal, even by luxury hotel standards. Philip's was a sumptuous affair, sunk into a floor of black marble, with walls zigzagging in red stripes. Still more water was needed to keep his gardens at a peak of perfection. The begonias, dahlias and shrubs were the envy of all horticulturists, and Austen Chamberlain often found relief from conferences by pottering about the magnificent rockeries. A vineyard and fig trees were hemmed between canyons of impeccably clipped yews and tall cypress hedges, but the flower-beds remained Lympne's special glory. A woman guest once expressed astonishment at the miraculous precision with which flowers seemed to appear in perfect condition and almost to order for some fête. Philip explained languidly: 'At twelve noon on the first of August each year, I give a nod to the head gardener who rings his bell and all the flowers pop up.'

The miracle needed taste as well as a millionaire's purse. Philip was so passionate about colour that he once bought several of Cartier's most costly cigarette cases in different shades so that his head gardener could use them as models before planting his beds. Fourteen gardeners and odd-job men tended the lawns and clipped the endless hedges. One of the drives ran a full half-mile under the cliffs. The tennis courts were kept up to Queen's Club standard. They were designed so that the sun would never be in the server's eyes. On the lake, as at Trent Park, many different species needed expert attention, notably rarities like the red-breasted geese from Siberia.

The main library was panelled in Wren period woodwork and painted in silver leaf. It was dominated by a superbly carved gallery. A smaller library was used by guests who desired to write letters or enjoy a snooze after the lavish meals. Philip would read there on the very rare evenings when he was not entertaining. He would wear his silk-lapelled, velvet smoking jacket and hand-made hide moccasins, looking as fastidiously elegant as ever, with only an admiring butler as audience.

Mrs Steadman, the housekeeper at Lympne, could rely on help from Sir Philip's sister and his cousin, Mrs David Gubbay, for elaborate fêtes and other special occasions. Sybil assisted her brother in his constituency despite the claims of her three young children, a busy social life and her continuing interest in the Wrens' Old Comrades Association. She also supervised arrangements for official banquets at Park Lane or Trent Park. But she had less time when the Fourth Marquess of Cholmondeley died from a riding fall. In addition to her recently acquired mansion in Kensington Palace Gardens, she then became châtelaine of the ancestral home, Houghton Hall in Norfolk.

Hannah Gubbay, who had no children, shared the duties of hostess with considerable flair. Her husband was now head of the David Sassoon firm and they entertained with quiet elegance at their house in Hertford Street, Mayfair. From her childhood in Bombay, she had played billiards like an expert and later blossomed into a first-class golfer, often partnering the Prince of Wales in mixed foursomes. A warm friendship with Queen Mary started through her work for the Needlework Guilds and developed with their common interest in collecting antiques, jade and pottery. A gifted needlewoman herself, she quilted a bedcover for Queen Mary and gave many exquisite examples of her work to other members of the Royal Family.

Sybil and Hannah Gubbay were both at Philip's side in May 1920 for the most dazzling hour in his political career. Lloyd George had arranged to meet President Millerand for a weekend conference at which they hoped to discuss Reparations and other delicate matters of post-war policy. Port Lympne was chosen as the meeting-place, and Philip set to work. His resources were admittedly ample, but he deserved credit for a brilliant feat of organization, down to the right size of a typewriter ribbon. He specially imported orange and lemon trees from Sawbridgeworth to decorate a house already resplendent in early summer glory. The conference proper was held in Sert's white drawing-room, where the Prime Minister installed himself with Austen Chamberlain and Lord Derby, the Ambassador to France. Millerand's smaller entourage included his Minister of Finance. Secretaries, translators, security men and minor aides were made comfortable in adjoining rooms, each directly linked by wire and telephone with the Quai d'Orsay.

Philip's French chefs delighted their countrymen with sumptuous menus, while the running buffet proved the liberality of a millionaire host. He was in his element as a witty conversationalist and mimic, with a wide repertoire of anecdotes told in perfect French. Sybil was equally fluent and vivacious. Billiards, superb brandy and a cinema show, put on at Lloyd George's special request, left everyone in splendid humour. After the first formal business, there were pleasant walks next day in the grounds with time to relax on the sunny terrace. Five of the host's Rolls-Royces stood ready to take the party on excursions through the countryside, then at its sparkling best.

This weekend meeting was preliminary to the full-scale conference arranged for June 20. Port Lympne had pleased the French so much that no other venue was contemplated. But this meeting would prove far less cordial. The agenda was weightier and the delegates, with their complement of aides, made extensive use of the direct links with Paris. Philip excelled himself in smoothly co-ordinating the mechanics of the Conference, but neither the *cordon bleu* gastronomy nor the ceaseless output of extra-mural charm from Sybil, Hannah Gubbay and himself could dissipate the tension. This time, Reparations were over-shadowed by the grave differences which split the Conference over the fate of the former Ottoman Empire. Lloyd George was strongly pro-Greek and nursed rosy visions of a Magna Graecia in Asia Minor. His view was not shared by Birkenhead, Churchill, Beaverbrook and Curzon, but their opposition only stimulated him to fiercer partisanship. With eyes crackling under his flowing white mane, and the familiar cape billowing in a gentle summer's breeze, he exuded supreme confidence. He hopped up and down the terrace, laughingly exchanging quips with Millerand, while Philip hovered to take a note or execute some last-minute commission for his guests' comfort. When Venizelos, the Greek Prime Minister, arrived, he was warmly embraced by the ebullient Welshman, but the French remained stiffly polite. Their delegation had been reinforced by Marshal Foch and General Weygand, who were known to have a respect for the Turk's fighting qualities only equalled by their Finance Minister's concern for French investments at the Sublime Porte.

The pleasantries at Lympne had deceived nobody. Venizelos was soon out of power. France, supported by the Italians and Soviet Russia, then threw her weight behind Kemal and a revitalized Turkey. Lloyd George's Near Eastern policy steadily collapsed and helped to widen his domestic breach with the Tories. If his chief often miscalculated, Philip Sassoon at least could never be faulted in his rôle of 'wonderful provider', as Beaverbrook called him. He not only fed Lloyd George scraps of gossip, but all his favourite Welsh dishes. The chefs were also instructed to prepare the 'virility' diets of offal, kidneys and liver which the philandering Prime Minister periodically demanded. Nothing was too much trouble for Philip, whether called upon to arrange a formal conference at Lympne or a series of intimate dinners at Park Lane when De Valera wished to discuss the Irish Treaty in privacy.

He enjoyed bringing important people together but remained in the background, like an alert but unobtrusive stage manager. It was not always possible. The San Remo Conference proved very different from the ambience salon of Port Lympne. Among many other prickly items on the agenda, the controversial Balfour Declaration finally came up for ratification. Feelings grew tense as Dr Weizmann and his friends lobbied for the Mandate to be handed over to Great Britain. Since Palestine was to be the last subject for discussion, they had to suffer in suspense, although comforted a little by Curzon's sympathy and some unexpected support from the Arab delegation. This made Sir Philip's conduct seem even more distasteful. Weizmann would later stress in his memoirs that 'the only man to ignore the whole business was Philip Sassoon, another of Lloyd George's secretaries – and as it happens, the only Jewish member of the British delegation'.

Philip felt more relaxed at a weekend party in April 1921. Lympne glowed in the bright Easter sunshine. Lloyd George chattered away and seemed to have forgotten all his problems, including the coal strike, while he made gallant remarks to Hannah Gubbay and Lady Ribblesdale. The Prince of Wales came over for Sunday dinner with Mrs Dudley Ward and laughed uproariously at passages from Lytton Strachey's *Life of Queen Victoria* which had so angered King George. Others who stayed for the weekend included the P.M.'s faithful confidant, Lord Riddell, and Sir Robert Horne who told excellent stories in the Scottish dialect and always gave Philip a good game of tennis. Another honoured guest was Haig's predecessor, now Lord French, who went off to Canterbury Cathedral on Good Friday with Lloyd George. Philip joined them on the Sunday at a Baptist Chapel service in Hythe. On the way back, he learned with delight that the Prime Minister had appointed him a Trustee of the National Gallery. It was one of his few honours which caused no cynical comment. Even Philip Sassoon's enemies had to admit his taste and discrimination in artistic matters. Yet even this handsome Easter egg was pierced by a goldfish almost before it was hatched.

Rachel Beer was indirectly responsible for the whole affair although, of course, quite unaware of what was going on. She had been living for years at Tunbridge Wells in considerable splendour which, together with her many charities, placed a burden on an estate already nipped by heavier taxation. It was decided to sell some of her pictures. The first would be Millais's 'Christ in the Carpenter's Shop' which was priced at 10,000 guineas. As no English collector came forward, it seemed destined to go to the United States. At this point, after hearing of Sir Philip's appointment to the National Gallery, Siegfried could not resist striking a blow simultaneously for Art and the Thornycrofts.

He wrote a letter to *The Nation*: 'I have heard that there is a grave danger that "Christ in the Carpenter's Shop" may leave this country for the lack of the few thousand pounds needed to acquire it. The picture is the property of my paternal aunt, Mrs Frederick Beer, whose estate has been under the administration of the Lunacy Commissioners for the past seventeen years. As a comparatively indigent member of the tribe of the Sassoons, I deplore the fact that none of my family have acquired the picture for the National Art Collection.

'In order to remind them of their responsibility in the matter, I have today placed one goldfish in the fountain in the entrance-hall of the Tate Gallery. I hope that the presence of this diminutive cyprinoid may induce some Sassoon, more affluent than myself, to come forward with the money needed to retain a pre-Raphaelite masterpiece in one of our National Art galleries.'

'An Angry Sassoon' answered. 'I was surprised and pained by the letter from Capt. Siegfried Sassoon. It is reported that when it was first suggested to a member of our clan that the "Christ in the Carpenter's Shop" should be presented to one of the National Galleries, he replied: "It is a subject which does not appeal to me." This tactful and ambiguous saying well sums up the family feeling on the subject. Capt. Sassoon should remember the fine old Norman-French motto of our ancestors, "Sassoon à son gout".

'Finally, may I say that I have examined Capt. Sassoon's goldfish and, in my opinion, it is not a genuine cyprinoid.'

This 'Angry Sassoon' turned out to be Osbert Sitwell, delighted to poke a little gentle fun at his old friend and fagmaster. The joke was only partially on target. Philip did not enjoy the pointed reference to himself, but chose to ignore it. The picture was saved for the nation by contributions from the public and various galleries.

Philip's monumental air of disdain was responsible for much of the unfortunate, and often cruel, publicity which pursued him even when he was being generous. He had sent two dozen of his Sargent canvases to the commemorative exhibition at Burlington House in 1926. They included his own portrait which admirably captured the pale, thoughtful face with its inescapable touch of aristocratic hauteur. E. M. Forster was among those who chose a quiet day after the fashionable opening. Drifting about under the lofty gaze of Sargent's duchesses, archbishops and generals, he found himself inspecting Philip's portrait with rather less reverence than 'a young Oriental, subtle and charming, and not quite sure of his ground, despite very horsy, impeccably cut tweeds. I complimented him in flowery words. He winced, he disclaimed all knowledge of the East. I had been speaking to Sir Philip Sassoon'.

Allowing for Forster's parody, one cannot miss the irritation which many felt on brushing Philip's invisible ruffs. Other rich men were extravagant during the years of unemployment and strikes, but few quite so airily impervious to criticism. Philip's first private aircraft was a case in point. Having developed a taste for flying during his cross-Channel errands for Haig, he could not rest until he had clipped half an hour off the journey between London and Lympne whose landing field was convenient for flights to and from France. He had bought himself an Avro in

September 1919 but ignored friends who expressed astonishment that he should indulge himself with such a lavish toy. 'You might as well ask me why I should buy a motor car,' he drawled. His only regret was that he could not share this hobby with the Prince of Wales whose father had sternly forbidden him to fly. This was the result of an incident towards the end of the war when the Prince had gone skylarking with a Canadian war ace who was photographed piloting the aircraft with his arm in a sling.

Philip made good use of his Avro, and not only for dashing between his three homes. He often flew down to his constituency with Sybil, who assisted at fêtes. He opened a free dental clinic at Folkestone and helped to maintain it for fifteen years, as well as building a model working-class housing estate of sixteen cottages and eight flats on the East Cliff near the Fish Market. He paid for this out of his own pocket, and Sybil laid the foundation stone. He also looked after trawlermen and widows or orphans who had suffered through U-boat action. He often threw open Port Lympne and its gardens to disabled soldiers and thoughtfully put up special planks for the wheelchairs.

A whisper would stimulate him to play Harun al-Rashid. He once heard that a political opponent was in financial trouble but, guessing that he would be too proud to accept help from him, arranged matters anonymously through an intermediary. Another Labour supporter in his constituency, who often made speeches attacking the rich and luxury-loving Member, was reported to be anxious to send his son to a certain public school, but could not afford it. Only after Philip's death, many years hence, was it disclosed that he had personally paid the boy's fees in the strictest secrecy. When he learned that Mrs Belloc Lowndes was trying to help someone get a job as a waiter but had difficulty in finding him an old dress-suit, Philip quickly telephoned to check the man's size. Within the hour, he had sent one of his own Savile Row creations with a slip of paper that read, 'Don't bother to acknowledge'.

If the gardens at Trent Park were looking specially attractive, he invited Servicemen due for posting overseas to bring their families for a day's outing. He usually pressed a crackling fiver into the children's hands as they left. His courtesy to rich and poor was infallible. He once arrived an hour late for a cocktail party near Folkestone and could only stay ten minutes. Before the party was over, his Rolls came back with a box of exquisite blooms from Lympne, together with a graceful note of apology for his lateness and unavoidably brief visit. On another occasion, when he had opened 25 Park Lane for one of his art exhibitions on behalf of charity, the waiting crowd stretched almost to Hamilton Place. Rather than push through and draw attention to himself, he stood patiently in the queue until he could pay his five shillings at the turnstile. Yet he could show an arrogance rare even among the brashest of *nouveau riche* million-aires. When Flt.-Lt. (now Marshal of the Royal Air Force, Sir) Dermot Boyle was giving him his first flying lessons, Philip wanted an aerial view of Blenheim Palace. It was a prohibited area but he insisted on flying low for a closer look. 'Very nice little place,' he commented, 'but did you not think the kitchen garden looked a bit pinched?'

Few outside the household or his immediate family circle guessed his inner unhappiness or the painful contradictions in his personality. Natur-ally shy, he was over-anxious to be liked, but this was concealed behind a mask of self-satisfaction. Outwardly he was the born *maître d'hôtel*, with equal proportions of disdain and deference, yet privileged by being unpaid and able to choose his own guests. He continually fed square meals into celebrated round holes and unrolled miles of red carpet without always acquiring the affection he craved. He preferred to dispense hospitality rather than disclose his own wounds on alien, possibly hostile territory.

Osbert Sitwell and others have acknowledged that they could always go to him with their troubles, certain of sympathy and a tonic gaiety. He would create a tactful diversion by asking them to help rearrange the furni-ture or books while he chattered away. He had a ready sense of caricature. It was typical of him to talk of a recent guest who had snored so loudly 'that the tiles flew off the roof like confetti'. As a travelling companion, says Sir Osbert, he was unique and delightful. He always seemed happiest when in motion. He needed the constant stimulus of new places and glamorous people to rescue him from a melancholia which had started in childhood and deepened when both his parents died of cancer.

His own premonition of an early death may explain an obsession for keeping fit and retaining his youth. He perpetually washed, bathed and swam. Every day of his life he shampooed his hair, taking remarkable pains to keep it sleek and dark. He drank and smoked with the moderation of an athlete always in semi-training. He ran round Lympne in shorts and prac-tised tennis and golf with his resident pros. Winter and summer, he played squash at the Bath Club and would drop almost anything for a polo match. He often visited his brother-in-law's private gymnasium in Kensington Palace Gardens and skated regularly with the Cholmondeleys at St Moritz.

He would always miss his adored mother, whose pearls he carried about with him, 'to keep them alive', as he once told Chaplin. From Aline he also inherited a passion for spiritualism. During his early flying days he was often piloted by a young airman who became a very dear friend. When he crashed in Egypt while on a flight to Australia, Philip was prostrate with grief. He turned in despair to Mrs Belloc Lowndes, who was not a convert but took a strong interest in psychical matters. He begged to be put in touch with a reliable medium who might help him to establish contact with the dead airman. Sir Oliver Lodge gave her the name of a woman in Notting Hill Gate, and a meeting was arranged in conditions of great secrecy. It seems that the phrase, 'flying boots', recurred constantly during the séance. Philip later bought a pair of his friend's boots and always treasured them as a sentimental relic, together with a portrait of the dead pilot.

He did not often show emotion in public and detached himself, almost clinically, from the heat of controversy. Yet when Lloyd George's stock began to slump disastrously, he had cause to be grateful for Philip's quick sympathy. In February 1922 eager for a diversion from the Irish troubles and mounting discontent among British workers, the P.M. went off to Boulogne to meet Poincaré, who had succeeded Briand. He hoped to agree an agenda for the forthcoming conference at Genoa which might soften the anti-German bloc on Reparations and, at the same time, secure recognition for the Soviet régime. He had no faith at all in Winston Churchill's highly risky manœuvres in support of the White Russians. Genoa appealed to him as a golden vision of peace and plenty in Europe.

He was disillusioned after only a few hours with Poincaré, who proved far more truculent than Briand about Reparations and seemed disinclined to talk of anything else. They had arranged to meet again in mid-April, but L.G. crossed from Boulogne with a heavy heart. He spent the night at Port Lympne where even Sir Philip's lively chatter and the excellence of his chef failed to rally him. The time had passed for sing-songs or whist-ling in the dark. L.G. retired early and stayed in bed until lunch. He came down after drafting a letter to Sir Austen Chamberlain, offering to resign as Prime Minister in his favour. Chamberlain refused the invitation, sus-pecting that he was being used as a pawn while the magician planned his next move.

Disasters followed in quick order. Genoa proved a failure, and Soviet Russia then made a pact of friendship with Germany at Rapallo. Kemal's triumphant armies shattered all Lloyd George's dreams for Greece. By the autumn, the British parliamentary Coalition was dead. The P.M. resigned and Bonar Law agreed to lead the Conservatives at the General Election. Philip's house in Park Lane, the scene of so many discreet little dinners during the years of triumph, was chosen for an election night party on November 15. His guests sat down to a magnificent banquet, reasonably confident that the 131 Coalition Liberal candidates could still bring the Tories down. Lloyd George, Birkenhead and other ex-Ministers grew noticeably more buoyant over their cigars and brandies as the results came in on the ticker-tape machine which Philip had installed. They chuckled when Bonar Law squeaked home in his own constituency on a minority vote, by only 2,500. While the footmen went back and forth with trays of drinks, Philip found himself so caught up in the excitement that he rushed across the room to take charge of the ticker. As the tape ran through his fingers, he called out the results with alternating joy and gloom. He had been returned by faithful Hythe but looked distressed as, one after another, his Coalition friends were slaughtered at the polls.

Lloyd George never held office again, but Philip would be back in less than two years. His brief exile was sweetened by a G.B.E., and there were other signs that his recent political affiliation would not disable him for life. He had neither the philosophy nor the depth of personality to create a political salon in the Edwardian tradition, but his very detachment made it easier for men of very different views to exchange gossip or hatch plots on more or less neutral territory while enjoying his splendid hospitality. Under his roof it became possible for Margot Asquith to meet her husband's bitterest enemy, Lloyd George, while Bonar Law's friends also found Philip useful for re-establishing contact with a number of Tories who had not survived the Coalition.

Sir Samuel Hoare, the new Secretary of State for Air, was among the Bonar Law supporters who began to appear at Trent Park and Lympne. A member of the distinguished banking family, he was a product of Harrow and Oxford where he had taken a Double First. His wife, Lady Maud, was a daughter of Earl Beauchamp. He was fluent in French and also shared Philip's enthusiasm for Proust, whom he once quoted to a rather startled House of Commons. He was an even more accomplished ice-skater, but they were well matched at tennis and often played hard-fought singles.

Hoare was bookish and a little prim in manner ('the last of a long line of maiden aunts', said Birkenhead). Philip, however, found him congenial, particularly when they discussed the future of the Royal Air Force which Trenchard and others were strenuously attempting to turn into a strong and independent Service. By May 1923 the Government had come round enough to give the Air Minister a seat in the Cabinet. A year later, after Ramsay MacDonald's short term in office, the Tories returned under Baldwin and Sir Samuel Hoare was back as Air Minister. He did not hesitate in choosing Philip Sassoon as his Under-Secretary. Like Lloyd George, he appreciated the amenities of Park Lane, Trent and Lympne, but his motives were not entirely social. Philip was learning to fly his own aeroplane and took a strongly practical interest in aircraft design. He also supported the new-born Auxiliary Air Force, a body of aerial 'territorials'.

One of the gayest groups of weekend flyers was No. 601 (County of London) Squadron, led by Lord Edward Grosvenor, a son of the first Duke of Westminster. Philip had known him at Eton and, like his other schoolfellows, had followed his career in the Foreign Legion, and afterwards in the R.N.A.S., with considerable fascination. 'Ned' Grosvenor was a rumbustious, hard-drinking giant who swaggered about in riding breeches and liked to fire pistols, but he demanded high efficiency from the bloods whom he recruited mainly from White's.

Hoare became the first Honorary Air Commodore of a Squadron which Philip found, to his delight, was often on his own doorstep. In the summer of 1923, they competed for the Grosvenor Challenge Cup over a 400-mile course which started and ended on an airfield just outside Port Lympne. When the Squadron began to run summer training camps, Philip kept open house for the pilots and ground crews. Grosvenor was at home anywhere, but some of his men were a little overawed at bumping into Winston Churchill, G.B.S., and the Prince of Wales who might be sunning themselves by the pool.

From the time he joined the Baldwin administration, Philip took to giving a weekly luncheon party in Park Lane after the Wednesday Cabinet meeting, and often invited witty back-benchers along. Winston Churchill, now back as Chancellor of the Exchequer, became a regular. Philip learned from him the habit of always memorizing his speeches, but without inheriting his tricks of oratory. He would always be plagued by his slight foreign accent and a nervousness of manner. He was saved by an excellent memory and would deliver the Air Estimates by heart in speeches running to six thousand words or more. The Press Gallery, supplied with copies in advance, rarely faulted him.

His interest in the family business had long been perfunctory. One of his rare interventions was to nominate an old army friend, General Sir John Davidson, to the Board of the parent firm and its subsidiary, the African Mercantile Company. Otherwise, he was content to draw an income more than adequate for the splendour of Park Lane and his two country houses. Thanks to David Gubbay who supervised his investments, and the appreciation of his own real estate holdings in China and Hong Kong, Philip's capital had actually increased, despite his princely style of living.

He was not tempted to make many visits to 9 King William Street. In the mid-twenties he appeared there so rarely that, on one occasion, the departmental managers were solemnly called into the Board Room and told to prepare for an 'inspection'. Robert Heathfield, the Import Manager for India, made an attractive display of jars of oilseeds, spices, stem ginger, gums and resins, while the Export Department laid out samples of metals, cotton goods, artificial silk, woollen yarns, together with the firm's individual brand of shirting material, known as 'Cash'. This had the figure of a Chinese coin stamped on each bolt and was sold by auction in Shanghai to private firms for distribution to the main ports and the far interior of Szechwan. The 'inspection', however, was not made by Sir Philip but the Prince of Wales. He was escorted by Hannah Gubbay, who had a quick eye for detail and knew far more about the staff and merchandise than her cousin.

The firm was flourishing, but its weakness in top personnel was beginning to show. David Gubbay had followed Frederick Sassoon most capably as head of the firm and a director of the Imperial Bank of Persia, but he was overworked and asthmatic. Cecil Longcroft, the senior executive director, was not dynamic enough to resist the combined challenge from Indian nationalists and Japan. Capable managers, like A. H. Compton and Robert Stock in Hong Kong, who handled shipping and a large turnover of yarn and produce, were often frustrated by a lack of enterprise and initiative at head office level. Philip remained a cipher, while Sir John Davidson's directorship was only one of several which he had picked up in civilian life together with a seat in the Commons.

The shining hope was Frederick's son, Ronald, whom David Gubbay had patiently groomed to succeed him as Chairman. He was only twenty-three when the war ended. His wound left him limping and ended his cricketing days, but he had not become bitter. Like his father, he had a way with the staff and could even charm a smile out of Longcroft. Since the latter refused to travel and Gubbay was finding it impossible to leave the bridge, Ronald attended the wool sales in Liverpool and kept a close link with the Manchester Cotton Exchange. He also made regular tours of all the firm's branches and agencies throughout the Middle and Far East. Such a stint would have been impossible for a married man or one with his family's taste for the fleshpots. Ronald, however, was a bachelor with an incisive business brain. Eton had blessed him with easy manners but withheld arrogance. He could even joke about his very prominent nose and seemed to have none of the racial inhibitions which had complicated life for Cousin Philip.

Unfortunately, he became the victim of his own zeal. In the summer of 1924, returning from Shanghai after a successful but strenuous tour of the Ports, he decided to call at Baghdad on his way home. The office there had wired him that the thermometer was registering 120° in the shade and suggested that he should postpone his visit. He insisted on keeping to his itinerary and died of a heart attack soon after arriving in the home of his ancestors.

His early death was an irreparable loss to the firm. In contrast, E. D. Sassoon & Co. acquired its greatest but least expected asset at this time. Sir Jacob's long-cherished hopes of Victor were about to be realized.

Chapter Fifteen

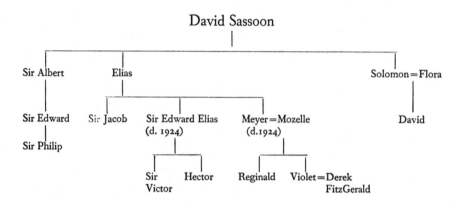

David Sassoon
- Sir Albert
  - Sir Edward
    - Sir Philip
- Elias
  - Sir Jacob
  - Sir Edward Elias (d. 1924)
    - Sir Victor
    - Hector
  - Meyer = Mozelle (d. 1924)
    - Reginald
    - Violet = Derek FitzGerald
- Solomon = Flora
  - David

On New Year's Day 1921, E. D. Sassoon was incorporated as a private trading and banking company. The former partners, Sir Jacob's three surviving brothers, allocated their funds between this company and the various concerns in which they had family holdings. It was the initial step in an extensive reconstruction made necessary by the post-war uncertainty in international trade and currencies. Rapid decentralization followed the higher taxation imposed by the British Parliament. A contributory factor was the attitude of Sir Edward Elias Sassoon, the Chairman, who had developed strong views on taxation during the war. Having made a liberal contribution to Government funds, he became highly incensed at being mulcted for his patriotism by an unsympathetic Inland Revenue. He took necessary precautions thereafter to protect the family business from what he considered the penal injustice of surtax and death duties. His Indian domicile enabled him to funnel his assets from England through an elaborate complex of Trusts. The Bombay Trust was incorporated in September 1920. The Hong Kong Trust was formed in the following July to carry on business as financiers and brokers. It had a paid-up capital of nearly £5 million sterling, plus a similar amount in reserve, with very wide powers to lend money in all parts of the world. The main objective, however, was to make fixed deposits with the Bombay Trust at a good rate of gross interest. This would then be remitted from Bombay to the Shanghai branch of the new banking house, which acted as intermediary.

Its directors, all members of the family firm, were also on the boards of the Trust Corporations. The offices of E. D. Sassoon & Co. were located in the same building as the Bombay Trust.

In some years, the Hong Kong Trust lent its entire paid-up capital and cash deposits to its Bombay twin. On 12 May 1926 the Secretary of the Hong Kong Company wrote to Bombay: 'I am instructed to inquire whether or not you will agree to accept one and a quarter crore (over a million sterling) from us on call as from the 1st June next at 5¼ per annum interest. If you are prepared to accept this sum on the above-mentioned terms, instructions have been given to the Bombay bankers, Messrs E. D. Sassoon & Co. Ltd to pay you this amount, in exchange for which please send us your acknowledgement.' The amount was automatically credited without any further written confirmation being considered necessary.

This system of transferring surplus assets at a lucrative rate of interest through the three main arteries – Bombay, Hong Kong and Shanghai – became highly effective at a time when E. D. Sassoon & Co. Ltd needed to be flexible. The war had ended with India's cotton factories making huge profits, yet the boom could not last. When the world slump came, India found herself with additional problems arising from her own internal strife and Japanese industrialization. After the Amritsar massacre, Congress fomented a campaign of strikes and civil disobedience which ended in the active boycott of Lancashire goods. With the Government confronted by an adverse balance of trade and a fall in the price of silver, the rupee was soon in danger.

E. D. Sassoon were conscious of their delicate position. They owned almost a dozen of Bombay's largest cotton mills and dye-works and had to keep wages stable among workers soured by a penal rise in the cost of living. Gandhi's home-spun might be only a temporary embarrassment, but the Japanese threat was more serious. Their cheap goods were flooding Indian markets and had already penetrated deep into China itself. Finer quality fabrics would have to be developed and costly equipment installed to defeat this competitor. It would not be easy, but a ready flow of capital could provide finance for business activities of every kind, more especially land development, by loans from the various Trust Corporations or bank overdrafts guaranteed by them.

China's land boom had finally convinced Silas Hardoon. He left the firm in 1920 to engage in large-scale speculations in property and public utilities. They would make him the richest and most controversial private figure in Shanghai. His millions spawned so many enemies that he was never seen in public without an armed Irish bodyguard. More than one attempt was made to murder him, but an undercover intelligence network, backed by his faith in divine providence, helped to protect him. He married a beautiful Chinese, Loo Chia Ling, and adopted ten youngsters, each of different nationalities, who were taught by private tutors to read and write English, Hebrew and Chinese.

The company replaced Hardoon by Meyer Sassoon's son, Reginald, a war hero, crack golfer and horseman but no commercial genius. He took a house in the French Settlement and spent every spare minute with the Paper Hunt Club. After winning his hunting 'pink', he became more ambitious and took fences, cossack-style, usually with his glasses hanging from one ear. In one race on the Kiangwan course, fringed by a golf links, he was leading the field when his pony landed him in one of the bunkers. His desk was invariably piled high with stud books and details of National Hunt records. He gave hours to schooling his horses on the tracks around Shanghai. One of his close friends was a police superintendent, M. O. Springfield, who recalls that, late one afternoon, Reggie was furious at missing his usual morning gallop and rode his hurdler into the setting sun. He was thrown, not for the first time. He awoke in the ambulance and murmured, 'Springie, you won't mind if I don't ride again this evening. I don't think I could do justice to my mount.'

He was determined to ride in the Grand National ('the only thing on earth I'm afraid of'), and completed the course on Ballystockart in 1927. He was the last to finish, but the crowd cheered him all the way back to the unsaddling-room. He came over to England every winter to buy bloodstock at the Sales and ride under National Hunt Rules. He once flew from Shanghai to London, via Siberia, specially to ride two of his horses, catching the next boat back to Bombay to keep an appointment with an industrialist. On another of his winter trips, he was in the saddle at Wolverhampton within a few hours of arriving from China.

He wore non-splinterable glasses at first, but later took treatment and remedial exercises until he could ride without them. Even so, he had five falls in as many weeks and probably broke more bones than any other amateur rider in history. After being carried off on a stretcher at one meeting, he was back in the saddle for the last race. An affectionate crowd roared him home with the customary, 'Come on, Captain!' He would arrange to have his chases filmed, whenever possible, and used to run them through again and again in slow motion, hoping to correct his errors.

His opposite number in Hong Kong also took his business responsibilities rather too lightly for the head office. This was Reggie's cousin, Hector, Sir Edward's younger son, who had survived his war in the Grenadier Guards. In 1921 he married the beautiful, petite Baroness Giulia Vici, daughter of an Italian nobleman. She was a first-class horsewoman, and

Hector delighted her by starting a stable and naming his thoroughbreds 'Roman Pride', 'Roman Victory' and so on in her honour. When not playing bridge or giving parties on the island, she was to be found on the Riviera, always followed by photographers who could not resist her scented black cigarettes, the pet leopard on a leash and her ropes of Sassoon pearls, as large as nuts. She was also a kindly soul and a particular favourite with her father-in-law, to whom she would read for hours when his sight began to fail.

Hector died suddenly in 1923 after an emergency abdominal operation, leaving his widow close on a million pounds, mainly in Hong Kong real estate, except his shares in the Company which passed to his brother, Victor. His will showed a characteristic touch; he bequeathed £37,000 for the benefit of first offenders, unmarried mothers and illegitimate children everywhere! Victor had the same sense of fun, but with a sharper edge of mockery. His war wound contributed to a natural cynicism. Genial and entertaining while free of pain, he would leave parties suddenly when a warning stab tore through his body. As a result, he soon gained a reputation for being brusque and irritable. He could only walk with two sticks and passed scarcely a day without spells of searing pain from his right hip. Manipulative surgery had not yet advanced enough to offer much relief, and he disliked taking drugs.

Bombay proved a welcome anodyne. He became almost obsessively eager to succeed, especially after his father's breakdown in health. Sir Edward Elias Sassoon had suffered a series of strokes which left him helpless and prematurely senile. It made Victor terrified at the prospect of himself becoming what he called 'a cabbage'. He vowed never to take to a wheelchair, even if he had to spend the rest of his life on crutches. Dancing and riding had to be put aside, and he could only swim by making a painful effort, but there was no bar to philandering. He became sexually voracious, partly no doubt to compensate for his disability. Philip did not apparently like women except as decorations, whereas his cousin remained a bachelor because, as he used to joke, he liked them too much! He often reminded himself and others of Nunkie's advice: 'If ever you find yourself in danger of committing matrimony, run like hell,' but his flippancy was a cover for something that cut much deeper.

He developed an almost neurotic horror of physical contact with anyone maimed or disfigured. It reminded him of his own handicap about which he became abnormally sensitive. 'If I had healthy and attractive children,' he once confided to a relative, 'I could not help becoming horribly jealous of them.' He convinced himself that nobody would ever marry him except for his money and position. However, there were consolations in plenty. He was still handsome at forty, and debonair enough to enjoy many love affairs, as well as the favours of a succession of mistresses who found him generous and meticulously tactful in his dealings. His *ménages* were always discreet and never attracted the scandal which pursued Nunkie. 'One of the reasons why I understand women,' he used to tell his bachelor friends, 'is because half my ancestors are women, after all!' A more cogent reason was a semi-oriental outlook which enabled him to keep his public and private lives rigidly apart.

Arriving in Bombay a year or so after the war, he quickly showed the staff that he would not become the rubber-stamping son of an absentee Chairman. He learned fast, aided by a grasp of office routine acquired in the Admiralty. He also had a practical bent for machinery and encouraged operatives and designers to suggest short cuts to increased efficiency. He would give time to photographing spindles and intricate pieces of machinery, later sending cables to the Manchester office with ideas for re-designing plant.

He could be quirky with any office colleagues who questioned his judgement. He had a cool head for figures and grasped balance-sheets with surprising ease. It was soon clear that banking and investment opportunities fascinated him more than routine marketing. He began to cross-examine the managers of overseas branches and agencies about industrial plants, insurance and real estate, and took special note of the overall political situation in their countries. Technicalities he left to accountants and local experts. He would listen courteously to advice, but rarely altered course once he had made up his mind. Within a few months of taking over in Bombay, few challenged his authority or dared go over his head to the London directors.

Victor could not have staged his entrance at a more challenging moment. An unsettled rupee had made importers nervous of taking heavy losses by the time their merchandise arrived. Many had good reason to fear that the post-war boom might subside and leave them in the kind of slump which had followed the feverish bonanza during the American Civil War. A universal political discontent did not help. The new and obviously conciliatory Viceroy, Lord Reading, landed at Bombay on 2 April 1921. He was greeted by bonfires of imported cloth and soon had to restore law and order by placing Gandhi behind bars. He also discovered that Lloyd George's pro-hellenic policy had inflamed the Moslems.

Lord Reading was a practical businessman as well as a distinguished lawyer and statesman. Setting a high priority on converting the Budget deficit into a surplus, he turned for support to India's leading businessmen. He was delighted when Victor accepted nomination to the new Legislative Assembly. Evidently he found this Sassoon more congenial than his recent host at Lympne, often inviting him up to Viceregal Lodge for private talks between the round of fêtes and garden parties.

Victor's monocle and two sticks made him conspicuous among the line of grey tropical suits and pith helmets waiting to greet the young Prince of Wales in Delhi in February 1922. He joined in the festivities but took a much more sombre view of the future than the complacent native potentates and some of the merchants. He felt acute embarrassment and anger when Gandhi's supporters quickly organized riots and strikes to wreck the royal goodwill tour. It reinforced his doubts about the Viceroy's attempts at pacification.

He found himself isolated between two irreconcilable forces in the Assembly. He thought Lord Reading's liberalism almost certain to be abused and preferred the paternalism which his own family had practised for generations in their factories, where labour conditions and wages were the best in India. Whatever his private doubts, he did not withhold support when the crusading Viceroy brought in a Factory Act which provided for a sixty-hour week and raised the minimum age of child workers to twelve. He was also in favour of India's first Workmen's Compensation Act, but suspected that it would become a dead letter in many parts of India. Worse, it might be used by up-country millowners to undercut their competitors in Bombay and Calcutta.

His bitterest opposition was directed at the new currency and excise measures which the Finance Minister, Sir Basil Blackett, was putting forward. They seemed so utterly wrong-headed that Victor swallowed his prejudices and briefly aligned himself with the Congress rebels. Thus he irritated a Government who had expected his unqualified support, while his temporary allies remained traditionally suspicious of the mill-owning caste.

Blackett had worked closely with Lord Reading during his wartime missions to the United States. But India, seething with a thousand and one complex resentments, proved a very different and far pricklier field. To achieve stability, he counselled retrenchment in expenditure and increased taxation. In his very first budget he doubled the hated salt tax which at once brought Victor to the support of his old enemies in Congress. He was even more critical of Blackett's heavy excise duty on Indian textiles. This was a reversion to a policy, long discredited, and one which had so nearly crippled the industry during the 'nineties. This time, fortunately, the Viceroy overruled his Finance Minister and repealed the excise.

Victor's heaviest guns were trained on the plan to stabilize the rupee at 1s. 6d. instead of 1s. 4d., which he and almost every other member of the trading community had thought satisfactory. He organized opposition and became Founder-President of the Indian Currency League, a powerful pressure group of merchants and millowners. In Delhi he sparked off one heated debate after another. Finally, he made a violent personal attack upon Blackett whom he accused of having 'the face of a cherub but the methods of a tank'. The President of the Legislative Assembly asked him to withdraw his remark. He preferred to walk out, not at all sorry to leave political life and return to his offices in Bombay. In any event, the death of his father a few months later would have made it impossible for him to continue his struggle against both the Viceroy and the Swaraj movement, much as he was enjoying the campaign on two fronts.

Sir Edward Elias's death in December 1924 had quickly followed that of his brother, Meyer. Probate on the latter's estate was granted in Hong Kong for $28 million, most of which was left to his widow, Mozelle, after various family legacies. The only figure published for Sir Edward's estate was £488,000 in English assets, but he also owned considerable properties in China, Hong Kong and India, where his domicile avoided heavy death duties. This left Victor and his Aunt Mozelle as the main beneficiaries of combined business assets then valued at £15 million. The new baronet did not confirm or deny this figure, which he passed off lightly by remarking that 'high estimates are always very good for one's credit'. In view of the declared assets of the two Trust Corporations in Bombay and Hong Kong alone, it was undoubtedly a conservative figure.

Victor's aunt was shrewd, but had no wish to follow the stormy precedent set long ago by Flora Sassoon. She would continue to take an extra-mural interest in the firm, but preferred to spend most of her time as a hostess of distinction in London and Dinard. She collected pictures, rare porcelain and old silver. She often held exhibitions at 6 Hamilton Place for charity, but her abiding philanthropic interest was in medical welfare. She financed and gave her name to a million-volt X-ray therapy unit at St Bartholomew's, and was a generous patroness of several other hospitals.

Her son, Reggie, was already a director in Shanghai and made frequent trips to England. Derek FitzGerald, her son-in-law, was now appointed to manage the London and Manchester offices and quickly impressed the new Chairman with his ability. Thus, with Hector dead and poor Reggie determined to kill himself at steeplechasing, Victor had virtually a free hand.

The transition from his rôle of easygoing man-about-town to that o tough-minded financier had started when he first deputized for his stricken father. When he became Chairman, it seemed like going back into the cockpit after years of being grounded. He was still in his early forties, but with experience of war, politics and international business already behind him. There were, of course, dangers implicit in an autocratic Chairman without strong directors to oppose him or even a wife to trim his ego. However, his judgement was usually cool and compassionate even if he could rarely resist a touch of irony in his dealings.

In the early days of the firm's entry into merchant banking, E. D. Sassoon discounted a bill drawn by a certain company in Shanghai on their U.K. correspondents. It was for an enormous shipment of Chinese eggs. The Shanghai office chartered the entire refrigeration space of a vessel and insured the cargo against the usual marine risks, including non-or-late arrival of the merchandise and a breakdown in refrigeration *en voyage*. The million to one chance occurred. The ship's refrigeration plant had not been used for some time before it arrived at Shanghai. Some ten days passed before it could be got to work, during which a hot mid-May sun beat down. The shipment was therefore in a highly volatile condition by the time it reached London. E. D. Sassoon had to face a substantial loss, but could not recover from shipowners protected by their Bills of Lading. Instead, they sued the firm whose bill they had discounted. The case was heard in Shanghai and went in favour of the Sassoons, but this was later reversed in the Hong Kong Court of Appeal.

The member of the Shanghai office who had handled this unfortunate transaction happened to be on leave in London when news of the appeal came through. Very distressed, he wrote an apology to Reggie Sassoon, his superior at the time, but quite unaware of all the details. Reggie replied with his usual courtesy and urged him to forget the unhappy affair. Mozelle Sassoon, however, heard about it and thought she would ask Sir Victor for information. His reply was typical, if rather hard on one whom he knew to be only technically responsible. He informed his aunt that it had cost the firm about £32,000, and would be written off as 'just another of Reggie's minor indiscretions'.

His light sarcasm once boomeranged with amusing results. Many years ago, the firm's auditors uncovered an ingenious scheme by which a bright, but over-ambitious, young employee was abusing his temporary power-of-attorney. He had found it convenient to allow E. D. Sassoon & Co. Ltd to take the losses on certain transactions in cotton while he pocketed any profits. It resulted in the 'misdirection' of several thousands of pounds before he was finally nailed.

Sir Victor found it distasteful to institute a prosecution which would inevitably have led to unwelcome publicity. The culprit was dismissed and approached another firm who agreed to engage him, subject to the usual reference from his previous employers. Victor wrote back: 'There is no question of "Mr X's" business ability; he should not however be empowered to sign cheques.' He was taken on, all the same!

When Victor succeeded his father, he also took over considerable tribal responsibilities. He was now the only surviving Sassoon resident in Bombay who could qualify as head of the Jewish community. Philip rarely visited the country, and Flora had severed her last direct link with India when she finally sold 'Il Palazzo' in 1920. She was now recognized in England as a leading authority on all matters of Sephardic doctrine and practice, and the Chief Rabbi has referred to her as 'a living well of Torah and piety'. But she was far from insular. Her butler in Bruton Street would in turn announce the Rani of Kapurthala, a rabbi from Aleppo and some Christian almoner from one of the many hospitals under her wing. Jew and non-Jew alike were welcomed for Sabbath-eve dinners at which her Indian servants produced a solid gold ewer and basin for the laving of hands before bread was broken. Flora then led the recital of grace in her sweet soprano.

The banquets that followed were so lavish, with the emphasis on a heavy eastern cuisine, that prudent guests would eat nothing for hours in advance. Nobody dared to refuse a dish at her table. Moreover, she had the oriental habit of passing titbits from her own plate. Her kinsman, Ralph Ezra, recalls that the fruit served was so enormous that many touched it unbelievingly to make sure it was not waxed.

Silver-haired, imposing, dressed with a regal elegance and always wearing the celebrated seven-roped pearl necklace, she kept open house at least once a week. Her salon welcomed the friendless as well as the socially favoured, each visitor in turn being invited to sit beside her for a few minutes. She seemed to know the family tree of every notable Sephardic family in a dozen countries. She was blessed with an unfailing memory and asked all the right questions in a direct but tactful manner, usually dismissing her guest with some practical advice or a promise to help. There was no need to take a note. It was all neatly pigeonholed for future action.

Her correspondence was prodigious. Postmen called every day with heavy bags of mail often simply addressed, 'Flora Sassoon, England'. She answered them all in her own hand and always on the day of arrival. From Russia, Persia and the Far East came pleas for funds from synagogues, and often agonized appeals for visas from the relatives of refugees who had already found sanctuary in England. Some wanted to trace a missing family or implored her help for orphans who needed to be adopted. Begging letters arrived by the score, including hopeful ones like that from a complete stranger in India who requested the 'loan' of £300 so that his daughter could have an operation. She replied courteously,

Sir Philip Sassoon, 3rd Bt. A drawing by Sargent, several of whose paintings were hung in a special room in the family's Park Lane mansion.

m. Siegfried Sassoon

A cartoon of Siegfried Sassoon in 1931 by his friend, Sir Max Beerbohm.
(From the *Spectator* Collection)

Port Lympne, April 1921. The British and French Prime Ministers meet for another series of talks on Reparations. Sir Philip Sassoon (left) acted as host, assisted by his sister, then Lady Rocksavage. Lloyd George was in genial mood but made little headway with M. Briand (extreme right). (*Daily Mail*)

The marble patio at Port Lympne, Sir Philip Sassoon's house on the Kent-Sussex border, from which guests had a superb view over the Romney Marshes and the Channel. It had a gallery of glazed tiles specially imported from Spain. (Copyright *Country Life*.)

Trent Park, Barnet, only twelve miles from London, stood in a 1,000-acre park and had a nine-hole golf course and private airfield. Here Sir Philip entertained royalty and many celebrities, including T. E. Lawrence and Bernard Shaw. It is now a training college for teachers. (Copyright *Country Life*.)

Sir Philip Sassoon, the Prince of Wales and Winston Churchill after a polo match at Roehampton. (*Tatler*, 8th June 1921.) Churchill often stayed at Trent Park of which he did several paintings.

even to silly correspondents, like the man in Shanghai who solemnly asked
her to decide whether Huntley and Palmer biscuits were *kosher*. She wrote
a sharp refusal to the impudent old *munshi* who had long ago given her
son lessons in Persian. He hoped she would show her 'gratitude' by sending him 2,500 rupees to settle his debts. She was kindlier to young
students from the European ghettoes in need of bursaries, and her heart
was always touched by pleas for dowries from some remote village in
Russia where life was hard.

Her son helped with this massive correspondence, although preoccupied with cataloguing his remarkable private collection of Biblical
codices and other rare liturgical manuscripts. It had grown so huge that
the two-volume catalogue, soon to be published under the title, *Ohel
Dawid*, would list over ten thousand poetical works alone in the index.
Among his illuminated manuscripts was the unique Farhi Bible, over ten
centuries old.* He had also made a major literary discovery by unearthing,
after centuries of oblivion, the lost corpus of poetry by Samuel Naghid,
the prince and scholar who flourished in eleventh-century Spain. This and
a MS. of Commentaries by Maimonides, written in his own hand, attracted
a stream of bibliophiles, among them Dr Davidson who came over specially from New York.

David Sassoon did not share his mother's tolerance of the London-
based members of the clan. A dedicated scholar and ultra-orthodox in
observance, he thought the Sassoon women blasphemous and could not
bring himself to be even formally polite to their husbands who went to
race-meetings on the Sabbath. Sir Victor was exempted from these stric-
tures by the austere bibliophile, who considered him a heathen, but good
natured. Unlike Philip and others, the baronet had fully accepted his communal responsibilities in Bombay and Shanghai, although he had long
divorced himself from the dietary laws and limited his synagogue attend-
ance to the most sacred Holy Days. However, he continued the firm's
practice of keeping all offices and factories closed on the Jewish Sabbath.
He took pride in his race and origin and always impressed on his co-
religionists the need to remain dignified in adversity and never to submit
meekly to unfair discrimination, however indirect. But he was careful to
avoid excessive parochialism. In memory of his father, he handed Lord
Reading a cheque for £37,500 to be distributed among India's needy and
destitute, whatever their creed.

* He negotiated patiently for ten years before buying it in Aleppo for £360. His
purchases between 1888 and 1919 cost him £2,304 13s. 3d. but the 506 manuscripts
were unique and chosen with remarkable discrimination. After the First World War,
when he paid as much as £1,500 for a Maimonides classic, the collection would have
cost him far more.

He maintained all his family's schools, hospitals and other endowments, but his cynicism did not always please the faithful. Some failed to appreciate his joke that 'there is only one race greater than the Jews, and that's the Derby'. His reawakened passion for the turf also invited violent criticism by Congress. 'Mr Eve' (the racing pseudonym adapted from his initials) had been interested in horses from his youth, but could only indulge himself freely after his father's death. He became friendly with Jimmy Crawford, a leading amateur rider in India, who returned to England to set up as a trainer. Among his first clients was Mr Goculdas, the Indian cotton magnate and sportsman, who had to retrench because of the post-war slump in textiles.

Victor took over all his racing interests, including more than a hundred horses in India and several in England, which he put into Crawford's charge at Bishop's Canning. Soon afterwards, he bought the famous Kingsclere stables where John Porter had trained many classic horses. Within a few months, fired with the ambition to breed his own Derby winner, he was pouring vast amounts into bloodstock. He spent 58,750 guineas in 1925, paying the then record sum of 12,000 guineas for a grey yearling filly. While at Doncaster Sales that same year, he bought two yearlings and happened to run into a bookmaker friend. He invited him to lay £1,000 to one against either of these horses winning the Derby. The bookmaker refused, but laughingly accepted the bet at a penny each way. One of the yearlings was later named Hot Night.

It was not these disbursements that aroused his critics so much as his decision, in July 1925, to spend £110,000 on a private racecourse. This was at a time when the Bombay mill industry was strike-bound by workers fighting proposed cuts in their wages. *The Times of India* condemned his racing plans as 'preposterous and deplorable', and denounced him for 'indulging in idle vanities and luxurious and extravagant tastes'. Victor went calmly ahead, building on a vast tract of land on the Sholapur Road in Poona. It was within easy access of his spacious bungalow, Eve's, which he used in the monsoon season when he was not occupying a suite at the Taj Mahal Hotel. Almost every day he would drive over in his huge yellow car, with the number plate EVE 1, to supervise the construction of three additional bungalows for trainers and jockeys, apart from excellent stabling for his growing string of horses.

Racing in Poona was on Wednesdays and Saturdays, and he would often be seen leading in a winner or two in his colours of peacock blue and old gold hoops and sleeves. In morning clothes and carnation, he always looked nonchalant and faintly contemptuous as he limped into the winners' enclosure, leaning on a silver-mounted stick while he held his horse's reins in the other hand. Usually hatless and monocled, with binoculars round his neck, he became a familiar if rather intimidating figure to his trainers and jockeys. They quickly discovered that he was just as autocratic about racing as business. He named all his fillies himself and invariably carried lumps of sugar about with him, but showed no charity towards jockeys who used the whip or otherwise disobeyed his strict riding instructions. He always loved to win but was superstitious about betting, convinced that any wager by him would prove a jinx.

He came over to England to see Hot Night run in the 1927 Derby. A few days earlier he called on his friend, Frank Curzon, who owned the favourite, Call Boy, but was too ill to go to Epsom. 'I just hope to live long enough to hear on the wireless that he's won,' he sighed. 'I hope so too,' murmured Sir Victor gently, 'and just to make sure, I will not back him as I always lose. But I'll break the rule of a lifetime and have a hundred on mine. That should settle it!' He was delighted for his old friend when Call Boy duly won in record time. It was a little disappointing to be cheated of his first Derby winner, but he did not regret keeping the whip off Hot Night, who ran second at 9 to 2. He was consoled by his bookmaker who had kept a record of the two-year-old bet and cheerfully paid over 249 pennies!

He now visited Shanghai regularly for two or three months each year. By the mid-'twenties it was booming. Godowns were roof-high with tea, silk, cotton, spices, rice, sugar and a dozen other commodities in which both Sassoon firms were still prominent. Yet there were many anxious moments. In May 1925 the killing of a Chinese millhand by a Japanese foreman led to a demonstration of workers and students who were fired on by Settlement police. The Chamber of Commerce called a strike next day in all foreign-owned factories. It ended with more shootings and a panic selling of shares. Among those who organized the riots was a former political chief of the Whampoo Military Academy, near Canton, who had lately returned from organizing a Communist cell in France. His name was Chou En-lai.

Shanghai now enjoyed a precarious calm. The Settlement became a sanctuary for discredited politicos and warlords anxious to protect their lives and fortunes. At the same time, swarms of peasant refugees from a dozen little wars were desperate to work in reasonable safety. They would need homes, as well as consumer goods and services on an enormous scale.

Victor had noted Hardoon's astonishing rise in property speculation. He too decided that bricks and mortar would be the most dependable and fastest growing field of investment in an unsettled country. Following the precedent set by his grandfather in the last century, he bought sites for development as factories and tenements, investing simultaneously in firms making building materials. He arranged to take over the old-established produce firm of Arnhold & Co., of Shanghai, with branches in Hankow, Tientsin and Canton, and offices in London. They also had useful interests in heavy engineering machinery, but Victor was even more attracted by their associated concern, the Cathay Land Company. This gave him control of several foreign-occupied apartment buildings and an hotel, as well as a sizeable number of housing estates in the French Concession. He now planned to add to the Company's site on the Bund in preparation for the hotels, office blocks and shops which would surely follow a thriving 'peacetime' economy. As part of this long-term strategy, he acquired holdings in laundries, breweries and flour mills, but the most substantial investment would be in short-dated mortgages on selected properties in the Chinese city.

The country was still far from pacified, and most factory workers went about looking sullen and potentially dangerous, but China had many attractions for expatriates living in the Settlements or the French Concession. Whisky out of bond was only two shillings a bottle, and the finest Manila cigars cost £1 a hundred. Servants were efficient and demanded little more than their keep and a roof. It was not surprising that Victor began to find Shanghai more truly his home than Bombay, where he was forced to spend most of the year. From the terrace of the Majestic Hotel or the Imperial he could see the rickshaws bowling along the Bund between elegant limousines on their way to the English Club, the Opera House, the Race Club or the gambling casinos on Bubbling Well Road. Some of the world's most *soignée* women danced in the arms of their white-coated partners after dining in the gilt and marble Empire Banqueting Room at the Majestic. Watching them waltz by in the light of coloured lanterns, with the scent of jasmine in the air, he never quite overcame a helpless sense of envy. That sunken courtyard was the scene of his gayest parties, but no pretty Chinese or European favourite at his side could compensate him for being unable to step on to the dance floor.

He was rarely seen at the races without some fashionably dressed woman on his arm. His stable was not on the same scale as his others in Poona and Newmarket, but it proved unexpectedly useful when Nunkie's visits to the Settlement began to coincide with his own. He had always understood and shared his uncle's weaknesses, but the ageing lady's man often acted too scandalously even for cosmopolitan Shanghai. Moreover, he expected to be consulted like an elder statesman at Sassoon House now that his favourite nephew was Chairman.

Victor manœuvred him away from the office by inviting him to manage his racing stable. This also became an embarrassment. Nunkie knew a good deal about bloodstock, and he was not the man to take kindly to 'Mr Eve's' forthright views on training and breeding. In a huff and determined to teach his nephew a lesson, he started up his own opposition stable under the name of 'Mr Morn'. He had very little chance against his well-established and richer rival, but they gave Shanghai racegoers some hilarious moments. Few would soon forget the meeting at which Wedding Eve ran a close finish with Dewy Morn.

Victor was often in too great pain even to go to the races. He would hobble from his office on the Bund to be driven home to his bungalow with the thatched roof. Lying outstretched on his bed in a darkened room, he would wait for the agony to subside. He sometimes found relief by fondling what he called his 'toys', the superb ivories which he had started collecting from his first days in China. He had sent his collector friend, Sydney Edward Lucas, and a number of agents on missions all over the country. From leading Manchu families they bought the ivory screens, trays and snuff-bottles which used to be exchanged between friends at times of rejoicing. Other valuable pieces were bought from Taoist and Buddhist priests who needed funds for repairing and restoring temples damaged by the wars or crumbling with age. One of Victor's special favourites was a steel-bladed knife worn by a former member of the Imperial family. Only $12\frac{1}{2}$ in. long, it had a jade handle and a scabbard of wood delicately inlaid with ivory.

The collection was still incomplete in 1927, when valued at over £100,000. It had been acquired with discrimination, often behind a heavy veil of secrecy. The pieces were usually offered singly or in pairs, but the bargaining became fierce when astute dealers put an inflated price on the last piece needed to complete a set. It was the kind of game which always amused and stimulated Victor. He would pay handsome sums for something he really wanted, but rarely allowed himself to be tricked or blackmailed.

A kinsman, who was not a member of the firm, once asked for a considerable loan to help him over his difficulties. Victor surveyed him with distaste through his monocle and cut the interview short by tossing his chequebook across the desk. 'Fill it out for what you need,' he snapped, 'but never come back.' The man hesitated before writing himself a cheque for a five-figure sum. It was generous, but well within the limits Victor had had in mind. As a seasoned poker-player, he had weighed the chances and gambled that the man would not risk too excessive a demand, thus leaving the door ajar for a return visit. He called back a few months later, as expected, but could not get past a stubborn, well-briefed secretary.

With all his shrewd psychology, Victor Sassoon sometimes went wildly adrift on political matters. He failed to make any distinction between the very different issues at stake in Shanghai and Bombay. He naturally took his stand with extreme reactionary opinion in the International Settlement where, for the better part of a century, his family had tasted the fruits of tariff concessions and all the other extra-territorial privileges enjoyed by foreign traders. One or more of the Sassoon nominees had always been on the Shanghai Municipal Council, a useful platform for lobbying or dealing with troublesome trade unions. It was also inevitable that a millionaire merchant and financier should support the Generalissimo and the police against Communism.

The Indian scene was far less clear cut, but Victor found ways of using his name and influence. When Lord Reading's Viceroyship came to an end in 1926, he agreed to serve once more on the Legislative Assembly. He was perturbed by the growing truculence of the Swarajists and did not trust Gandhi who addressed the new Viceroy, Lord Irwin, as 'Dear Friend' while directing his *khadi* campaigns and continuing to needle the adminis-tration.

Victor tended to over-simplify the causes of India's malaise. He was bedevilled by factory strikes and boycotts which made him even more impatient of hints about 'Dominion Status'. At Viceregal Lodge, as well as in the Legislative Assembly, he came to be regarded as a last-ditch reactionary. He seized an opportunity in 1927 to bait his fellow-members by entering the Chamber in full racing regalia of grey top-hat, morning coat and carnation. In a hubbub of protest and abuse, he looked about him with studied distaste and very leisurely removed his topper just before being called to order. It was done for rather a childish bet, but he had established himself as the first European to appear in the Assembly with his hat on.

He was now the leading millowner in Bombay. The E. D. Sassoon United Mills operated 6,500 looms and 250,000 spindles, in addition to the Alexandra, the Edward Sassoon and Meyer Sassoon Mills and various dye-works. But increasing taxation, higher production costs and constant strikes were making it difficult to withstand undercutting by foreign manufacturers and equally relentless competition from Indian-owned mills who often paid wages equal to only six annas in the rupee demanded in Bombay. His solution was to modernize plant and increase efficiency. He wanted to see fewer, but more skilled and better-paid, operatives in Indian mills.

He was almost alone in pouring money into capital development when other industrialists were either closing their plants or withdrawing funds altogether. He increased his spindles, replenished stocks and constantly experimented to improve the quality of the cloth. He overruled the grumblings of his United Mills shareholders, who had seen no dividends since the 1924 slump, and went ahead guaranteeing bank loans and 'forgiving' interest until the mills could be restored to a paying basis. By the end of the decade, the ten-rupee Deferred Shares had fallen to under a rupee, but there were encouraging signs that output and quality might slowly check Japanese competition.

United Mills were under the supervision of a dynamic figure, Frederick Stones, who later earned a knighthood for services to the Indian textile industry, as well as his championship of welfare schemes, including crèches and other amenities, in all the E. D. Sassoon plants. He had joined the firm in 1920 from the Bombay Dyeing Company, and became Victor's right-hand during the troubled years that followed. Standing over six foot two and weighing twenty-four stone, he was a gigantic personality in every sense. He hid a kind heart behind his ruthless drive for increased production, but could be equally blunt with the Viceroy or some troublesome foreman when the time came to deliver home truths in his broad Lancashire accent.

In the final analysis, however, neither his practical common sense nor the Chairman's financial flair could succeed without the goodwill of the workers. Congress showed no change of heart, and Victor's temper, always at low boiling point, became more violent with every turn of Gandhi's hand loom. He dismissed all India's aspirations to self-government as clear evidence of the 'Red Hand'. His three years in the Legislative Assembly, followed by his appointment to the Royal Commission set up in 1929 to investigate labour conditions, might have proved more valuable without his rather petulant outbursts. 'It is my firm conviction,' he once declared roundly, 'that the agents of Communism in India are making any grievance, real or imaginary, the excuse for the further spread of Moscow doctrines, the industrial agitation being but a cloak for a far wider and more sinister move.'

Congress leaders, who had welcomed the new Labour Government in Britain, grew restive when the Simon Report was published. The abortive series of Round Table Conferences in London was followed by Gandhi's spectacular march to the sea in symbolic protest against the Government's salt monopoly. Victor became even more intractable when demonstrations started at his mill gates. In Shanghai, he was used to playing the mandarin. Here in Bombay, where his great-grandfather had settled a century before, he resented being denounced as a 'foreign' exploiter of labour.

Both the Sassoon firms were inevitably hit by the world slump, but even harder by the political upheavals in India. They reacted quite differently.

E. D. Sassoon elected for expansion, and would profit indirectly from the depressed cotton industry. They bought one of Tata's mills and picked up several others cheaply when their owners went bankrupt or were forced to sell to settle their debts. The original firm decided to retrench.

Not for many years, and only after millions had been made or lost, would it become possible to judge the wisdom of either policy.

Chapter Sixteen

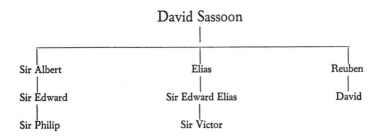

David Sassoon

Sir Albert — Sir Edward — Sir Philip

Elias — Sir Edward Elias — Sir Victor

Reuben — David

E. D. Sassoon & Co. paid £250,000 in 1929 for a largish site on the Bund, earmarking a further three-quarters of a million to convert it into an ultra-modern building. Formidable difficulties had first to be overcome. Shanghai's mud could not take the mighty skyscraper which Sir Victor had planned to put up on the New York model. After experiments with ingenious new engineering and drainage ideas, he compromised with a ten-storey building constructed from huge slabs of ferro-concrete. It would be known as Sassoon House and occupy almost an acre of ground.

British trade interests in China were then worth some £300 million, two-thirds of it concentrated in Shanghai. Speculators were eagerly pulling down dingy buildings and replacing them by apartment houses. Tenants seemed happy to pay high rents for modern amenities like lifts, plate-glass windows and reliable heating. Victor did not ignore this field, but concentrated most of his working capital on the Bund, the business heart of the city. Sassoon House would be ideally placed near the Custom House an such prominent office blocks as the Hong Kong and Shanghai Bank.

It was completed, as planned, by March 1930. The ground floor was rented by two banks behind which spread a network of shopping arcades. Two floors were let as offices, while the whole of the third would be occupied by E. D. Sassoon and Arnhold & Co. The fourth went quickly to the American Women's Club of China. The rest of the building accommodated the new Cathay Hotel.

Before the end of 1929, Victor had persuaded Carrard, the manager of Bombay's Taj Mahal, to go out and supervise the opening of the best-appointed hotel in the Far East. Three floors were given over to lavishly panelled rooms and suites with service even superior to that of most luxury hotels in Europe and the United States. Guests could summon a drinks waiter, room boy, maid, dry-cleaner, valet and laundryman by telephone. The vast marble baths had silver taps supplying purified water from Bubbling Springs Well outside the city. On the eighth and ninth floors were the sumptuous ballroom with its sprung floor, the restaurant, grill-room and kitchens.

Sassoon House was to become Sir Victor's headquarters. The Bombay mills would continue to be operated, in the full knowledge that only loan money and interest could be expected until the political situation improved. Cotton apart, the firm's other assets would be taken out of Indian ownership. These, together with the family's considerable private holdings and hard currency securities, would be removed from Bombay at once and absorbed in a vast reconstituted Hong Kong Trust. It was planned to re-invest mainly in Shanghai, but substantial deposits would later be made in the United States, mainly with the First National Bank of Boston. The firm's long-established export business in produce, linseed oil and the like was to be handled mainly by the Arnhold associate company, but would be allowed to run down slowly.

To finance the large-scale investment planned outside India, it was decided in 1930 to register a new concern in Hong Kong, the E. D. Sassoon Banking Co. Ltd. Half the £1 million capital was issued and paid up. Victor became Chairman, with Reggie Sassoon and Derek FitzGerald as fellow-directors. The Company took spacious offices at 85 Gracechurch Street in the City of London, where its European interests would be efficiently handled by FitzGerald. The firm's banking interests in London, Manchester and Hong Kong were taken over and rapidly expanded, but Shanghai's real estate development remained the main objective, despite civil war and the continuing threat of Japanese aggression.

David Sassoon & Co. were also suffering heavy losses in India, but they decided to sell some of their properties rather than move into an unsettled market. Their traditional operations had always been based on trading rather than merchant banking, and there seemed even less reason to change during a world depression. Another important factor was the death of David Gubbay in 1928, when executive control passed mainly into the hands of Cecil Longcroft. He was shrewd and reliable but had never, even in times of comparative security, shown much appetite for risky speculation. One of the firm's rare attempts to diversify during the 'twenties had been the opening of a branch in Buenos Aires. It lost money and was hurriedly closed down. Faced with strikes and boycott in India, Longcroft met little opposition when he chose to rein in. The Bombay cotton mills would continue, but on a far more restricted scale than that planned by the other firm. Longcroft hoped instead to develop reliable lines like soya beans, Chinese eggs, wood oil, spices, rice and other produce.

From Manchester to Canton, every branch of David Sassoon soon became uncomfortably conscious of this extreme cautiousness at head-office level. Sir Philip's chairmanship was always nominal, and the last family link had virtually been snapped with the loss of David Gubbay who had managed so capably after Ronald Sassoon's early death. Many employees began to ask themselves if the old initiative had not been buried with them. This was not quite fair to the Board.

Longcroft kept a tight hold on investment, content to export produce which did not involve too heavy a capital outlay. Before the world stock market began to collapse, the firm was quick to sell shops and office buildings at good prices, including Philip's valuable land in Icehouse Street, the site of the Hong Kong Stock Exchange. They preferred to take office space at economic rents and thus increase the company's liquid assets when others were holding on too long or pouring good money after bad.

It seemed a sound enough policy. Philip, for one, did not object. His share holdings, admirably handled by David Gubbay, Longcroft and professional investment counsellors, had been nourished by useful legacies from time to time. When Reuben's son, David, died in 1929, leaving half a million, £150,000 went to Philip, plus shares equal in number to those already held by him in the firm.

The third baronet's way of life demanded a very substantial income. Port Lympne had cost him the better part of a quarter of a million before he was even reasonably satisfied. Improvements never ceased. Guests would show no surprise at seeing Rex Whistler climb a chimney-piece to add some filigree of fantasy to a mirror in the Painted Room. This was situated between the gardens and the reception-room and had been artfully converted into a 'tent' with striped silk awnings. Whistler's attractive townscapes depicted scenes from Wren's London, Palladian Dublin and Park Lane in its eighteenth-century glory. A secret panel in the painting of a lady in a barouche opened to a marble cloakroom. Philip had paid his young artist friend a fee of over £800 and thought it well spent, even in the middle of the depression.

Trent Park took an estimated £10,000 a year to run, exclusive of frequent structural alterations. Philip scrapped the wrought iron gates at the entrance to his drive in October 1928. He substituted oak ones adorned by the urns which had long stood outside Devonshire House. He enjoyed pointing out the marks of damage done during the Corn Law riots and also some scratches reputedly left by George III's coach on one festive Christmas Eve.

He and the Prince of Wales were often joined by visiting Walker Cup teams who liked to practise on the excellent course at Trent. Philip once partnered the U.S. amateur champion, Harrison R. Johnston, against the Prince and Bobby Jones. Trent Park now had its private airfield and guests were encouraged to use the owner's new Super Moth, fitted with all the latest gadgets and expensive heating equipment. It was painted black, with pale blue stripes at the regulation spacing ordained for Old Etonians. He sometimes flew up from Port Lympne to breakfast with his sister at Houghton Hall and then dashed off to see the opening of a new play in Paris. In a mere twenty-five minutes he could hop from Trent Park, 'just to see how the flowers are doing at Lympne', and hurry back to London for a concert in Sybil's duck-egg blue ballroom or to join the Prince of Wales at the Embassy Club.

When the Prince bought himself a small D. H. Gypsy Moth, he started almost a shuttle-service between Fort Belvedere, his house near Sunningdale, and Trent Park. He found the Fort a delight after the gloomy formality of York House, and Philip suggested many of the splendid herbaceous borders as well as the layout of the rock garden. Norah Lindsay, Lady Diana Cooper's aunt, was in charge of this replanning, and would often come over to Trent to advise Philip on his own gardens and lawns. He became fascinated by her views on spiritualism. They used to walk together for hours, Philip completely absorbed in her stories about Conan Doyle, while she stepped out resolutely, an unforgettable figure in leopard-skin trousers and rows of baroque pearls dangling over a jazzy tunic.

He had grown almost morbidly superstitious and insisted on having his large silver cobra mascot on every car, motor-boat or aeroplane he owned. He qualified as a pilot a few months after the Prince of Wales, but needed almost twice his friend's flying hours. He once crashed while landing at Cranwell but stepped out unhurt and imperturbably telephoned Hendon for a replacement. He fretted so much at being wingless that he had himself photographed for a Christmas card while 'leading' 601 Squadron. The picture was faked. It was shot just as the pilot ducked out of sight to reveal Philip alone in the cockpit. It provided Sir Victor with one of his favourite anecdotes.

But the gay youngsters in 601 made allowances for their C.O., who took over when Grosvenor died in 1929. Philip was always a generous and friendly host. He presented them with new aircraft and could even laugh when someone made a forced landing and buckled the propeller of his Moth. Tom Moulson, the Squadron's excellent historian, tells us that Drogo Montagu once dived over Trent Park but forgot to wind in his wireless aerial. It made quite a splash in the lake and caused a number of casualties among the rare wild fowl. Philip took it gracefully, as usual.

Once qualified, he loved to lead the Squadron on bombing manœuvres and aerobatics. When official duties made him give up his command, they made him Honorary Air Commodore. His dinner parties for the flying boys became the envy of other squadrons who took to 'dive-bombing' Lympne with old cans, eggs, dead poultry and bags of soot. Even without such gate-crashers, the dinners often became so riotous that he was forced to lock away anything fragile or valuable.

He gave his warmest support to weekend pilots and private aero clubs, but did not neglect his official and more irksome duties as Under-Secretary of State for Air. Many sniggered about his effeminacy and joked that his baroque was worse than his bite, but they did less than justice to the serious way he tackled his unpaid job. His House of Commons manner remained unfortunate. Standing on one foot at the dispatch-box, like some exquisite heron who had alighted direct from the Burlington Arcade, he lisped through his statistics and often had a difficult time with hecklers. The R.A.F. was still the poor relation of the Services. It had simultaneously to resist the Cabinet's economy drives and Socialist clamours for disarmament.

The Opposition always made a point of singling Philip out for attack. They could never forgive reports of his sunken marble baths, the private airfield at Trent or his offhand purchase of an £8,000 Gainsborough from America while so many workless families were on short rations. The little red-headed Labour M.P., Ellen Wilkinson, declared that 'Sir Philip makes one want a revolution just to see him for once in an environment that has not been planned with perfect taste, but even if the Westminster Soviet made him carry coals, he would do it with a delicate air'. He would probably have resolved Marie Antoinette's dilemma by sending out a footman with a silver tray of *petits fours* for the starving.

His fastidious taste was best seen at the exhibitions in aid of hospitals and other charities at 25 Park Lane. Georgian art, painted fabrics, needlework, furniture and rare plate were periodically displayed to the public in settings which showed true artistry. For an exhibition of English Conversation Paintings, several from his private collection, he wrote the preface to the catalogue and filled the house with magnificent flowers from Trent Park. Queen Mary paid several visits and always stayed to tea.

His skill in arranging lighting and other novel effects would have done credit to a professional interior decorator. When his friends arrived for a

series of Roger Fry lectures on Cézanne, they notice that he had added a
background of red velvet to the statue of Diana that graced a niche in the
hall. Pots of hyacinths gave the impression that she stood in a garden. The
effect was enhanced by green pots of dark purple flowers which lined the
marble staircase leading to the peach and gold satin benches in Sert's
music-room.

Philip only seemed fully happy when on the move, restlessly rearranging
his *objets d'art* and guest-lists. Lady Horner, who had never forgotten her
promise to mother him and was constantly seen at his dinner-table, once
declared with complete sincerity that 'few rich men so understood how to
share enjoyment'. She and Mrs Belloc Lowndes were among many gentle
elderly women who soothed him when he seemed dejected over a badly
received speech in the House or was going through some emotional crisis.
At such times he reassured himself by filling his homes with people
slightly over life-size. Celebrities of every kind had become irresistible
to a man who almost appeared to live in italics.

Winston Churchill liked to relax at Trent, and his painting of the Blue
Room was the fruit of several visits. When he went into a London nursing
home for a throat operation, Philip invited him to stay at Park Lane with
his wife until he was fit enough to return to his own home in Kent. At Trent
Park, Lord Balfour could be seen dozing in a deckchair after playing tennis
with Boussus; G.B.S. and Lady Astor would be locked in two mono-
logues; while Thornton Wilder, promptly captured after the success of
The Bridge of San Luis Rey, was kept busy autographing copies for the
rest of the house party.

A visit to the Embassy Club or the Kit-Kat usually followed dinner if
the Prince and his younger brother, George, were guests. Philip was not
fond of dancing but dutifully accompanied them to nightclubs and the
more tedious charity balls. One of the latter provided a rare touch of the
unexpected. The Prince was patron of a Derby Ball at which a grandstand
box at Epsom was being auctioned for a deserving cause. The bidding
had started at only a fiver. Impatient to depart, the Prince at once bid £150
and smiled across at Philip, who quickly put it up by £10. Nobody else
intervened while the two kept bidding against each other. When it reached
£200, Philip dropped out inexplicably. The Prince looked surprised but
appeared to see the joke. Philip did not make it a precedent.

His ministerial job satisfied his taste for perpetual animation. He visited
Canada and the United States in 1927 to study developments in military
and commercial aeronautics. While in Detroit, he asked to see a new Ford
model but learned that it was still on the secret list. He sent Henry Ford a

personal note which at once brought a mechanic to drive him round the city. 'What do you think about it?' asked the manufacturer. Philip lightly nodded approval. 'I'm glad you think so,' laughed Ford. 'The car is now yours.'

He flew to Rome a few months later to see Marshal Balbo, his opposite number, and also had an audience with the Pope. While kicking his heels waiting for Mussolini to return from Milan, he hopped down to Naples for lunch and dazzled the natives with his elegance. For days afterwards, they could speak of nothing but his clothes, especially the magnificent pearl he wore as a shirt button. Back in Rome, the newspapers voted him 'the best-dressed Englishman' and started a vogue for copying his hats, ties and suits.

That autumn he set off on a seventeen-thousand-mile tour of inspection in India and the Middle East. It was almost a test flight for the huge Ibis flying-boat, but also gave him an opportunity to see remote R.A.F. stations very much off the usual inspection beat. Philip wrote an account of this trip which was later published under the title, *The Third Route*, and offered some unconsciously revealing glimpses of the author. In Baghdad, so long the home of his ancestors, he showed no desire to see the original source of his fortune or to search for family relics. 'Of course, I went to the Horse Show and wandered about a little in the bazaars and by-ways of the city,' he reports languidly. He disregarded the left-handed compliment of an admiring local journalist who described him as 'a true Baghdadi'. Basra, where his great-grandfather had once found brief sanctuary, he flicked off as 'a charming place – like an Eastern Venice'.

Between all the formal inspections and a warm reception at Viceregal Lodge in Simla, he did a painstaking and serious tour of duty. A former R.A.F. man, C. Stobart, can well recall his visit to Shaibah in Iraq. The temperature was 127° in the shade, morale was low, and the camp without radio and other comforts. The Under-Secretary slipped away from the officers' mess and appeared unannounced in the airmen's billets. He sat informally on the edge of a bed and chatted away about camp life. 'He sorted things out and cheered us up,' reports Stobart. Official action soon followed to improve the poor lighting and similar hardships.

He also visited Miranshah Fort on the Afghan border, where he met 'Aircraftsman Shaw', otherwise T. E. Lawrence. Dressed in soiled shorts and a faded open shirt, 'Shaw' was rather nervous of his visitor and attempted to break the ice by talking warmly of Siegfried who had given him much encouragement. Philip preferred to mention his subscription copy of *Seven Pillars*, and Lawrence lost his shyness as he talked about *The Mint* which he was then writing. What he wanted most of all, apparently, were some books and the gramophone which G.B.S. had promised him but forgotten to send. Philip hastened to put this right.

They became good friends, each perhaps sensing the unhappiness and darker undertones in the other. Philip could never resist a professional hero, particularly such a romantic figure, but showed genuine loyalty when Lawrence fell under the blackest of official clouds. When he was brought back to England after rumours that he was acting as a spy and generally fomenting trouble in the Middle East, he was welcomed at Trent during his leaves. He always enjoyed talking to Bernard Shaw, Chaplin or guests like the King and Queen of the Belgians, who came to stay incognito.

He was soon back in hot water. In September 1929 he manœuvred himself into a job as groundsman at Calshot so that he could enjoy the Schneider Cup Race. Senior officers looked horrified when he began to hobnob with visiting dignitaries. He was carpeted by Sir Hugh Trenchard, Chief of the Air Staff, who threatened him with instant dismissal if he approached Sir Philip Sassoon, Sir Austen Chamberlain, Winston Churchill, Lord Birkenhead or Lady Astor.

By this time Philip was no longer Under-Secretary, although again returned for Hythe when the Labour Government took office. He startled a few veteran constituents at his adoption meeting by denouncing Lloyd George as 'a self-appointed worker of miracles', but they were delighted when he was restored to his post within two years. He missed Sir Samuel Hoare who had moved to the India Office, but it seemed very much like old times when the Prime Minister, Ramsay Macdonald, arrived to spend a restful weekend at Trent Park after kissing hands at Buckingham Palace.

Philip did not desert Lawrence who, although a sore trial to the Air Ministry, remained an honoured guest at Trent and Lympne. Wearing his thick aircraftsman's uniform even on the hottest day and with his bull terrier at his heels, he liked to joke with the uninhibited pilots of 601 Squadron and talked earnest shop with Amy Johnson. She was made much of by Philip after her solo flights but, oddly enough, was never allowed to fly one of his own planes. Always sensitive to such things, he may have had a premonition that she would crash to her death.

T. E. Lawrence, however, could have asked for anything. He was particularly grateful for Philip's sympathy when he was twiddling his thumbs for months on end in dull maintenance work. He tried to kill the monotony by translating *The Odyssey*, but wanted desperately to work on flying-boats. Unseen officials seemed to block him at every point. He resigned impulsively from the R.A.F., then changed his mind and poured out his distress to Philip. Before very long, no doubt through his friend's discreet pressure at the Air Ministry, he was transferred to the Marine Craft Station at Felixstowe. He was practically looping the loop with joy when he arrived at Trent for tennis and a swim on his next leave.

Philip's return to office almost coincided with his cousin's formal departure from the Bombay scene. As an earnest of his affection for the country which he was leaving with genuine regret, Victor opened a fund to endow prizes for Indian pilots with a lakh of rupees (then £7,500). He had long supported flying clubs, an interest which softened him a little towards Sir Philip. Neither he nor Reggie had, however, forgiven the 'highly-polished' staff officer. When anyone introduced his name in conversation, they tended to shrug but made no comment outside the family circle.

Victor's decision to make Shanghai his headquarters came as a shock to many. The Sassoons from Baghdad had seemed almost as much a part of the Bombay scene as the numerous local monuments to their generosity. The Stock Exchange, aware of the steady transfer of assets and the significance of the new Company registered in Hong Kong, was rather less surprised. Besides, rumours had been flying about ever since Hardoon's death in June 1931. It was whispered that the E. D. Sassoon Banking Co. was planning to take over his property empire in the International Settlement.

On July 17 Victor crisply explained why he was leaving the country. 'There will be less scope in India for a foreigner in the future because of the cut-throat competition with Indian firms, who have less overhead charges, and because of the anti-foreign prejudice. It looks as if India under Swaraj will have a great deal of internal trouble. On the other hand, China is now getting over her civil wars and other troubles. China offers a better field to the foreigner because the Nanking Government realizes the necessity for foreign finance.'

It seemed a perfectly sound and valid prophecy at the time.

Part Five (1931–1949)

Chapter Seventeen

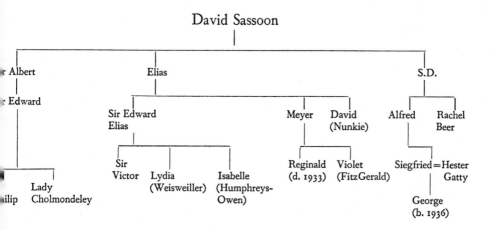

Almost from its opening day, the Cathay Hotel became a formidable rival to the Majestic where Chiang Kai-shek had held his £10,000 wedding reception. Its restaurant and the Horse and Hounds Bar were soon the venue of Shanghai's highest society. The world's leading cabaret artists performed in the ballroom where slender Chinese girls in brocaded satin *cheongsams* blended with the elegant and cosmopolitan beauties who came on from Settlement parties and race-meetings. Among the first guests to spread the fame of the new hotel was Noël Coward who, however, was laid low by an attack of influenza soon after arriving from Peking. Before sailing on to Hong Kong, he luxuriated in the room service. Propped up in bed, he completed the draft of *Private Lives* within four days.

The Cathay's success had stimulated the firm to start building a rather less opulent, fourteen-storeyed Metropole Hotel. Sites were also bought for several apartment and office blocks. Grosvenor House, Embankment House, Cathay Mansions and Hamilton House would, between them, offer tenants one thousand air-conditioned bedrooms and suites, with bathrooms and other comforts up to the highest standards of the West.

Few conservative banking houses would have approved such investments during a world depression. Moreover, China's top-heavy military budget and a disturbed currency had made her even less attractive than India and the oil-rich Middle East. Victor preferred to gamble on a speedy return to normal. Even if that were delayed, the Settlements still offered excellent prospects. The threat of Communism had brought in more and more Chinese capital for safe keeping, while office and factory space was soon at a premium.

Hardoon had left an estate valued at over £15 million, mostly in sites near the Bund, as well as across Soochow Creek in the Chinese industrial area. The honey from Shanghai's richest beehive would, however, have to be distributed to meet death duties in Hong Kong and elsewhere, apart from maintaining his lavish endowments. The E. D. Sassoon Banking Company was quickly on the scene. It underwrote an issue, greatly over-subscribed, for a public company to buy a slice of Hardoon's richest property for eighteen million Chinese dollars (about a million sterling), mostly on debenture stock.

Land prices in the Settlements were already climbing when Japanese troops moved into Manchuria in September 1931. The adventure was timed precisely when both Britain and the United States were financially strained and in the mood for disarmament. While the League of Nations debated and eventually sent out an exploratory Commission to Manchuria, the Japanese became resentful of the boycott of their goods and planned to move into China proper.

The times were propitious. That winter had been abnormally cold. Heavy flooding in the interior was followed by a famine which brought desperate refugees into the already overcrowded towns. Hundreds of corpses were being picked up each week from the pavements of Shanghai. Another convenient 'incident', this time the murder of one of their nationals by a mob, gave Japanese marines the signal to land under aircraft cover. Several bombs were dropped on the Settlement which also came under heavy shellfire.

Victor was lunching in the Cathay when the Chinese exploded a mine fifty yards from the Japanese flagship in the harbour. The ferro-concrete building seemed to sway, but he could find no sign of a crack when he made his rounds. Now and then a stray piece of shrapnel peppered what he called 'the front row of the stalls'. This made him so eager to see the war on the other side of the road that he picked up his ciné camera and limped out to take photographs. A Chinese soldier took him for a sniper and fired. The bullet passed over his head and shattered a window in one of the banks.

'On the whole the war kept its place,' he said later. 'Everything was most gentlemanly.' A Chinese general sent a perspiring A.D.C. with a packet of sweets as a peace-offering, followed by flowery regrets for the conduct of the soldier who had been punished. Not to be outdone, the Japanese authorities expressed their regret in the name of the Emperor for any damage inflicted on the most honourable and beautiful Cathay. However, it would be six long weeks before the Chinese retreated and the invaders were ready to discuss a truce.

Victor was under almost intolerable strain but managed to look cool and amused while ordering magnums of pink champagne for his guests in the Horse and Hounds Bar. Not for some time would his mother and sisters learn something of the truth. Alone in his office on the third floor of Sassoon House, he had spent long nights seeking ways and means of salvaging his affairs. Each burst of gunfire seemed to remind him that he had gambled with an empire painfully built by his ancestors and now in serious danger of collapse. His family and many other shareholders had followed him without question. If the 'incident' developed into a full-scale war, he alone would have to take full responsibility for what some would condemn as the reckless folly of an autocrat.

In later years he could joke about those endless hours when he kept reproaching himself and was 'almost' tempted to use the Service revolver in his desk. He was not helped by the acute attacks of pain in his hip joint which seemed always to coincide with business pressures. After a snatched sleep, he sometimes found relief by going out to the stables to feed sugar to his horses and make plans for their evacuation if the Japanese took the city.

He seemed as jaunty as ever when he arrived in London in May 1932 after a visit to the United States. He went to see his mother and also called on his sisters, Lydia and Isabelle (who had qualified as a doctor). Their pretty daughters were in the throes of the Season's dances and loved to tease him about his 'arrest'. When the steamer *President Coolidge* had docked at Honolulu, a woman revenue officer came aboard, impounded a trunk of wines and spirits in his stateroom and took him into custody. Since she was charming as well as pretty, he went cheerfully ashore to put up $150 in lieu of a fine. He was then permitted to return to the ship, a free man. 'I had no idea I was busting any of your jolly old United States laws,' he told reporters at San Francisco before hurrying on to New York.

But the strain of the past few months had left a mark. One of his wards, now Mme Zola Ponzio, can still recall her shocked surprise when she greeted him in London. After a year's absence, his hair had lost its sleek blackness and was liberally spattered with grey. The lined face was that of a newly old man who now looked the full fifty on his birth certificate.

He had only been back in Shanghai a few months when Reggie left on his usual trip to buy English hunters and have a few rides. On 16 January 1933, Victor was handed a cable and publicly burst into tears for the only time on record. Reggie's horse had hit the top of a fence and rolled over him during a steeplechase at Lingfield. He was rushed by ambulance to a London nursing home but died after a blood transfusion. In his memory, his mother built and endowed a working-class block of flats in Peckham to be let at nominal rents. Several of his brother-officers in the Irish Guards and a number of amateur riders subscribed for the R. E. Sassoon Memorial Cup in an annual race at Lingfield.

Reggie would be missed more for his gentle and delightful personality than his business capacity. As it happened, a far more efficient member of the family had reported for duty in Shanghai only a fortnight before Reggie was killed. This was Lucien Ovadia, Victor's cousin (their mothers were sisters), who was in fact returning to the firm. After a banking training, he had first joined E. D. Sassoon's Manchester branch in 1921, but grew bored with testing cotton and preferred to work with the Banque Belge Pour l'Etranger in London.

Ovadia was born in Egypt of Spanish nationality and educated in France. He was a true cosmopolitan who got on equally well with Europeans, Americans and Chinese. Heavily built and bald, he looked every massive inch the Sassoon Tai-Pan. Within a few years he had become the firm's number one in the Far East, specializing in finance.

He arrived at Sassoon House precisely when the firm was doing a very substantial business in foreign exchange and arbitrage. They had the largest sterling cover in the market, with an average quarterly turnover of well over £3 million. Sterling would be crossed against local currency and U.S. dollars to yield considerable profit, but there were also heavy losses through underwriting bad loans and indulging in over-speculative risks. During the early 'thirties, vast sums estimated at not far short of a million sterling would be lost by poor judgement. Although Sir Victor left the running of the business mainly to the management, he would sometimes be tempted to make snap decisions on projects that excited his imagination.

Ovadia's main function, apart from dealing in foreign exchange, was to assess risks and act as a brake on hasty action. He often crossed swords with Victor who had made it plain that he did not want him as yes-man but nevertheless disliked having his decisions questioned. Everyone kept well clear when the cousins were closeted in heated debate. They would eventually emerge for tiffin, all smiles.

One difference of opinion almost ended in Ovadia's resignation. During 1936, the director of an associate company entered Sir Victor's office in some excitement. It seemed that he had had the offer of all the best molybdenum deposits in a vast area west of Hangchow. Victor, always attracted by something new, was eager to buy at once. Ovadia was much less enthusiastic and insisted on making further inquiries, while his cousin hopped about, impatient to conclude the deal before some rival snapped it up. Ovadia had soon found several holes in the proposition. No foreigner could own these mines which would have to be sub-leased from, quite literally, hundreds of small tenants. Worse, the deposits were being hauled manually to the port, over two hundred and fifty miles away, by bamboo relays.

'This is crazy,' declared Ovadia, rightly pointing out that the half-million pounds or so asked might only prove the down payment on a most hazardous purchase.

'Buy,' snapped Victor. 'Go to the Chartered Bank at once and borrow the money.'

'I couldn't face the Bank with such a scheme,' objected his cousin. 'It would make us look fools. If you feel so strongly about it, I suggest *you* ask for the loan.' The argument became so heated that Ovadia offered to resign. Victor then ordered him out of his office. By next morning, he had quietly dropped the whole project.

With all his personal quirks, he was always a good man to have in one's corner when the fight was going badly. Ovadia remembers a nightmarish experience over one deal that had seemed almost routine. A Chinese Bank official brought in a government functionary who wished to buy certain properties in Hankow. The price was settled at £140,000 in American dollars, and one of the firm's managers left at once for Hong Kong to transfer the title-deeds. Ovadia preferred sterling at this time and speedily arranged to sell the dollars to the well-known exchange brokers, Swan, Culbertson and Fritz, on the floor below. They agreed to credit the firm with sterling in London, in exchange for the dollars payable in New York. Next day, to Ovadia's horror, the Chinese Bank announced that they would pay in sterling. This left the Shanghai office short of the dollars which they had already sold in advance and in good faith. To add to their misery, the rate of exchange had meantime changed against them. Ovadia sent an anxious cable to Victor, simply asking him to remit the requisite amount of dollars to New York and adding, 'Letter follows'. A cable came back by return. 'Remitted.' No questions were asked.

Victor could forgive honest errors of judgement and also gave extensive powers of attorney to Ovadia and one or two others in his confidence. But he had no patience with lesser men who committed the crime of not briefing themselves thoroughly in advance. He was charming to specialists who did not waste his time and gave him the answers, particularly if they chimed with his own views. One with the additional advantage of not being in his employ was Lewis Holt Ruffin, a handsome and debonair American who was not only a scratch golfer and socially prominent, but the youngest manager ever appointed by the National City Bank of New York. He later became a partner in Swan, Culbertson and Fritz and was a frequent guest at Victor's parties in Shanghai and Bombay. Victor turned more and more to him for advice on investments and the transfer of funds into sterling or dollar currencies. Ruffin had exceptional qualifications. He was closely identified with Wall Street as well as China; he had served in Rangoon and Manila, and moreover he was knowledgeable about Latin America, soon to become increasingly attractive to the E. D. Sassoon group.

The Chairman was himself a valuable roving ambassador, with high-placed contacts in government and banking circles in every continent. But his greatest asset was a team of specialists hand-picked for their knowledge of the complicated Far Eastern scene. Lucien Ovadia acted as the firm's 'insurance' risk assessor and underwriter in the Far East. In Bombay, Stones was the hard-headed, textile administrator and technician who blasted his way through labour difficulties and was unexcelled in dealing with government departments, from the Viceroy down to some obstructive *babu*. In 1932 Victor was fortunate enough to enrol W. B. Bryden, a young Scots chartered accountant from a leading firm in Calcutta. He would become his chief *aide* in the intricate banking operations now unfolding.

There was plenty of capital for investment. The Shanghai properties would almost treble in value by 1935. The hotels, office blocks and apartment houses all yielded handsome revenues, while several acres in the Chinese city would be added to the property empire when many mortgages were foreclosed during the acute currency crisis of the early 'thirties. It was not all smooth sailing. When Nanking's silver reserves dwindled, a paper dollar note was issued. Worth only 1s. 2½d., it failed to arrest an adverse trade balance, since the price of silver abroad still kept falling and inevitably caused China's exports to decline in value.

These currency troubles hit all the business houses, but E. D. Sassoon was more than compensated by Shanghai's buoyant land values. Several solid interests were also acquired in the Union Brewery, laundries, lumber and transport companies. Competitors soon began to circulate the bitter half-truth that one went by a Sassoon tram to a brothel rented from the firm, who also took a percentage from every glass of beer served there. Revenue came from many more reputable sources. In 1935 the Banking Company made a private-issue loan of £238,000 to the Hwai River Conservancy Board to finance its construction work on the Chiangpa Regulator. It was secured by the British portion of the Boxer Indemnities remitted to China in 1922. This issue was placed privately in London and regularly serviced and amortized until just before the war, when the Japanese troubles prevented the remission abroad of the necessary sterling.

Sir Victor was now being freely spoken of as 'the J. P. Morgan of the Orient'. When he sailed from Hong Kong, his own launch would come out to take him into Shanghai, thus sparing him irritating formalities at the Customs. Few politicians and industrialists in the International Settlement or the French Concession ventured to move without privately canvassing his views in advance.

He became a close friend of the Generalissimo's brother-in-law, Dr H. H. Kung, the Finance Minister, a stoutish Yale-educated man with whom he was often closeted. He was delighted when Dr Kung insisted on personally presenting him at the Cathay with a gold medal for his liberal endowments to the Chinese Red Cross Hospital.

He was now dividing his time between the hotel and Eve's, his bungalow off the Hungjao Road overlooking the golf course. It was built in the Old English style on the model of a Sussex house where he had stayed with friends. From the courtyard one entered a raftered lounge hall with a vast open fireplace and inglenook seats. There were only three very modest bedrooms because, as he frankly admitted, he wished to discourage too many people from intruding on his privacy! He developed an enthusiasm for gardening and experimented with various species of carnations, but soon gave this up for sailing. He had a small yacht built in Norway and shipped out to him. It was at once christened *Eve*, and won many races, but he did more entertaining on his houseboat which was ideal for duck-shooting. When he tired of this, he stayed mainly in his suite at the Cathay, while Mr and Mrs Ovadia took over the bungalow.

In the hotel he gave some of the most lavish and almost legendary parties of the pre-war decade. For one 'shipwreck' fancy dress ball, the guests were bidden to come as if they had just taken to the lifeboats. The first prize went to a couple with a small hand towel between them. They were apparently taking a shower together when the ship's 'alarm' went! For a circus party the guests turned up as clowns or performing animals, while Victor acted as ringmaster. Whatever the *motif*, he insisted on reasonable decorum and had no patience with tipsy and unruly guests, male or female, who were never asked again.

There was rarely a shortage of pretty girls at his parties. Chic women from the legations brushed bare shoulders with delicate Eurasian beauties, and the host often escorted a partner from a light opera company that toured the East every year. One or two selected ladies from the chorus always seemed to leave the troupe in Shanghai. Victor would engage them as temporary members of his secretarial staff and often dropped them off in Bombay when he flew there.

Frederick Stones was making excellent progress in pulling the mills back into shape, although labour troubles still handicapped output. The replacement of out-of-date machinery also caused a constant drain on capital. By contrast, the David Sassoon firm continued to apply the brake and closed down their Manchester office in March 1934. The Shanghai, Calcutta and Karachi branches discontinued trading altogether in textiles, but maintained offices for transacting import–export business in produce and collecting rents from the various family properties.

Aware of these policy changes, Victor began to send out feelers. By 1937 he had acquired several of David Sassoon's residential sites in the Treaty Ports, including their main office building at the corner of the Kiangse and Kinkiang Roads in Shanghai. The price of nearly £140,000 turned out to be a pleasant little windfall for various members of the other clan who had drawn steady but modest incomes over the years. 'I had quite forgotten we still had any interest in Hankow doss-houses,' Siegfried laughed when this writer recalled the transaction. In fact, Victor had not bought as an investment but mainly because he disliked seeing any Sassoon landmark go out of the family.

A David Sassoon branch still flourished in Hong Kong where the firm had been prominent from its first days in China. On the eve of the depression, Longcroft had thought of closing it down but was dissuaded by the two local managers, A. H. Compton and Robert Stock. They held on grimly and were able to expand the produce trade, especially in sugar and rice. It was not easy and often called for on-the-spot initiative.

When the Chinese Government decided to tax sugar in the mid 'thirties, there was a frenzied rush by importers on the mainland to stock up. One of the firm's chartered ships, *Cape Cross*, was actually on its way from Java to London when the forthcoming duty was first announced. Stock and his colleagues hastily radioed the captain in mid-ocean and ordered him to change course for Hong Kong. There it was surrounded by a swarm of junks waiting to unload. Merchants scrambled to buy up the cargo and sail it up the coast before the tax came into force.

David Sassoons had always enjoyed a close connection with old-established sugar firms in Sourabaya and such leading rice exporters as Blackwood, Ralli in Burma. The Hong Kong branch established almost a trading monopoly in rice when they switched their main imports from Saigon to Rangoon. The Burmese paddy market prices had to be watched on a vigilant day-to-day basis with the aid of the Reuter's cable service. Before long, it became impossible to close the office on Saturdays, as the Sassoons had always done, and the branch had to fall into line with other local firms except for the sacrosanct Day of Atonement.

When Japan made war on China in 1937, the Cantonese authorities were naturally anxious to lay in heavy stocks of rice. A Chinese giant of a man once burst into the Hong Kong offices of David Sassoon & Co. and offered to buy up their entire stocks from Burma. He claimed to be acting unofficially for Canton and explained that he was working through nominees, a Dutch bank, to avoid diplomatic complications. He agreed to buy 50,000 tons at £7 per ton *c.i.f.*, but only if it could be delivered very quickly. Longcroft was cabled but showed a natural distaste to place so much business in one market, however lucrative. It seemed altogether too hush-hush and risky for his taste. He was only persuaded when the Dutch nominee proved to be above reproach, but remained reluctant until the Hong Kong and Shanghai Banking Corporation agreed to help underwrite the transaction.

Stock promptly chartered six P. & O. steamers who shipped the whole 50,000 tons from Rangoon to Hong Kong within a month. There were some anxious moments. The three-funnelled S.S. *Talemba* was the very first ship to arrive, with even her passenger cabins stuffed to the ceilings with rice. A typhoon then blew up, and she and other vessels were ordered out to Junk Bay to make more room in the overcrowded harbour. The *Talemba* drifted and went aground. Two thousand tons of rice were destroyed, but all dealings were covered up to 90 per cent by Lloyd's who settled quickly. Apart from this single mishap, the whole transaction went off smoothly and showed the firm a healthy profit.

Victor often made flying visits to Hong Kong, where his Banking Corporation was registered. At his headquarters in Holland House, Victoria, he and Bryden organized and allocated investment capital for a network of subsidiaries, but neither could afford to stay away too long from Shanghai where Victor now faced problems outside his business interests. A number of Central European Jews had made for the Settlements as soon as Hitler came to power. As persecution mounted, hundreds more escaped each month to Italian ports and embarked for China. By the end of 1937 something like twenty thousand had arrived in Shanghai, many with only the ten marks which the Nazis allowed them to take. Since they could not land without the regulation minimum of £100, Victor Sassoon, Ellis Hayim and other wealthy co-religionists had to allocate substantial funds as caution money.

Food, shelter, medical care, schools for children and houses of worship had also to be provided, and Victor made himself personally responsible for providing free milk to all refugee families. Jobs were, however, the top priority. He placed many immigrants in his own offices and associated concerns, while using gentle pressure on other employers. It was characteristic of him to remind the refugees, many of them stateless, that they now owed loyalty to those who were giving them sanctuary. As a result, about two hundred and fifty fighting men were soon being trained under a Jewish commander for the Shanghai Volunteer Corps.

Victor's attitude to the ancestral faith showed a slightly erratic sense of logic. He was never a practising Jew but did not renounce his religion. When in England during his mother's lifetime, he always respected her feelings by avoiding business and race-meetings on the strict Holy Days. His secretary once grew alarmed at having innocently booked him seats for a first night on the eve of the sacred Yom Kippur. He brushed aside her apologies and went off to the theatre as his mother was no longer alive. Similarly, 'out of respect for my forbears', he left instructions that a rabbi was to say a prayer over his grave but expressed no wish to be buried in a Jewish cemetery.

He admired Flora Sassoon, who signed scores of guarantees and relentlessly bombarded the Home Office with letters on behalf of many refugees seeking asylum in Britain. At the same time, he did not share her passion for Palestine and remained openly sceptical of Zionism as a solution to the Jewish problem.

On one visit to England, just after Flora's death in 1936, he received her grandson, Solomon, who had graduated from a rabbinical seminary in North London and was now actively engaged with his father in refugee work. He called rather nervously at 85 Gracechurch Street to enlist help for four relief organizations in desperate need of funds. Victor was kindly but abrupt. He cut short his young kinsman's explanation of why the money was required and quickly wrote out four cheques, each for £1,000. Solomon thanked him profusely and declared that his work for refugees in the Far East was 'full of virtue'. Victor shook his head. 'I'm a wicked man,' he said with a smile, 'and the last to be accused of virtue.' Rabbi Sassoon went off, greatly relieved at not having been pressed for details. Two of the cheques had been privately earmarked for the Holy Land.

Philip may possibly have contributed anonymously to refugee causes, but it is doubtful. He signed a naturalization certificate for Richard Tauber, who repaid his kindness by often giving after-dinner recitals of his *lieder* on the terrace at Lympne, but Philip saw nothing wrong in sailing to America in a new German liner. He infuriated his co-religionists even more by paying a private courtesy call on Goering early in 1933, during an official visit to Berlin to discuss aerial disarmament. Goering only discovered afterwards that his 'Parsee' guest was a member of the hated race.

Philip was finding life more confusing and difficult, despite his customary air of detachment. He once told Anthony Eden that he had given up reading newspapers because 'entertaining gives me all the news worth hearing without the trouble of reading what the Press has to say'. Nevertheless, he was sensitive to criticism and suffered acutely during his difficult time at the Air Ministry. He made strenuous tours of overseas stations, diligently visited aircraft factories and championed civil aviation, but it was becoming more frustrating to have to stand up to an unfriendly Commons. A stronger man was needed to plead for increased Air Estimates while his own party remained apathetic and the Opposition was campaigning passionately against an armaments race. Above all, his explanations withered under repeated blasts from Winston Churchill.

Introducing the Estimates in 1935, he was almost howled down when, in reply to Churchill, he declared that the country was stronger in the air than Germany. All his critics jeered at being reminded that 'actually, in terms of first-line aircraft, our strength is nearly four times that of Rumania'. Some months later, he told Mr Attlee, 'I do *not* think Coventry is so very vulnerable', and strongly recommended its use as a shadow factory centre.

He was far happier playing host to admiring friends who enjoyed his smalltalk. They liked to hear about the fox who had eaten 'two of my costly little ducks at Trent' and relished his account of a bumpy flight to Singapore when his teeth 'had chattered like dice in a box'. As in the days of Lloyd George, if now less frequently, he was delighted to provide a venue for some secret parley. In mid-June 1935 he entertained Sir Samuel Hoare, Anthony Eden and Sir Robert Vansittart at Trent Park. During that weekend, the plan was drafted to yield to Mussolini and buy off the unfortunate Abyssinians with a strip of sea outlet from British Somaliland.

When Eden succeeded Hoare, he would often rush from the Foreign Office to Trent for a game of tennis or a refreshing swim. He liked Philip with whom he had enjoyed working as a co-Trustee of the National Gallery. Others, however, found him intolerably irritating. Sir Harold Nicolson has described him in his diary as 'the most unreal creature I have ever met', and even his intimates could not always resist teasing him about his lion-hunting. One Easter he received a telegram from a woman who said, 'Christ is risen. Why not ask Him to lunch?'

Characteristically, he could not help warming even to his rebel cousin when he re-emerged as a literary celebrity after almost a decade of semi-obscurity. Siegfried's war anger had dissolved into the bitterness of peace. His satire, directed at the privilege and philistinism of the 'twenties, proved that the sullen eagle's talons were far from blunted, but the slim volumes of verse were privately printed and read only by friends and others who cherished the earlier poems. His convictions remained as impassioned and confused as ever.

He had lost his taste for doctrinaire Socialism but not his deep humanity or his sympathy for the underdog. The General Strike plunged him into his worst fit of despair since the dark days at Craiglockhart. He shared with Osbert Sitwell a disillusionment with trade union intransigence. Both saw the tragic hopelessness of the class struggle but could do little. Late one night in May 1926, they called together at Beverley Baxter's flat in Chelsea. Almost in despair they appealed to him to put the strikers' case in the *Daily Express*. Baxter found Sitwell easier to pacify than 'the gallant eccentric', who, as he later recalled, kept marching back and forth, 'brandishing his fists at the ceiling'.

In one of his poems at this time, Siegfried poured scorn on the Mayfair sybarites who indulged themselves while miners went hungry. His own needs were small. He had his gramophone and the baby grand on which he played Chopin long after midnight. He enjoyed his pipe and a glass of wine with fellow-writers, and he liked to go over to Fenner's or any County ground where there was promise of good play. In the season he always turned first to the cricket column in *The Times*. His memory of pre-war players, complete with initials and individual performances, was encyclopaedic.

Rachel Beer died in 1927, leaving £318,000. After death duties, the residue was divided between Siegfried, his brother, Michael (who had returned from Canada and settled at Matfield), and other survivors of the Ashley Park branch. His legacy of £30,000 or so enabled Siegfried to live in a little more comfort and privacy. It gave him the chance to travel abroad and visit the Bayreuth Festival, and also to see old friends like Max Beerbohm at Rapallo. After a time, he left Weirleigh (where his mother remained until her death in 1947) and settled in an immense rambling house near Warminster, with a park backing on to the Wiltshire Downs. Among his books and manuscripts, with his grand piano and a glowing oil painting of Aunt Rachel over the fireplace, he lived very quietly and saw few people. He continued to write ironic verse, but was being urged by Sir Edmund Gosse to attempt a more substantial poem incorporating his youthful experiences of country life.

It would prove an exhilarating challenge for a reserved man who had never outgrown his roots. After the harshness and feverish uncertainty of post-war England, this nostalgic retrospect of his old life in the Shires took on an idyllic and comforting aspect. His vignettes of half-remembered days began to take shape, not however as verse, but in crisper prose. He could still not bring himself to write in the first person and decided instead to tell his story in semi-fictional form through a narrator, 'George Sherston'. Even so, he needed encouragement. Glen Byam Shaw has recalled the time when he was at the Oxford Playhouse with J. B.

Captain Reginald Ellice Sassoon, M.C., Irish Guards. He rode in the Grand National and died after a fall at Lingfield where an annual race is run for a Cup in his memory.

The Marchioness of Cholmondeley (right) on the Admiralty roof with the Director, W.R.N.S., Dame Vera Laughton Mathews. Lady Cholmondeley, a leading figure of this Service in both wars, was made a C.B.E. in 1946. (Photo: Cecil Beaton)

Sir Victor Sassoon leads in Pinza at Epsom, 1953. It was a first Derby triumph for both owner and jockey, Sir Gordon Richards. The latter retired to set up as trainer, but Sir Victor won three more Derby victories.

Sir Victor and Lady Sassoon, his former nurse from Dallas, Texas, at London Airport in September 1960. She shared her husband's interest in the Turf and maintains the famous racing colours, as well as his many charities.

Fagan. Siegfried used to come backstage and, after much persuasion, diffidently read one or two pieces he had sketched out.

Memoirs of a Fox-Hunting Man appeared anonymously in October 1928 and delighted the public with its sensitive charm and wit. The critics rhapsodized over such gems as 'The Flower Show Match' and 'The Colonel's Cup', and first editions soon changed hands at inflated prices. It won the Hawthornden Prize for the author who could not, however, face the ceremony and begged Edmund Blunden to represent him. Two years later, following the success of war books by Blunden, Graves and Richard Aldington, he published a sequel. The whimsical cricketer and steeplechaser was now in the trenches, recalling his experiences of the Somme and Arras with an understatement and integrity that have stamped *Memoirs of an Infantry Officer* as a modern classic. It brought him a far wider and more appreciative public than his poetry.

Before embarking on the final stage of his trilogy, *Sherston's Progress*, he began writing poems in which he prophesied the coming of a more devastating war than the last. As he sat at his desk in the library at Heytesbury, he could hear the drone of engines above Stonehenge. His verses were published in 1933 under the title, *The Road to Ruin*, but attracted little attention except among those who, like himself, had signed the Revd 'Dick' Sheppard's Peace Pledge. He was almost regretting his war poetry which had invested him with a dated and quite distasteful glamour. 'I only wrote those poems,' he now insisted, 'to make people remember how utterly ghastly war is, and to stop criminally senseless people, like American film directors, from pretending that war is a romantic picnic.'

He was in a gloomy frame of mind when, out of the blue, an invitation came from Port Lympne. Surprisingly, he accepted curious to meet this cousin who seemed to be liked by some and loathed by many others, but mainly to inspect the new murals painted by a mutual friend, Rex Whistler. The latter and T. E. Lawrence were almost the only people he knew among the crush of celebrities from the political and sporting worlds. He soon retreated into a corner where he was joined by another lost-looking soul. This was a sad young Rothschild from Frankfurt, who told him of his humiliation by the Nazis. Siegfried listened sympathetically but soon made his escape from Lympne which was altogether too shrill and opulent for his taste. He afterwards told his brother of the eeriness of a 'country retreat' where, almost before one took out a pipe, half a dozen flunkeys pounced with matches and ashtrays.

Perhaps he sensed the pathos of Philip's life behind all the glitter and social feverishness. He could never grow close to one who spent so lavishly on creature comforts while thousands of unemployed workers and their children went hungry, but came to think more kindly of him.*

In December 1933 Siegfried married Hester Gatty, whose family included several distinguished lawyers. Only a few relatives and intimate friends were present, among them T. E. Lawrence. Philip sent a charming letter of congratulation and Siegfried thanked him with a picture postcard on which he wrote: 'There'll always be a plate of porridge for you at my fireside.'

But Philip, a diner-in by preference, had little time for excursions into remote Wiltshire. If his ministerial duties grew more trying, his stock with the Royal Family had never stood higher. He was always available. He took the Duchess of York's young brother back to Eton after the holidays and lent Trent Park to the Duke and Duchess of Kent for the second part of their honeymoon. Soon afterwards, he called at Fort Belvedere with some prize delphiniums from Trent Park and delighted Mrs Simpson with the gift of a dachshund puppy. On this occasion, the boot of his Rolls-Royce was so crammed with packages that the Prince of Wales raised a questioning eyebrow. Philip explained. 'Sir, as I was going to be in the neighbourhood anyway, I thought it would be just as easy to include a few presents for the King and Queen at Windsor Castle, and for your brother (the Duke of York) at Royal Lodge.' The Prince watched the car receding and murmured to Mrs Simpson, 'Philip certainly isn't missing any tricks this morning. He's just about filled a royal flush.'

This was not one of Philip's happiest days. Instead of being content to deliver the delphiniums, he had also brought along his gardener to plant them. The Prince thought he should have been consulted and rather testily had them uprooted and replanted, only a yard or so away. 'As a matter of fact,' he confided to Mrs Simpson, 'he picked out the best place, but I couldn't resist being a little difficult all the same.'

Snubs of this kind were rare, and Philip showed himself a loyal and helpful friend when the Wallis Simpson affair became delicate. The Cholmondeleys' villa near Cannes was taken for the summer of 1935 by the Prince and a house party of friends, including Mrs Simpson, whose husband was also invited but declined. Later that year, the Prince spent the weekend at Trent Park with Mrs Simpson before departing for a strained Christmas at Sandringham.

The death of King George V in January 1936 indirectly strengthened Philip's links with the Royal Family. The hereditary office of Lord Great

---

* In a letter to the present writer, he commented, 'I know Philip was an easy target, but I have no sympathy for the hedonists who accepted his lavish hospitality, and then made fun of him.'

Chamberlain passed to his brother-in-law, the Marquess of Cholmondeley, whose ceremonial duties would include the care of Westminster Palace and control of all State Ceremonies therein, notably the Opening of Parliament, when he would sit on the Monarch's left. He would also play an important rôle at the Coronation of the new Sovereign.

Philip's part in the Abdication crisis was limited to that of a friend who could only offer deep sympathy on his visits to the Fort or when the Prince came to Park Lane for a quiet dinner followed by a film show in the private cinema. At Trent Park, he entertained the Duke and Duchess of York who appreciated a short respite from the intolerable strain and uncertainty of those anxious weeks. They had always been close to Philip and his cousin, Hannah. When they first moved into 145 Piccadilly, Mrs Gubbay had advised them on the decorations and furnishing schemes. She also made many of the clothes for Princess Elizabeth's layette, as well as the lace cushion covers for the Duchess's bedroom.

Philip endeared himself to the young Princesses by many little acts of kindness. While visiting the Regent's Park Zoo with her sister and mother, Princess Margaret Rose had become so infatuated with a peacock that she refused to leave without it. Her mother told her firmly that this was out of the question, and the Princess had departed in a flood of tears. She was comforted a day or so afterwards when Philip sent two peacocks from Trent Park, one for herself and the other for her sister. Later, he enchanted them with some rare water fowl from Lympne for a garden pond recently dug in the grounds of Buckingham Palace.

His resilience was remarkable. He saw nothing wrong in inviting his friend's *bête noire*, Mr. Baldwin, to spend Easter 1937 at Trent Park. When the Coronation excitements were over, he flew off from Lympne with gay Tyrolean costumes in his bag to join the Windsors in Austria. The imposing gates of Trent Park were daubed by yard-high swastikas in his absence. He seemed more irritated by the aesthetic outrage than any personal significance.

If anything, he felt as carefree as at any other time in his life. The trials and perplexities of the Air Ministry were behind him, now that he had become First Commissioner of Works in Neville Chamberlain's administration. Even his premonition of an early death temporarily subsided after a lucky escape in an air crash. He was not strapped into the back seat of his new two-engined Perceval which tore through a hedge and overturned into a dyke while landing at Trent in a heavy rainstorm. The aircraft was badly damaged and Philip had a moment of terror when the exit door jammed.

His new post was completely congenial and satisfying. It kept him prominent in high places but without responsibility for unpopular policies.

He now had full outlet for his connoisseur's flair in art, tapestry, decoration and landscape gardening. His staff at Storey's Gate, Westminster, was soon infected by an enthusiasm which would make Coronation Year, his first in this office, memorable for taste and beauty.

He started with the House of Commons during the summer recess. Structural alterations were made in the kitchens, dining-rooms and 'servery'. The lighting in the Chamber was softened, the seating remade and ventilation generally improved. Members of all parties rejoiced at the way dark corridors were suddenly transformed into handsome lounges by stripping the varnish from oak panels. Himself the possessor of an exquisite collection of clocks and watches valued at £25,000, Philip delighted his colleagues by installing several more timepieces, including one in the Press Gallery shaped like a dartboard, with another over the Speaker's Chair.

His touch was also felt in the State Apartments at Hampton Court Palace before they were reopened to the public. The ugly Victorian black pipes were ripped out and replaced by concealed panels in the floor. Even the fire-fighting apparatus was artfully concealed in window-seats. New furniture was brought in, and pictures rehung with all the artistry which Philip gave to his own homes. Every day or two he would arrive to rearrange a vase or point out where the velvet of a beautiful settee was going threadbare. He inspected everything personally. Those responsible for liveries and plate at Foreign Office and other official banquets quickly became aware of an exacting, fastidious taste behind the scenes. He helped design picturesque uniforms for the footmen and, for one India Office reception, lent his own Louis Seize chairs from his mansion in Park Lane, now renumbered 45.

He restored Thornhill's Painted Hall at Greenwich and set about removing some of the sombre heaviness from Admiralty House. Under the hall floor he had the linoleum scraped away to reveal some exquisite eighteenth-century stone. When Sir Samuel Hoare moved from the Admiralty into the gloomy Home Office, Philip at once replaced the Home Secretary's ugly writing-table and also disposed of a grim desk calendar which had made him shudder. It was still marked in red ink to denote execution dates after the statutory three weeks for reprieve had elapsed.

He advised Mrs Neville Chamberlain to redecorate some walls at Number Ten in gay yellows and pinks. The three drawing-rooms were refurnished with eighteenth-century settees and Regency sofas. He had a suite of furniture formerly owned by Clive of India upholstered in red, and arranged for the National Gallery to lend works by Turner and Claude Lorrain to brighten the room. He also used his imagination to transform a small passage into an elegant and intimate room, where Mr and Mrs Churchill would often dine together during the war years.

He opened a campaign against litter in London's Royal Parks. To stimulate civic pride, he planted bright crocuses on the grass verges and installed comfortable wooden benches made from old ships' timbers. They were replicas of those at Trent and Lympne. He was soon earning more praise for his hard work as First Commissioner than ever before in his career, yet would never overcome his fatal assiduity to please.

After the Coronation, it was decided that those present in the Abbey would be permitted to buy their chairs and stools as keepsakes, while other historic relics were to be sold to the public. Bernard Newman, the author and lecturer, was then in charge of sales at the Office of Works. He began to notice that several of the titbits seemed to be reserved for Sir Philip's friends. Resenting such favouritism, he made strenuous efforts to save at least the golden Throne carpet from ending in some peer's country house. He finally checkmated his Minister by disposing of this particular treasure to Winchester Cathedral.

As peace hopes faded, the Sassoon cousins reacted quite differently. Sir Victor was fighting tenaciously to defend his interests in Shanghai against renewed attacks by the Japanese. The birth of a son, George, in 1936, gave Siegfried delight, but it also made him agonize over the world's imminent catastrophe. 'If I had a son of military age,' he told an interviewer, 'I should leave him free to decide for himself. I should hope that anything he did would be courageous, but I should not be proud of him if he dropped bombs on babies.'

Flora's son, David, was another gentle soul who came near to despair. He prayed ceaselessly for peace and spent much time and money helping refugees from Germany. His collection of Bibles and scrolls was almost as dear to him as his own children, and he suffered great anguish at having to leave them in a London safe deposit. That night he wrote sadly in his diary, 'I embraced and kissed them and reflected whether I should ever set my eyes on them again.' Five sealed cases of manuscripts were also sent to the National Library of Wales at Aberystwyth.

Philip remained a slightly wistful anachronism to the end, yet he too must have had private misgivings. He made his last will and testament in the summer of '38. The time had passed for worrying about whether to have mauve or white crocus beds in the parks. The Houses of Parliament were being sandbagged and people seemed more interested in the safety of air-raid shelters than their artistic appearance. However, he continued to do his duty and took exceptional pains to ensure that the French President's

State Visit in March 1939 went off without a hitch. He closed Westminster Hall to the public while it was reheated, briskly rebuking a Socialist M.P. who wanted to know why the stoves had to be lit so far in advance. 'I am trying in three weeks to counteract the chill of nine centuries,' replied Philip.

A few days later, he gave a lantern lecture to the Eton Archaeological Society on the preservation of ancient monuments. In mid-April he had a severe attack of influenza. Although barely recovered, he spent the whole of the 21st at Windsor Castle as he was anxious to see the King and Queen before they left for their tour of Canada and the United States. He then departed for France where his temperature rose alarmingly from a streptococcal infection in the throat. He flew back to England when it spread to a lung.

Philip Sassoon died peacefully in Park Lane on June 3. He was only fifty, but his death spared him the ugliness and horror of a war in which he could only have played an unhappy spectator. Lord Boothby has rightly observed that 'he was the end, not only of a line but an era. His death, like everything else about him, was well timed'. No memorial service was held, by his own request. His ashes were scattered from the air over Trent Park, while fighter aircraft from 601 Squadron circled and dipped in final salute.

He left estate valued at £1,980,892, on which duty of close on £800,000 was paid. Hannah Gubbay was the main beneficiary, inheriting Port Lympne, Trent Park and an annuity of £11,000. The original of Earl Haig's Order of the Day went to the British Museum. Sargent's oil portrait of Philip was left to the Tate Gallery who, however, rejected the same artist's charcoal drawing of the Prince of Wales as being 'of insufficient merit'.

Various handsome bequests were made to hospitals, and more than a hundred servants received a year's salary. The R.A.F. benefited by £5,000, to be applied to a half-yearly prize for the best cadet at Cranwell, excepting the winner of the Sword of Honour. Philip did not forget little Miss Skey who had mothered him so long ago at Eton. She inherited an annuity of £100 and remembered his charm and kindness to her over the years. 'I always knew he would do well in the world,' she declared with pride.

Chapter Eighteen

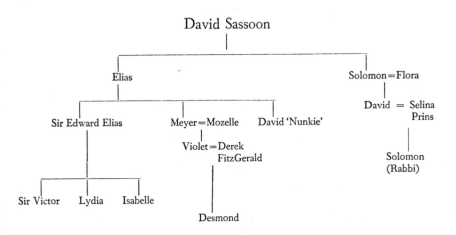

Coronation Year seemed to Victor symbolic of peace and plenty. After civil war, slump and intermittent threats from Japan, all his argosies were at last coming into port. A central national bank had been set up in China, and even the paper dollar was looking less dog-eared. Dr Kung was in Europe busily negotiating loans for financing railway construction and the purchase of war materials. His country's internal ulcers seemed to be healing. Chiang Kai-shek had not found it easy to parley with the Communists, but he was realist enough to see the short-term virtues of a common front. This watchful love–hate relationship now had the doubtful blessing of Moscow, who sent military supplies and 'advisers' to Peking. Such a situation was not ideal, but the merchants and bankers of Shanghai still welcomed the prospect of a more settled economy. An average of thirty large ships docked every month in the Liverpool of the East. It seemed that United China must grow progressively stronger and better equipped, materially and psychologically, to repel any hostile move from Tokyo.

The Indian industrial front was less stable, with nine million workdays a year lost through strikes. In the February provincial elections, the Congress Party had made substantial gains and was able to form a ministry in Bombay. Nevertheless, Victor was in optimistic mood when he arrived for his annual visit in the early summer of 1937. His mills were turning out more yarn of improved quality, while a protective tariff was also helping them to compete in price with the Japanese product. Significantly, the 10–Rupee shares of United Mills, so long at zero, had slowly climbed to three rupees.

Victor had arrived in Bombay, still glowing with his first English classic success, the One Thousand Guineas, soon followed by victory in the Oaks. He now planned to add to his studs by heavy purchases of bloodstock in the hope of leading in his first Derby winner. On July 8 the ticker-tape machine in his office on the Ballard Estate announced that Japanese and Chinese troops had clashed on the Marco Polo Bridge outside Peking. Within twenty-four hours, Japanese troops were rushed to Manchuria and were heading for Peking under an umbrella of heavy bombers.

An armada of enemy troopships, supported by cruisers and destroyers, was steaming for Shanghai, while low-flying bombers strafed the Chinese territory around the port and the columns of refugees streaming across the countryside. In the Japanese part of the International Settlement some four thousand of their troops exploded out of their barracks and were fiercely engaged by Chiang's forces beyond the Shanghai perimeter. They were joined on August 11 by Japanese marines.

The French Concession and the International Settlement (policed by British troops and American marines) felt secure behind their barbed wire and sandbags. But this time it would be no comic opera affair of a few broken windows, settled by apologies and a bag of sweets. On the morning of August 14 1937, henceforth known as 'Bloody Saturday', Chinese aircraft attacked the enemy flagship *Idzumo* moored just below the Japanese Consulate-General. Hundreds of terrified Chinese, joined by foreigners from the northern and eastern districts, poured over the bridges leading to the Bund which was soon jammed with refugees.

Shortly before four-thirty that afternoon, two Chinese planes were greeted by a hail of ack-ack from the men-of-war in the river. It seems that they panicked or lost control. They jettisoned their bombs. Two fell in the river, one just opposite Sassoon House on the Bund. A bomb struck the roof and top storey of the Palace Hotel which became a sheet of flame in minutes. Another glanced off the side of the Cathay, cracked the canopy covering the entrance to Sassoon House and burst in the street, killing hundreds who thronged Nanking Road.

Ovadia was working in his office while the gunfire was going on. Two of the windows were open when the first bomb fell, and the blast hurled him across the room. He picked himself up as the phone rang. Suter, the Swiss manager, reported that the hotel entrance had been hit. Ovadia went down by lift and found the canopy wrecked and the arcade a mass of broken glass and shattered lalique. Luckily, a party of twenty-four American schoolteachers who were having tea in the lounge had left the

Arcade only a few minutes before the explosion. Bodies lay thick among the masonry and glass in Nanking Road, where several wounded had their clothing torn off by the blast and were screaming for help. By nightfall, hundreds of corpses were stacked like grotesque sandbags in the street. Within the next two days, many more sprawled in death opposite the racecourse where a few enterprising citizens were knocking rough coffins together.

The Cathay began to count heads and glasses, but damage was light. The front of Sassoon House was boarded up, and a section of the Volunteer Corps guarded the Arcade. The company's excellent Chinese personnel had responded well, and it seemed that Mayor O. K. Yui was keeping down panic and defeatism in Greater Shanghai. Parties of British and Americans were still being evacuated. Shoppers occasionally had to duck to avoid stray bullets from some pilot taking a rooftop joyride, but no significant incident had occurred since Sir Hughe Knatchbull-Hugessen, the British Ambassador, was machine-gunned on August 26. *En route* from Nanking, he was about fifty miles from Shanghai when two Japanese planes dive-bombed his car and seriously injured him in the spine. The enemy had apparently mistaken his car for that of Chiang Kai-shek who passed through only a few hours later.

The main Sassoon properties were inside the Settlement and the French Concession where blast was quickly made good by the firm's various associates in the building trade. They were spared the bitter fighting in Chapei and Nantao where the population suffered incessant bombing, followed by looting and atrocities wherever the Japanese took a sector. Whole buildings were stripped down to the last nut and bolt before being set alight by the soldiers.

Victor flew from Bombay to Hong Kong towards the end of September to meet Lucien Ovadia and Bryden. They reported that business and social life in Shanghai had returned to a slightly feverish normality. The Cathay Hotel had only been briefly put out of action, and all services were restored within hours of the bombing. The fighting was still continuing outside the Settlement when Victor arrived back there later that autumn. British and American patrols, backed by the reinforced Shanghai Volunteer Corps, maintained order on the fortified perimeter, and people went about their business with more confidence. The import and export trade had of course suffered but the port remained open, although ships were anchored for safety at Woosung farther downstream. The firm's major interests in transport and other public services remained unaffected. On the third floor of Sassoon House, the company's real estate department was being flooded with inquiries for apartments, offices, shops and godown space at almost any price.

The property shortage became a famine when the war started to run strongly against the Nationalists. By early November, after heavy slaughter on both sides, Chiang had to withdraw from the Shanghai triangle. Japanese troops marched through the International Settlement in a Victory Parade on December 3 when a hysterical onlooker tossed a bomb as they passed the Sun Sun department store. Little General Iwane Matsui, who weighed only seven stone and used to read lengthy chauvinist poems to his suffering officers, was now less amiable. He insisted on access to the International Settlement at any time without advance notice to the Municipal Council, also claiming the right 'to investigate and examine suspects' within its confines. Crossing the Garden Bridge over Soochow Creek, elderly Chinese had to bow to the Japanese guards, who often prodded them with bayonets or playfully threw them into the water, watched by indignant but helpless British sentries.

The Japanese would make a show of force by raiding a hotel or two on Nanking Road and removing a few servants for questioning. They also took their time searching people crossing their sector to and from the Settlement, but still said 'please' to Europeans. In the Cathay the mood remained cheerful, despite the grim news from the front. The invaders took Nanking by mid-December, indulging in vicious atrocities against the civilian population. The Generalissimo fell back but went on fighting, holding up the enemy by a scorched earth policy and vigorous guerrilla tactics.

Morale-boosting parties were held nightly in the Cathay, where the drinking became heavier and less relaxed as stories of the Nanking horrors began to come through. However, the pink champagne bubbled and frothed with every report that the Nationalists had 'consolidated their positions'. If any business friend expressed gloom, Victor would rally him with a joke or offer to buy him out. He had absolutely no doubt at this time that Chiang would triumph. In office conferences and at public meetings he made provocative comments which were duly reported back to General Matsui's intelligence officers. He repeatedly predicted that the Japanese Army would bleed to death in China.

He also pooh-poohed timid strategists who feared that the Japanese might take Canton and then turn on British Malaya. He was more disturbed by the wanton sinking of the U.S. gunboat *Panay* and foresaw a future collision between the United States and Japan. Like so many others, he was convinced that the new docks planned for Singapore would make Malaya impregnable, and nothing could ever shake his faith in the R.A.F.'s ability to counter any threat to Hong Kong.

It was still obviously prudent to plan an overall financial strategy for what he always referred to as '*my* companies'. In fact, since the death of

Sir Edward and Meyer Sassoon, the holdings in the major concern were shared almost equally between Victor, his mother and sisters on the one hand, and Mrs Mozelle Sassoon and her family. The ratio, however, always remained slightly in his favour. In the E. D. Sassoon Company, this was 56 per cent against 44. In the Banking Company, his family owned 50,000 shares of which 10,000 were held by him personally in one of his trusts. His Aunt Mozelle held 49,990 shares. He kept the remaining ten to give himself effective control.

As early as 1936 Victor had gathered his rupees, sterling and Shanghai dollar assets into a non-dollar 'O' (Omnibus) Trust, known as the Victoria Holding Company. Through this concern he sold half his assets from the various trusts originally left in India and China under his father's will. This allowed him a personal capital credit of £2,800,000, up to half of which he could raise under the terms of the original family trust. It also enabled him to maintain his racing studs and stables, while separate accounts, under the secret pseudonym of 'Val Seymour', were used to help Jewish refugee organizations by putting up guarantees or paying passage money for those anxious to seek new homes in the Far East.

As a hedge against currency upheavals, he invested substantial capital for himself and the various family concerns in American stocks and international bonds which offered good gross returns. One of his most profitable coups was the purchase of a huge block of Australian Bonds offered to him in Shanghai, in 1937, by a broker at about 40 per cent discount. In the mid-'thirties he also bought the controlling interest in a small French bank, the Société Parisienne de Banque, from Sir Basil Zaharoff. He continued to dabble in scores of other projects and was always eager to invest in new inventions. Hearing that some Austrian refugees had experimented with plastic tubes, he quickly financed a manufacturing company and opened handsome offices in Rockefeller Centre.

But these were relatively minor operations in a vast and intricate complex. The firm's fourteen mills in Bombay would obviously become vital in wartime. However, much of the machinery was obsolete, and administration far from efficient. Victor decided to send Bryden to join Frederick Stones. They were instructed to build up maximum stocks, replace equipment and prepare for capacity output. Consequently, the Bombay mills had impressive reserves, including a valuable 100,000 bales of fine-staple American cotton, when more cautious competitors were either running down or operating on an almost month-to-month basis.

The firm's property holdings in Shanghai had actually increased in value as a result of the Sino-Japanese war, but nobody could guess the future while the Japanese held the docks, the post office and the Customs. If the fighting went against them, they would surely check the outflow of currency and print 'occupation' yen. The Sassoons and other prominent business houses decided to play safe by shipping millions of dollars to Hong Kong. Further, Sir Victor considered this the right moment to make a tour of the Western Hemisphere. Apart from brushing up on the military and diplomatic situation, he hoped to find attractive investment pockets outside the sterling area. 'A good desk has plenty of drawers of all sizes,' he often reminded himself and his advisers.

On 31 March 1938, he flew from Hong Kong to Mexico City by Pan-American China Clipper. He then made his way through Panama and spent some weeks in Chile and Peru where he attended many parties but had time to see local bankers and industrialists. It seemed to him that one could not go far wrong in following conquistadores like Bethlehem Steel, the Guggenheims and Standard Oil of New Jersey. In Buenos Aires he was fêted by the snobbish *estancieros*. He visited their vast ranches, although far more fascinated by their horses than the endless vistas of pedigree beef. During this time, however, he became decidedly uneasy about the growing influence of the German colony whose propaganda was being blatantly directed against Britain and the United States.

He flew up to New York via the West Indies and Florida. He had already part-formed the general plan for establishing a powerful 'V' Trust in Latin America with surplus dollar assets, should his position become untenable in China. That seemed remote, but he thought it practical to sound out Holt Ruffin who had specialized knowledge of this hemisphere's involved financial structure. In the Bahamas, he was enchanted equally by the climate and the obvious tax attractions. He made a mental note of this potential cache for sterling before heading north from Miami.

He played the gay, debonair millionaire bachelor in New York and was guest of honour at all the best parties, but corporation lawyers and brokers discovered him to be anything but a dilettante over investment prospects. His portfolios were fairly considerable but well spread. He was seen with so many film stars that it was wrongly thought he might be planning to buy into Hollywood, but he was more interested in reports of what Du Pont were doing in synthetic fibres. Plastics, insurance and the currency market all claimed his notice.

He took every chance to give his forthright views on the Far East crisis. Even if Chiang Kai-shek were defeated, which he doubted, the enemy would still need British and American financial help to remain in control unless a military clique seized power and did 'something rash'. He hinted to friends in Wall Street and the State Department that an Anglo-American-French economic embargo could soon drive the Japanese out of China. This incensed their Consul-General in New York who pointed out that Sir Victor had cleared his assets from China and was no longer qualified to express such views. Since the firm's property holdings in the Settlement alone had only recently been valued at well over £8,750,000, this riposte cut little ice with the Americans. Nor was it apparently taken too seriously by the Japanese themselves. They soon redoubled their efforts to win his support.

Victor's overseas interviews were extensively quoted in Shanghai, often to the embarrassment of his associates who were trying to maintain a precarious 'neutrality'. As a result, he once surprised the San Francisco reporters with a rare 'no comment' and professed to know nothing about what was going on in the Settlement. When he opened his newspaper in the St Francis Hotel next morning, he was furious to read a headline, 'Sir Victor Sassoon knows nothing'.

He flew back to China early in 1939, stimulated by a social tour which was also a useful dry run for future investment. The only sad note had been a cable informing him that Nunkie had died in Shanghai. They had had their differences, but the old *bon vivant* had always proved more congenial than other relatives who were inclined to be over-critical when their annuities and dividends seemed to be in any danger. Nunkie, flamboyant to the end, had left instructions for his burial in a most elegant casket of crystal and gold. As soon as Victor reached Shanghai in February, he visited the cemetery which his grandfather, Elias, had built in the mid-'sixties.

He was quickly besieged by refugee leaders who welcomed him back almost like a messiah. One desperate plea came from a Jewish doctor with a polio patient. Victor, himself a cripple, was sympathetic and wasted no time in importing the first iron lung into China. To avoid causing anti-Jewish feeling, he made it plain that any European, American, Chinese or Japanese hospital would be free to borrow it. Such a problem, however, was more easily solved than the plight of hungry refugees who were herded into blitzed and insanitary Hongkew, held by the Japanese. They were not allowed to move to the Settlement or the French Concession and were constantly being warned that relatives from Europe would not be given landing passes as freely as before.

Victor's work on the Committee for Assistance to European Refugees ('Comar') helped him to pierce an elaborate smoke-screen. The Japanese had never practised anti-Semitism, but in Manchuria and later in Shanghai they set up committees to report on any possible advantages from the 'problem'. Some eighteen thousand refugee Jews, mainly Ashkenazim of German origin, were living in Shanghai. Few had much capital, but Tokyo thought their skills might be 'co-ordinated' into the new sphere of Co-Prosperity. If they were kept out of the Settlements, it was hoped that these stateless Jews, many without strong religious ties, would turn pro-Japanese. A liberal policy towards them might also make a good impression abroad, especially in the United States. With the pressure alternately applied and relaxed, they could have a hostage value as far as their richer brethren in the Settlement and the French Concession were concerned. The main problem for the Japanese was to win over old-established Sephardic clans like the Sassoons, Ezras and Kadoories, who not only exercised international banking power but, unlike the refugees, had strong British affiliations through nationality or tradition. By working on their sympathy for Hitler's victims, it was hoped to use their financial backing and perhaps even wean them from Chiang Kai-shek.

Victor was as adept as any Oriental in maintaining a bland façade. After his return from New York, he became aware of a distinct coolness towards him, but hid his feelings. While there was any prospect of squeezing concessions for the refugees or the Settlement's business community, he remained the soul of courtesy towards the Japanese. Their officers were treated with scrupulous politeness when they dined at the Cathay, now the main rendezvous of the various military and diplomatic colonies, not excluding a swollen army of spies and police informers.

As war came nearer, discouraging reports about him were going back to Tokyo. It now appeared certain that he could not be relied upon for neutrality, let alone pro-Axis support. He was becoming almost deliberately provocative. On 13 July 1939 he flew to Hong Kong and stopped off *en route* for a few hours in Tokyo, where he stunned a passport examiner by roundly indicting the Government for the decline in Anglo-Japanese goodwill. While gaping officials edged nearer, he hinted strongly that if their countrymen continued to make business conditions difficult in the Settlement, he and many others would not hesitate to move lock, stock and barrel to Hong Kong. He seemed quite unconcerned and rather amused that police agents followed him from the moment he left the airport to go shopping and sightseeing.

Soon after war started, he sold two valuable sapphires and a number of jade necklaces in the United States and gave the proceeds to the R.A.F. for the purchase of fighter aircraft. While in New York, he read out a telegram sent to him by Jewish refugees in Manchuria, protesting against their brutal treatment by the authorities. He also told a radio audience that the Japanese people must soon revolt against a power-mad military clique. This naturally aroused fury in Tokyo where some newspaper commentators called for his arrest if his plane landed there. He took this as a challenge to return by the same route. Nothing happened at the airport, but this time he did not go shopping.

He supported the newly opened British War Fund in Shanghai with a single personal gift of £20,000. One of the most painful moments of his life was to wave farewell to the Seaforth Highlanders who departed for Singapore and other strategic points where the British were thin on the ground. They embarked with grim faces while the U.S. Marine Band played 'Will ye no' come back again?' American and Japanese forces would now share patrols of the British sector.

While Tokyo remained outwardly polite, the Nazis were irritated by Victor's exuberant faith in their certain defeat. They had noted his extensive preparations to build up an arsenal of goods in Bombay, and Goering evidently thought him important enough to denounce on the radio as a mischievous 'Hollywood playboy'. This amused him, but he considered the enemy was going a bit far in resurrecting poor Philip! On 9 January 1940 the *Volkischer Beobachter* informed its readers that 'Sir Philip Sassoon remains at his important post as director of war production in spite of the dimissal of Hore-Belisha'.

Even more curious is an episode recalled by Louis Polak, a distant kinsman of Flora Sassoon's daughter-in-law, the former Selina Prins of Amsterdam. Early in the war, the Germans in occupied Holland thought they might gain a propagandist advantage and possibly some useful foreign currency by establishing links between Dutch Jewry and any rich connections abroad. The Polaks naturally included the Sassoons in their list, but a German official explained self-righteously that this family would be unacceptable as sponsors because 'they had dealt too much in opium'!

The Japanese were less fastidious in Shanghai where they had tried in vain to gain control of the Settlement. The membership on the Municipal Council was comprised of two Japanese, two American, two British and one European (usually Swiss), together with seven Chinese. The British Chairman exercised a casting vote. Since the voting qualification was based on property ownership, the Japanese saw a chance of sweeping the coming election with docile voters from occupied Hongkew. The big companies countered by promptly splitting all their own properties into small groups and handing them over to a body of directors for a nominal transfer. Victor's holdings in the Far Eastern Development Co., together with Mozelle Sassoon's, produced hundreds of votes alone, and the Municipal Council was elected as before.

The Japanese tried another tactic. They approached Sir Victor late in 1940 with the polite suggestion that he should join an Anglo-Japanese property combine to 'safeguard' foreign real estate. He wanted to turn this down flat, but was restrained by the British authorities who thought it might be practical to keep them on a string. This manœuvre worked up to a point, but the Japanese finally began to press for a decision. It was learned over the bamboo telegraph that they were proposing to put up several run-down properties in Hongkew as their side of the amalgamation, hoping to secure the far more valuable Sassoon shops and houses in return. Ovadia promptly made out a list of rat-infested tenements which were either derelict or notoriously bad rent risks.

A Japanese colonel duly arrived at Sassoon House with his *aides* and two armed sergeants. After much bowing, he produced a list which confirmed previous rumours of its worthlessness. Ovadia then handed over his schedule. The colonel glanced at it briefly. 'This is an insult to Japan,' he snapped, jumping to his feet. 'We will never forgive you.' It was no idle threat.

The Settlement was ideal soil for a gangster-style 'protection' technique. Vincent Sheean used to say that Shanghai was unique in two respects: great wealth, and an even greater fear of losing it. A third unenviable distinction was its underworld's 'tariff' for murder. In pre-war years, thugs had quoted £1 for killing a Chinese and £5 for a foreigner. The Japanese were more subtle in their approach. They professed complete innocence of arson and other outrages on property by organized gangs, but lost no time in inviting leading merchants to 'contribute' sums to help maintain law and order in the Settlement. Victor scoffed at these manœuvres and refused to pay over a single paper dollar. Indirect threats soon reached him that his properties might be 'transferred' in the interests of efficient administration if he remained unco-operative. 'Splendid,' he told an emissary. 'I've been trying to get rid of them for four years.'

A conciliatory Japanese officer then gave a private dinner party in his honour at the Cathay. Over the brandy he paid his guest flowery compliments, but hinted very gently that the mighty Sassoon empire would undoubtedly collapse when the Chinese dollar became worthless. 'It doesn't concern me,' said Victor serenely. 'I have a very large overdraft.'

'An overdraft? A Sassoon with an overdraft?' His host shook his head in disbelief.

'Of course,' said Victor, taking out his monocle which was handy for just such occasions. He polished it carefully, before fixing it in his eye. 'You must understand that no one with any sense keeps money around when robbers are ravaging the neighbourhood.'

The dinner ended in outraged silence while the junior officers waited for their chief to recover from his loss of face. He picked his teeth and managed a smile. 'Tell me, Sir Victor,' he asked in a low voice, 'why exactly are you so anti-Japanese?'

Victor clipped a fresh cigar and took his time. 'I am not anti-Japanese at all,' he replied. 'I am simply pro-Sassoon and very pro-British.' Yet he did not minimize the danger of his own situation or that of his colleagues. In January 1941, W. J. Keswick, the head of Jardine, Matheson & Co. and Chairman of the Shanghai Municipal Council, addressed a ratepayers' meeting at the Racing Club. He was severely wounded by four shots fired by the Japanese spokesman.

The Horse and Hounds Bar was now the scene of some rather desperate drinking, but the foolhardy were bundled off before they talked too much. Agents and double agents of all nations operated an almost round-the-clock service. In his office, Victor continued to work under considerable difficulties. In 1940 he had set up two Bahamian companies, one of which would later take over all his British racing interests. The outflow of capital from the Settlement was still gathering momentum, and in this respect he was in a favourable position. Being a resident of Shanghai, his holdings there were outside Sterling Control. He could move these assets freely, while those in the huge Hong Kong family trust might also be invested in American securities.

Although considerable capital was deployed to Manila, Boston, New York and elsewhere, the Bombay mills would not be stinted for money, stocks and enthusiasm. Derek FitzGerald arranged in London for the purchase of the Indian cotton output and also shipped out textile machinery and replacements. However, since the outbreak of war, the E. D. Sassoon Banking Co. had inevitably to limit its energies to serving the family interests. Desmond FitzGerald was already in the Irish Guards, and many of the staff at 85 Gracechurch Street followed him into the Services.

Victor's situation in Shanghai grew daily more precarious after the Keswick outrage. He had a suspicion that his telephones were being tapped and took to keeping his revolver handy to 'repel boarders', as he put it. He seemed to thrive in this atmosphere of danger and habitually wore his old R.F.C. tie. He radiated confidence at parties and ordered his executive staff to winkle out suspected spies and rumour-mongers from the organization. In the Cathay ballroom they regularly showed the latest British and American films, but tried to avoid those which might provoke the Japanese into retaliation. However, diplomatic restraint had its limits. The performances usually ended with a sing-song of favourites like 'We'll Hang out our Washing on the Siegfried Line'.

In the spring of 1941 Victor was strongly advised by Ovadia to get out of Shanghai. He flew to San Francisco where again he discounted Tokyo's capacity to be of much help to the Nazis. Equally, he pooh-poohed any suggestion that the Japanese could pursue a successful militaristic policy on their own. Like so many others, he became a victim of euphoric jingoism. Any Kuomintang advance was always magnified in the Settlements, and notably in Hong Kong, which was then seething with speculators making quick fortunes from tungsten and other war materials in short supply. Victor was more interested in boosting confidence. 'The internal situation in Japan is anything but good,' he assured American journalists. 'Labour is short and inefficient and machinery lies useless for lack of repair.'

He thought it a huge joke when the F.B.I. insisted on giving him two stalwart shadows in New York. There had been whispers of possible danger from members of the Nazi Bund or perhaps Japanese gunmen who might wish to silence him. Washington, anxious to avoid any embarrassing incident on American soil, remained unmoved by his protests. He finally acquiesced and enjoyed playing hide and seek with his bodyguards whom he managed to slip for a night out in Harlem. He was in more serious mood when he took off from Los Angeles that June. He declared at the airport that 'the sure way to stop Hitler' was to form a world democratic federation between the United States, Britain, Australia and Canada.

It was his good fortune to be in Bombay after Pearl Harbor, when the Japanese took over all Shanghai's foreign banks, commercial concerns and shipping. Several of his executives were hustled off to Bridge House which the secret police specially favoured for Gestapo 'inquisitions'. Harry Arnhold of the associated company was interned there, while his brother Charles was rounded up in Peking and put behind barbed wire. E. G. Smith-Wright was one of several unfortunates captured in Shanghai. A most capable manager, he had been recruited to Sassoon House after all-round service in the Bombay office and the petroleum drilling company which the firm had developed in Burma. Many others escaped to Hong Kong but were trapped there when the Japanese marched in on Christmas Day. Robert Stock, who had held on so grimly to the David Sassoon branch throughout the difficult 'thirties, was among those interned in the Argyle Street and Shanshuipo camps.

The Japanese had soon emptied the Shanghai bank vaults, smoothly taking over any business which might help their economy. It gave them no pleasure to learn that Sir Victor Sassoon had slipped away and was already working his Bombay mills at full blast. Anxious to fortify working morale after the bitter news of Pearl Harbor and Hong Kong, he decided to give a mammoth party to celebrate his sixtieth birthday on 30 December 1941. He invited four thousand senior members of his staff to a garden party on Bombay's spacious Maidan. After the speeches and junketing, it was back to work in double shifts, but the atmosphere was soon poisoned by defeatism. When Burma and Singapore fell, many Indians feared that the enemy would take Ceylon to secure their flank. Gandhi was preaching pacifism and civil disobedience, claiming that the presence of British soldiers was an open provocation to Japan. He demanded that they should quit the country and jeered at Sir Stafford Cripps's promise of post-war independence as a 'post-dated cheque upon a bankrupt Empire'.

Victor was equally contemptuous of Cripps and the Mahatma. The former seemed to him a woolly idealist, and he thought all Congress leaders would be safer behind bars. In a broadcast from Bombay he proposed that a national emergency should be declared and the Viceroy, Lord Linlithgow, given dictatorial powers for the duration. He accused Congress of hating England so much that they would even abandon their country to the Japanese.

Lucien Ovadia's absence from Shanghai was the result of a happy accident. During the summer of 1941 he had been actively negotiating with the American Consulate who were anxious to buy the Metropole Hotel. The sale had almost gone through by the end of September when the Americans suddenly stipulated that payment would have to be effected in sterling and the final arrangements made in London. Ovadia then embarked for San Francisco in the *President Harrison*, made his way overland to New York and crossed the Atlantic. He was told in London that the Metropole deal had fallen through. He decided to sail back to Shanghai, via the United States. His ship was north of Iceland when the radio announced the bombing of Pearl Harbor. He therefore found himself temporarily stranded in New York where he used his full power of attorney to clear a mass of frozen dollar assets from Shanghai and Hong Kong. He also had useful meetings with Holt Ruffin who was preparing to set up his own brokerage business in Uruguay.

In February 1942 Ovadia was joined in New York by Victor who had made another spirited attack on the Government of India before sailing. He indicted Delhi for using red tape to strangle those, like himself, who were trying to feed the Allies with oilseeds, cotton, grain, timber, tea and mineral ores. 'There is nothing wrong with the people, in spite of their so-called leaders,' he said sharply. In America he saw agents, stockbrokers and bankers and arranged for cotton supplies and machinery before going to the Argentine to confer with Holt Ruffin. They discussed in broad outline the prospect of establishing a series of trusts in Latin America after the war, while making interim arrangements to invest dollar assets. Before leaving, he asked Ovadia the ritual question which his financial associates had come to expect from time to time. 'What am I worth?' It was not a miserly weakness for counting his money but the kind of information he always liked to have, even in round figures, before making any important move.

Ovadia told him, 'You have the Hong Kong Trust Corporation money, some five million dollars worth of first-class securities in America, as well as the Shanghai properties, plus the assets in India.' 'You can forget China,' said Victor gloomily. 'It's lost.' Ovadia tried to comfort him by pointing out that the Indian mills were now flourishing and might be worth quite a lot of money. Victor doubted this. He pointed out that much of the machinery was out of date. There were also formidable production and shipping difficulties still to be overcome. 'I'm worth about $10 million in all,' he decided after making swift calculations on a blotter. By that he meant the firm, as usual. Ovadia knew him too well to argue. He had personally not written off China and suspected that Victor was of the same mind. Moreover, he disagreed profoundly about the potential of the cotton mills.

In Bombay, Stones, so deservedly knighted for his services to India, had almost quadrupled the output of the United Mills and the other factories. Over forty thousand workers on three shifts were producing vast quantities of khaki drill, shirts, tropical underwear, sacks, sandbags, camouflage material and webbing. Within a year, the mills were able to pay off an overdraft at the Imperial Bank of India of over £2 million. This was mainly due to Stones, who had placed all the firm's resources at the Government's disposal at cost plus 5 per cent. The turnover was enormous. With the Mediterranean blocked, the huge cargoes for the Middle East were sent to South Africa and trans-shipped mainly from Durban, which became the firm's busiest entrepôt.

Before returning to India in October 1942, Victor stayed for two months at the Ritz in London. He conferred with Derek FitzGerald, who was briskly engaged on the British end of the cotton business. He also visited his racing studs and then went down to Bournemouth where his mother, a lively octogenarian, was staying. She still kept open house for the Forces in Belgrave Square and had converted part of the mansion into a Red Cross supply depot.

From her he learned with regret that Flora Sassoon's son, David, had recently died. His family were bombed out of Bruton Street and had settled in Letchworth, Herts., where he exhausted himself by working impossible hours for refugee causes.

Siegfried had withdrawn further into the quietude of rambling Heytesbury House to play his piano and escape into yet another volume of nostalgic autobiography following *The Old Century* of 1938. Four years later he published *The Weald of Youth*, a prose idyll of his mid-twenties in Kent, but the rogue poet had grown sadder and more contemplative. His marriage had drifted into the limbo of friendly separation. He now addressed their young son in verses which showed far more tenderness than anything he had written in the angry past. He was trying

> To find rewards of mind with inward ear
> Through silent hours of seeking,

as he wrote in *The Tasking*. It became more difficult when he read the casualty lists and mourned the death of friends like Rex Whistler, who fell in Normandy.

Port Lympne was requisitioned by the Army, and 45 Park Lane was being converted into an American Officers' Club, many of Philip's art treasures having previously been removed to Houghton Hall. On her brother's death, Sybil had been invited to succeed him at Hythe, but she was always far less interested in politics than music and the arts. When her two sons went into the Forces, she had promptly volunteered for the W.R.N.S. and became an outstanding deputy to the Director, Dame Vera Laughton Mathews. Contemporaries have paid tribute to a forceful but persuasive personality who often presided at the Selection Board for Officers at Greenwich and accompanied Dame Vera on many tours of inspection. She was witty and sensible in committee and also dealt briskly with Press or film people.

She surprised many who had expected a haughty marchioness. She could laugh at herself and once described her married name as 'a bad music-hall joke'. She proved a natural liaison with the Royal Family on ceremonial matters and kept a friendly eye on V.I.P. officers, but she was never starchy. Behind the blue-rinsed coiffure and the lapis lazuli cuff-links which matched her Wren stripes and the office carpet, she was anything but an elegant amateur playing at war. She stood no nonsense either from highly-placed, but obstructive, Admiralty officials or juniors who took things a little too casually. Second Officer Nancy Spain was never easily abashed, but she would fly at the double almost before her Superintendent's 'exquisite Persian hand' was off the button. From Kensington Palace Gardens, where she did much inter-Service entertaining, Lady Cholmondeley used to drive her tiny maroon Fiat to Queen Anne's Mansions where even the rubble, blood and broken glass failed to disturb her invincible calm after a buzz-bomb had shattered her office.

Although the two family branches had not been close for years, Victor privately admired Sybil Cholmondeley's poise and elegance. His own wartime schedule would have daunted a younger and able-bodied man, but he thrived on the adrenalin of risks and pressure. He made strenuous trips to South Africa, the U.K. and the United States, but Bombay remained his very active base. He lived at the Taj Mahal Hotel but found time in the season to go up to Eve's in Poona, where Gandhi had been interned in the Aga Khan's neighbouring villa.

Sharp at 10 a.m. every day, he would stump into his office where he stayed until seven, with usually a break for one of his long tiffin parties. Arrangements would be made by his personal assistant, Captain A. K. McEwan, formerly A.D.C. to Lord Willingdon. The guest-list often included prominent British Service chiefs, like Sir William Slim, as well as high-ranking American officers. There would sometimes be a gay leavening of Ensa touring stars, with Bea Lillie and other witty actresses much in demand. Aly Khan, who was then serving with the Wiltshires, was a particular favourite. As a fellow-connoisseur of horses and women, Victor always had a special affection for him. Aly was one of the few rival owners permitted to examine the stud books which, complete with photographs, Victor had meticulously assembled since his first racing days in the mid-twenties. He confessed that luck had not so far been with him, but stuck to his theories. 'From a close study of my own family tree,' he told Aly, 'I have become aware of the dangers of too much inbreeding and will not make the same mistake with horses when I start again.' He was already bristling with plans to rebuild his studs and one day breed a Derby winner from a Derby winner, his dearest ambition.

Nothing seemed impossible as the war news brightened from Europe and the Pacific. Almost miraculously, his health had improved during the past few years. This was largely due to his little Italian masseur, Valvosone, who was with him for years in Shanghai. His manipulative techniques proved of lasting benefit. Some nights Victor was able to throw away his sticks and even take a few 'victory rolls' round the dance floor of the Taj Mahal. Occasionally he paid for over-confidence. A thud would be heard from the private office when his eagerness to walk ended in a crash landing.

He was not an easy man. Bryden, Ovadia and Frederick Stones knew how to handle him, unlike less cautious colleagues who soon felt the sting of his sarcasm when their familiarity went too far. He saw through sycophants and snubbed managers who unwisely attempted to further social relations with him beyond the office sphere. He demanded quick action in business and expected his people to be fully briefed at all times. He had as little use for subordinates who were too pushing as those who nervously kept away in the hope that he would make the decisions for them. This was fatal, as many discovered. He preferred a man to admit a mistake but abhorred indecision or attempts to cover up sloppy 'homework'. Although he had a constant turnover of executives, due to a certain machiavellianism when he thought his authority was being even remotely challenged, he gave unlimited trust to a few tried colleagues. Even with them, however, he could be finicky to the point of peevishness, if not brutality, yet few merchant princes were readier to give extensive powers of attorney.

He could be quixotically generous when his sympathies were touched by the sick or physically handicapped, but grudged spending an extra rupee on formal dinners for people who meant nothing to him. He could never bring himself to play the courtier even when it could have been achieved without loss of dignity. His collection of ivories had been stored in London vaults during the war. To celebrate their survival, he decided to publish a superb three-volumed catalogue, bound in vellum, for the benefit of connoisseurs. The price was 100 guineas, and he presented a complimentary set to Queen Mary who thanked him most warmly. It was later reported back to him that the Queen might perhaps have appreciated one of the ivories, but he preferred not to take this seriously.

He disapproved of over-generosity and would never compete with the Aga Khan who once gave a girl caddie at Mougins a two-seater car as a tip. Victor rewarded good service with a sense of proportion, if not always on the scale expected of a multi-millionaire. The hall porter of the London Ritz, George Criticos, often placed bets for Aly Khan, and Victor also used him now and then. On a rare occasion when he decided to back one of his own horses, his bookmaker offered him ten to one. Dissatisfied, he asked the porter to try and improve on these odds. The horse won at 100 to 8, which netted Victor an extra £300. He gave Criticos a five-pound note, whereas Aly would probably have parted with at least a 'pony'.

Shortly after the war, when the British Government was restricting dollar transfers, a friend called at Gracechurch Street and pleaded for a loan of £3,000. Victor was just leaving for a day's racing. He shouted out over his shoulder: 'As a banker, I'm unable to do it, but I'll make you a gift of it instead.' He then told a secretary to make the arrangements with the New York office. When his friend arrived there, he was duly issued with travellers' cheques for that amount. Enclosed was an invoice for the stamp duty, 'with the compliments of Sir Victor Sassoon'.

His fussiness over quite minor sums dated back to his own hard-up schooldays, but it was partly rooted in his father's obsession with the iniquities of taxation. Bred into a tradition of patriarchal philanthropy, Victor would never wholly reconcile himself to handing over what he considered largesse to some wasteful and anonymous government department. This attitude, which hardened and mounted over the years, once led him into a Gilbertian situation. In the pre-war epoch when the Bombay mills were losing heavily, several executives had agreed to take salary cuts. As the mills started to flourish, Stones drew Ovadia's attention to a clause in his contract which gave him a percentage of any profits. This amounted to several thousands of pounds by 1942, and few men had more richly deserved their reward.

On Victor's return from the United States early in 1943, Ovadia reminded him of this contract which he had apparently quite forgotten. He was particularly incensed over the commission clause and curtly reminded Stones that much of it would be absorbed in taxation. Supported by Ovadia, Stones insisted and finally resigned in a fury when payment was still held up. He was quickly charmed back by Victor who agreed to the payment but hated to give way. 'Fred has behaved stupidly,' he told Ovadia privately. 'I wanted him to have his few thousand, of course. And he would have had it *all* as part of his pension.'

Taxation was only one of the many forms of 'waste' which horrified him. In 1946 he decided to sell Eve's, Poona, and set up a trust fund from the proceeds to help Indian ex-Servicemen. It was characteristic of him to remind Mrs Bryden that there was a certain amount of linen which might fetch a little for the benefit of one of his Jewish charities. 'Don't give it away,' he kept reminding her. '*Sell*, even if you only get six annas. People never appreciate anything they don't pay for.'

He liked his philanthropies to be personal and saw no virtue in merely adding his name to subscription lists. He wanted to see exactly how the money was spent, ensuring if possible that it was neither squandered nor diverted by careless organizers or tax 'sharks'. If the public supported some cause, he preferred to look elsewhere. 'Everything I put into a charity,' he used to remind his colleagues, 'must double or treble itself by wise investment, or at least encourage others to contribute.'

British and Indian troops were crowded into wretched camps in Bombay towards the end of the war. Many suffered worse hardships than anything they had experienced on the battlefields. Victor heard that money was needed for comforts and promptly made out a cheque for £30,000. Within a few days, he became impatient of delays and red tape. He cleared his godowns and stocked them with cable, thousands of chairs and bales of curtain material. In double-quick time he also recruited stevedores, skilled carpenters and a corps of handymen to work a crash programme. His policy soon justified itself. Seeing the camps transformed, other merchants and philanthropists promptly followed his example.

Long before D-Day, he had already begun plotting his firm's post-war course. His early gloom about the future of the Bombay mills had been spectacularly confounded. The firm now owned a quarter of the textile plant in the Presidency and turned out over 7 per cent of all India's cotton goods. By the end of 1943 the United Mills shares had shot up to well over par. Sir Frederick Stones shrewdly recommended that this might be the ideal time to sell these mills and dispose of the others piecemeal. Victor agreed, convinced that foreign millowners would be in for a difficult time once independence was granted. He was already haunted by the prospect of post-war government controls and his old spectres, taxation, tariffs and death duties.

The sale would not be easy. Would-be buyers knew that much of the machinery was run down and must speedily become out of date. But Bryden, Ovadia and Stones were quick to point out that they were selling a balance-sheet, not machinery. The greater difficulty was first to secure a quotation on the Bombay Stock Exchange, since 99 per cent of the holdings were jointly owned by the Oriental Investment Co. (Victor's side of the family) and the Asian Finance Corporation, controlled by his Aunt Mozelle.

The purchasers were the Mawaris, 'the Scotsmen of India', a hard-headed breed, but so superstitious that they would only sign the final purchase agreement when the stars were favourable. Even when the price and all other terms were agreed after strenuous bargaining, the delays still seemed endless. Ovadia was getting into bed late one night when his telephone rang. It was Goodbody, the broker who acted as intermediary. He announced that the Mawaris would sign at *exactly* 2.47 a.m. Ovadia protested at first that he could not sign without the firm's legal department. He hurriedly agreed to act on his own after being warned that the stars might not be in the right place again for some time to come.

The Mawaris arrived at his flat in force. At 2.45 a.m. he took out a sheet of the firm's notepaper and wrote: 'I, L. I. Ovadia, by virtue of my full powers of attorney in E. D. Sassoon & Co. and the Asian Finance Corporation, hereby sell – shares (except 200,000 which were in the market) to – for the price of 3 crores 995,000 rupees on the basis of the appended balance sheet.' He signed exactly two minutes later, followed by the purchasers who saluted him solemnly, picked up their copies of the agreement and filed out.

Ovadia passed a sleepless night and reported early next morning to the office lawyers. They thought it highly unorthodox, if not insane, but confirmed that the transaction was fully legal. The Mawaris duly paid the purchase money of close on £4 million which, by arrangement with the Government, was converted from rupees into sterling and allowed to be remitted out of India. The only proviso was an undertaking by the firm that the sterling would be invested in gilt-edged securities in London for the duration of the war and a period of six months thereafter. The remaining plants would be sold in the course of the next few years at even better prices.

The proceeds from the United Mills sale were not the firm's only liquid assets. After tiffin one day, Victor turned suddenly to Bryden and drawled, 'The news seems a bit better from the Philippines. I wonder what happened to our gold-mining shares. Didn't we have a small lot?' Bryden confirmed that they were worth about a couple of hundred thousand pesos. At the last return, some of the shares were with the Chartered Bank in Manila and the others with the brokers. 'Ring up someone and find out exactly where they are,' snapped Victor, impatiently ignoring that they were still in the middle of a war.

As it happened, the impossible became a matter of routine. Bryden telephoned his friend, Laidlaw, the manager of the Chartered Bank in Bombay. He was out, but another voice came on the line. It was a Mr Cooke who had only recently been transferred from Manila. Yes, he remembered the gold share certificates perfectly well. In fact, he had personally put them aboard an American submarine just before the evacuation. 'They'll be in the States by now,' he said confidently.

Bryden wrote to the Chartered Bank in New York who at once confirmed their safe arrival. They were available for sale within a fortnight. It was a freak chance, but the kind of instant service Victor demanded.

He was in his sixty-fifth year when the war ended. He arranged annuities for his mother, his sisters and other members of his family, having previously made over the Eve Stud near Newmarket to his niece, Denise Fitzpatrick, from whom he would lease his horses. 'I shall act as banker, adviser, secretary and friend,' he explained genially. He was eager to end his long exile now that India was moving rapidly towards independence. He had no wish to remain as the tolerated and over-taxed guest of Congress. China had also become far less attractive with the loss of extra-territorial rights. With a view to basing his future financial strategy on the Americas, he therefore instructed his associates to dispose of suitable Settlement properties as soon as they were derequisitioned and repaired.

After staying a few weeks at the Ritz in London, he flew to New York in May 1946 to see bankers, corporation lawyers and investment brokers. With them he studied reports about the Bahamas, where income tax and death duties were almost invisible. The climate in winter was delightful, and land might prove a splendid investment if the expected tourist boom materialized. With two of his companies already registered in Nassau, the Bahamas could become a natural reservoir for the firm's considerable sterling assets. He and Bryden meantime arranged for Holt Ruffin to manage the firm's vast trust funds in South America.

Victor spent two months in England where he conferred with the FitzGeralds and bought a few horses at the July Bloodstock Sales. After a short stay in Shanghai, he left for Bombay where he reminded the Government that India deserved a full share of the dollar pool promised to the Dominions for post-war reconstruction. Sir Frederick Stones had now retired, and Bryden was commuting briskly between Shanghai, Bombay, Hong Kong and New York. Ovadia had briefly served the Government of India as Controller and Purchaser of paper supplies, chemicals and other commodities, but there was little for him in India once the mills were sold. It was decided that he should return to China.

When Ovadia arrived in Shanghai early in 1946, he found the city racked by a black market. There was a desperate shortage of fuel, and the railway system had broken down. Currency inflation was creeping in, and money-lenders in the slums were charging their victims up to 500 per cent per month. Not surprisingly, Red propaganda found many a willing convert.

The firm's Chinese-occupied properties in the International Settlement and the French Concession had fared better than those occupied by foreigners. The Sassoon hotels and elegant apartment blocks were in poor shape. The Japanese had ripped out boilers and radiators for scrap. Fittings had disappeared or were ruined, and few of the luxurious carpets could be salvaged. It took almost a year to find heating and other essential equipment.

Bookings were plentiful for the still-requisitioned Cathay, but it was difficult to persuade the Americans to leave. General Wedemeyer, who had replaced Stillwell and now occupied Sir Victor's suite, was not an easy man to dislodge, but this was only a minor piece in the whole chaotic jigsaw. Inflation was making itself felt on the Stock Exchange where share dealings gradually became a free-for-all which degenerated into crude bartering. With dollars frozen and the Nationalist armies crumbling, many were frantically realizing assets and shuffling balances around.

Until the end of 1948, the Sassoons were fairly well inoculated against this gangrene. In the immediate post-war period they were still fulfilling contracts amounting in value to several million sterling, covering the import of capital goods from the United Kingdom. But the exchange and arbitrage business was ending. Ovadia concentrated on reducing the firm's property investments in Shanghai, Hankow, Tientsin and Canton. The difficulty was to find buyers in conditions which deteriorated every day. The Shanghai properties had been valued after the Occupation at about £7½ million, Sassoon House alone being estimated at £1 million, but the market was shrinking all the time. One of the first sales effected was for the old David Sassoon building, but it proved more difficult to dispose of others. A director of the Bank of China almost bought the Union Brewery but changed his mind at zero hour. Several of the Chinese properties had to be sacrificed for what they could fetch, and it was not easy to secure realistic prices for any of the valuable hotels, shops and apartment houses in the Nanking Road area and the French Concession.

As currency slumped, property dealings called for a steady day-to-day appraisal. The atmosphere, tense enough when the Communists subdued Manchuria, reached near panic with the capture of Peking and Tientsin. The foreign merchants in Shanghai could no longer trade peacefully behind the perimeter of their Settlement. In such circumstances, Ovadia needed all his nerve and negotiating skill to dispose of some £1,400,000 worth of the firm's properties.

During these salvage operations, Victor could be very trying. His moods alternated between despondency (*Après moi le déluge* had become one of his constant expressions) and a light-heartedness which covered an inner anxiety. During one of his visits to Shanghai in 1948, the city was in such a fever of inflation that a sackful of paper dollars could hardly buy a packet of butter. In Sassoon House, as elsewhere, the staff refused to take their wages entirely in notes and insisted on part payment in rice, pieces of cloth and almost anything else edible or wearable. A substantial amount of bulky currency still had to be kept on hand for workers who insisted on being paid every three days.

One pay-day the Sassoons found themselves temporarily short of enough currency in the safe to make up the staff salaries. When Ovadia arrived, he was taken up by an unnaturally surly liftman. Rumours were flying about that the offices had been burgled and the staff would not be paid. The atmosphere became so tense that the Sassoon Labour Union decided to hold an emergency meeting in the Cathay ballroom. Ovadia sat on the orchestra platform, flanked by hotel chefs armed with choppers. Cash reinforcements arrived several hours later. It turned out that Sir Victor had gallantly emptied the night safe to help a Frenchwoman and her daughter return to Europe!

A sick man at this time, he was himself anxious to leave Shanghai where he was not getting proper attention. A few days later, he sailed off to the United States with a heavy heart. After so many years spent in patiently building up one of the richest property empires in the Far East, he was horrified by the attitude of the Chinese staff with whom the management had long had excellent relations. But, as always, he was resilient and stimulated by a change of scene. Following the grant of independence to India and the sale of the rest of the Company's mills, he decided that the time had come to establish his domicile in the Bahamas where the climate and business possibilities were equally attractive.

At the end of 1948, E. D. Sassoon & Co. Ltd of Bombay was put into voluntary liquidation. By the following April Shanghai was doomed. Tank traps had been set up on the golf course and advance patrols were within fifty miles of the city. Nobody was deceived by the cheery notice outside the Country Club, 'Tennis courts will be open from May.' By then the Communists had taken Shanghai which was soon being bombed by Chiang Kai-shek's pilots.

Victor was sitting in his lawyer's office in New York when the news came through that Shanghai had fallen. He closed his eyes for a moment, then managed a smile. 'Well, there it is,' he said quietly. 'I gave up India and China gave me up.'

Part Six (1949–1961)

Chapter Nineteen

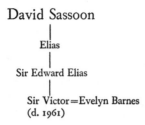

David Sassoon
|
Elias
|
Sir Edward Elias
|
Sir Victor=Evelyn Barnes
(d. 1961)

Mao Tse-tung proclaimed the People's Republic of China on 1 October 1949. The Communist Mayor of Shanghai exhorted Europeans to carry on as before, but apart from a few optimists, the majority prepared themselves for a hopeless rearguard action. There were some brave gestures. The British Consul gave his usual At Home to celebrate the King's Birthday, tea-dances were held at the Y.M.C.A., and a few of the hardier souls arranged one or two cricket matches. None doubted, however, that factory slogans like 'Down with foreign imperialism' would soon be translated into action.

The bureaucracy now dedicated itself to a take-over which would be slow, bloodless and without any hope of escape. The screws were gradually tightened through a series of new levies payable at very short notice. In the case of property owners, a heavy land tax was imposed; failure to settle on time would be punished by fines at the rate of 1 per cent, compounded daily. A firm with E. D. Sassoon's property assets inevitably faced immense bills which could only be met by remitting funds from abroad. This they declined to do, certain that the first down payment would merely stimulate the dragon. The taxes mounted and the game went on. It was played with two separate sets of rules. The take-over of urgently needed foreign holdings in transport, power, telephones and dockyards had top priority. Most of these concerns were so harassed by restrictions and self-appointed 'caretakers' that they were glad enough to hand over their assets in exchange for exit permits.

For non-essential assets such as hotels, shops and apartment houses, the technique was different and the tempo slower. Foreign firms were reminded that their senior executives would be held personally responsible for taxes. In the Sassoons' case, Ovadia soon discovered that he would not be given his visa before all the firm's liabilities had been met. He was held as hostage because a replacement of sufficient seniority and acceptable to the authorities was not available.

He tried vainly to square the circle. To meet tax demands, one had obviously to raise revenue, but this was made hopeless under current trading conditions. The import business was gradually being liquidated. The luxury hotels had quickly lost most of their guests, while the tenants of the large apartment houses simply melted away, those remaining soon finding it impossible to pay their rent. Many of the office buildings were half empty. Meantime, the firm had to foot a wage bill for some fourteen hundred employees formerly working on the administrative and clerical side or in now unproductive non-office jobs.

It was relatively simple to deal with the foreign personnel who had contracts of employment, but the numerically larger Chinese staff could not be discharged, reduced or laid off, even by payment of compensation. Each of Ovadia's representations was politely stone-walled. He was informed that any former agreements on staff redundancy had been superseded by new regulations to protect workers against foreign exploiters. He argued in vain that dues, now amounting to several hundred thousand pounds, could only be met if unusable labour were discharged. The Tax Bureau officials shrugged. They were interested in arrears of taxes, and nothing else.

This slow-drip bureaucratic torture went on, month after month. Each department either professed complete ignorance of what the others were doing or insisted that it had no jurisdiction to intervene. When Ovadia made out a case to the Foreign Affairs Bureau, which had been set up to act as trouble-shooters during this interim period, he was bluntly advised to import foreign funds. Similarly, his offer to hand over various local assets in settlement of taxes and fines was repeatedly declined.

His personal situation became delicate in the extreme, although he was spared the fate of Robin Gordon of Jardine, Matheson who was thrown into a cell for six days with thieves without a word of explanation. Ovadia had to accustom himself instead to being disturbed in the middle of the night at his flat in Grosvenor House. Two secret policemen would stolidly ask him to fill in a questionnaire giving his name, place of birth, education and so on, which he had already completed half a dozen times. In time, he and other heads of foreign firms reacted philosophically to this war of nerves, but their Chinese friends were in constant terror. More than once, Ovadia had to meet lawyers and contact men in dark alleys because they could not risk being seen with him.

The Communist officials constantly devised new techniques to sap the morale of foreign managements. Several were Western-educated and spoke fluent English and French, but insisted on all conversations being conducted in Chinese through an interpreter. At one meeting over the perennial question of tax arrears, Ovadia's inquisitor became aggressive and made such a preposterous demand that he turned sharply to the interpreter and snapped: 'Tell him that this is no longer negotiation. It's blackmail.' The official jumped to his feet and hissed in perfect English; 'Mr Ovadia, let me warn you that the word blackmail must not be used in Communist China. This meeting is now over.'

Blackmail or not, the tissue of legality continued to be used as a protective wrapping in all dealings. By the spring of 1951 the Foreign Affairs Bureau had contrived an almost foolproof formula. They advised Ovadia to approach the Bank of China who apparently had worked out a solution to his firm's problems. It was a courteous invitation to lease Sassoon House to the Government for a period of three years from June 1, the rent to be payable in advance. Ovadia was in no position to disagree. He signed the lease and duly received a cheque for the rent, which was then calmly taken out of his hand by a waiting representative of the Tax Bureau. Oddly enough, it tallied *exactly* with the amount claimed for land taxes and fines in default! Since the owners and not the lessees would remain liable for Land and Property Tax during the next three years, he had no doubt that the ritual would be repeated when the lease came up for renewal in 1954. The firm did, however, secure one useful advantage from this remarkable transaction. It enabled them to discharge the maintenance and hotel staff on payment of their retiring allowances.

A month later Ovadia at last secured a replacement acceptable to the authorities. His name was published in the weekly official list of foreigners who could apply for an exit visa, but his troubles were not yet over. It would be a full year before he could leave China, even though he was now a private resident and barred by law from attending the office where his replacement was in charge. Someone in authority, either in Shanghai or perhaps in Peking, apparently saw a chance to enjoy himself at the expense of this former Sassoon Tai-Pan. A number of trumped-up claims for compensation were filed against him personally by Chinese ex-employees. Some of them had been discharged or made redundant before the Communist régime, and others even before the war, but the relevant Authorities insisted that each individual case would have to be thoroughly investigated. The claims would not be withdrawn for several months. But the remaining members of the staff were still reluctant to see him depart. He was arraigned by a newly appointed Committee of the Sassoon Labour Union early in 1952. They now objected to his being allowed to leave the country until he had arranged for the remittance from abroad of some

£125,000. It would be held in escrow for the benefit of any Chinese staff still in the firm's employ, who *might* become redundant if and when the State took control of their remaining properties!

This demand was so impudent and brazen that Ovadia had difficulty in keeping his temper. He made a formal objection to the legality of the claim and pointed out that he was no longer in charge of the firm's affairs. The matter was considered important enough to refer to Peking. Four months later, on June 12, the Shanghai authorities called a committee meeting of the Labour Union and curtly ordered them to withdraw their claim which had been ruled illegal by the higher authority. Ovadia was then summoned to the local police bureau dealing with aliens. He was handed his exit permit and told to collect a one-way railway ticket for Canton. He asked for a few days to arrange his affairs but was ordered to leave within forty-eight hours.

He flew from Hong Kong to London to report to Sir Victor and hand in his resignation. He had suffered a three-year nightmare and now wished to settle in France where he could enjoy life again and devote himself to his banking interests. He might possibly have remained with the firm had it not already been decided that the new E. D. Sassoon Banking Co. would take over all the assets and liabilities of the Hong Kong concern which would be controlled, like the London and Manchester branches, from Nassau. He considered it a mistake to cut down so drastically in Hong Kong where the firm still held lucrative agencies for Metropolitan-Vickers, Textile Machinery Makers and others, but his cousin had made up his mind to leave the Far East for good.

Ovadia had a farewell lunch at the Ritz with Victor who had spent a busy morning rattling off letters and memos into his two dictaphones. He was bristling with plans for the new private Banking Company of which he was governing director, with Derek FitzGerald, his son Desmond, and W. B. Bryden on the board. The authorized capital was £1 million in £10 shares.

Victor had quickly bought and converted an old colonial house in Nassau as a residence. On the remaining part of the lot he built a compound to accommodate various business concerns, including the E. D. Sassoon offices and a real estate company, Grosham. Meantime, the Danish architect, Frederick Soldewell, was putting up a huge corner block of apartments, 'Victorcourt', in the downtown area of Nassau. It would become the hub of a property and insurance empire in which the E. D. Sassoon Banking Co. planned to invest vast sums over the next decade. Housing sites were still low-priced but already rising steadily, and the property tax only $2\frac{1}{2}$ per cent.

The London branch under Capt. FitzGerald had moved to 37 Upper

Brook Street in Mayfair, where a separate department was set up to deal with the quickly expanding Bahamian interests as well as merchant banking in Europe and Africa. Victor was meantime maintaining the closest personal supervision of his various stables and studs directed by Norman Bertie, Harry Peacock, Capt. Elsey, R. C. H. Laye and Nora Wilmot. To the original Eve's Stud at Newmarket, owned by a company registered in the Bahamas, he added in 1951 the Earl of Fingall's 550-acre estate in County Meath which he would convert into a stud farm. He was at last realizing his ambition to breed the finest thoroughbreds, but it demanded endless concentration as well as a long purse. The days were over when a horse could be kept for five guineas a week. Victor estimated that he would need a minimum of £100,000 a year in prize money, a rare possibility indeed, to cover the expenses of his racing establishments, not counting his disbursements for top yearlings.

Ovadia found his cousin as mentally nimble and brisk as usual, but more irascible than during the worst crises in Bombay or Shanghai. He was now using a wheelchair, the result of slipping a disc a few months earlier in New York. This permanently damaged his good leg. The pain was often so acute that he would leave his guests and retire to work on his papers, while drinking huge quantities of black coffee. He had his morning massage and manipulation by a physiotherapist, and in time even the wheelchair became something of a blessing. It increased his mobility and gave him an escape from bores.

Nevertheless, to one who had preserved his millions after so much effort and personal danger in the Far East, the timing of this new blow seemed particularly cruel. He had mapped out his life on luxurious and congenial lines. In winter, he would relax in the Bahamas where he could entertain his American and European friends and sail or bathe in the warm waters of the Caribbean. For several months each year, his suite in the London Ritz would be his base for the office, race-meetings, bloodstock sales and the studs where he would keep his trainers and jockeys on the hop. Instead, at the age of seventy, he saw himself condemned to a life of semi-invalidism which would be hard to endure without his excellent Chinese servants.

He appealed for help to the vivacious American nurse who had been with him constantly after putting him in traction in New York. Her name was Evelyn Barnes from Dallas, Texas, where her family had farmed and were now active in land development. She was thirty, a petite blonde whose brisk efficiency had impressed him. 'The Southern hill-billy,' as she described herself, hesitated at first to undertake the full-time care of an autocratic millionaire used to instant obedience, but he soon proved one of the easiest patients she had ever had. Although inclined to make too much use of the wheelchair which he enjoyed propelling at high speed, he could often walk with one stick. 'Barnsie' had some difficulty in persuading him that two sticks would help to keep his leverage. It proved a success. Equally important was the companionship of a young woman who handled him with such good-humoured firmness.

Miss Barnes had expected a rough passage but quickly discovered that her patient could be charming and considerate. His talk was witty, and few nurses ever enjoyed more stimulating anecdotage about exotic places or celebrities in varied social spheres. He seemed younger than his years when he tinkered with a new polaroid camera or spent hours testing the very latest type of tape-recorder. Before long she was caught up in his twin enthusiasms for photography and racing.

In his folding wheelchair, with a bag like a barrister's slung over the back to hold his notebooks, he would inspect the paddocks at the Doncaster yearling sales in the coldest weather. He used to take pictures of anything that caught his eye and compared notes afterwards with Barnsie, who soon picked up much turf lore. He made a point of buying in the mornings, wherever possible, because he found that the auction was apt to become euphoric after lunch. He would pay 13,000 guineas and more for a yearling but used to stop bidding as soon as prices became disproportionate.

Racing was more than a millionaire's hobby with him. He applied himself to it with a dedication which often had a touch of ruthlessness. He dismissed one trainer because the stable did not seem happy. His instinct told him, rightly as it turned out, that the horses would quickly improve in other hands. He always took the horse's side in any dispute with a trainer. He studied breeding strains with infinite care and was a superb race-reader, but after spending half a million pounds – his own estimate – in seeking a Derby winner, he had finally to confirm Aly Khan's faith in the luck factor. Learning that Fred Darling, an astute trainer and breeder whose judgement he respected, was putting a yearling up for sale, he decided to bid. He was by Chanteur out of Pasqua which fitted in with Victor's theories of pedigree. The colt was big, powerful and awkward looking, more like a Grand National hope than a flat champion, but might be worth a thousand. Victor had to go up to 1,500 guineas for the yearling who was sent to Norman Bertie's stables at Newmarket.

It seemed as if he had wasted his money. Pinza was erratic in training gallops and often unseated the stable boys, but his owner came to love him. Whenever he took out his camera, Pinza would rear on his hind legs and pose like some Hollywood equine star. As soon as Barnsie or any other admiring woman approached, he practically rolled his eyes.

He won a few useful races as a two-year-old but only settled down when Gordon Richards, who had also taken a strong liking to him, offered to school him for the Derby. The big fellow almost gave him a hernia, he used to recall, but he had never ridden an animal who accelerated more like a fire-engine.

Sir Victor began to be hopeful, but could not restrain private doubts about Richards whose Derby 'hoodoo' was notorious. However, it seemed a good augury when the jockey was given a knighthood. Another favourable omen was Fred Darling's death-bed vision of Pinza passing the winning post with Sir Gordon in the saddle. Pinza duly won that Coronation Derby of 1953 like a champion, giving both owner and jockey their first triumph in the race. Victor was jubilant after over a quarter of a century's racing but gracefully commiserated with the Queen who sighed, 'Why ever did Pinza have to come on in the same year as Aureole?' Pinza knew his manners. When the Queen later paid him a visit, he shook his mane and all but curtseyed.

He went on to win the King George VI and Queen Elizabeth Stakes at Ascot and seemed a certainty for the St Leger until he strained a tendon. Sir Victor's prize money that year was £58,579, a satisfactory sum if well short of his expenditure on yearlings and his network of stables. But he refused an American offer of a million dollars for Pinza who retired to stud. He decided instead to form a forty-share syndicate at 5,000 guineas a share, retaining twenty-three nominations for himself. One of the shares went to the Queen and another to the Princess Royal.

There was some surprise when Sir Victor transferred his horses from Norman Bertie's care to Noel Murless, but he always followed his instinct when others might have hedged. That was never his way, either in racing or business affairs, yet he could show remarkable generosity. When Sailing Eve was in foal to Pinza, he sold her to Sir Alfred Butt's stud and handed the proceeds of 4,300 guineas to the Hungarian Relief Fund. Soon afterwards he donated his well-bred Elopement, fourth in the 1954 Derby, to the National Stud. He gave 4,000 guineas for a nomination to Persian Gulf, then a British record fee, because the proceeds would go to the Animal Health Trust for equine research.

His first Derby triumph stimulated him to buy more bloodstock for the Eve Stud, and he added further to his empire by buying the late Lord Derby's fine Thornton-le-Street stud near Thirsk. With the faithful Barnsie vainly attempting to slow him down, he moved ceaselessly between Nassau and England, often flying over to France to see his horses run and rarely missing a sale wherever good yearlings were on parade. He continued to expand his real estate holdings in Nassau and, with Barnsie's help, developed Eve's, his home at Cable Beach, into a pink and white showplace. It was started as a beach-house to entertain guests at luncheon parties. Victor loved a daily sea bathe, but thought it prudent to build a heated oval-shaped pool where he could swim in all weathers. Here he sun-bathed and talked on the plugged-in telephone while the house was going up. Eve's was encircled by gardens foaming with bougainvillaea and hibiscus and overlooked a large sandy beach which reached up to the house and was protected by a high sea wall. As it was built on two floors, Victor had a small lift put in to take his wheelchair. Between the pool area and the beach he laid out a breezeway, 'The Stables', lined with sculptures of his favourite horses. In every room he had paintings, framed photographs, cups, lamps and even waste-paper baskets with turf associations, but his most cherished mascots were ash-trays made from his classic winners' shoes.

He enjoyed giving parties at Eve's for friends who came from many parts of the world to stay in the separate two-storeyed guest house. Sitting on his huge terrace from which half a dozen stairways led down to the beach and pool, he personally mixed the cocktails and always seemed in high spirits. His temper had mellowed, thanks largely to his nurse who humoured him but had to be firm when he over-excited himself. With one of the three or more cameras constantly round his neck, he took candid shots of his guests. They included Richard Fairey, the aircraft manufacturer; the Duke of Sutherland; the former Governor of Jamaica, Sir John Huggins; Charles Hughesdon and his wife, Florence Desmond, the actress; and always a number of American and Nassovian friends.

Nothing could restrain his lifelong passion for gadgets. He was so delighted when a friend made an engraving of his profile over a replica of his signature, that he often used it to stamp all his business letters. In London and New York he was well known in several stores who specialized in the latest radio and photographic equipment. He was fascinated by electronics and never tired of experimenting with tape-recorders. He had a gift for being able to dictate, glance at notes and hold several conversations at the same time, darting from one visitor to another in his chair. But he was conscious of one handicap. He bitterly resented his inability to remember names or telephone numbers automatically. He tried any number of mind exercises, spent long hours with *The Super Power Memory Book* and unsuccessfully attempted Yoga. Otherwise, for a man in his mid-seventies, his vitality and *élan* were phenomenal. On the spur of the moment he would decide to fly to Miami for a day's racing, and on to New York for a show, often touching down at Dallas on the way back to buy nylon shirts. He hated to miss the racing at Laurel Park and relished shoptalk with Ambrose Clark, Paul Mellon, Elizabeth Arden and many other breeders in Virginia and Kentucky. An impulse would send him flying down to Rio to see Holt Ruffin who had remained a valued associate and personal friend. Another was 'Bill' Bryden who was used to his sudden whims. Arriving one afternoon at Eve's, he was casually asked what he had had for lunch. 'Shepherd's pie,' he replied. Victor almost exploded. 'I'm a rich man and *never* get shepherd's pie which I happen to love. My food bills are enormous, but I'm not lucky enough to get anything made up from the night before.'

Evelyn Barnes came to understand changes of mood which might have daunted anyone less patient and devoted. He had moments of deep depression. The news from China that the State Enterprises Company had finally seized the rest of his firm's properties touched a still raw nerve. In Sassoon House the take-over officials had been greeted with applause, gongs and cymbals by the Chinese staff who lined the corridors jeering at the European employees as they signed their resignation forms and then walked out of the building in disgust. The Cathay was renamed Peace Hotel and henceforth welcomed visiting dignitaries from the Iron Curtain countries and any Westerners who might be nibbling at trade prospects. The Shanghai Club became the headquarters of the Seamen's Union, and Victor could not help smiling at reports that the famous Long Bar now served only soft drinks and the watery near-beer, *pejo*.

Barnsie had a gift for keeping him cheerful, although at times he laughingly protested at becoming 'a trained seal'. He needed firm discipline when he became too wound up over racing. They would talk for hours about bloodstock until she became something of an authority herself and looked forward to the annual visit to England almost as much as her patient. Early in 1957 he seemed almost to paw the ground as the days drew nearer for Epsom.

A thoroughbred can only win the Derby once, a supreme and unique day in its life. For some lucky owners their first win can be repeated but never quite equalled, yet Sir Victor Sassoon was now hoping for a greater triumph than Pinza's victory. His big chestnut entry, Crepello, had been bred at the Eve Stud. He was sired by elderly Donatello II out of Crépuscule who was by Mieuxcé, a great sire of French brood mares, and one of Victor's best pre-war buys. The purists might have disagreed with him, but he was emphatic that France's long line of successes was due to breeding horses who had speed without sacrificing stamina. He encouraged Noel Murless who brought Crepello along very smoothly to win the Two Thousand Guineas in style. With Lester Piggott aboard, he would have a splendid chance in the Derby, although some critics thought Crepello's nonchalant temperament a pointer to stamina rather than pace.

Victor's pride in Crepello was tinged with some anxiety for the punters.

At 6 to 4 he was the shortest-priced Derby favourite since the war. A fortune rested on his nose. His owner did not have a bet himself and refused, even provisionally, to order a celebration dinner at the Savoy for Derby Night. He placated the gods instead by booking a table at a Mayfair restaurant, explaining that he might have to cancel if luck went his way. Crepello won from a bad draw in the fastest time since Mahmoud's victory in 1936. As his horse crossed the line, Victor almost catapulted from his seat in the stand and hurried off to lead in his winner. That night the winning owner's table in the Savoy Restaurant was decorated in the Sassoon racing blue colours.

Victor went off to Monte Carlo where he had a heart attack. It brought him still closer to Barnsie who nursed him through many bouts of pain. A tenderness had slowly developed between them. She occupied many sleepless nights by making gay sports shirts for her patient as well as designing her own clothes. After treatment in Paris, Victor stayed in the Curzon Street flat which had replaced his suite at the Ritz. He was strictly forbidden by his doctors to leave his bed for race-meetings, sales and anything else that might further damage his heart. He had to console himself with his battery of dictaphones and kept in close touch with the Nassau office. He also studied reports from the stables in Newmarket, Yorkshire and Ireland and issued detailed instructions to his trainers, while ticking off likely buys from the sales catalogues which Barnsie read out to him.

He might be 'barred' from racing by doctors' orders, but used his enforced rest to supervise the matings of his mares. Having refused an American offer for Crepello, he started working out details of a scheme by which breeders unable to afford 3,000-guinea fees might benefit from nominations to top-class stallions. He invited Lord Rosebery, Noel Murless and Peter Burrell, manager of the National Stud, to visit him in Nassau where they discussed the allocations to suitable breeders. As a result, he gave away five shares in his Derby winners to create a Small Breeders' Trust.

He won £58,522 in prize-money in Crepello's year and was runner-up to the Queen as leading owner. He was ploughing it all, and more besides, into bloodstock but always with a discriminating hand. When the Aga Khan's Irish and French studs came up for sale at Newmarket, he was greatly tempted by a splendidly bred Mieuxcé mare, Mehmany, especially after his successful hunch about Crepello's staying power. Rival owners were therefore astonished when he allowed the fourteen-year-old mare to be led out of the ring after failing to reach her reserve of 14,500 guineas. He bought her privately next morning for 14,000.

He made a point of buying a few mares or some promising yearling from the smaller studs in need of support, but expected little return from these low-priced purchases, even though Pinza had so handsomely recouped his modest 1,500 guineas. On one spectacular occasion, however, the million-to-one miracle came off. Victor flew over to the Balls-bridge Yearling Sales in Dublin in 1956, and was much taken with a lop-eared dark bay colt, sired by Hard Sauce out of Tout Belle II. Hard Sauce had produced some fairish sprinters and the dam had claims to ancestry, but the yearling was lethargic and looked anything but a potential Derby candidate. Victor thought otherwise. On the other side of the rostrum, his trainer Mick Rogers was bidding modestly up to 270 guineas when it was pointed out that he was up against Sir Victor whom he had failed to spot. He stopped bidding and the yearling was knocked down to Sir Victor at 280 guineas (the buyer later complained in fun that he might have had Hard Ridden for 120 guineas but for the mis-understanding!).

Mick Rogers tells the rest of the story. Immediately afterwards, 'The owner sent for me, and we went and had a cup of tea. I never saw Sir Victor so delighted with any purchase he had made. He even predicted that this could be his best bloodstock purchase. He said that he would send the horse to me to train. At the same time he gave me very definite instructions. I was to enter him in all the English and Irish classic races in 1958, and on no account to strike him out at any of the forfeit stages. I was to concentrate all his training on his three-years-old career with particular emphasis on the Derby. If I wished, I could give the horse one race only as a two-year-old at the fall of the year, just for experience. I might add that if I had purchased Hard Ridden that day in September 1956, I should never have entered him in the Derby!'

Hard Ridden improved well enough to take the Irish Two Thousand Guineas, but few had given him any chance of staying the Derby course, let alone winning the race. In an undistinguished field, Smirke made a brilliant late sprint to drive him past the post. Victor was well pleased with his 18 to 1 outsider, but almost as gratified at having bred the second horse, Paddy's Point, whom he had sold as a yearling. Leading in his third and most unexpected Derby winner in five years, he kept chuckling like a schoolboy. In the Royal Box he laughingly suggested that his phlegmatic horse would be ideal for Trooping the Colour. 'I'd be much too nervous to ride a Derby winner,' said the Queen.

Hard Ridden sprained a tendon during training and then stood at the Killeen Stud in Ireland. Noel Murless sent his owner a wire, reporting a handsome overseas offer for the horse and requesting a cabled reply by return. He heard nothing from Nassau for a fortnight. Then came a letter which only mentioned the offer in a curt postscript. Sir Victor 'thought it was understood' that British breeders would always have the opportunity of using his Derby winners. It was typical of his brusque kindliness.

Later that year he seized another opportunity to assist less affluent owners. The Philadelphian building magnate, John McShain, was proposing to sell his 'wonder horse', Ballymoss. It seemed certain that his countrymen would buy it for stud, but the Queen Mother had hinted that this would be a sad loss to British bloodstock. The National Stud, however, decided against paying £250,000 even though McShain could have made much more from an American syndicate. Sir Victor and William Hill, the bookmaker, therefore decided to guarantee three-quarters of the price by joining forces in a syndicate of forty shares. The owner retained ten shares, Mr Hill took a similar number, and Victor bought twenty, half of which he sold to other breeders.

But 1958 had been a strenuous season. He was taken ill at Ascot and spent more time in bed than in his wheelchair. The doctors had cut him down to two Havanas a day and warned him off racecourses. Back in Nassau, he was soon swimming again and sunning himself while working through a mass of correspondence. Having discovered that an occasional brandy was considered medically beneficial, he was presented with a gadget that gave him immense pleasure. His friend, Tom Slick, the oilman and airline magnate, fitted his two sticks with hollow tops from which he could take nourishing nips.

The rupees from the Bombay mills had transplanted admirably to Bahamian soil. Victor founded investment banks and expanded the company's real estate holdings to include some of the best business and residential sites in the islands. Among his major plans was the building of a five-storey luxury apartment block of eighty-four flatlets and suites in the Cable Beach area. It would have a central recreation area and a heated swimming pool. Victor spent many long hours working on the blue prints with George R. Davis, the head of a Florida construction group associated with the project. He made time, however, to fly up to New York with Barnsie and saw *My Fair Lady* once again, afterwards paying Julie Andrews the tribute of naming one of Pinza's fillies in her honour.

The Nassau house was rarely without guests, among them Noel Murless for whom Victor felt great affection and admiration. Lester Piggott and his wife spent their honeymoon at Eve's, and Barnsie was godmother to their first daughter. Victor appreciated the dedicated professionalism of his leading trainer and jockey and, according to informed racing experts, would probably have kept them together had he lived.

He was gay and hospitable, but close friends knew better than to intrude when he retreated behind his black cloud or made one of his chronic self-appraisals. After his last illness he was doing some hard private thinking. He had suffered acute physical agony, yet at times experienced more peace and happiness than he had known in all his thrusting years in the East. He had loved many women, but his liaisons had all been temporary since his crash in the First World War. With Barnsie he had found companionship and a rare understanding which mellowed into affection. She had saved his life during more than one heart attack, but his feeling went deeper than gratitude. He decided that the time had now come for marriage. 'After all,' he explained laughingly to a friend, 'seventy-seven years of bachelordom are essential to acquire enough judgement to choose the right wife.' His affairs were in order and uncomplicated by the elaborate *ménages* which many cosmopolitan millionaires maintained. Eve's was well-appointed without being lavish, and the flat in Curzon Street sufficed for his London visits. He had no yacht, private aeroplane or fleet of limousines. He refused to collect paintings for snobbish satisfaction and would not hoard his ivories, which he put on public exhibition in several British and American cities.

Despite heavy losses in Red China, he had preserved the family inheritance in thirty years of wise and often daring administration. His mother, who died in 1955, had lived in considerable style and acted as guarantor of many favourite causes, notably the Symphony Orchestra at Bournemouth, where she spent her last years. His two sisters were comfortably off and enjoyed handsome annuities. He had also provided for his nieces, godchildren, wards and many refugees, Jews and gentiles alike, who had come out of China and Germany and needed funds to make a fresh start in the United States or Latin America. He had increased his charitable settlements in England, India and the Bahamas, and his nurse shared his passionate new interest in cardiology. He donated heart machines to several hospitals and research centres in the United States.

He wished Barnsie to inherit his name and wealth, assured that she would continue the many philanthropies with which she was now almost as familiar as himself. Above all, he had no doubt that she would keep his racing colours flying. He did not make a formal proposal, and the matter remained so much a secret between them that guests in Nassau, including Florence Desmond, were surprised when they announced their intention to marry on the first of April, 1959. Victor explained that he had chosen the date because it was easy to remember and also happened to be the anniversary of the founding of the Royal Air Force.

He and his bride wanted no fuss. The platinum ring was simple and unpretentious, and a plain oyster-coloured wedding gown was bought off-the-peg from Neiman-Marcus. The ceremony was performed by a local magistrate at Eve's and Victor insisted on standing throughout and helped to cut the wedding cake. The thirty-eight-year-old bride was given away by her brother, a building contractor from Texas, and Lewis Holt Ruffin flew up from Rio to be best man. The bride's young nephew, R. E. Barnes, Jr., produced a perfect *non sequitur* for the occasion. 'Uncle Victor *can't* be seventy-seven as it says in the paper,' he protested indignantly. 'He's only just taught me to play poker.' One of the scores of leg-pulling cables came from Tom Slick who wired, 'You must have run out of shoe-leather,' reminding Victor of Nunkie's advice to 'run like hell' when threatened by matrimony.

The couple left for a short honeymoon in Miami where they went to the races at Gulf Stream Park for the Florida Derby. They came over for Epsom, as usual, but their colt, Love and Marriage, had not proved good in the trials and was scratched. They sunned themselves on the Riviera where they were joined by Lady Sassoon's two nieces from Dallas, and returned to England for the Newmarket yearling sales. They became excited when the Murless-trained St Paddy won the Royal Lodge Stakes at the September Ascot meeting. The handsome bay colt was admirably bred, a son of the Queen's Aureole out of a mare by Bois Roussel, winner of the 1938 Derby. Victor began to hope secretly that he might win the race for the fourth time in eight seasons. St Paddy was a January foal, now well grown, and a stayer with the right turn of speed, if at times temperamental. He was not in the Crepello class and would obviously need all Noel Murless's handling to give him anything of a chance.

Thoughts of the Derby were dismissed that autumn, when Lady Sassoon had a major operation in New York. Her husband turned male nurse with a gentle efficiency that surprised their friends. They sunbathed on the terrace at Nassau and celebrated their 'anniversary' every Wednesday with a bottle of champagne and an exchange of presents. They were happy and at peace together, rarely going out in the evenings. Victor's business associates discovered a new gentleness in him – until they stepped out of line or forgot to brief themselves – but his sarcasm had lost much of its sting. It was now reserved for trainers and stud managers who disputed his judgement or decisions. Racing had become a passion, sharpened by success.

In March 1960, he heard that Martin Benson's Beech House stud was up for sale at Newmarket and could not resist adding it to an empire of sixty horses in training, eighty brood mares, and some of the finest stallions in the world. When he and his wife arrived for their annual visit to England, they hurried off at once to see St Paddy. He had come on splendidly but had some formidable Derby rivals. Victor was cautiously optimistic, encouraged by the coincidence that St Paddy was No. 20 on the card and Derby Day happened also to be his brother-in-law's twentieth wedding anniversary. With some hesitation he placed a few pounds on St Paddy *each way* for some American friends and ordered a dress in peacock blue and gold which he hoped Lady Sassoon might wear at a victory dinner party.

He was depressed to see newcomers in the next-door box which Aly Khan would have occupied but for his fatal car accident three weeks earlier. He was still fretting over Aly's absence when the horses came under orders. Through his glasses he watched the parade and picked out Piggott's very individual stance. Suddenly, as he recalled afterwards, he had absolutely no doubt that St Paddy would win. He jumped from his chair and snapped the finish through his telephoto lens as his horse swept past the line three lengths ahead of the Irish-trained Alcaeus. His chauffeur wheeled him into the lift and on through a wildly cheering crowd to the unsaddling enclosure. Noel Murless led in the winner, Victor following on his two sticks. 'This has taken more out of me than my horse,' he panted as he climbed to the Royal Box. When he had his breath back, he thanked the Queen for her share in his victory, a graceful reminder that St Paddy was sired by her Aureole.

Lester Piggott and his wife were at the celebration dinner that night. It took some persuasion to overcome the jockey's shyness, but Victor insisted. He also had his way in setting up a trust fund for the jockey instead of giving him the customary 10 per cent of the prize money as a taxable present.

St Paddy himself played host at a unique dinner. The Guinea Pig Club of Allied airmen, former patients of Sir Archibald McIndoe, always held their annual reunion at East Grinstead. The famous plastic surgeon normally gave them dinner but he died earlier that year. When Sir Victor heard that funds might not be available, he at once arranged that the celebration should be 'on' St Paddy. In a room decorated in his racing colours, he sat down to dine with a hundred and fifty men who, like himself, had crashed, survived and could still laugh.

(St Paddy would be syndicated as a stallion and one annual nomination made over in favour of the Guinea Pigs. Knowing that it was her husband's dearest wish, Lady Sassoon later made all the arrangements by which the club fund would benefit by some £3,000 a year throughout the stallion's stud life.)

After St Paddy's triumph, Victor was becoming excited over an ambition which he had privately nursed ever since Hard Ridden's surprise win. With four Derby victories now behind him, he had more than an outside chance of equalling and perhaps beating the Aga Khan's record of five, although one had been half owned by Leon Volterra. It would be a remarkable feat, since the Aga's stables and bloodstock were worth £4 million and he had won over a million sterling in stakes in England alone. By contrast, Sir Victor's seven establishments collectively were never estimated at more than a million and a half in value, even at their peak.

He was suddenly hopeful that a Pinza colt, Pinturischio, might win him his fifth Derby but it was most doubtful if his doctors would allow him to risk the excitement of Epsom. Instead, he made plans for a four-month trip round the world with his wife. In January 1961 they were in San Francisco on the first lap when he suffered a severe heart attack. Lady Sassoon arranged for oxygen equipment and had him taken to St Luke's Hospital.

Her prompt action had again saved his life. He remained in bed for an impatient six weeks. On his first day up he popped a carnation into his lapel and hobbled into a fashion show in the St Francis Hotel. He was delighted when the chef, who had worked in London and remembered his tastes, prepared shepherd's pie specially for him.

He flew down to Dallas where he learned with astonishment that the British public had made his horse favourite for the Two Thousand Guineas and the Derby although he had never run a race. It showed extraordinary faith in his now legendary winning combination with Murless and Piggott, but Pinturischio fell ill and had to be scratched. His owner soon recovered his spirits and astonished his friend and cardiologist, Dr Alfred Harris of Dallas, by laughing and joking although both knew he was a dying man. He refused to be separated from his new white stetson when he and his wife flew to Nassau in mid-May, planning to spend the summer quietly.

He remained almost boisterously cheerful even in moments of acute pain. He spent hours with his nephew, showing him his collection of silver taels, explaining the Chinese inscription with all the old dry humour. And he fretted at not being allowed to go and see a troupe of Japanese acrobats who were performing at the local theatre which was not air-conditioned.

His wife was not misled by his high spirits. She became anxious and secretly telephoned Dr Harris. Together they concocted an excuse for him to come to the Bahamas and 'call in' at Eve's. Victor may have seen through it but showed no alarm. 'Maybe Al will take me to see the acrobats,' he chuckled. The doctor humoured him, and they thoroughly enjoyed the show together.

On the Saturday night, a week before his death, Victor had arranged a dinner party for the Governor of the Bahamas, Dr Harris and his wife and other friends. Lady Sassoon hinted gently that it might be postponed but he would not hear of it. 'I can't do them out of their curry just because I'm not quite up to the mark,' he said firmly. He dressed very carefully in white coat and black tie, examined himself in the long mirror and asked his wife, as usual, 'Do I look all right?' He was in excellent form and kept his friends laughing all through dinner.

He spent the next six days in his oxygen tent. By Saturday, August 12 1961, there was no hope for him, but he would not permit any tearful death-bed scene. He was a brave man, and always practical. When the time came for another injection, he looked up with a faint smile and murmured, 'I'm not going to need that one, Barnsie.'

Epilogue

The publication of Sir Victor's Will aroused international interest, although only the naïve expected a complete picture of his estate. He and his advisers had planned long and strenuously to prevent his family assets from being butchered to make a tax-collector's holiday. Nevertheless, the provisional valuation of his various properties proved surprisingly low. It did not take into account his five racing studs in England and Ireland, his banking interests in the Bahamas, the 'V' Trust of non-sterling assets set up in Panama and Uruguay at the time of his marriage, or the numerous subsidiaries established in other parts of Latin America after the Second World War.

His estate in England was valued at only £12,602. The Eve Stud Company was an English concern, but the shares worth over £1 million had long been held by a company in Nassau. Otherwise, they would have been liable to a punitive estate duty.

A Will made on 28 May 1959 had disposed of assets in a trust fund set up in New York. After bequests to the value of £178,000, the widow was to receive the income from the remainder, together with securities and £214,000 in trust. Another Will admitted to probate in the Bahamas, showed credit balances in various companies and shareholdings to the value of £230,000. No real estate in Nassau was held in Sir Victor's name.

Lady Sassoon received all the shares in her husband's stables and studs, together with the balance of his estate after expenses. She undertook responsibility for the lavish benefactions set out in his British Will. A niece, Elizabeth Humphreys-Owen, was left £200,000, and two others £50,000 each. His sisters, Lydia and Isabelle, would continue to receive their allowances of £7,500 and £6,500 a year respectively, while other generous sums, annuities and gifts were bequeathed to friends and employees. Noel Murless received £5,000, W. B. Bryden £15,000, and Charles Hughesdon was delighted to have Nuage Rouge, half-sister to Crepello's dam.

Sir Victor's death ended both the baronetcy and the last family connection with his companies in the direct male line. In 1963, his widow sold the FitzGeralds her half interest in the Banking Company and also resigned from the board. The company, whose headquarters in Nassau, are now the imposing E. D. Sassoon Building, was revitalized in 1967 –

exactly a century since Elias Sassoon first broke away from the founder firm in Bombay.

Captain FitzGerald had left the Board on reaching retiring age. He died suddenly while watching the racing at Royal Ascot. His son, Desmond, is now Chairman. The share capital has been re-organized by Ralph C. Yablon, the new Vice-Chairman. In association with the Crown Agents and the powerful Continental Illinois Bank of Chicago, the firm's merchant banking operations, including Foreign Exchange, are being greatly expanded. Under its new structure, the Banking Company is concentrating on export finance and the management of international investment accounts.

The name-plate of David Sassoon & Co. in St Swithin's Lane also reminds Londoners of the once powerful oriental trading firm which changed so dramatically in scope and policy after the sale of its Indian interests and the seizure of assets by Communist China. It is now a private company with issued capital of £500,000, and remains active in the import and export field, covering a wide range of merchandise. The firm holds several important agencies and does considerable business in almost every part of the world. On the merchant banking side, it finances ship-building, estate development and a wide complex of engineering projects within the United Kingdom. The family link is preserved through Sybil's son, Lord John Cholmondeley, the present Chairman.

Since her husband's death, Lady Sassoon has herself set up a private banking and real estate organization with Holt Ruffin as general manager and her brother, Ernest Barnes, as one of the directors. Lady Sassoon Enterprises now includes two investment banks in Nassau, each with a subscribed capital of £200,000, a property company with apartment buildings and estates in the Bahamas, and a general insurance agency which represents Lloyd's of London and other leading companies.

Lady Sassoon spends several months of the year in Nassau and the rest of her time in Dallas, Texas and Europe, but her various business interests and philanthropies take her often to South America and India. She maintains the racing studs and stables in England and Ireland, and she has had several turf successes, notably the Ascot Gold Cup in 1963, but without so far finding another Pinza or Crepello to overtake the Aga Khan's Derby record.

Apart from many other welfare trusts, she created and maintains the Sir Victor Sassoon Heart Foundation in her husband's memory. A clinic in Nassau cares for young victims of the disease, while a close liaison is kept with the Children's Hospital in Miami and cardiac centres in other American cities. The first benefit was a film première at which Joan Crawford made a personal appearance. Since then, Meyer Davis has played at three gala balls.

The peacock blue and old gold colours still remind racegoers of Sir Victor's astonishing series of Derby victories, while his cousin's name is preserved in the race run annually for the R. E. Sassoon Cup at Lingfield. But there are surprisingly few other relics to recall the legendary past.

There is no monument except in the affection of his relatives and a small surviving circle of friends, to the kindness and hospitality of Sir Philip Sassoon. Port Lympne has long since vanished from the social scene. Trent Park, where Hannah Gubbay still occupies the lodge, is now a teachers' training college. By a cruel irony, 45 Park Lane has become the home of the Playboy Club. 'Bunnies' and blackjack have exorcized the ghosts of Sargent, Melba and A. J. Balfour.

Except to a nostalgic minority, Sir Philip's name will mean far less than that of Vidal Sassoon, the contemporary hair stylist, who does not claim descent from the Baghdad dynasty. His father was born in Turkey where many Sephardic Jews found sanctuary after the Spanish Inquisition.

By a strange paradox, the two outstanding survivors of the dynasty since Sir Victor's death have been a rabbi and a Roman Catholic convert. Neither is remotely identifiable with a tradition of vast mercantile power, even less of social grandeur. These great-grandsons of David Sassoon, both men of commanding height and with the aquiline features and deep-set eyes of their ancestor, led very different lives, yet with points of contact in mind and spirit which recall the patriarch.

Solomon Sassoon, Flora's grandson, has settled in the Garden City of Letchworth in Hertfordshire. He became a rabbi and teacher of Hebrew at the age of twenty. Like his father, he is dedicated. He is also a distinguished scholar who has edited and published many learned works on the Scriptures. After India became independent, he made himself responsible for the welfare of several hundred Jews who came over to England from Bombay and Calcutta. He is President of the largest Sephardic seminary in the world, now in Israel.

He maintains a strictly orthodox Jewish household where, as in the days of David Sassoon, visitors are welcomed from far-off communities. The library of rare Hebrew and Samaritan manuscripts attracts scholars who also show much interest in the Holy Ark, the Scrolls and other relics which Reuben collected, unaware that they would provide a more lasting memorial than his friendship with King Edward VII.

There is an oriental, synagogue-like bustle at Letchworth. The telephones are busy with calls from bibliophiles, scholars and members of the three congregations which the rabbi supervises.

He hopes his two sons will follow a religious vocation. The other surviving branch shows an equally emphatic leaning towards the Thornycrofts. One of Michael's boys, Hamo, has made a brilliant reputation as an archaeologist in Tanzania. Siegfried's son, George, now works in Cambridge as a research engineer and specializes in electronics.

At Heytesbury House, during Siegfried's last years, one had a feeling of corduroy rather than gaberdine. The poet, still lean and athletic-looking in his eighty-first year, usually wore a faded college blazer and silk muffler over undergraduate grey flannels or patched riding breeches. Until a short time before his death in September 1967, he still played cricket occasionally for the Downside Ravens and was not easy to dislodge except by bumpers.

After being received into the Catholic Church in 1957, he wrote much devotional verse for limited editions. His conversion gave him peace without driving him deeper into retreat. His front-door bell was still out of order, but there was a warmer welcome for a few old friends who delighted in his table talk, salted with puns. Sometimes he drove over to Mells or Downside Abbey in his vintage Humber, and 'he was enticed from his idyllic retirement', in the words of the Public Orator of Oxford University, to receive the honorary degree of D.Lit.

He helped to buy Edmund Blunden's cottage in Long Melford, Suffolk, by advancing part of the money he intended to leave him. 'I thought it would be handy,' Blunden laughingly explained, 'just in case he wanted to look in on passing through to visit the nuns at Bury St Edmunds.'

In the library at Heytesbury House, as at Letchworth, one felt completely remote from the opium clippers nosing into Shanghai or the pulsating cotton mills that enriched the Sassoons of Bombay. But the eye was soon caught by the vivid painting of Rachel Beer over the great fireplace. Siegfried spoke of her with affection as he caressed a small silver trinket shaped like a brazil nut, a souvenir of another aunt, Mozelle. During my last visit he shot abruptly from the room to return with some carefully preserved photographs of David Sassoon. 'He was really the one that counted,' he said thoughtfully.

From their great-grandfather he and the Rabbi of Letchworth both inherited an idealism which other Sassoons missed in their pursuit of wealth and righteousness.

Bibliography

In addition to the family papers in the custody of Rabbi S. D. Sassoon of Letchworth, special acknowledgement is due to Cecil Roth's *The Sassoon Dynasty* (London, Robert Hale, 1941), David Solomon Sassoon's *Ohel Dawid* (London, Oxford University Press, 1932) and *A History of the Jews in Baghdad* (privately published, 1949).

Other sources consulted or quoted are listed below in alphabetical order.

Asquith, Cynthia *Haply I May Remember* (London: James Barrie, 1950; New York: Scribner's, 1950) and *Remember and Be Glad* (London: James Barrie, 1950; New York: Scribner's, 1952)

Asquith, Margot *Autobiography* (London: Eyre & Spottiswoode, 1962; Boston: Houghton Mifflin, 1963)

Baxter, Arthur Beverley *Strange Street* (London: Hutchinson, 1935; Toronto: Ryerson Press, 1935)

Beaverbrook, Lord *The Decline and Fall of Lloyd George* (London: Collins, 1963; New York: Duell, Sloan & Pearce, 1963)

Belloc Lowndes, Mrs *A Passing World* (London: Macmillan, 1948)

Bernhardt, Sarah *My Double Life* (London: Heinemann, 1907)

Bibesco, Marthe *The Veiled Wanderer* (London: Falcon Press, 1949)

Boothby, Lord *I Fight to Live* (London: Gollancz, 1947)

Cecil, David *Max* (London: Constable, 1964; Boston: Houghton Mifflin, 1965)

Chaplin, Charles *My Autobiography* (London: Bodley Head, 1964; New York: Simon & Schuster, 1964)

Charteris, Evan *John Sargent* (London: Heinemann, 1927; New York: Scribner's, 1927)

Churchill, Randolph *Winston S. Churchill, Vol. I* (London: Heinemann, 1966; Boston: Houghton Mifflin, 1966)

Collis, Maurice *Wayfoong* (London: Faber, 1965; New York: Humanities Press, 1965)

Dicker, Herman *Wanderers and Settlers in the Far East* (New York: Twayne Publishers 1962).

Divine, David *These Splendid Ships* (London: Muller, 1960)

Forster, E. M. *Abinger Harvest* (London: Penguin, 1967)

Graves, Robert *Goodbye to All That* (London: Cape, 1929; New York: Blue Ribbon Books, 1931) and *Poems, 1914–1926* (London: Heinemann, 1927; New York: Doubleday, 1929)

Hahn, Emily *China Only Yesterday* (London: Weidenfeld & Nicolson, 1963; New York: Doubleday, 1963)

Haig, Douglas *Private Papers, 1914–19* edited by Robert Blake (London: Eyre & Spottiswoode, 1952; Toronto: Collins, 1952)

Harris, F. R. *Tata* (London: Oxford University Press, 1925)

Hassall, Christopher *Edward Marsh* (London: Longmans, 1959). Published under the title *Biography of Edward Marsh* (New York: Harcourt, Brace, 1959)

Horner, Frances *Time Remembered* (London: Heinemann, 1933; Toronto: Ryerson Press, 1934)

Kipling, Rudyard *The Irish Guards in the Great War* (London: Macmillan, 1923; New York: Doubleday, 1923)

Lawrence, A. W. (Editor) *Letters to T. E. Lawrence* (London: Cape, 1962; Chester Springs: Dufour Editions, 1964)

Lawrence, T. E. *Selected Letters* edited by David Garnett (London: Cape, 1938; New York: Doubleday, 1939)

Lloyd George, Richard *Lloyd George* (London: Muller, 1960)

Lucas, S. E. *Catalogue of Sassoon Chinese Ivories* (London: Country Life, 1950; New York: Scribner's, 1950)

Magnus, Philip *King Edward the Seventh* (London: John Murray, 1964; New York: E. P. Dutton & Co. Inc., 1964)

Marsh, Sir Edward *A Number of People* (London: Heinemann, 1937; New York: Harper, 1939)

Minney, R. J. *The Edwardian Age* (London: Cassell, 1964; Boston: Little, Brown, 1965)

Morris, James *Oxford* (London: Faber, 1965; New York: Harcourt, 1965)

Morton, Frederic *The Rothschilds* (London: Secker & Warburg, 1962; New York: Atheneum, 1962)

Moulson, Tom *The Flying Sword* (London: Macdonald, 1964; Toronto: Nelson, 1964)

Munz, Sigmund *King Edward VII at Marienbad* (London: Hutchinson, 1934)

Newman, Bernard *Speaking from Memory* (London: Herbert Jenkins, 1960; Toronto: Smithers & Bonellie Ltd., 1960)

Nicolson, Sir Harold *Diaries and Letters, 1930–39* (London: Collins, 1966)

Osborn, E. B. *The New Elizabethans* (London: John Lane, 1919)

Painter, George D. *Marcel Proust, Vol. II* (London: Chatto & Windus, 1965; Boston: Little, Brown, 1965)

Petrie, Sir Charles *Scenes of Edwardian Life* (London: Eyre & Spottiswoode, 1965)

Pound, Reginald and Harmsworth, Geoffrey *Northcliffe* (London: Cassell,
1959)

Pound, Reginald *The Lost Generation* (London: Constable, 1964; New
York: Coward-McCann, 1965)

Reed, Sir Stanley *The India I Knew* (London: Odhams, 1952).

Riddell, Lord *More Pages from My Diary* (London: Country Life, 1934;
Toronto: The Copp Clark Corp. Ltd., 1934)

Sassoon, Sir Philip *The Third Route* (London: Heinemann, 1929)

Sassoon, Siegfried
   The Old Huntsman (London: Heinemann, 1917)
   War Poems, 1919 (London: Heinemann, 1919)
   Counter-Attack (London: Heinemann, 1918)
   The Old Century (London: Faber, 1938; New York: Viking, 1939)
   Siegfried's Journey (London: Faber, 1945; New York: Viking, 1946)
   Memoirs of an Infantry Officer (London: Faber, 1931; Toronto
      Ryerson Press, 1934)
   Collected Poems, 1908–1956 (London: Faber, 1961)
   Rhymed Ruminations (London: Faber, 1940; New York: Viking,
      1941)
   The Weald of Youth (London: Faber, 1942; New York: Viking, 1942)
   The Memoirs of George Sherston (London: Faber, 1937; Harris-
      burg: Stackpole, 1967)

Sitwell, Edith *Taken Care of* (London: Hutchinson, 1965; New York:
Atheneum, 1965)

Sitwell, Osbert *The Scarlet Tree* (London: Macmillan, 1946; Boston:
Little, Brown, 1946)

Spain, Nancy *Why I'm Not a Millionaire* (London: Hutchinson, 1956)

Springfield, Maurice *Hunting Opium and Other Scents* (Halesworth:
Norfolk & Suffolk Publicity Services, 1966)

Sulivan, R. J. F. *One Hundred Years of Bombay* (Bombay: Times of
India Press, 1937)

Taylor, A. J. P. *English History, 1914–1945* (Oxford: Clarendon Press,
1965)

Terraine, John *Douglas Haig* (London: Hutchinson, 1963). Published
under the title *Ordeal of Victory* (Philadelphia: Lippincott, 1963)

Thomson, Malcolm *David Lloyd George* (London: Hutchinson, 1948)

Thornycroft, Elfrida *Bronze and Steel* (Shipston-on-Stour: King's Stone
Press, 1932)

Thorpe, Michael *Siegfried Sassoon – A Critical Study* (London: Oxford
University Press, 1966)

Untermeyer, Jean Starr *Private Collection* (New York: Knopf, 1965)

Weizmann, Chaim *Trial and Error* (London: Hamish Hamilton, 1949; New York: Harper, 1949)

Windsor, Duchess of *The Heart Has Its Reasons* (London: Michael Joseph, 1956; New York: David McKay, 1956)

Young, Kenneth *Arthur James Balfour* (London: Bell, 1963)

Index